Identity and Agency in Cultural Worlds

as transformation of cul

Identity and Agency in Cultural Worlds

Dorothy Holland
William Lachicotte Jr.
Debra Skinner
Carole Cain

HARVARD UNIVERSITY PRESS
Cambridge, Massachusetts
London, England

First Harvard University Press paperback edition, 2001

Library of Congress Cataloging-in-Publication Data

Identity and agency in cultural worlds / Dorothy Holland . . . [et al.].
    p. cm.
    Includes bibliographical references and index.
    ISBN 0-674-81566-1 (cloth)
    ISBN 0-674-00562-7 (pbk.)
    1. Culture. 2. Identity (Psychology) 3. Agent (Philosophy)
I. Holland, Dorothy C.
HM101.I28935   1998
306—dc21   98-19269

Contents

Preface

In *Marxism and Literature* Raymond Williams says:

> The strongest barrier to the recognition of human cultural activity is this immediate and regular conversion of experience into finished products. [. . . It is misleading to habitually project endings] not only into the always moving substance of the past, but into contemporary life, in which relationships, institutions and formations in which we are still actively involved are converted, by this procedural mode, into formed wholes rather than forming and formative processes. (Williams 1977: 128–129; quoted in Harvey 1996: 24–25; interpolation by Harvey)

Williams's admonition is important for cultural studies of the person and for our focus on identity. Identities—if they are alive, if they are being lived—are unfinished and in process. Whether they be specific to the imagined worlds of romance or the careers of mental illness, or generic to ethnic, gender, race, and class divisions, identities never arrive in persons or in their immediate social milieux already formed. They do not come into being, take hold in lives, or remain vibrant without considerable social work in and for the person. They happen in social practice.

Cultural studies of the person, in particular, need to move more solidly to process. They must be predicated upon continuing cultural production: a development, or interlocking genesis, that is actually a co-development of identities, discourses, embodiments, and imagined worlds that inform each moment of joint production and are themselves transformed by that moment. It is this processual understanding of identity and agency that we seek to build, through concepts offered by two scholars of society and the person, whose work began in the aftermath of the Soviet Revolution of 1917, L. S. Vygotsky and M. M. Bakhtin.

Although not, as far as we know, directly intertwined, the intellectual lives of Bakhtin and Vygotsky were influenced by the same currents of thought in 1920s Russia. The two men addressed the common questions and objectives that characterized the great ferment of social theory about the "new society" and its inhabitants, the new "socialist man." Each had a thoroughly sociocentric view of human thought and feeling, and both saw speech, language, literature, and art as the pivotal media through which consciousness and subjectivity develop. Bakhtin relied upon some of the same concepts as Vygotsky did, such as the important notion of "inner speech," but Bakhtin's center of gravity remained in the areas of sociolinguistics and literary criticism, while Vygotsky turned to the task of building a sociohistorical school of psychology. Bakhtin's search was less for a social science of what we will call heuristic development—the contingent formations of subjectivity over time—and more for the social grounds of "personal" creativity and authority. Vygotsky and Bakhtin together articulated a powerful version of human life as necessarily mediated: as produced by social interchange among persons whose activity, however circumscribed by material and social circumstances, and however cast in forms of discursive and practical genres, nonetheless remakes these conditions. Theirs is a social world that is necessarily personal, not automatic; a world of agents and of hope carried forward from the Revolution. It still has much to say to us today.

Williams's admonition against supposed endings reminds us of our manuscript. This book has been in process for a long time, and the intellectual projects it reflects are certainly not finished. Carole Cain, Dorothy Holland, Renée Prillaman, and Debra Skinner started talking about the subject matter more than ten years ago. Because of work and family obligations, Renée Prillaman had to drop out of the project, but the book profited from her ideas. Meanwhile, William Lachicotte joined our discussions and writing.

The plan for the book has remained fairly constant. We wanted to develop our ideas about identity collectively through our discussions of other scholars' writings and through our own research projects, which we undertook individually or in pairs. The result is a book that sometimes plays havoc with current notions of authorship, just as our view of subjectivity must surely grate against common ideas of identity and personhood.

If authorship of a collective venture is hard to square with individualistic notions of cultural production, so too are our acknowledgments. A multitude of people have contributed to our field research, among them the residents of the area in Nepal where Holland and Skinner lived and worked, the members of the Alcoholics Anonymous groups attended by Cain (especially those we call Hank, Ellen, and Andrew), the clients and staff members of mental health institutions who gave their time and assistance to Lachicotte, and the students of the two universities where Holland learned about the figured world of romance. A host of readers, listeners, and partners in discussion have also been crucial to the development of our ideas. We cannot name them all. Our solution is to thank the following people, who have significantly aided one or more of us: G. B. Adhikari, Richard Ashmore, Alan Benjamin, Katherine Bunting-Howarth, Roy D'Andrade, Robert Daniels, Mary Des Chene, Margaret Eisenhart, Glen Elder, Sue Estroff, Terry Evens, Judith Farquhar, Alison Greene, Marilyn Grunkemeyer, Erin Hannan, Jean Harris, Peter Hervik, Lee Jussim, Willett Kempton, Jean Lave, Bradley Levinson, Robert Levy, Tanya Luhrmann, Donald Nonini, Alfred Pach III, Maheswor Pahari, Steven Parish, Jim Peacock, John Peterson, James Poling, Laurie Price, James Reeves, Bob S., Sapana Sharma, Claudia Strauss, Renu Lama Thapa, Julia Thompson, Jaan Valsiner, Joanne Waghorne, and several anonymous reviewers.

Funders for our research projects were crucial as well: the National Science Foundation (BNS-9110010), the Fulbright Foundation, the National Institutes of Mental Health (Grant RO1 MH40314), the National Institute of Education, the University Research Council of the University of North Carolina at Chapel Hill, and the University of North Carolina at Chapel Hill Dissertation Fellowships. Thanks also to the Nepal Offices of the United States Educational Foundation and Save the Children, U.S.A.

We dedicate this book to some special people whose voices we brought with us to our task: Ashby Gaines Holland; William S. Lachicotte Sr.; Willard Skinner; Mack and Delores Cain. They are part-authors of this story and shape it still in ways not even we can fully tell.

Identity and Agency in Cultural Worlds

I

On the Shoulders of
Bakhtin and Vygotsky

1

The Woman Who Climbed up the House

People tell others who they are, but even more important, they tell themselves and then try to act as though they are who they say they are. These self-understandings, especially those with strong emotional resonance for the teller, are what we refer to as identities. A man interviewed by Lachicotte, Roger Kelly,[1] diagnosed as having a mental disorder, struggled with who to be: "I'm only 35. I mean I wi—kind of wish I was 60, and I was done with all . . . It would make things simpler, you know, 'I'm disabled. I'll just live out my last few years and do a little good works and try to enjoy my day.' But when you're only 35 there's pressure to get back in there and try it again. I've tried four or five times. I've been up in the hospital five times now. How many more times do I have to try?"

Tika Damai, a girl of fifteen in a community in central Nepal, when asked by Skinner to tell about herself and her life, answered by singing a series of folksongs, which began:

> Parents have earned a little money,
> But my life will be spent in cutting grass and wood only.
> Daughters are married off, crossing nine great mountains,
> But the sons are always kept at home.
> Mother, am I not your daughter,
> Am I not your daughter?
> Brothers are given wealth and property, but nothing is given to
> me. (Skinner, Valsiner, and Basnet 1991: 19–20)

Although from widely divergent cultural worlds, Tika Damai and Roger Kelly were engaged in similar identity-making processes. They

3

were producing, from the cultural resources available to them, under-standings of themselves that seemed to be not only "of" (about) them-selves, representing the dilemmas of their respective social situations, but also "for" themselves. These productions figured in their communi-cation with themselves about their past and present actions. We picture Roger, Tika, ourselves, and other individuals and groups as always en-gaged in forming identities, in producing objectifications of self-under-standings that may guide subsequent behavior. This vision emphasizes that identities are improvised—in the flow of activity within specific social situations—from the cultural resources at hand. Thus persons and, to a lesser extent, groups are caught in the tensions between past histories that have settled in them and the present discourses and images that attract them or somehow impinge upon them. In this continuous self-fashioning, identities are hard-won standpoints that, however de-pendent upon social support and however vulnerable to change, make at least a modicum of self-direction possible. They are possibilities for me-diating agency.

Identity and Its Theories

"Identity" is a concept that invokes and relates theories from various streams of psychology, social psychology, anthropology, sociology, and now from such interdisciplinary fields as cultural studies. Our own take on this concept is at heart an anthropological and cultural studies adaptation of sociogenic concepts of personhood developed within the American school of social psychology that claims G. H. Mead as its founder.

Mead began with humans' instinctual ability to coordinate their ac-tions and traced the career of this coordination through the person's engagement in social life. Self-consciousness and self-reflection develop in the active child as the product of a social history. The person acquires the ability to take the standpoint of others as she learns to objectify herself by the qualities of her performance in and commitment to various social positions (for example, in the United States, mother, activist, black woman, Marxist anthropologist, student, environmentalist, public ser-vant, good person).[2] Such objectifications, especially those to which one is strongly emotionally attached, become cores of one's proactive identities.

Identity is a concept that figuratively combines the intimate or personal world with the collective space of cultural forms and social relations. We are interested in identities, the imaginings of self in worlds of action, as social products; indeed, we begin with the premise that identities are lived in and through activity and so must be conceptualized as they develop in social practice. But we are also interested in identities as psychohistorical formations that develop over a person's lifetime, populating intimate terrain and motivating social life. Identities are a key means through which people care about and care for what is going on around them. They are important bases from which people create new activities, new worlds, and new ways of being. In some chapters we will pay great attention to the ways in which persons are malleable, changeable, and subject to discursive powers. In others we will show more respect for persons' generativity, their capacities—embedded always in collective meanings and social relations—to imagine and create new ways of being. Human agency may be frail, especially among those with little power, but it happens daily and mundanely, and it deserves our attention. Humans' capacity for self-objectification—and, through objectification, for self-direction—plays into both their domination by social relations of power and their possibilities for (partial) liberation from these forces.

The "metatheoretical" shift to practice, coupled with what might be called the critical disruption in the social sciences, the humanities, and some areas of psychology, has cleared a space for new understandings of persons. Cultural studies, joined to feminist theory's engagement with issues of identity, invite us to see persons taking form in the flow of historically, socially, culturally, and materially shaped lives.[3] At the same time, a more sociogenic approach to personhood has developed. The task we undertake here is inspired not only by contemporary cultural studies but also by the intellectual tradition that includes the great Soviet psychologist L. S. Vygotsky, his students, and other members of what has come to be called the cultural-historical or sociohistorical school of psychology. Equally important to our tradition is another figure from the same period and place, the critical theorist and semiotician M. M. Bakhtin. To comprehend and articulate a vision of both person and society true to the parts played by cultural forms, the machinery of power and social positioning, and the continual processes of identification, we join the work of Bakhtin, Vygotsky, and their colleagues to contemporary debates (a link that, especially in the case of Vygotsky, has been made before; see, for example, Gergen 1994; van der Veer and Valsiner 1991; Wertsch 1991).

Bakhtin's work was inspired by a neo-Kantian tradition of philosophy that emphasized aesthetics.[4] But Bakhtin did not rest content with this difficult kind of idealism. He took his work in two directions, both of which were more concerned with specific practices and persons than with the generic practice of abstract (indeed quasi-transcendental) subjects. First, he studied literature and verbal art, looking most closely at the means for representing characters and (therefore) authors. Second, he began, with V. N. Voloshinov, a study of the sociology of human expression, which also became a social psychology. Their works of 1929, *Marxism and the Philosophy of Language* and *Problems of Dostoevsky's Poetics,* intertwine these two lines to create an understanding of human expression that seems more at home in the cultural studies of today than in either the social science or the literary studies of the time.

Vygotsky came to his study of persons from interests in literature, art, and linguistics. His 1925 dissertation, *The Psychology of Art,* included an analysis of a short story, Bunin's "Gentle Breath." His fascination with the way the closing image of the story transformed the whole feeling of the piece was part of his more general engagement with the potential of symbols to affect and reorganize experience. He carried this fascination with symbols into his psychology and organized his later studies around it. He construed symbols, particularly cultural symbols learned through social interaction, as so many ways in which people free themselves from the tyranny of environmental stimuli. But this work of freedom, for Vygotsky, demanded an appreciation of time and timing. He took a genetic or developmental approach because, in his handling, it was difficult, if not impossible, to understand a person's behavior without knowing the opportunistic history of its formation.

Bakhtin's concern with the social weighing of expression and the creative life of association, combined with Vygotsky's emphases on historical development and on the potentiality of symbols for (re)formation, affords a means by which "cultural studies of the person" may avoid a common conceptual dilemma—one that traps persons permanently, either in "cultural logics" or in "subject positions" or in some combination of the two. This is our objective here: to respect humans as social and cultural creatures and therefore bounded, yet to recognize the processes whereby

(. agency
v cul constraint

human collectives and individuals often move themselves—led by hope, desperation, or even playfulness, but certainly by no rational plan—from one set of socially and culturally formed subjectivities to another.

Our view of identity and human agency differs in some important ways from two interrelated and influential streams of work that have also treated these issues. When anthropologists and other contributors to cultural studies of the person write about "identities" they are usually concerned with "cultural identities," identities that form in relation to major structural features of society: ethnicity, gender, race, nationality, and sexual orientation. Our concept of identity is both broader and more particular. We focus on the development of identities and agency specific to practices and activities situated in historically contingent, socially enacted, culturally constructed "worlds": recognized fields or frames of social life, such as romance, mental illness and its treatment, domestic relations, Alcoholics Anonymous, academia, and local politics.

Identifications of people within these worlds are often, if not always, structurally marked. That is, they may be divided by gender, race, ethnicity, or any other durable structural feature of the society. We address the structural aspects of world-specific identities in Chapter 6. There are also culturally constructed worlds where "woman" or "lesbian" or "white woman" is a salient identity in and of itself (for example, some worlds of feminist debate) or where "wife" or "daughter" or "daughter-in-law" is practically coterminous with female as a general status. Chapters 10 and 12, on Nepal, address the latter case. Still, we are always interested in the grounding of cultural identities in the specific worlds of which they are a part.

Cultural studies of the person—including a significant proportion of the anthropological research on (cultural) identity—share an opposition to a general "Western" notion of identity that takes as its prototype a coherent, unified, and originary subject (see, for an extreme example, Stuart Hall 1996). The projects of these newer studies are quite unlike that of Erik Erikson (1963, 1968), for example, with its focus on the tasks any person must successfully accomplish to resolve the psychodynamic dilemmas of maturation and thus establish a consistent identity. Instead the newer studies rely upon feminist and later psychodynamic approaches, both of which recognize those social forces which make such an integrated subject an extremely unlikely occurrence.

At this point we differ. It is not that we have an inclination to the idea of a unified subject; we conceive persons as composites of many, often contradictory, self-understandings and identities, whose loci are often not confined to the body but "spread over the material and social environment," and few of which are completely durable. We also concur with the emphasis on cultural forms and the inevitable importance of socially distributed power. But we take a different path to theorizing identities and processes of identification. Though we share an interest in many of the same issues and a critical focus on the importance of cultural forms in the production of subjectivities, we develop different aspects of the relation between society and subjectivity. We do not attend to the psychodynamic processes that may lead to the identification of self within the structural inscriptions of gender, race, and so forth. Rather we build upon notions of inner activity and inner life, drawn from Bakhtin and the sociohistorical school, that cast the development of self-understandings (identities) on intimate terrain as an outcome of living in, through, and around the cultural forms practiced in social life. Bakhtin and Vygotsky give us a means of theorizing history-in-person that allows us to conceive of identities as always forming, but that differs from history-in-person conceived primarily through psychodynamics (see Chapter 2).

The case studies we employ to trace out these processes include culturally constructed worlds in the United States: the world of Alcoholics Anonymous, the world of romance and attractiveness, and the world of mental health care. They also cross what are usually considered more profound cultural boundaries into the constructed worlds of domestic and political relations in Nepal. How do these culturally constructed worlds become matters of desire? How do people's senses of themselves in these worlds become engaging? How do persons become agents in these worlds? How do these worlds become prisons? How do people together create new cultural worlds? How do their subjectivities expand or reform so that they are able to inhabit new worlds? These are the sorts of questions that we try to answer through alternating expositions of concepts and the ethnographic details of the case studies.

Our frame is what might be called, following Bakhtin, a dialogic one; following Vygotsky, a developmental one. We aim to build upon and move beyond two central approaches—the culturalist and the constructivist—to understand people's actions and possibilities. All the perspectives we discuss assume, at least implicitly, that behavior is mediated by senses of self or what we call identities.[5] In the older of the two approaches that we work to transcend, the person is driven by an internalized cultural logic; in the more recent, by social situation. In order to communicate what we find important about these two approaches, we simplify them to two ideal types.

Two Perspectives on Identity

An incident told from Dorothy Holland's perspective can be used to exemplify the two approaches.[6] The incident happened in Naudada, a rural hill community in central Nepal:

Debra Skinner and I were interviewing people for a small research project. Debra had been carrying out ethnographic fieldwork in the community for about a year and a half. I had recently joined her.

Naudada was occupied by people of different *jat* (caste/ethnic groups). Since we wanted to interview people from a range of jat, we had asked members of the various castes, from the highest (Bahun) to the lowest (Damai), to come to Debra's house to be interviewed.

In Naudada, persons of lower caste were usually prohibited from entering the houses of those of higher caste. Food and cooking were considered especially vulnerable to pollution, and, since the only entrance to most houses was on the first floor, where the hearths were, people of lower castes kept away. Under normal village circumstances, then, lower-caste people would have expected to be barred from Debra's house. She was accorded, in most contexts, a status analogous to that of a higher-caste person, and, in addition, her Bahun landlord lived on the terrace above her, practically next door. Debra, however, throughout her residence in Naudada, had insisted that lower-caste people enter her house to talk. People all around had come to know of her unusual practice.

One day we were interviewing on the second-floor balcony of the three-story house. We were in the process of interviewing a woman of the Sunar caste—historically associated with the occupation of goldsmithing and considered "untouchable." The woman seemed uncomfortable. We guessed that her discomfort was due to the proximity of the next person to be interviewed, a Chetri (higher-caste) woman, who was sitting around the corner of the balcony.

About that time another woman arrived at the house to be interviewed. The new arrival, Gyanumaya, a woman in her late fifties, was also of the Sunar caste. Debra called down to Gyanumaya that we wanted to talk to her on the balcony, and went down to greet her, intending to bring her through the kitchen and up the stairs. However, as Debra was on her way downstairs, Gyanumaya took a different route: she scaled the outside of the house. She somehow crawled up the vertical outside wall, made her way around the balcony to an opening in the railing, came through the opening, and sat down. Gyanumaya knew that Debra did not prohibit lower-caste people from entering her kitchen, but she found a way to get to the place of our interview without going through the house.

I later questioned Debra about her knowledge of the community. Did she know of other people who scaled the outside of houses to get to the second floor? Was Gyanumaya in particular known to enter houses in this way? As far as we could discern, no community members were accustomed to getting to the second stories of houses by climbing up the walls. Nor did Gyanumaya have a reputation for whimsical or unusual behavior.

How Gyanumaya herself interpreted her climb we do not know. We did not ask her to explain her action. For me, her climb became an icon of limitation—an example to use in writing, in talks, and in teaching to point out the limitations of culturalist approaches (see, for example, Holland 1992b). Here the story lends itself to both a culturalist and an opposing constructivist interpretation. Gyanumaya had undeniably climbed above a culturalist approach, but her actions raise issues about the constructivist one as well.

After I had said to myself, "Yes, she really did climb up the house!" my next thought was about caste. I had an image of caste identification, ingrained in the Sunar woman, propelling her away from the sin of polluting another's hearth, to the extreme that sent her up the wall. I tried in vain to think of a culturally given sense of myself that could have moved me to such a physical feat. My image, rapidly conceived in reaction to a startling event, provides a good caricature of the culturalist approach. Culture—the cultural significance of caste and pollution learned from childhood—was an essential force inside Gyanumaya, directing her behavior.

According to this first interpretation, Gyanumaya's climb lent dramatic corroboration to a culturalist theory and justified careful and painstaking attention to all of the details of caste, pollution, sin, dharma, and other related concepts. It demonstrated the potency of cultural "meaning systems." My attention, for a time, was directed toward a deeper understanding of caste. Only later did other aspects of the situation begin to intrude on my attempts at culturalist analysis, accumulating as contradictory evidence, until the incident slowly became for me a reminder of lacunae in the culturalist approach.[7]

I remembered, for instance, that Debra and I had attributed the discomfort of our other Sunar interviewee to the presence of the Chetri woman. We had also wondered, in retrospect, if Gyanumaya had somehow been reminded of the close proximity of the Bahun landlord's house. This was another way to understand Gyanumaya's action. Perhaps the presence and proximity of these higher-caste persons evoked an implicit discourse of caste that held sway in many contexts of life in Naudada, a discourse about relations between members of different castes. In avoiding the kitchen Gyanumaya conformed to the positioning that the discourse of caste imposed upon her and the other Naudadan participants in the situation. Had the social situation been different—had Debra been there alone, for example—then perhaps Gyanumaya would not have been obliged to take up her caste position; rather she would have complied with Debra's wishes, entering through the kitchen and using the stairs. But as the situation stood, Gyanumaya was liable to construal, and subordination, by the discourses of caste that were hegemonic there and then.[8] Her behavior was not an index of the cultural impetus of a caste identity *embodied* in her, but of the social significance of a caste identity *imposed* upon her. She was propelled up the house, not by cultural tenets that long ago had formed her outlook on hearths, food, and pollution, but by the social forces that determined whether the discourse of caste would be salient in that particular situation.

The constructivist position emphasizes the social positioning that goes on whenever people interact. Constructivists extend to all behavior the point that sociolinguists and ethnographers of communication have made about linguistic behavior. No matter what one person says to another, there is always more to the message than its semantic content. How the message is said—through accent, tone, or tempo, what language or dialect it is said in, what style (formal or informal), what mode (whether phrased as a question or command)—all these index the relationship among speaker, addressee, and audience and constitute signs of the speaker's claim to social position.

Irvine (1980) is one of many who makes this point. Her elegant example addresses the social meaning of asking a favor in Wolof. One day early in her stay in Senegal, she asked a woman, very politely, to make room for her on a bench. Taking pity on her ignorance of sociolinguistic convention, a bystander pointed out that she should not put such small requests in such polite form. In fact, the request should not even be phrased as a question ("Would you please do x?") but as an imperative ("Do x"). Her request was more than a simple indication of need. It was also an indication, inexplicit to be sure, of her status relative to that of the other woman. And, Irvine later learned, she made three mistakes in the space of one short utterance, twice claiming a lower status than she merited and once a higher status. To give another example, Lutz (1987) argues that Ifaluk attributions of emotion were not just about feelings, but also about social position. To attribute *fago* (glossed in English as compassion/love/sadness) to another or oneself was to make a claim of high social position. Only a person of accomplishment, status, or wealth could have cultivated the sort of sensitivities, and carried through the kinds of action, that *fago* required.[9]

Gal (1987) and Irvine (1985) point out that studies of language use show situation to be extremely important; people usually command a range of alternative ways of speaking, which they vary in response to social situations. It is not that American women, for example, use hedges and other linguistic markers of deference automatically, as though they were characteristically deferential. Both women and men use deferential markers when and only when they are in situations that demand their deference (O'Barr and Atkins 1980).[10]

Social constructivists urge the same conclusion with respect to other behavior. For Hindu Nepalis, approaching the hearth of someone whose caste is higher than one's own—no matter whether it is an act significant in a moral world—is a sign of and a claim about social position. In Gyanumaya's case, entering through the kitchen could be construed as claiming a higher-caste status than she was known to have. She avoided such a claim by avoiding the kitchen. According to constructivists, Gyanumaya and others from Nepal, like everyone else, are always propelled by their "subject position" within the social situation in which they find themselves.

Cultural Logic or Subject Position?

It is possible to think of linguistic behavior from a culturalist position, explaining how one speaks (for example, saying "please" when asking for favors) as reflecting precepts learned in childhood about conducting (and thus identifying) oneself as a moral person. One strives to say whatever upholds the culturally constructed, moral world. A constructivist approach, in contrast, would emphasize that linguistic behavior depends upon maneuverings, negotiations, impositions, and recreations of relations of status and entitlement. Saying or not saying "please" makes a social claim about one's status or relationship vis-à-vis one's addressee. It is as though a speaker is always of two minds, attending to two consuming concerns. The culturalist speaker seeks to conduct herself so as to do right by a preconstituted, culturally given, and moral world. The constructivist speaker responds instead to the social claims implied by the utterance, making and sustaining the claims that the particular situation allows.

Bourdieu (1977a), for one, has shown that the two perspectives we have considered cannot be collapsed into each other. Culturalists might be tempted to claim that they can encompass the constructivist position. They might say that, as a child, Gyanumaya learned a context-sensitive cultural principle: in the presence of higher-caste persons, ideas about the hearth and pollution are important; otherwise, they are not. But this argument by "context rule" turns out to be unending, impossible. We know from our ethnographic research in Naudada that certain caste-related restrictions are contested and often not followed in the local schools. Does this mean we should add another aspect of context sensitivity: when in school ignore the former context-sensitive rule? We know that Debra, who was neither within nor without the caste system, invited people of lower caste into her kitchen. Had the lower-caste people who came into her kitchen really learned context-sensitive rules to take care of such an eventuality? Bourdieu explains that context-sensitive rules are impossible because situations always arise that do not fit the rules. It is simpler to admit the possibility that different discourses can be hegemonic in different locales, an admission that obviates the need for a myriad of context-sensitive rules.

Once culturalists admit that people use culturally meaningful behavior to bring about contested social ends, they have stepped outside their own position. Disagreements over (and even recognitions of) a person's social position, relative status, and relationships belie the possibility that the social uses of culture can be totally dictated by cultural logics. Instead differences are resolved by other means. The constructivists suggest that power makes a difference as to whose version will prevail.

Yet the culturalist position cannot be totally rejected, as it might be by a radical constructivist.[11] Clearly there is more to saying "please" in Wolof than one more way of indicating one's social position. No doubt for Gyanumaya there was more to her climb than simply indicating to the Chetri woman that she knew her place. Culturally constructed moral worlds, aside and apart from how their discourses can be used to position others, have a persuasion of their own.

In a familiar optical illusion, two faces, silhouetted in profile, look at each other across a small space. But looking again we see the space in the middle as not-space, and the lines of the faces disappear into the lines of a vase. The extreme culturalist and constructivist perspectives on behavior are also a sort of interpretive illusion. In the extreme culturalist vision, Gyanumaya, the person, is a bearer of "culture"—historical events and conditions that have been distilled through group processes into culture and passed somehow into her mind/body. In the radical constructivist vision, Gyanumaya is an instrument and an outcome of "the situation," a person pushed first into one subject position (when Debra's greetings and invitations positioned her as a person whom Debra welcomed into her house) and then into another (when the higher-caste woman saw Gyanumaya, and, perhaps through posture or movements, communicated to Gyanumaya that she saw her as a bearer of pollution). Looked at from the culturalist position, behavior follows cultural principles; it falls in line with heartfelt moral precepts that transcend the actual people with whom one interacts and the actual situations surrounding those interactions. From the constructivist position, behavior instead is the acting out (or refusal) of subject positions; it is pushed into line by relations of power and influence that obtain in the venues where, and among the particular people with whom, one interacts.

What propelled Gyanumaya, then? Must we choose one perspective or the other? Are we doomed to oscillate between the two visions of what we all "know" to be a continuous field? The answer, we think, is clearly no. These perspectives can be separated, and indeed we have found it immensely helpful to recognize dimensions missing from the culturalist perspective and offered by the constructivist one, and vice versa. But there is no reason to pretend that they are so separate in action. Gyanumaya was no doubt swayed, as most of us are in any situation, by multiple and mixed thoughts and feelings. Dialogic perspectives, such as Bakhtin's (1981), explicitly free us from the idea that we as a group or as individuals can hold only one perspective at a time. Humans are both blessed and cursed by their dialogic nature—their tendency to encompass a number of views in virtual simultaneity and tension, regardless of their logical compatibility. Our own perspective puts together the culturalist and the constructivist positions in a dialogic frame.

Improvisation and Heuristic Development

Gyanumaya's climb can also introduce another parameter of our dialogic position. It brings into focus the iconic potential of both the behavior and the artifacts that are produced in interaction, and the roles these symbols may play in changing or preserving identity and subjectivity. Again, the move to such a perspective depends upon entertaining the wisdom of both the culturalist and the constructivist.

As the vision of Gyanumaya being propelled up the house by the cultural principles of caste identity faded, I (Holland) began to marvel at the improvisational nature of her entry onto the balcony. Gyanumaya was, as far as we could learn, not accustomed to making her way to the second stories of houses by scaling exterior walls. Instead she had come up with a spectacular improvisation in the face of a problematic situation. The house belonged, in her eyes, to an upper-caste person, and thus—at least in the usual circumstances of community life—she would not be allowed to enter. Yet she needed to get to the second-floor balcony. She devised the solution of climbing up the outside of the house.

My original training as an anthropologist did not direct me to attend to such improvisation. Rather I was taught to attend to culture, to common conventions, to shared organizing themes. Even though ethnographic studies invariably noted variations and sometimes marked dissent, the job of the anthropologist was to find the culture. One of my first experiences with fieldwork took place in Trinidad, where I went in 1967 to study the religious practices referred to as Shango. At first, as I attended Shango ceremonies around the island and talked to leaders and participants, I was greatly impressed by the differences among the ceremonies and the ideas and practices of the leaders. Within weeks I was mired in a crisis of confidence. I had been taught that people followed cultural patterns. Where were the obedient pattern-followers? I even began to doubt that anyone ever coordinated his or her behavior with anyone else. If the newspaper reported that two people had engaged in the same activity, I was skeptical.

But I continued to attend Shango feasts. After several more weeks I calmed down and concentrated on the commonalties I had started to notice across the Shango practitioners. I noted the conventionalized emphases and understandings that threaded their way through the cacophony of differences. I was at last a successful anthropologist: I had found the culture that was there. Other truths—a great deal of improvisation, provoked by a great variety of social and material conditions—became evident (see Holland and Crane 1987). The connections of the forms created by the participants to postcolonial relations, to the location of the particular groups in relation to urban centers, and to the position of Shango in relation to the larger field of religious activity (including the established churches, Spiritual Baptism, and a more secretive activity, "circle-side work") are all clear in hindsight. But in my writing I paid little attention to these features and instead distilled "the culture of Shango" and detailed "its" effects, reshaping the values and lifestyles of participants.

Gyanumaya's climb up the house repeated, in microcosm, the same opportunity to focus on commonalities and forget the differences. One could ignore the improvisational character of her feat and instead wonder, as I first did, at the power of the cultural proscriptions of caste, the products of collective social history, to guide an individual's actions.

Constructivism takes the opposite tack. It invites notice of the improvisation as a sign of positioning by powerful discourses. Gyanumaya then becomes an instrument and an outcome of the situation, a person pushed first into one subject position (as a welcome guest) and then into another (as a bearer of pollution). In the extreme, especially in circumstances deemed postmodern, according to constructivists, people constantly face such disjoint situations. Feminist poststructuralists emphasize that women and other oppressed people are especially subject to situations like Gyanumaya's, situations replete with contradictions. Oppressed people are constantly climbing up houses.

We advocate paying more attention to the improvisation itself, to what was produced. We try to see both culture and subject position at the same time. We do not look directly at either cultural logic or subject position as a phenomenon unto itself. Instead we consider the practical artifacts of the moment—the verbal, gestural, and material productions—emerging from the situation, and ask how, and to what end, these artifacts might be taken up and, in later events perhaps, become conventionalized or made into culture. In our vision, Gyanumaya and the rest of us, individually and collectively, are not just products of our culture, not just respondents to the situation, but also and critically appropriators of cultural artifacts that we and others produce.

By climbing up the house Gyanumaya produced an unusual form of behavior, one that did not, but conceivably could have, become an icon for reflection. There were other such productions as well. Debra and I, together with the people of Naudada, co-constructed the interview situation, making Debra's house a somewhat unusual social space in the community and a notional artifact perhaps more appealing for future appropriation than the idea of climbing up houses. The space was one where prevalent caste restrictions were not authorized by the person who was at least in nominal charge.[12] The situation also figured in various improvisations: of material that could be incorporated into later gossip sessions about the strange foreigners, of research materials for later use by Debra and me, and, obviously, of an icon that could be useful for our purposes in this chapter.

Constructivists think of improvisation as an expected outcome when people are simultaneously engaged with or pushed by contradictory discourses. They view it as an endpoint, however, not a beginning. Others have attempted to connect culture and subject position conceptually in order to understand people's behavior. Bourdieu has made one of the most significant efforts in this regard, and his metatheory of practice has been extremely consequential for anthropological theories of culture. Under the tutelage of Bourdieu and others, anthropological attention has turned from the analysis of culture as an objectified and abstract system to the immanent analysis of cultural forms, of their constant improvisation within ever-changing social and material conditions (see Ortner 1984 for an early review).

Gyanumaya's climb up the house, no matter how striking and dramatic an improvisation, is, in the regard of Bourdieu's practice theory, characteristic of everyday behavior. Improvisations are the sort of impromptu actions that occur when our past, brought to the present as *habitus,* meets with a particular combination of circumstances and conditions for which we have no set response. Such improvisations are the openings by which change comes about from generation to generation. They constitute the environment or landscape in which the experience of the next generation "sediments," falls out, into expectation and disposition. The improvisations of the parental generation are the beginning of a new habitus for the next generation. *Pace* Bourdieu, we suggest that the process is also condensed into the space of a lifetime. In our view, improvisations, from a cultural base and in response to the subject positions offered *in situ,* are, when taken up as symbol, potential beginnings of an altered subjectivity, an altered identity.[13]

Such productions, we believe, are always being appropriated by people as heuristic means to guide, authorize, legitimate, and encourage their own and others' behavior. As an often unintended but sometimes purposive consequence, there is a continual process of heuristic development: individuals and groups are always (re)forming themselves as persons and collectives through cultural materials created in the immediate and the more distant past. In this process of heuristic development, culture and subject position are joined in the production of cultural resources that are then subjectively taken up.

The possibilities of heuristic development do not mean that humans are free to develop whatever subjectivity they wish and to do whatever strikes them at the moment. Far from it. One's history-in-person is the sediment from past experiences upon which one improvises, using the cultural resources available, in response to the subject positions afforded one in the present. The constraints are overpowering, yet not hermetically sealed. Improvisation can become the basis for a reformed subjectivity.

The ethnographic case studies we present in later chapters range widely in their subjects—from persons coming to identify themselves as non-drinking alcoholics to women workers and students living and sometimes resisting the cultural politics of gender that position them; from Roger Kelly, assembling identities from his psychiatric diagnoses, to Tika Damai and other young women in Nepal imagining, through songs, a world in which women escape patriarchal control. The conceptual discussions interspersed among these ethnographic chapters emphasize not only the contemporaneous processes but also the long-term, developmental character of identity formation as it moves through improvisation, conflict, embodiment, and dialogue in social and historical time.

2

A Practice Theory of Self and Identity

Discourses and Practices of the Self

In all places across the world—in Nepal, for example, or American Samoa—there are ways of talking about what we might call a person's self (or selves). That is, there are conventional means for representing the intrinsic capacities and processes that are presumed to shape a person's actions. These intrinsic capacities and processes are implicated in reflexive mediation of behavior, the objectifying, monitoring, and evaluating stances that a person sometimes takes toward his or her own behavior.[1] This talk of, this discourse about, what we will call selves takes many forms. It may consist of expressions implying a subjective sense of oneself as an actor/subject; it may be embedded in claims about others or expressed directly in pontifications about the self by specialists. Nepalis and Samoans have ways of talking about selves, but their discourses differ from those prevalent in the United States. They also engage in activities thought to affect the self, "practices of the self," that are not necessarily common in the United States (see, for example, Clement 1982 on Samoan therapeutic procedures for mental disorders).

Parish (1991, 1994) has written about people living in the Kathmandu Valley of Nepal who identify themselves as members of the Newar ethnic group.[2] At the time of his fieldwork in the 1980s the Newar people he met did not use any term that might be easily glossed in English as "self," but they talked about the heart in ways akin to our talk about the self.[3] Memories, thoughts, and feelings were stored in the heart (*nuga*); willful actions came from the heart. English speakers in the United States sometimes say things like "Who knows what's in his heart?" but the

Newars talked about the heart in ways that would be readily understood in English. They spoke, for example, of someone with no ability to commit himself or follow through on moral action as lacking "heart blood." Furthermore, the self/heart was an abode of the sacred. They spoke of a deity residing in their hearts and dictating morally commendable actions.

Parish's account of a distinctive self-discourse is not without company. Fifty years of research by anthropologists and other cross-cultural researchers have provided examples from all parts of the globe. It is now clear that there exists a huge variety of discourses, practices, concepts, means, and modalities of the self.[4] The question now is not so much whether there are differences but rather what they signify. At issue is the role of historical, social, and cultural phenomena in constituting the self. How, if at all, do they inform the self that is their object? Stances toward the ontological status of these self-discourses and practices lie at the heart of the debates in the vast literature on the self.

The Universal versus the Culturally Specific Self

Before the 1970s, anthropological work on culture and the self, like other cross-cultural inquiries, developed primarily through a dialogue, sometimes implicit, sometimes explicit, between universalist and culturalist perspectives.[5] The oft-remarked division of labor between anthropology and psychology (for example, Bloch 1985, Miller 1988) cast psychology and psychologists as the champions of universalist perspectives and anthropology as the bastion of culturalist positions, but the dialogue was also conducted within anthropology.

The debate is very familiar and can be recounted quickly. The point of particular importance is the status attributed to specific discourses and practices of the self. For those who assign theoretical priority to the "natural self," culture is subordinate to universal properties of human psychology. The human self is, first and foremost, a complex of natural, species-given structures and processes. The selves found in Samoa are simply refractions of an underlying natural self, as are those in Nepal. Pliant to scientific probing, the natural self exists beneath the sometimes dazzling but always thin overlay of cultural expression, of the ways of enacting and talking about the self—much as the species-given human body exists beneath culturally variable kinds of clothing.

In this view, the natural self is akin to the heart or the liver. It is as invariant as these organs and for the same reason: its ontology is that of a natural phenomenon. From such a perspective, culturally distinct discourses of the self are simply more or less correct, more or less productive of scientifically sound interventions, but scarcely significant in any other way. Even in the field, we could often amalgamate the understandings of different groups to our own. So the Newars of Nepal talk about a deity in their hearts. Could we not simply say that they have a metaphorical way of talking about the superego? Misguided childrearing practices may lead to pathologies of the natural self, just as poor eating habits affect whether the heart becomes diseased, but the relationship is the same no matter what the culture. One's "cultural background" may affect such things as whether one's self-esteem is high or low, yet self-esteem remains not only ascertainable but also a significant correlate of other aspects of the person, no matter the culture. Whether in a given culture there exists a comparable concept, a similar discourse about self-esteem, is irrelevant.

Countervailing culturalist positions cannot be captured by the clothing/body analogy. For them, culturally specific concepts are not coverings of the universal self. Instead they are indicators of contours of culture that shape the self in profound ways. South Asian religious and philosophical writings and pronouncements on the self, for example, have been read by anthropologists such as Dumont (1980) and Marriott (1976a, 1976b) as indicators of a culture deeply at odds with Western culture. These anthropologists argue that South Asian cultures, especially dominant Hindu forms, grant value principally to the collective. The culture derogates individuals to the point that, especially for Dumont, the Western concept of the individual is not very helpful in the study of Indian societies.

Culturally variable discourses and concepts of the self are, in the culturalist view, not simply more or less accurate maps of the same territory, but different maps that bespeak a difference in the territory. Shweder and Bourne (1984), summarizing a large amount of cross-cultural literature, identify two ideal types of self: a "Western" concept that is autonomous, acontextual, abstract, and independent; and a non-Western notion that is context-dependent, concrete, and socially defined: "To the question 'Does the concept of the person vary cross-culturally?' our answer is obviously 'yes'; we have tried to identify two major alternative conceptualizations of the individual-social relationship, viz., the 'ego-centric contractual' and the 'sociocentric organic'" (193).

For many anthropologists this research implies the proposition that culture profoundly shapes selves.[6] Different cultural conceptions of the self are treated as indicators of underlying cultural themes that affect not only conceptions of the self but also conceptions of emotion, child development, and mental disorders, as well as individuals' patterns of cognition and affect. As Miller (1988: 280) puts it, "the studies imply that cultural content must be regarded as an essential influence on the patterning of psychological structures and processes." The differences in collective meaning systems, in other words, are productive, and therefore indicative, of profound and thoroughgoing differences in the selves of those who are cultured in these systems. These cultural discourses and their relationship to the self are not like the relation of the clothes to the body, but more like that of a bottle to the liquid it contains. Self-discourses and practices must be scrutinized, for they are clues to the contours of the bottle—the culture—that shapes the malleable self.

Few anthropologists, if any, fully embrace the extremes of either the universalist or the culturalist position. Rather they try to reconcile the tensions between universalism and cultural specificity. For example, Hallowell (1955a, 1955b), who pioneered anthropological theories of the self, argued that every person anywhere had a sense of himself or herself as a separate being and could thus become an object to himself or herself. For Hallowell, self-awareness and self-reflexivity were universal, species-given characteristics.[7] He pointed out other invariant aspects of selves as well, yet argued that many seemingly natural aspects of the self are, in fact, culturally shaped and cannot be universally interpreted.[8] For instance, in a culture where demons are taken seriously, a feeling that one is being threatened by demons is indicative of culture, not of pathology as it probably would be in a demonless culture.

More recent approaches to the problem of articulating the universal with the cultural include the work of the anthropologist Gananath Obeyesekere (1981), who builds upon psychodynamic theories an account of important, universal structures and processes that, at the same time, emphasizes cultural symbols. In his view, individuals appropriate cultural symbols to assuage and manage the psychodynamically generated dilemmas that we all face.[9] The medical anthropologist Thomas Csordas (1994) draws upon the phenomenological psychology of Merleau-Ponty to articulate a notion of the self embodied within—that is, universally oriented to—an experiential world that is deeply and inevitably informed by its particular cultural environment. He too seeks to reconcile the universal and culturally specific aspects of self.

In this debate, then, we see broad differences in the assessment of culturally specific discourses and practices of the self. From the universalist position these discourses are largely irrelevant; from the culturalist they are indicative of key contours of cultures. The more recent perspectives (introduced in Chapter 1) certainly consider these discourses relevant, but they do not take them to be indicators of an underlying, pervasive culture. Rather they conceive them as what we will call living artifacts or living tools. Obeyesekere's conceptualization of cultural symbols—as "therapeutic media" taken up by individuals faced with psychodynamic dilemmas—hints at this direction, but the new development moves outside the old issues.

The Critical Disruption

Roughly two decades ago powerful cross-currents began to disrupt the universalist-culturalist debate. Anthropology entered into a period of critical examination of its relations with its subjects. The discipline came under sustained criticism from within. The critics reflected upon the collaboration of anthropologists with colonial powers (Asad 1973), for example, and upon the tendency of anthropological fieldwork to focus myopically on men and male-centered activities (Weiner 1976; Reiter 1975). Somewhat later, anthropologists began asking questions about their representations of others. What messages were conveyed by anthropological writing practices? Clifford (1988), Fabian (1983), and others harshly judged the device of the "ethnographic present" (writing in the present tense) used to describe peoples who were actually studied during a particular period. Such usage suspended these peoples in time, removed them from history, and treated them as though they were simply pliable specimens of science, comparable to other "cultural species."

Anthropologists, along with some psychologists, also adopted Foucault's work, especially his formulation of power/knowledge, as an impetus for critical reflection. Foucault depicted social and psychological sciences as constructing, rather than objectively studying, their subjects. In the post-Enlightenment West, the scientific management of populations places people in categories that determine the treatment they receive in such institutions as mental institutions, prisons, and schools. Technical categories, such as "schizophrenic" or "at risk" children, the argument goes, also enter into or return to everyday discourse, and so are used in schools and other institutions. People learn to treat one another and themselves according to these categories.

This traffic between the scientific and the institutional, between the scientific and the popular, belies the possibility that social scientists could be what they claim to be: non-interfering, truth-telling observers. Instead scientists, most obviously those whose "findings" enter directly into institutional treatments, become implicated in a kind of forced reductionism. Local knowledge is disregarded and replaced by scientific categories imposed by those with power. No matter how scrupulous the attempts of individual researchers to be objective, social scientists, today as in the past, are studying what their field of study has helped to create. In this Foucauldian vision, unreflexive claims to "objectivity" are hollow at best; at worst they are a self-serving means by which science rhetorically claims authority.[10]

This critical stance has had a number of ramifications in anthropology. For one, "culture," that is, anthropological descriptions of cultures, was subjected to scrutiny and seen to be suspiciously entangled with systems of power/knowledge. Looking back to past collaborations with colonial governments, for example, anthropologists analyzed how anthropological constructions of the colonized informed governmental actions. Governments' efforts to subjugate their colonized populations powerfully constrained these peoples to reconstruct themselves, either in embrace of or in opposition to the categories used to describe them.[11] The guise of scientist has thus become suspect to the point that many anthropologists meet claims to scientific objectivity and authority with incredulity, if not antagonism.

Feminists too have rigorously criticized past representations of culture, claiming that anthropologists often put forward patriarchal and thus partial accounts. Twenty-five years of feminist scrutiny have made it impossible to ignore the importance of gender in *all* societies or to avoid the recognition that what men may take to be important may well be experienced in quite different ways by women. Twenty years ago Geertz (1973a) could get away with analyzing the cockfight in Bali, a solely masculine activity, without paying particular attention to the social significance of its gendered quality, of who participated and who did not. Today it is clear even to those who are not engaged by feminist theory that women have different perspectives on the apparatuses of male privilege—such as men's houses in Amazonian cultures—than men do; and that their perspectives are not necessarily those which men wish them to adopt (Gregor 1977). Clearly one's social position—defined by gender, race, class, and any other division that is structurally significant—potentially affects one's perspective on cultural institutions and the ardor of one's subscription to the values and interpretations that are promoted in rituals and other socially produced cultural forms.

These feminist critiques see many cultural discourses as impositions, pushing women and men to behavior compatible with the structures and institutions that favor members of one social category over another. Feminists, then, provide yet another basis for suspecting descriptions of seemingly holistic, coherent, integrated cultures. They ask: Whose account of "the" culture is being privileged? Whose view is being constructed as though it were the only one? And they answer: Not the view of those in positions of restricted privilege. Accounts of culture that ignore the importance of social position surreptitiously participate in the silencing of those who lack privilege and power.

The critical disruption has further affected the writing of ethnographies across cultural boundaries. Texts, when conceived consistently with a Foucauldian logic, invite the reader to regard anthropological subjects from a certain perspective. Thus the writings of contemporary ethnographers, as well as those of researchers in other fields, are now vulnerable to criticism of their "textual strategies." These strategies include more than theories about significant structures and processes important to the question at hand; they also include the text's implications about the position of the researcher relative to the people being studied and relative to the reader. Ethnographic accounts are now critically read for their portrayal of the relationship between anthropologist and subject, and many texts now include explicit sections that problematize these relationships (for early examples see Favret-Saada 1980; Crapanzano 1980). It is now common for writers to consider critically the perspective that they convey.

This critical disruption has a number of implications for comparison across cultural boundaries. The very conceptions of culture have changed drastically. Anthropology no longer endeavors to describe cultures as though they were coherent, integrated, timeless wholes. The object of study has shifted away from Samoan culture, or American culture, or any culture taken as a whole. Anthropology is much less willing to treat the cultural discourses and practices of a group of people as indicative of one underlying cultural logic or essence equally compelling to all members of the group. Instead, contest, struggle, and power have been brought to the foreground. The objects of cultural study are now particular, circumscribed, historically and socially situated "texts" or "forms" and the processes through which they are negotiated, resisted, institutionalized, and internalized. As Foucault insisted, significantly for the study of culture and self, "cultural forms" are presumed to affect and shape subjectivity, and these cultural forms come in great variety.[12]

The Socially Constructed Self

In addition to bringing about a refiguring of culture as an object of study and of the scientist's position with regard to those being studied, the critical disruption in anthropology and other fields has had a powerful impact on dialogues about the self. Discourse or discursive theory, as Foucauldian and related understandings are sometimes called, has provoked a new concept of the self—as socially constructed. Here we return to the consideration of constructivism we began in Chapter 1. The discourses and categories dominant in a society, the argument goes, are "inscribed" upon people, both interpersonally and institutionally, and (as we shall see later in this chapter) within them. Selves are socially constructed through the mediation of powerful discourses and their artifacts—tax forms, census categories, curriculum vitae, and the like.

To reiterate, social constructivists emphasize that our communications with one another not only convey messages but also always make claims about who we are relative to one another and the nature of our relationships. When we speak we afford subject positions to one another. In this chapter we afford certain positions to anthropologists and others to psychologists, those who identify themselves as scientists, those who suspect scientific representations, those who subscribe to older anthropological views of the self, and so on. In like manner, genres such as censuses or curriculum vitae require us to present ourselves according to categories obligatory to the form. Resistance to such affordances is possible, of course. But the texts and other cultural media we create constrain, according to social constructivists, "readers" to two choices: to comply or to resist. Perhaps the discourses we use here are not hegemonic, and perhaps we lack even momentary power to make the constraints we place on our readers chafe; nonetheless, there exist other texts and other discourses that cannot be similarly put aside. The "subject" of the self is always open to the power of the discourses and practices that describe it.[13]

The social constructivist position cannot be contained by the terms of the prior universalist-culturalist debate. Indeed, from the standpoint of constructivism all the phenomena addressed (and differentiated) by the participants in that older debate might as well be collapsed into one construct, an "essential self." This essential self, a durable organization of the mind/body, is perennially suspect as a product of "essentialist" thinking, while the socially constructed self remains a paragon of anti-essentialism.

The culturalist versions of essential selves have been especially subject to criticism. Envisioned as stable and enduring characters set in place (by the end of childhood) through rituals and other socializing practices that distill and inculcate the core values of what were assumed to be pervasive cultures, they are anathema to constructivism, a kind of double essentialism. Such selves persist through time, regardless of change in social and material conditions. Socially constructed selves, in sharp contrast, are subject to positioning by whatever powerful discourses they happen to encounter—changing state policies that dictate new ways of categorizing people in the census, educational diagnostics that label some children "at risk," or new forms of racist discourse taken up from right-wing talk shows. Perhaps they are resistant to such social forces; they nonetheless remain provisionally at their mercy. Social constructivism conceives discourses and practices to be the tools that build the self in contexts of power, rather than as expressions of stable interpretations of world and values that have been imparted to the person through enculturation.

Indeed, the universalists and the culturalists (insofar as they still exist) find themselves unwitting allies, cast into the same essentialist camp. The heated debates now concern the degree to which the essentialist self is important at all. Again, when portraying this second debate, one must not imagine two exclusive categories but rather a continuum between an extreme essentialist view, which pays absolutely no attention to the socially positioning power of discourses, and an extreme constructivist position, which has no interest in any durable aspects of self. Most if not all actual statements lie somewhere along the continuum and seek to reconcile the tensions between what can be depicted as incompatible views.[14] One finds social constructivists, such as Hollway (1984), who, despite their emphasis on discursive positioning, consider Lacanian concepts useful to delineate parts of the embodied self that endure and make a difference in capitulation or resistance to social positioning—or even Foucault (1978) himself, who finds, beyond the discourses of sexuality, a "surplus" of experience in the sexual pleasures of the body (Harvey 1996).

Emerging Directions in the Study of the Self

The critical disruption has, to put it mildly, interfered with the kind of questions posed by Shweder and Bourne (1984) in their summary of cross-cultural variation in concepts of the person. The intellectual and political climate within anthropology has decisively changed, affecting the questions that those of us engaged in studies of self and identity are now pursuing.[15]

The newer research, in combination with past work, provides a basis for a practice theory of self, one informed and fundamentally reformed, but not determined, by the extreme versions of the critiques mounted in the last twenty years.[16] The more recent inquiries, though not always undertaken in the name of critical psychological anthropology, nonetheless reflect dimensions of the critical disruption. We can discern at least three interrelated components of a theoretical refiguring of the relationship between culture and self. First, culturally and socially constructed discourses and practices of the self are recognized as neither the "clothes" of a universally identical self nor the (static) elements of cultural molds into which the self is cast. Rather, differentiated by relations of power and the associated institutional infrastructure, they are conceived as living tools of the self—as artifacts or media that figure the self constitutively, in open-ended ways. Second, and correlatively, the self is treated as always embedded in (social) practice, and as itself a kind of practice. Third, "sites of the self," the loci of self-production or self-process, are recognized as plural.

Sites of the Self

The idea of plural, even competing sites of the self, is now common to a variety of disciplines (see, for example, Smith 1988). In anthropology the demise of the privileged concept of bounded, discrete, coherent cultures has made room for the recognition that people are exposed to competing and differentially powerful and authoritative discourses and practices of the self.

A series of articles in the journal *Ethos* in the early 1990s made this point. This series challenges Shweder and Bourne's separation of a Western "egocentric" or independent self from a non-Western "sociocentric" or interdependent self. The articles particularly attack any monolithic, essentialist version of the "Western" self. Their arguments take us through some of the same terrain we have already explored. For instance, Ewing (1990) and Murray (1993) inveigh against the past tendency of anthropologists to write as though cultural discourses and practices of the self could be taken as indicators of core cultural themes whose internalization yielded "culturalized" selves. But they resurvey this ground with specific reference to culture and self, and they illustrate the conceptual move to plural sites of self-fashioning. They call for the "disambiguation" of the sites or sources of the self and imply that the works drawn from these different "production sites" of self-discourses and practices are not necessarily complementary.

Ewing, for example, says that the authoritative discourses on the self found in religious and philosophical texts hardly exhaust the sites of self-production. Popular discourses about the self are another important locus. Anthropologists like Marriott and Dumont, Ewing argues, fail to take account of the self as it is expressed by individuals in everyday talk and action. Hence their account of "self" in South Asia, derived from analyses of the talk and texts of specialists, is always partial and may not coincide with the self construed by popular genres of speaking and acting. In particular, Ewing turns her criticism to the depiction of the Western self. Although Western representations of the self found in philosophical and psychological texts may indeed bespeak a person who is autonomous, bounded, and transcontextual, people's representations of themselves in the stream of everyday life reveal a multitude of selves that are neither bounded, stable, perduring, nor impermeable. Spiro (1993), addressing a broader set of topics, makes some of the same points to support his thesis that the differences between the West and the non-West have been greatly exaggerated.

Murray (1993) speaks to a different point. His argument has to do less with discrepancies between selves founded in authoritative discourses and selves depicted in everyday talk than with discrepant characterizations within Western authoritative discourse on the self. Western philosophy, Western psychology, and Western religion do not, he argues, present a unified conception of the self. He cites David Hume as a major philosophical figure whose depictions of the self were quite at odds with those which supposedly characterize the West. If even authoritative sources are far from being in agreement, where then does a "Western" conception of self live?

Holland and Kipnis (1994) return to the venue of popular discourse. They describe everyday discourses on embarrassment in the United States and analyze the cultural model of self that underlies this talk. The self that gets embarrassed is a "sociocentric" or, to use Markus and Kitayama's (1991) terms, an "interdependent" self. Western ethnopsychologies, Holland and Kipnis conclude, like Murray's formal psychologies and philosophies, do not uniformly posit an egocentric self. Americans engage in discourses that are not consistent on the subject of sociocentrism/egocentrism. Some posit a sociocentric or interdependent self; others, an egocentric or independent self.

Selves in Practice

These articles do not say that differences we think of as cultural are insignificant. Nor do they deny the utility of the distinction between sociocentric and egocentric. Self-discourses and practices do vary across cultures in ways that may be, for some purposes, usefully glossed as sociocentric and egocentric. Markus and Kitayama, for example, are convincing in their argument that accommodating one's self to others is important in Japan, and Kondo's (1990) ethnography, also set in Japan, vividly communicates the same valuing of accommodation. In some of our own research in American Samoa on interpretations and treatments of mental disorders (Clement [formerly Holland] 1982) we found that Samoan cultural models of mental problems rested upon a notion of persons affected more by their social situations than by their enduring intrapersonal conflicts or tendencies.

As Miller (1988) points out in her review of the anthropological literature on concepts of self, these findings fit the generalization that some groups emphasize more relational notions of the self while others, such as those of the West, emphasize more individualistic ones. The caveat is that such characterizations lend themselves to reification. We must take care that "American culture" and "Americans," for example, are not construed in our specialist discourses as inherently egocentric or independent, or that Samoans' culture and Samoans are not treated as though they were, in essence, sociocentric or interdependent. Behavior is better viewed as a sign of self in practice, not as a sign of self in essence. It is sometimes useful to extract from the flow of events and discourses in a particular locale important conceits or concepts—recurring conventions of thinking and behaving and constantly defended values. But the further step—assuming that this abstraction, this "culture" or "the self" associated with it, has an essence, an impetus of its own that will continue through time, absent any social machinations—has been decisively challenged (White 1993).[17]

Whether subject to direct criticism or not, any anthropological idea of an unproblematic relation between culture and self would have no doubt eroded on its own. The relationship between cultural forms and personhood is no longer taken for granted, and as a result subjectivity is both more significant and more interesting. Persons are now recognized to have perspectives on their cultural worlds that are likely to differ by gender and other markers of social position.[18] They are no longer considered to be unproblematically shaped by rituals and other key events of an enculturation that solely reflects cultural ideology. If public institutions and the rituals they stage are important to, but not determinant of, subjectivity, then researchers need to address personhood directly. If people are not seen simply as living enactments of core cultural themes, then anthropologists are free, indeed pushed, to ask a broader range of questions about experience and subjectivity and the role of cultural resources in the constitution of this experience.

New ethnographers of personhood have begun to ask such questions.[19] They share some implicit or explicit components of a theory of the relationship between culture and self. All of them emphasize specific cultural discourses and practices. All of them show interest in the plurality of sites of the self. They do not regard these discourses and practices as indicators of essential features or themes of the cultures in which they work. Rather, and these particulars are important, they treat these discourses as the media around which socially and historically positioned persons construct their subjectivities in practice. The critical developments of the past twenty-five years not only have revived anthropological interest in culture and self but also have fundamentally shifted anthropologists' view of the relationship between the two. The new ethnographers of personhood describe how specific, often socially powerful, cultural discourses and practices both position people and provide them with the resources to respond to the problematic situations in which they find themselves.

Subjectivity, in these works, is seen to be developing at an interface, within the interplay between the social and embodied sources of the self, in what might be called the self-in-practice or, to use a label inspired by Bakhtin, the authoring self (see Chapter 8). This self-in-practice occupies the interface between intimate discourses, inner speaking, and bodily practices formed in the past and the discourses and practices to which people are exposed, willingly or not, in the present.[20] It authors or orchestrates the products of these sites of self. These ethnographies sidestep a possible impasse between social constructivist and embodied views of the self,.and see instead a mediation between them—a mediation produced, in part, by a developing self-in-practice.

A Next Step

This view of self and identity emerging from ethnographic studies speaks to the critical concerns of our postmodern disciplines. Our purpose in this book is to extend, through concepts drawn from Bakhtin and Vygotsky, the lessons learned from anthropological encounters with self and identity to a cultural studies of the person. Our theoretical path diverges from, though it may ultimately be compatible with, other efforts in cultural studies.

Hall (1996) provides a state-of-the-art account of efforts to overcome a problem left by Foucault's success in killing off the Western concept of the integral, originary subject. Foucault persuasively detailed the historical processes "of subjectification by discursive practices, and the politics of exclusion which all such subjectification appears to entail" (Hall 1996: 2). But he died early in the process of correcting an over-emphasis on the determinants of the subject. Subjects, especially in his earlier writings, were left with no "surplus" (Harvey 1996) by which to escape complete and utter domination and compliance. "The notion that an effective suturing of the subject to a subject-position requires, not only that the subject is 'hailed,' but that the subject invests in the position, means that suturing has to be thought of as an *articulation*, rather than a one-sided process, and that in turn places *identification*, if not identities, firmly on the theoretical agenda" (Hall 1996: 6).

To solve this problem of why and how the subject invests in discursively afforded positions, cultural studies has embraced psychoanalytic theory. Hall situates this choice in the prehistory of present-day theorizing about articulation. He goes back to debates over Althusser's essay on "ideological state apparatuses" and its reliance upon a Lacanian vision of the psychodynamic constitution of the subject. For many reasons, this approach proved deeply flawed. Modifications and reformulations have overcome some of the central critiques and show promise, in Hall's estimation, for avoiding the older vision's shortcomings: lack of a developmental perspective (identifications happened all at once in early childhood); and insufficient attention to whether psychodynamic understandings of sexual and gender identifications could be extended or otherwise prove useful in accounting for racial identification, for instance, or national identity. He mentions the work of Butler (1993). Identification, as reworked by Butler, is a promissory note for a productive theory of "articulation," "a suturing [of subject and discursive practices], an over-determination not a subsumption. There is always 'too much' or 'too little'—an over-determination or a lack, but never a proper fit, a totality" (Hall 1996: 3).

Our plan is to follow a different possibility for understanding the "suturing" of person to position. From a Bakhtinian-sociohistoric perspective, persons develop through and around the cultural forms by which they are identified, and identify themselves, in the context of their affiliation or disaffiliation with those associated with those forms and practices (see Chapter 8). A better metaphor for us is not suture, which makes the person and the position seem to arrive preformed at the moment of suturing, but codevelopment—the linked development of people, cultural forms, and social positions in particular historical worlds.[21]

Building a Bakhtinian-Sociohistoric View of Self

Our notions of the role of cultural forms in the heuristic development of identity are strongly influenced by a stream of thought that began in postrevolutionary Russia and matured there in the late 1920s and 1930s. The sociohistorical school of psychology was the product of an earlier critical disruption. Its members took as their task the creation of a psychology founded upon Marx's historical, social, and economic precepts, a psychology that would nonetheless give proper attention to the (always relative) autonomy of "personal," cognitive, affective, and conative phenomena. Vygotsky and his followers were not alone in their search for an understanding of persons that took Marx into account. Among the many philosophers, writers, artists, and "human scientists" who considered it, Bakhtin and the friends who wrote with him (Voloshinov preeminently) contributed one of the most significant explorations of personhood— one that is socially and historically construed, yet creative. Although they worked virtually contemporaneously, there is little evidence that the two groups of theorists knew much of one another.[22] Their similarities are a testament to the shared problematics of the postrevolutionary intellectual milieu.

The period in Soviet history immediately following the 1917 Revolution was one of intense intellectual as well as social ferment. Utopian conceptions of the "New Men" that must populate a new world arose in many fields and ranged from the romantic and heroic to the scientistic and systematic. In the arts, cubism, futurism, even "suprematism" sought to break the old forms of perception and replace them with newly expressed and various understandings of the sensuous. Symbolists and formalists debated the forms of literary expression proper to the new order, weighing poetry against prose and the intuitive and spoken against the structural and written. Philosophical schools and the sciences, both social and natural, strove to come to terms with a Marxist tradition that had yet to solidify. And all these idioms and ideologies were intended to inform the living world, the lives of people beyond the rings of intellectual debate.

Marx's followers had never settled on a common understanding of human beings apart from the necessities of political economy and revolutionary action. After a successful revolution, however, a new establishment awaited, one whose concerns no longer had to adhere to the exigent but could (indeed must) expand to the horizons of the everyday. Others have interpreted this move as a return to the broader, more philosophical concerns of the young Marx. But that work was little known, and it was unfinished in comparison to *Kapital*. An old problem remained, which we might now call one of social psychology. What was the proper relation of the social realm to the psyche, to the interior life of people? If Marx had said, in the theses on Feuerbach, that "the human essence is no abstraction inherent in each single individual . . . in its reality it is the ensemble of social relations," he had not said how this ensemble was composed (Marx 1975). Vygotsky and his students, Bakhtin and his collaborators were among the many who attempted to meet this problem (see Joravsky 1989; Luria 1979). In the remainder of this chapter we will focus on the answers proposed by Vygotsky and the sociohistorical school; the wonderful complications drawn by Bakhtin and Voloshinov will meet fuller exposition in Chapter 8.

Semiotic Mediation

Vygotsky was primarily interested not in conceptualizing activity (or practice, in today's terminology) but in the process of "semiotic mediation," and in the development of voluntary control over behavior—the hallmark of "higher mental functions"—through this mediation by cultural devices. Vygotsky formulated his thoughts in opposition to the stimulus-response psychology of his day. For him the key to human existence was the ability of humans to escape enslavement to whatever stimuli they happened to encounter. And the way they did this was (broadly) linguistic, that is, through the active construction and use of symbols.[23] Just as humans can modify the environment physically—thanks to their production of and facility with tools and symbols—they can also modify the environment's stimulus value for their own mental states.

In devising his concept of mediating devices, Vygotsky drew from Engels's ideas about the role of the making and use of tools in the history of the human species. Engels had observed that tool use, over evolutionary time, changed not only human environments but human physiology as well. Musculature, cerebral architecture, and other biobehavioral systems—Engels's example was the hand and "handedness"—were shaped to the tool as effectively as the tool was shaped to human purpose. Vygotsky drew an analogy between tools and signs, suggesting that the use of signs altered not only the social "environment" but also the very behavioral architecture of the users. Cross-cultural studies assured him that the analogy could be fruitfully applied. The descriptions available to him, drawn from the work of Levy-Bruhl, Thurnwald, and Taylor, proved to Vygotsky (1930) that human beings frequently use culturally constructed "external" objects as signals to control their own psychological processes. Vygotsky especially liked examples of mnemonics. He cited these techniques—from the elaborate mnemonic objects used by messengers in traditional cultures to the contemporary Westerner's knot in her handkerchief—to show that mediating devices signal a turning point in human cultural history: the transition from the *use* of one's memory to *active control* over it.

A typical mediating device is constructed by the assigning of meaning to an object or a behavior. This symbolic object or behavior is then placed in the environment so as to affect mental events. Vygotsky, however, saw these tools for the self's control of cognition and affect as, above all, social and cultural. "Assigning meaning" and "placing in the environment" are not just individual acts. Rather mediating devices are part of collectively formed systems of meaning, products of social history. Although individuals constantly construct and reconstruct their own mediating devices, most of their constructions are not original. They have been appropriated in the course of social interaction with others who, in turn, had appropriated the devices from others. Even productions we might call innovative have developed in the flow of social interaction and depend intimately upon it for their significance (and hence their effectiveness). Mediating devices (Bakhtin and Voloshinov will cap the argument in Chapter 8) develop within a locus of social activity, a place in the social world, that identifies and organizes them.

Vygotsky (1960) used the example of tying a knot in a handkerchief to remind oneself of something. The knot is given meaning for the purpose of organizing a mental event, for remembering. Yet the meaning depends upon a collectively remembered history of use and interpretation that is a common part of the social commentary that accompanies most interaction. Similarly, the dieter uses a mediating device when he tapes a picture of an obese person to his refrigerator door; the purpose of the image is to affect his intentions toward the refrigerator's contents. But these intentions did not originate with the dieter, they were once social contentions in the discourses relating objects and desires.

At first, in the development of a mediated complex of thought and feeling, mediating devices may be tangible, used voluntarily and consciously: a word said to oneself to encourage oneself to action, a piece of music to which one listens to change one's mood, a chart that one consults to know what to do next in a work routine. Repeated experience with the tangible device may eventually become unnecessary, and its function may be "internalized" (Vygotsky 1978; Wertsch 1985b). The sign-image, that is, its representation within the "inner speaking" (and more generally, inner activity) that constitutes whatever substance there is to self-consciousness, comes to evoke the routine originally organized in relation to the external sign. Finally, the process of self-training may even be forgotten, and the evocation of control may become automatic (see Hutchins 1986). Even the sign-image escapes notice, and the behavior becomes in a translation of Vygotsky's Russian, "fossilized."

Although Vygotsky stressed the construction of "higher psychological functions," such as purposive remembering, the idea of mediating devices is appropriate far beyond the domain of humans' control over their memory and even their problem-solving and inferencing. Luria (cited in Cole 1985), for example, gives a case of the mediation of will, and Vygotsky (1984: 379) discusses the development of a "logic of emotion." Through signs and words, children learn to talk about, compare, classify, and thus manage their own emotions. These ideas inform more recent studies of and popular notions about artifices for modulating emotion.

Arlie Hochschild (1983) describes the training of flight attendants and the devices they were taught to use to control their anger at obnoxious passengers. They were taught to imagine that something traumatic had happened in the passenger's life, or to remind themselves that the passenger was behaving childishly because of his fear of flying. Hochschild shows that these devices were carefully inculcated and continually reproduced in practice, under a regimen of training that was instituted and maintained by the corporation but supported as well by a popular tradition of such means to self-control. So successful was this training that many flight attendants began to lose any sense of their own anger, on or off the job.

Another example could be taken from Spradley's account of urban nomads in Seattle. Spradley (1970) describes a part of the nomad tradition that had to do with surviving incarceration. He details the degradation and brutality that urban nomads faced at the hands of the police, and he recounts the nomads' response, a way of organizing thoughts and feelings that they taught one another so as to do "easy time." Easy time was a way of minimizing the effect of incarceration, a sign-routine mediating interpersonally the course it would take, and "inner-actively" the cognitive-affective response to it. In Vygotskian theory, humans often develop qualitatively different mental functions as a result of learning to use collectively derived symbols in regulating their own behavior. Supported in using these tools by their fellows, Spradley's urban nomads were able to learn to organize and, to some extent, consciously control their thoughts and emotional reactions to jail.

Semiotic Mediation and Agency

Semiotic mediation provides for the capacity that may be called symbolic bootstrapping. One of the convincing points about this tool of agency, this tool for gaining control over one's behavior, is its appropriate modesty. It is an indirect means—one modifies one's environment with the aim, but not the certainty, of affecting one's own behavior—and it requires a sustained effort. As Hochschild observed among the flight attendants, by relying first upon "training wheels" of a symbolic sort, one can learn to ignore aspects of situations to which one would have previously responded.[24] One can even, through similar processes, master one's history of alcohol addiction (see Chapter 4). But the process involves effort, may not succeed, and, except for rather small-scale changes, is clearly beyond the ability of any individual to accomplish alone. These tools of agency are highly social in several senses: the symbols of mediation are collectively produced, learned in practice, and remain distributed over others for a long period of time.[25]

Activity and the Self in Practice

The sociohistorical school's vision has points in common with that of Bourdieu. For instance, compare the work of Vygotsky's influential student A. N. Leontiev (1978) with Bourdieu's concern with the concept of "practice." Leontiev—a figure often associated with the sociohistorical school[26]—has insisted on the importance of "activity" in understanding human behavior.

According to Leontiev, accounts of behavior by anthropologists, sociologists, and psychologists tend to reduce to two terms only: person (or group) and environment. Ordinarily in these accounts the person "reacts" to the conditions of the environment, which are conceived to vary freely—reminding us of the stimulus-response pairs of behaviorist psychology. Culture, for Leontiev, does not qualify as a third term because, in its anthropological renderings, it simply becomes a "reading," a conceptual figuration, of the environment.[27] Nor do psychodynamic processes count as a third term; they simply explain the complexities of response formation in the person.

The third term Leontiev proposed to add indicates that people respond to what they find in the environment in the context of a historical, socially and culturally constructed form of social (inter)action that he called an *activity*. In the two-term accounts, persons *passively* encounter things in the (culturally interpreted) environment to which they, for psychodynamic or other reasons, are sensitive. Then they react. Activity theory instead views people as *actively* engaged with the environment. They are always in the flow of doing something—the something being a historical, collectively defined, socially produced activity—and it is within this meaningful intent toward their surroundings that they respond to whatever they encounter in the environment. (Indeed, the fact of an "encounter" with an environmental "stimulus" is itself mediated by the activity.) Tomorrow they may be engaged in another activity in which the same object, for example, will be used in a different way, if noticed at all. Practice theory shares this understanding of people as actively engaged with their environments. Bourdieu (1977a) highlights the similarities between the two theories when he explicitly describes "practice" as a third way to grasp social action, one that mediates between objectivism (environment) and subjectivism (person or group).[28]

One significant entailment of the activity theory described by Leontiev is the implied dialectic of person and environment within the context of activity. The boundary between person and environment becomes less definite, especially when viewed over time. Persons oriented toward their surroundings by desire for food, for example, have that desire shaped in relation to the food they encounter and become familiar with. The desire is objectified or made more concrete through encounters with possible objects that could satisfy it in the particular environment.

Bakhtin's associate Voloshinov (1986) provides an even more important example of this process for our purposes because he addresses the social aspects of the environment that affect the objectification of hunger.[29] He made an extended argument that experiences, even of internal sensations such as hunger, are formed in and so bear the marks of social context (see Chapter 8). Utterances about one's hunger, even those which never quite become public utterances, are shaped to the social situation, and they in turn affect one's subjective sense of hunger. Hunger when one feels no right to request food from one's hosts is likely to feel different from hunger when one is a customer in an expensive restaurant and the food has been inordinately delayed. There is, in each instance, a microgenesis, a microdevelopment as the person goes from a personal, subjective sense to its objectification, responding to and drawing upon past experience as well as the resources and demands of the particular situation.[30] The ultimate behavior—whether an expression of hunger, a solution to a problem, a climb up a house, or a work of art—is a product of the person-in-practice. This product, in turn, can become a symbol or icon important in the mediation of future behavior. The process is one of heuristic development.

The Heuristic Development of Identity and Agency

Vygotsky's exposition of semiotic mediation as a means to agency gives us a good vantage on the social and historical creation of identities as means to self-activity. "Heuristic development" clearly directs attention away from the extremes of cultural determination of behavior on the one hand and situational totalitarianism on the other. Rather it directs attention to two processes: (1) the genesis of the products (improvisations) that come from the meeting of persons, cultural resources, *and* situations in practice; and (2) the appropriation of these products as heuristics for the next moment of activity. To the extent that these productions are used again and again, they can become tools of agency or self-control and change.

Persons develop more or less conscious conceptions of themselves as actors in socially and culturally constructed worlds, and these senses of themselves, these identities, to the degree that they are conscious and objectified, permit these persons, through the kinds of semiotic mediation described by Vygotsky, at least a modicum of agency or control over their own behavior.[31]

Significant to our concept is the situatedness of identity in collectively formed activities. The "identities" that concern us are ones that trace our participation, especially our agency, in socially produced, culturally constructed activities—what we call figured worlds—such as the worlds of romance and therapy in the United States or the expected life path of women in Nepal.

The concept of figured worlds, which we elaborate in Chapter 3, clearly draws upon Leontiev's notion of activity, and helps us make several points about the heuristic development of identities and their significance. First, figured worlds are historical phenomena, to which we are recruited or into which we enter, which themselves develop through the works of their participants. Figured worlds, like activities, are not so much things or objects to be apprehended, as processes or traditions of apprehension which gather us up and give us form as our lives intersect them.

Second, figured worlds, like activities, are social encounters in which participants' positions matter. They proceed and are socially instanced and located in times and places, not in the "everywhere" that seems to encompass cultural worlds as they are usually conceived. Some figured worlds we may never enter because of our social position or rank; some we may deny to others; some we may simply miss by contingency; some we may learn fully.

Third, figured worlds are socially organized and reproduced; they are like activities in the usual, institutional sense. They divide and relate participants (almost as roles), and they depend upon the interaction and the intersubjectivity for perpetuation. The significance (indeed the existence) of cultural worlds in our lives does not derive from holding them "in mind" as some whole image (we may or may not do this), but from re-creating them by work with others.

Fourth, figured worlds distribute "us," not only by relating actors to landscapes of action (as personae) and spreading our senses of self across many different fields of activity, but also by giving the landscape human voice and tone. This last point goes beyond Leontiev, recalls Voloshinov, and presages Bakhtin. Cultural worlds are populated by familiar social types and even identifiable persons, not simply differentiated by some abstract division of labor. The identities we gain within figured worlds are thus specifically historical developments, grown through continued participation in the positions defined by the social organization of those worlds' activity. They are characteristic of humans and societies.

"Figured world" then provides a means to conceptualize *historical* subjectivities, consciousnesses and agency, persons (and collective agents) forming in practice. It also provides the terms for answering a conundrum of personal agency.

Inden (1990: 23) defines human agency as

> the realized capacity of people to act upon their world and not only to know about or give personal or intersubjective significance to it. That capacity is the power of people to act purposively and reflectively, in more or less complex interrelationships with one another, to reiterate and remake the world in which they live, in circumstances where they may consider different courses of action possible and desirable, though not necessarily from the same point of view.

The conundrum is the seeming contradiction between humans as social producers and as social products. Inden continues: "People do not act only as agents. They also have the capacity to act as 'instruments' of other agents, and to be 'patients,' to be the recipients of the acts of others."

Case Studies

Along with our theoretical discussions, we include case studies of identity in lived worlds: the constitution and interpretation of personal action in historically circumscribed, though never closed, venues of social activity. We tell of romance at two universities, of drinking and not drinking in a chapter of Alcoholics Anonymous, and of the treatment of mental illness, all in the United States, and of gender relations in Nepal. Participants in all these worlds undergo processes of heuristic development which result, for some, in identities: of self as a romantic type, as a non-drinking alcoholic, as a manic-depressive or borderline, as an unjustly treated woman.

Hannerz (1983) describes various "tools of identity," notably the mirror, whose importance he noted during his research among the Fulani of Nigeria. His conception of identity indexes a *general* notion of oneself. The tools of identity that we examine are those of *particular* lived worlds. In Alcoholics Anonymous, for example, participants are coached to tell their lives according to a format, a genre of story, that has been collectively developed from the beginnings of AA in the 1930s. These emblematic narratives become a major means of the symbolic bootstrapping that creates a revised sense of self. Through their forms, participants develop an understanding of themselves as persons who are, and always will be, sensitive to drink. They learn to shun alcohol or else lead a life controlled by it. Chapter 4 is devoted to a close examination of this heuristic development organized around life stories.

Other tools of identity we explore include the lexicon of types from the world of romance ("jerk," "nerd," "fox," "loose woman," "dog") by which American women and men position one another and, in the process, themselves. A lexicon of gender types is also an important tool of identity in Nepal (*sande aimai*, "bull woman"; *aputri*, "barren woman"; *alacchini*, "woman who brings bad luck"; *nathi*, "flirt"), especially as it is realized through songs and the "internalized interlocutors" (personified forms of inner speaking) that originate from scoldings and gossip (see Chapter 10). Songs are, of themselves, also important tools of identity for women in parts of Nepal. When Skinner asked young girls to tell about themselves and their lives, they often replied with lines from folksongs. Both girls and women sing songs to themselves, among themselves, as one means of objectifying their senses of who they are and the kinds of lives they lead (Skinner 1990; Holland and Skinner 1995a; see Chapters 10 and 12).

Diagnosis is an obvious tool of identity in the figured world of mental illness. But diagnoses are not necessarily "subjectified" (personalized, drawn into inner speech) by the persons who are their "targets" in ways that fit the descriptions authorized by the DSM-IV, the diagnostic manual of the American Psychiatric Association. In Chapter 9 we describe the identities that one man, Roger Kelly, formed around the diagnoses he received in the course of his treatment—first as a manic-depressive, then as a borderline. With Roger's case we begin to see the "play" that there is in symbolic bootstrapping, and the interplay that sometimes takes place among different sites of identity, different venues of self-fashioning. Roger arranges, indeed counterposes, these diagnostic tools of identity strategically, to his advantage in the fields of activity and the relationships that compose his social world. His various identities serve as complicated mediating devices, yet, like all such works of heuristic development, they take on a life of their own, whose effects cannot be reduced to Roger's intentions.

In Chapter 6 we return to the issue emphasized by constructivists, that of "positionality," and its relationship to figured worlds and to the narrativized identities shaped within such worlds. Positionality refers to the fact that personal activity (the identified action of a person) always occurs from a particular place in a social field of ordered and interrelated points or positions of possible activity. In Harré's work (1979, 1984), perhaps the most rigorous theoretical exposition of a constructivist (social) psychology, a "person" is really only this, a position that locates an act within a universe of possible locations defined by discourse.

A person engaged in social life, a person involved in an activity or practice, is presumed to have a perspective.[32] One looks at the world from the angle of what one is trying to do.[33] Postmodernists and feminists also attend to perspective, especially to the perspectives that come from being treated according to broad social divisions such as gender, race, class, ethnicity, and sexual orientation. Persons look at the world from the positions into which they are persistently cast.

We are especially interested in the ways in which people's perspectives develop over time. We explore, particularly in Chapters 6 and 7, the degree to which, and the conditions under which, experiences of being positioned (which often occur out of awareness) develop through symbolic bootstrapping into identities that afford a modicum of control over one's own behavior. In the figured world of Alcoholics Anonymous, the newcomer is discursively positioned as an alcoholic, an identity that most newcomers are reluctant to accept. And not all newcomers end up developing a sense of themselves as an alcoholic. How do we understand the various courses people take from the social work of positioning to the cultural means of its figuration? How do people come to terms with their lot in order to do something?

Another type of placement is at least as important as narrativized or discursive placement: positioning by access to space, to associates, to activities, and to genres. Women of Naudada, Nepal, were largely barred from certain governmental and ritual activities. Lower-caste people were usually not allowed to enter the kitchens of higher-caste people. We discuss these forms of social positioning by inclusion and exclusion in Chapter 6. Perspectives are tied to a sense of entitlement or disentitlement to the particular spaces, relationships, activities, and forms of expression that together make up the indices of identity. In Chapter 7 we sketch the heuristic development of women's positionality in the world of romance, where attractiveness mediates one's access to partners of higher or lower status as well as one's entitlement to good treatment from men. The positional aspects of perspective are often less symbolized, less developed as explicit aspects of one's identity than narrativized aspects. Thus, behavior that proclaims these socially defined entitlements may be less susceptible to voluntary control.

Still, position is not fate. Cultural resources, including the activities and landscapes—the figured worlds—that give meaning to people's interaction, change historically in ways that are marked by the political struggles and social valuation of their users. The particular inspiration that we draw from the sociohistorical school is its attention to *continuing* adjustment, reorganization, and movement. This continual development contrasts with Bourdieu's conception: for Bourdieu, the improvisations that are characteristic of all social behavior make a difference to the habitus of the *next generation*. That is, the forms of novel activity created by a senior generation provide the experiential context in which their children develop the habitus of the group. Such innovation has little impact on the established habitus of the elders. For proponents of the sociohistorical school, in contrast, improvisations make a difference for the *next moment* of production.[34]

It is not impossible for people to figure and remake the conditions of their lives. Bakhtin shows that, from the very fact that cultural resources are indelibly marked by social position, people can reassert a point of control through the rearrangement of cultural forms as evocations of position (see Chapter 8). The equation of the means of expression and social force—the notion of voice—works both ways. It positions persons as it provides them with the tools to re-create their positions. The fields of cultural production that circumscribe perspectives become, in Bakhtin's handling, spaces of authoring.

Groups of women in Naudada joined together at the yearly festival of Tij and produced songs that described and analyzed the sad and unfair position of women in Nepali society (see Chapter 12). The women narrativized and symbolized their social positions in the family and in society, and through the activity and around its productions they were developing both critical understandings of their position and new identities related to their Tij groups. Small groups like these develop heuristically as well.

In fact, we believe identity formation must be understood as the heuristic codevelopment of cultural media and forms of identity. In Chapter 11 we discuss the ways in which the development of courtly love in the eleventh and twelfth centuries, its activities (the "courts of love"), and its songs envisioned not only new forms of association among men and women but also new figures of possible selves-in-practice. The opening of an originally specialized, nearly ritual, performative world into the everyday—a long transformation—is part of what has made possible the American world of romance that we studied in the 1970s and 1980s. We also discuss Anderson's (1983) "imagined communities," the grounds of modern nationalism, in that chapter.

Heuristic development results in persons whose "history-in-person" is likely to have an agenda and momentum of its own. Persons do bring a history to the present—an important aspect of which is usually an untidy compilation of perspectives, some developed into symbolized identities.[35] Even in the face of powerful situational determinants, such as inducements to drink among members of Alcoholics Anonymous, these identities, especially when supported by others of like perspective, afford some self-control and agency. Nonetheless persons remain susceptible to the situational determinants of their reproduction, including the subject positions foisted upon them. The process is a composite one of slow, sometimes erratic, but continuous change. History-in-person collides with combinations of circumstances that are by degree precedented and unprecedented. The behaviors, the products of the moment, then become available as mediators to change oneself and others, and perhaps even the figured worlds in which one acts. Culture and subject positions are important components of the working of identity, but cultural production and heuristic development are the keys to its analysis.

II

Placing Identity and Agency

3

Figured Worlds

John Caughey (1984), among others, has remarked upon humans' penchant to enter into imaginary worlds—via dreams, daydreams, or spectatorship (films, sports events, reading). He sees the significance of this as twofold. By modeling possibilities, imaginary worlds can inspire new actions; or, paradoxically, their alternative pleasures can encourage escape and a withdrawal from action. Benedict Anderson (1983) draws out yet another significance of human fantasy by understanding nationalism as participation in an "imagined community." Many of the activities that engage human energy and interest have an imaginative component.

Figured worlds rest upon people's abilities to form and be formed in collectively realized "as if" realms. What if gender relations were defined so that women had to worry about whether they were attractive? What if, as in the Trobriand Islands described by Weiner (1976), bundles of banana leaves were so important that older women spent much time and energy assembling them?[1] What if there were a world called academia, where books were so significant that people would sit for hours on end, away from friends and family, writing them? People have the propensity to be drawn to, recruited for, and formed in these worlds, and to become active in and passionate about them. People's identities and agency are formed dialectically and dialogically in these "as if" worlds.

Toward the end of his life, Vygotsky (1978) wrote a paper in which he expanded his notion of children's potential for development. In that paper we see Vygotsky's usual fascination with the ability of humans to manipulate their worlds and themselves by means of symbols. In it he analyzed young children's play and their later abilities with games. Early

49

in life children begin a type of play in which the everyday meaning of objects is suspended and new meaning is assigned. Behind the couch becomes the bad guy's hideout, under the table becomes the jail. Or perhaps a certain set of everyday meanings is retained and highlighted, and other features drop away; Vygotsky describes two sisters playing at being sisters.

In either type of play, meanings are manipulated to point to other (absent or distilled) social settings, and one's motivations and feelings are geared to participation in that scene. Children use a piece of candy to represent, say, a jewel that robbers have stolen, and treat it as a jewel. They resist the temptation to eat it. Children may also ignore pain and fatigue for the purpose of continuing play. When they run a race, the goal of winning the race, or at least reaching the finish line, overcomes any desire to stop from fatigue. Sometimes children do stop before the race is over, or eat the candy, or tire of playing sister. But remarkably often they do not. They learn to detach themselves from their reactions to their immediate surroundings, to enter a play world—a conceptual world that differs from the everyday—and to react to the imagined objects and events of that world.

Vygotsky gave central place to collectively developed signs and symbols as the media by which children's mental and emotional faculties were culturally formed.[2] He paid special attention to the role of tangible objects, made collectively into artifacts by the attribution of meaning, as tools that people use to affect their own and others' thinking, feeling, and behavior. Through habitual use these cultural tools become resources available for personal use, mnemonics of the activities they facilitate, and finally constitutive of thought, emotion, and behavior. Describing how children develop the ability to enter into an imagined world, Vygotsky speaks of a "pivot," a mediating or symbolic device that the child uses not just to organize a particular response but to pivot or shift into the frame of a different world. Toys, even sticks assigned the status of horse, can be the pivots. The tangible symbol may eventually be discarded and the child may be able to enter the play world without physical props.

Games with more explicit rules and less concrete fantasy become more prominent as children grow older. Still the children must shift themselves to a conceptual world beyond their immediate surroundings in order to become actors who submit to the game's premises and treat its events as real. A child's desires become related to "a fictitious 'I,' to her

role in the game and its rules" (Vygotsky 1978: 100). It is this competence that makes possible culturally constituted or figured worlds and,
consequently, the range of human institutions. Lee (1985) points out the
definite link between play worlds and institutional life. Fantasy and
game play serve as precursors to participation in an institutional life,
where individuals are treated as scholars, bosses, or at-risk children and
events such as the granting of tenure, a corporate raid, and the self-esteem of at-risk children are taken in all seriousness. But to see imagination extended so is simply to recognize that it pervades cultural life.

Under the rubric of culturally figured worlds or figured worlds we
include all those cultural realms peopled by characters from collective
imaginings: academia, the factory, crime, romance, environmental activ-
ism, games of Dungeons and Dragons, the men's house among the Mehinaku of Brazil (Gregor 1977). These are worlds made up of Geertz's
(1973b) "webs of meaning." Figured worlds take shape within and grant
shape to the coproduction of activities, discourses, performances, and
artifacts. A figured world is peopled by the figures, characters, and types
who carry out its tasks and who also have styles of interacting within,
distinguishable perspectives on, and orientations toward it.

Consider the cultural world of Alcoholics Anonymous (explored in
Chapter 4). In AA meetings participants tell stories about their lives
before they joined the organization. They collect tokens for the periods
of time they have remained sober. They come to name themselves, and
often to see themselves, as "alcoholics" and not just drinkers. All these
elements of AA are meaningful in, relevant to, and valued (or not) in
relation to a frame of meaning, a virtual world, a world that has been
figured.

When Cain did her research the tokens used to mark length of sobriety were the same plastic chips sold for playing poker. In the world of AA
these chips were not won by holding a straight flush. Rather, they were
meaningfully revalued to a world where the stake, the thing at wager,
was staying sober; the chip became an emblem of a different achievement, another kind of success. On the store's shelf a poker chip is worth
little, but within the world of AA the significance of a chip, color-coded
for length of time without a drink, is great. The difference between
picking up and not picking up a chip is, for some, the difference between
a good and a bad life.

Likewise, the stories that AA participants learn to tell, about their former lives and their current temptations, are revalued because they signify experience and place in a world that differs from that of the non-alcoholic. These life stories, too, take on the extended meanings characteristic of play and are thus re-formed within the larger frame of reference, the figured world of AA. They become the cultural resource that mediates members' identities as "non-drinking alcoholics."

These socially generated, culturally figured worlds, many linguists believe, are necessary for understanding the meaning of words. When talking and acting, people assume that their words and behavior will be interpreted according to a context of meaning—as indexing or pointing to a culturally figured world. Violations of this assumption cause confusion and prevarication. Fillmore (1975, 1982), a key figure in the development of "frame semantics," asked his readers to consider the word "bachelor." Why is it confusing to ask if the Pope is a bachelor? After all, a bachelor is an unmarried man and the Pope is an unmarried man. Yet there is something peculiar about referring to the Pope as a bachelor. The problem is that "'bachelor' frames . . . a figured world in which prototypical events unfold: men marry at a certain age; marriages last for life; and in such a world, a bachelor is a man who stays unmarried beyond the usual age, thereby becoming eminently marriageable" (Quinn and Holland 1987: 23). The Pope, under a vow of celibacy, is not a relevant character in the cultural world of marriage—of marriageable men, and of not-yet-married bachelors. Asking if the Pope is a bachelor is akin to trying to redeem one's poker chips for money at an AA meeting. The questioner and the would-be redeemer have both mistaken the relevant figured world.

By "figured world," then, we mean a socially and culturally constructed realm of interpretation in which particular characters and actors are recognized, significance is assigned to certain acts, and particular outcomes are valued over others. Each is a simplified world populated by a set of agents (in the world of romance: attractive women, boyfriends, lovers, fiancés) who engage in a limited range of meaningful acts or changes of state (flirting with, falling in love with, dumping, having sex with) as moved by a specific set of forces (attractiveness, love, lust).[3]

These collective "as-if" worlds are sociohistoric, contrived interpretations or imaginations that mediate behavior and so, from the perspective of heuristic development, inform participants' outlooks. The ability to sense (see, hear, touch, taste, feel) the figured world becomes embodied over time, through continual participation. One can, in the current state of technology, put on a bulky headset with connections to computers, television cameras, and "data gloves," and enter into a virtual reality. A figured world, too, is played out; a frame becomes a world—a space and time established imaginatively—that one can come to sense after a process of experiencing, acting by virtue of its rules (see Shotter 1982). No technology, no headset is necessary. Players become ever more familiar with the happenings of a figured world—the stories told in AA, for example—and learn to author their own and make them available to other participants. By means of such appropriation, objectification, and communication, the world itself is also reproduced, forming and re-forming in the practices of its participants.

Cultural Means

Figured worlds could also be called figurative, narrativized, or dramatized worlds. "Figurative," according to *Webster's Third International Dictionary,* means transferred in sense from literal or plain to abstract or hypothetical; representing or represented by a figure. The production and reproduction of figured worlds involves both abstraction of significant regularities from everyday life into expectations about how particular types of events unfold and interpretation of the everyday according to these distillations of past experiences. A figured world is formed and re-formed in relation to the everyday activities and events that ordain happenings within it. It is certainly not divorced from these happenings, but neither is it identical to the particulars of any one event. It is an abstraction, an extraction carried out under guidance.[4]

"Narrativized" and "dramatized" convey the idea that many of the elements of a world relate to one another in the form of a story or drama, a "standard plot" against which narratives of unusual events are told.[5] For example, Holland and Eisenhart (1990) and Holland and Skinner (1987) found a taken-for-granted sequence of events in the world of romance on two university campuses; we present it in Chapter 5.

Skinner's studies in Naudada, a mixed-caste, predominantly Hindu community in central Nepal, provide another example of a figured world organized around a sort of narrative. For Naudada's women the figured world of domestic relations was dominated by a narrativized account of the life path of a good woman. This life path was set forth in the Hindu moral and religious texts that were read in Naudada and explicated by priests, and so had more of a prescriptive flavor than the taken-for-granted sequence of romantic relations. Along this life path (Skinner 1990: 73–77):

> Girls are good, hard-working, and obedient daughters.
>
> Eventually they marry, leaving their natal homes *(maita)* for the homes of their husbands *(ghar)*.
>
> At their *ghar,* good daughters-in-law are obedient, respectful, and diligent in their household and agricultural duties, laboring from dawn to dark for their in-laws.
>
> As wives, women devote themselves to their husbands, seeing to their needs and obeying their demands.
>
> A good woman bears sons to carry on the patriline.
>
> As she gives birth to and raises sons, she attains more status in the household.
>
> After the marriage of her own sons, she directs the activities of the daughters-in-law.
>
> A good woman dies before her husband does.

Again the storyline was not prescriptive but was significant as a backdrop for interpretation. The meaning of characters, acts, and events in everyday life was figured against this storyline. *Radi* (widow), for example, was used as a general term of insult for women and girls of any age, even very young girls. Its connotations were definitely and potently negative because of its relation to the life path of a good woman: a widow was a woman who had decisively departed from the course of the moral narrative by outliving her husband.

The conceptual importance of figured worlds has been emphasized in anthropology for some time. Hallowell (1955a) argued that individuals live in worlds that are culturally defined and understand themselves in relation to these worlds. In a classic article, "The Self and Its Behavioral Environment," he notes that, for those whose cultural world gives them credence, ghosts and other nonmaterial beings have a psychological reality that denotes nothing about a person's sanity or insanity—as it might in a culture where such beings are considered figures of fantasy, imagination, and superstition. Shweder (1991) devotes much space to "intentional worlds," a concept reminiscent of Hallowell's behavioral environment. Quinn and Holland and other authors in their edited volume (Holland and Quinn 1987) similarly write about simplified worlds, taken-for-granted worlds that are culturally modeled.

Cultural schemas or cultural models are stereotypical distillates, generalizations from past experience that people make. They are akin to what Crapanzano (1990), speaking about the processes that maintain the self in continual change, calls "arrests"—representations of self at a particular time that people try to reassert, even under new conditions.[6] According to the cognitive architecture currently theorized for them, cultural models (conceptualizations of figured worlds) certainly may and are likely to change (see D'Andrade 1995; Quinn and Strauss 1994), but here we emphasize figured worlds that have some durability; those that are, for various reasons, reproduced socially. In such cases these culturalist perspectives offer an important grasp on lived worlds.

Beyond Imagination

Despite the importance of these "as if" meanings, these figurings, through which lived worlds are interpreted and taken to heart, we cannot stop with culturalist perspectives. We must also appreciate what social constructivism and practice theories tell us about the imagined worlds in which we conduct our lives. Figured worlds *happen,* as social process and in historical time. For instance, Favret-Saada (1980), in a vivid practice-theoretical account of witchcraft in the Bocage of France (ca. 1970), describes the social construction, through discourse, of certain people in the region as actors in a figured world populated by witches, unwitchers, and the bewitched. She shows how she herself inadvertently entered the practice of witchcraft by the simple act of questioning. The kinds of questions she was asking were, it turned out, meaningful as acts—and markers of identity—in the figured world of witchcraft. Only gradually did she realize—a realization of great moment to her ethnography—that she had become (that is, become construed as) an actor in that world.[7]

Favret-Saada makes crucial points about living the figured world of witchcraft. Acts in the world of witchcraft (or any figured world) happen in time. Caught in the moment, far from a timeless omniscience, the participants in witchcraft's world experience degrees of uncertainty. They worry: Will I die from the witchcraft I suspect has been worked upon me? Do these people suspect that I am a witch? Am I suffering misfortune after misfortune because someone wishes me ill?

Another part of this uncertainty is the very multiplicity and partiality of the figured worlds that hedge the interpretation of action. It is often unclear which (or how many) figurations are instanced by interaction. Was that person's intent gaze a sign of witchcraft directed at me, a mark of interest in the color of my dress, or simply an accidental glance, looking through me to the thought beyond? Was she (at this time, in this place) acting as a witch, an admirer or critic, or an uninterested bystander?

Favret-Saada's work dramatically exemplifies the ways figured worlds are encountered in day-to-day social activity. Her work, with its constructivist dimension, directs attention to the living of figured worlds through practices and activities. Holland and Eisenhart (1990), in their ethnographic study at American universities, found that women spent a great deal of time, alone and together, in activities devoted to improving their bodies and appearance. Motivations for these "beautification" practices were expressed via the discourse of romance. Attractiveness to men was an important quality in the students' world of romance. A woman's prestige derived largely from the treatment she received from men, and that treatment was formative of and responsive to her attractiveness. Attractiveness was, in Bourdieu's terms, a symbolic capital of the field. The endless energy and hours spent on beautification made sense in such a world.[8]

Activities as a meaningful context of action have been a traditional theoretical concern of the sociohistorical school for some sixty or seventy years. Leontiev and many others have conceived people's actions and their individual development within the larger frame of a historically assembled, socially and culturally constructed *activity*. These activities (work, play, teaching are often the matters of interest in this literature)[9] establish particular sets of roles, actors, institutions, settings, durations, and organizational requirements (see Wertsch 1981; Engeström 1990, 1992).

Drawing a link between identities and activities similar to the one we propose, Lave and Wenger (1991) begin to explore the consequences of self-development in and through activities. Lave and Wenger are concerned with "situated learning" in "communities of practice"—that is, with how newcomers are inducted into socially enduring and complex activities. They conceive learning as simultaneously a form of association (situation), an act of recruitment, and a (re)constitution of the basis for communities. They follow the learning of neophytes brought into communities of practitioners who may tailor in Liberia, deliver babies in the Yucatán, or navigate large vessels in the U.S. Navy. "Communities of practice" recast the practices and productions of working groups as power/knowledge (to use Foucault's term), that is, as knowledge which cannot be divorced from position, and as position married to knowledge, within social groups. Identities become important outcomes of participation in communities of practice in ways analogous to our notion that identities are formed in the process of participating in activities organized by figured worlds.

Goodenough (1994) suggests that we should theorize culture in relation to activities. People's activities—even within the small, isolated communities, crisscrossed by multi-stranded social relations, so familiar to ethnographers—demand and are organized around different sets of situated understandings and expectations. There is, Goodenough concludes, no uniform, consistent, or coherent set of meanings—no "culture"—that applies equally in every activity. Goodenough's notion of activities is reminiscent of the concept defined by the sociohistoric school, and it has inspired intriguing work on the development of consciousness (see Amit-Talai 1995).[10] But the sociohistorical school's concept of activity remains more useful to us. Because of its roots in Marxian analyses of capitalism and other historically specific modes of production, activity theory pays more attention to the articulation of activities within larger systems of power and privilege.[11] This embedding of activities is central to an understanding of figured worlds as well: as we shall see in Chapter 7, the world of romance and attractiveness plays a prominent role in the production and reproduction of gender privilege in the United States.

Power and Privilege

The relationships of the practices and activities that instance figured worlds with larger, institutionalized "structures" of power confer a depth to figured landscapes that extends beyond the immediate order of interaction. Imagined acts, courses and places of action, actors, and even the whole of a figured world take on an element of rank and status according to this relational hierarchy. None of the concepts we have so far used to elucidate social construction in figured worlds accounts well for this aspect of hierarchy and status. Bourdieu's concept of field helps to bring out this additional aspect of figured worlds.

Like habitus, field is too potent and pervasive a theme of Bourdieu's thought to be precisely delimited. Bourdieu uses the world of authors and writings as an example:

> What do I mean by "field"? As I use the term, a field is a separate social universe having its own laws of functioning independent of those of politics and the economy. The existence of the writer, as fact and as value, is inseparable from the existence of the literary field as an autonomous universe endowed with specific principles of evaluation of practices and works. To understand Flaubert or Baudelaire, or any writer, major or minor, is first of all to understand what the status of writer consists of at the moment considered; that is, more precisely, the social conditions of the possibility of this social function, of this social personage. In fact, the invention of the writer, in the modern sense of the term, is inseparable from the invention of a particular social game, which I term the literary field and which is constituted as it establishes its autonomy, that is to say, its specific laws of functioning, within the field of power. (1993: 162–163)

Fields are not absolutely autonomous, for they subsist in what Bourdieu calls the field of power, which is itself an aspect of class relations. They are instead relatively autonomous, for the relationship any field has to other fields or to the field of power is refracted by the mode of cultural production specific to the field. In this sense the field is a game like the games Vygotsky described. Bourdieu further intended the concept to be a kind of translation of "structure" that would not stand apart from persons. A field is "structure-in-practice," and as such is a world of relationships, of social positions defined only against one another (Bourdieu 1985a). It is also a peopled world; its positions, which are producers as well as products, are also social personages. Field thus closely parallels our notion of figured world and elucidates our later emphasis on positionality (Chapter 6).[12]

Bourdieu elaborated the concept from his sociological studies of French arts and letters and the French academic scene as it was in the 1960s. The concept of field directed attention to the aspects of the collec-

tively defined activities that make up the arts and the academy that relate
to what Weber (1978) would have called "status."[13] Had Bourdieu mediated his understanding through "figured world" instead of "field," he
would have told us more about the discourses of academia and the
cultural constructions that constituted the familiar aspects of academic
life: the taken-for-granted generic figures (professors, graduate students,
undergraduates, provosts, secretaries) and their generic acts—both such
formal tasks as giving tutorials, administering tests, firing, hiring, and
granting degrees, and the less formal stories of tenure granted, tenure
denied, and teaching responsibilities juggled against writing and schol-
arly research—as situated in a particular institution.[14] He would have
more closely detailed the terms of academic discourse—such as "quality," "originality," and "brilliance"—as ways in which academics come to
evaluate their efforts, understand themselves, and interpret the positions
they hold in the academy.

In *Homo Academicus* Bourdieu directed his field analysis less to these
day-to-day aspects of cultural figuring than to social relations among the
more powerful and influential players. He paid attention to the positions
of academic personages and institutions in the French educational hierarchy, the markers of position, the symbolic capital accruing to the scholars and institutions, and the cultural productions created by them.[15]
We learn much from *Homo Academicus* about the interrelations of scholars and institutions in France according to their relative prestige and
influence; we learn much less about the day-to-day content of activity—
and the ways positions of prestige play out locally—for the vast number
of academics. Hence we miss, for French academics, the focus that
Favret-Saada provides for French witchcraft: the everyday construction
of actors.[16]

Although Bourdieu's interests in *Homo Academicus* were directed toward the prominent men and women of the system, a field analysis is
relevant to any figured world.[17] Indeed, as we have said, lived worlds
are organized around positions of status and influence (in the case of
American college students, attractiveness and prestige; in the case of the
Naudadans of Nepal, caste and wealth as well as gender) and the cultural
narratives that posit particular sorts of characters and their dealings with
one another (the loving boyfriend and the flirt; the attentive therapist
and the recalcitrant "borderline"; the Naudadan husband who threatens
his wife by telling her he will bring another woman into the house).

We agree with Bourdieu's vision: the as-if character of possibility that marks fields (and figured worlds) is not an indifferent, "mental" abstraction, an "imaginary" in its usual sense, but a social reality that lives within dispositions mediated by relations of power. This point is most clearly made in Bourdieu's analyses of "silencing" or self-censorship, a theme later amplified by Skinner and Holland in their exploration of women's experience in Nepal. Indeed, positions that have become dispositions, of privilege and prestige are especially important to our case analyses of the worlds of romance in the United States and gender relations in Nepal.[18] Identities form in these figured worlds through the day-to-day activities undertaken in their name. Neophytes are recruited into and gain perspective on such practices and come to identify themselves as actors of more or less influence, more or less privilege, and more or less power in these worlds.

As we situate it among the related concepts of fields, practices, activities, and communities of practice, the place of figured worlds takes a clearer shape. It is a landscape of objectified (materially and perceptibly expressed) meanings, joint activities, and structures of privilege and influence—all partly contingent upon and partly independent of other figured worlds, the interconnections among figured worlds, and larger societal and trans-societal forces. Figured worlds in their conceptual dimensions supply the contexts of meaning for actions, cultural productions, performances, disputes, for the understandings that people come to make of themselves, and for the capabilities that people develop to direct their own behavior in these worlds.[19] Materially, figured worlds are manifest in people's activities and practices; the idioms of the world realize selves and others in the familiar narratives and everyday performances that constantiate relative positions of influence and prestige. Figured worlds provide the contexts of meaning and action in which social positions and social relationships are named and conducted. They also provide the loci in which people fashion senses of self—that is, develop identities.

Artifacts and Materiality

Figured worlds rely upon artifacts. The sociohistorical school has long emphasized the importance of artifacts as mediators in human action, as "psychological tools" (Kozulin 1986). We followed this lead in Chapters

1 and 2. Now we are in a better position to explain the significance of this point. Figured worlds are evinced in practice through the artifacts employed by people in their performances. Such artifacts are *pivotal* in the sense Vygotsky attributed to them in play. Artifacts "open up" figured worlds. They are the means by which figured worlds are evoked, collectively developed, individually learned, and made socially and personally powerful.

Cole (1996) provides a useful discussion of artifacts. In his conceptualization, cultural artifacts—whether the poker chips and life stories of Alcoholics Anonymous, the "sexy" clothes and gender-marked stereotypes of the world of romance, or patients' charts and medications in the world of mental health care—have "developmental histories" by virtue of the activities of which they were previously a part and which they mediate in the present. They have been manufactured or produced and continue to be used as part of, and in relation to, intentional human actions. Hence artifacts assume both an obvious and necessary material aspect and an ideal or conceptual aspect, an intentionality, whose substance is embedded in the figured world of their use. By the same token they are both instrument and collective remembrance.

Holland and Cole (1995: 482) suggest that we consider a hammer as a tool/artifact/mediator:

> The generic function of hammers is to connect two or more objects by driving a nail (or its equivalent) through them. Although hammers can be used for a (restricted variety) of other tasks (those where hitting something is functional, as in war; as a door jamb or a paperweight), their shapes are predominantly shaped by their nail driving function. In Gibson's (1979) terms, hammers "afford" hitting nails.
>
> In this respect, every hammer can be seen as an encapsulated "theory of the task" and simultaneously a "theory of the person" who fulfills the task. The head of the hammer is typically made of a hard material so that it does not shatter when used. The handle is shaped to fit the human hand. Such "tailoring" can be quite specific, but it can never be totally general. A tack hammer has not only a small head, but a small handle that affords light tapping. A railway hammer (a sledge hammer) has not only a large and heavy head, but a handle of such a shape and such a length to accommodate a person of sufficient strength and falling within a height range holding it with two hands and swinging it after raising it over the head with legs spread apart.

Note that mediation through artifacts applies equally to objects and to people. Consider poker chips as they are ordinarily used in Alcoholics Anonymous. Consider, too, the pronoun most husbands used to address their wives in Naudada: *ta* (you), the least respectful form employed also for children, animals, and other "inferiors." Poker chips and pronouns, through their collective use in common practices, have come to embody for, and so impose on, people in AA and in Naudada a conception of the tasks to which they are put, and a conception of the person(s) who will use them and be the object(s) of them.[20]

This vantage on cultural artifacts has also been shaped by the critical disruption and inspired by Foucault. Discourse (or discursive) theory emphasizes many of the aspects of cultural resources that we discuss here, especially their existence as public forms and social tools. Discourses and their categories are like the artifacts that Cole describes. They originate outside their performers and are imposed upon people, through recurrent institutional treatments and within interaction, to the point that they become self-administered. Categories carry an association to those who use them and are subject to them—an association with power—as artifacts do an association with tasks and those who perform them. In fact, for a Vygotskian like Cole, categories of expression and more tangible artifacts like hammers are the same.[21] They "afford" ways of doing not only things but also people.

Social constructivists or discourse theorists point to important aspects of figured worlds and the cultural artifacts that are associated with them. Although they have usually considered only privileged or hegemonic discourses, their points apply equally to all cultural artifacts—from hammers, poker chips, clothing, and psychiatric diagnoses to advertisements and films. All these have a history of development in relation to particular tasks, undertaken by people in particular environments.

Just as films afford particular "gazes" on their subject matter (see Traube 1992), poker chips, in their association with the figured world of Alcoholics Anonymous, afford certain ways of thinking and feeling about sobriety and about the people who employ them to mediate their relation to alcohol and drinking. Of course, some AA members-in-the-making do at times let go of the meaning of the chip, tire of being sober, or wander away to other pursuits. The point is how often they do not. They learn to detach themselves from their reactions to earlier understandings of poker chips, to enter the world of AA—a conceptual world that differs from what they knew before—and so learn to react to objects, to events, and to themselves as figured in that world. Just as a child enters into a game.

Cultural artifacts gain a kind of force by connection to their social and cultural contexts, to their figured worlds. These artifacts and people's relationship to them are decidedly unlike the artifacts and relations in the scenarios of problem-solving, or the conduct of other goal-directed tasks, imagined by those who subscribe to the dominant perspectives in psychology. They are very unlikely to be the product of a lone individual's conscious contemplation, of the solution to a problem rationally defined.[22] Rather, as Davies and Harré (1990: 48) put it, actions become "determinant" for participants as acts that position them in relation to the "local expressive order which they presume is in use and towards which they orient themselves."[23] In our terms, the actions, the deployments of artifacts such as pronouns and chips, evoke the worlds to which they were relevant, and position individuals with respect to those worlds. It is their pivotal role, as Vygotsky called it—their capacity to shift the perceptual, cognitive, affective, and practical frame of activity—that makes cultural artifacts so significant in human life.

To attend to the materiality of cultural artifacts is also to recognize the force of their use in practices—practices responsive to changing historical circumstances (see Holland and Cole 1995). The conceptual and material aspects of figured worlds, and of the artifacts through which they are evinced, are constantly changing through the improvisations of actors. This context of flux is the ground for identity development. It sets the conditions for what we called in Chapter 2 the authoring self—what in Chapter 8 we will expand to call the "space of authoring."

The Paradoxical Possibility of Self-Control

The authoring self becomes a possibility because of another aspect of cultural artifacts. Cultural artifacts were central to Vygotsky's conceptualization not only because they could be the media of consciousness, of "higher mental functions," but because, as such, they could serve as tools of liberation from control by environmental stimuli. As we use artifacts to affect others, we become, at some point in our growing up, aware of and capable of using artifacts to affect ourselves. We achieve self-control, albeit of a very limited sort, by the mediation of our thoughts and feelings through artifacts. We learn how to control our-selves from the outside, so to speak (Vygotsky 1978); we learn how to position ourselves for ourselves.

Social constructivists consider discourses principally as the means by which power/knowledge (or some equivalent) inscribes bodies and (thus) creates persons. Vygotsky conceived cultural artifacts as learned within social interaction; they serve first as interpsychic tools and only afterward—when one takes them as meaningful for oneself—do they function on intimate terrain. Although Vygotsky and the other members of the sociohistorical school sought to build a psychology in accordance with Marxist thought, they emphasized a side of Marx's work that is often forgotten these days: the possibilities for *becoming*, and the sense of freedom so pervasive in the period immediately after the Revolution. They paid most attention to humans' potential to expand, rather than limit, their abilities and horizons. Foucault (among others) would later elaborate the controlling aspects of human artifacts, the inscriptions of discourses and the impositions of discipline. The sociohistorical school, initially at least, took the path of optimism, and explored the potential for the liberation and expansion of human capacities that artifactual mediation afforded. Its members mapped the routes of escape from the tyranny of environmental stimuli (including, presumably, the stimuli of the social environment).

Here we have a paradox. As Shepel (1995: 428) puts it: "The accumu-lation and mastery of a cultural tool kit and its use in overcoming the dependency on a particular culture is one of the basic contradictions of human development." How does liberation from the particular determi-nations—the entrapments—of our cultural worlds come about through the tools shaped in those worlds for their perpetuation? In our case studies we follow this paradox and play out this contradiction. By creat-ing and embracing an identity in the world of Alcoholics Anonymous, the former drinker can achieve a modicum of control over his relation to alcohol, but in so doing he learns a kind of discipline, a way of looking and behaving that often condemns what his friends, and often his "other selves," would have him do. Through participation in the women's groups that create songs envisioning a new world of gender relations in Nepal, individual women find a place to stand, a perspective on them-selves and their lives not otherwise offered in the texts and rituals of their daily lives. They achieve their standpoint, however, only by submitting themselves to another set of cultural forms that have their own peculiar limitations and constraints (see Chapters 10 and 12).

The next two chapters concern the lived worlds of romance and Alcoholics Anonymous, and how people take form, building understandings of themselves as agents, patients, and instruments[24] in these figured worlds. These understandings—these identities—are unstable, especially as people are first inducted to a figured world, and they continue to undergo heuristic development in concert with people's acclimation to new spheres of activity. They remain multiple, as people's trajectories through figured worlds neither take one path nor remain in the ambit of one cultural space, one figured world. Nonetheless, identities constitute an enduring and significant aspect of history-in-person, history that is brought to current situations. They are a pivotal element of the perspective that persons bring to the construal of new activities and even new figured worlds.

4

Personal Stories in
Alcoholics Anonymous

Consider a group of men and women who are becoming alcoholics, not by drinking, but rather by learning not to drink. These individuals have decided to stop drinking because they have come to understand that "alcohol is controlling their lives." The change they undergo is much more than a change in behavior. It is a transformation of their identities, from drinking non-alcoholics to non-drinking alcoholics, and it affects how they view and act in the world. It requires not only a particular understanding of the world but a new understanding of their selves and their lives and a reinterpretation of their own pasts. They enter, or rather are recruited to, a new figured world, a new frame of understanding. One device in particular that helps one identify oneself in this world is the telling of a particular sort of personal story.

The identity and interpretation at which these men and women arrive are ones defined by the self-help group Alcoholics Anonymous.[1] In this sense AA has created a cultural world, albeit a limited one, which is its institutional reason for being. AA has constructed a particular interpretation of what it means to be an alcoholic, what typical alcoholics are like, and what kinds of incidents mark a typical alcoholic's life. This cultural knowledge about alcoholism and the alcoholic shared by members of AA differs both from the cultural knowledge of alcoholism shared by those outside of AA and from the self-understanding of most potential members before they enter AA. The self-understandings of the individuals who join AA must come to reflect and incorporate the knowledge organized within AA's figured world; cultural knowledge must become self-knowledge. For some, though not all, self-understanding is transformed.

One symbolic device that helps mediate this transformation is the "personal stories" told by members of Alcoholics Anonymous.

In the culture of middle-class America drinking is ambivalently viewed. In many contexts it is a marker of adulthood and a frequent part of social interaction. But drinking too much or too often, or behaving inappropriately while drinking, may place one in the stigmatized status of "problem drinker" or "alcoholic." No distinct line runs between "social" or "normal" drinker and "problem drinker" or "alcoholic," and different sectors of U.S. society do not agree on what these terms mean.

In the past alcoholism was widely interpreted as a defect of character or moral weakness. To some extent this view persists (Robins 1980), but since the early 1940s an interpretation of alcoholism as a disease has largely replaced it. This reflects the general Western trend toward medicalizing deviance (Conrad and Schneider 1980). Alternative interpretations are possible. Like the mentally retarded people Edgerton (1967) describes, whose disorder is largely an inadequacy in social conduct, the alcoholic fails to meet social obligations. Alcoholics are labeled alcoholic by others when their behavior becomes problematic by normal standards, not on the basis of the volume of alcohol drunk or the frequency of drunkenness. "Alcoholism" describes a tendency toward inappropriate, out-of-control behavior.

Nor is the deviance simply a quality of the acts or behaviors so labeled. It is a consequence of the breaking of rules and sanctions created by a group that is in a position of power, and that finds the behavior "unsettling." Deviance is a matter of politics (Schur 1980). As MacAndrew and Edgerton (1969) argue, drunken comportment is learned, and varies cross-culturally. Americans' "drunkenness" is a learned behavior and has its appropriate and inappropriate forms. Alcoholics are a labeled group of people who behave inappropriately after drinking alcohol.

There is disagreement on who should be categorized as a problem drinker or alcoholic. A successful writer who finds she writes better with a few drinks, a college student who only gets drunk on the weekends, a businessman who drinks to loosen up in social situations—these people may not consider themselves alcoholics, but those around them may consider them so. Certainly there is a significant difference between members of Alcoholics Anonymous and the urban nomads described by Spradley in *You Owe Yourself a Drunk* (1970). Yet the people in both groups are labeled "alcoholics."

Once the drinker is labeled as an alcoholic he may or may not accept this label himself, and it may or may not become an identity. Even should he accept this interpretation of his drinking behavior, so long as the interpretation remains unassimilated to a figured world such as that created by AA, he need not see it as an aspect of himself that carries over into other areas of his life. He may even learn about AA without that knowledge reorganizing or transforming his own understanding of himself.[2] By "identity" we mean the way a person understands and views himself, and is often viewed by others, at least in certain situations—a perception of self that can be fairly constantly achieved (see Schwartz and Merten 1968). These forms of self-understanding are always construed relative to a figured world of social life. "An alcoholic," "a father," and "a judge" are all particular answers to the question "Who am I?" (Kuhn and McPartland 1954), where the implicit condition is "relative to such and such a social world."

These identities affect how a person acts in the world. If a drinker does accept the label of alcoholic as applying to himself, and accepts and acts on the identity of an alcoholic, this transformation of identity, from a drinking non-alcoholic ("normal drinker") to an alcoholic, requires a radical reinterpretation of who he is, of "self." It requires a new way of figuring the activity of drinking, those who drink, and the place of drinking in a broader social and personal context. This process of reinterpretation of self, the formation of a new identity, is a major component of Alcoholics Anonymous.

AA and the Disease of Alcoholism

Members of Alcoholics Anonymous have found a particular definition of a problem and a particular way to deal with it. AA constitutes a figured world, a meaning system within a meaning system. It draws upon specific sets of interpretations and assumptions which circulate alongside many others in the United States. AA is the best-known program for attempting to deal with alcoholism and is widely held to be the most successful, although there is no agreed-upon way to measure this claim. Many of its principles, and often the program itself, are used in treatment centers for alcohol and drug addiction.

From its beginning AA used an illness model to describe alcoholism. Peterson (1988) traces this terminology to AA's roots in the Oxford Group Movement of the 1930s. This religious movement in the United

States and England drew an analogy between sin and illness in a program of personal evangelism. Early AA members, including the founders, participated in Oxford Group meetings and were influenced by the oral tradition and terminology and the methods of personal contact. The original medical model of alcoholism used by AA was borrowed from the medical model of sin popular in the Oxford Groups. The original methods section of *Alcoholics Anonymous* (published in 1939) uses the words "illness," "malady," and "habit" to describe alcoholism; the word "disease" appears only once, to describe alcoholism as a "spiritual disease" (Peterson 1988: 5). Later, as the medicalized view of alcoholism as a disease became popular, it spread back to AA from the medical profession (John Peterson, personal communication).

AA members are told that alcoholism is a progressive and incurable disease that, if unchecked, is fatal. The drinking alcoholic is powerless over alcohol, and out of control. Once one becomes an alcoholic, one's whole life is centered around alcohol, and once the drinking alcoholic takes one drink, she cannot resist the next, or the next . . . The disease affects all areas of one's life, and evidence for alcoholism cannot be found in any one symptom but rather in the life as a whole. The only way to arrest the disease is to stop drinking completely, and since the alcoholic is powerless to resist alcohol, the only way to do this is to turn one's life and will over to a Higher Power. The individual's Higher Power may be God, the AA group, or any other conception of something larger than self. The surrender must be complete, and can only be accomplished when the drinker is ready to stop drinking, when she admits not only that she may have a problem with drinking but that she is powerless over alcohol and that her life has become unmanageable (AA 1976). For this reason the drinker must "hit bottom" before she can stop; it is not enough that others want her to stop. The bottom is not directly determined by how much one drinks, but by what alcohol has done in one's life:

Whether or not you are an alcoholic is not determined by where you drink, when you started drinking, how long you've been drinking, with whom you drink, what, or even how much. The true test is in the answer to this question: What has alcohol done to you? If it has affected your relationships with your family, friends, former or present employers; if it has influenced the way you schedule your days; if it has affected your health; if it determines or affects your nondrinking moods or your state of mind; if you are in any way preoccupied with alcohol—then the likelihood is that you have a problem. (AA 1979c: 3)

Hitting bottom is a point of crisis in the drinker's life. It is a point at which life apparently cannot go on as it has. And if the drinker can understand drinking as the source of the problem, then drinking is the behavior that must change. One way AA members deal with their problem is to stop drinking. But becoming sober in AA involves much more than not drinking. Since drinking affected all areas of one's life, sobriety must also affect all areas of life. "Sobriety," when talked about by AA members, means a new way of life, with spiritual aspects of surrender to God or a Higher Power, humility, trust, honesty, and making amends for wrongs committed in the past or present. The self-understanding, the identity of a sober AA alcoholic ideally includes all of these as well as a particular drinking history. There are therefore two aspects important to membership in AA: qualification as an alcoholic, based on one's past, and continued non-drinking behavior, or effort at not drinking, which is a negation of the behavior that first qualified one for membership.[3]

Since alcoholism is an incurable disease, once one is an alcoholic one remains an alcoholic for the rest of one's life. The AA member comes to see not only his drinking as alcoholic but his self as an alcoholic. The disease is a part of one's self. Alcoholism is not something one has; rather an alcoholic is what one is. This is a situation in which many of one's basic assumptions must be changed or reorganized, in which one must learn a new understanding of one's problem, one's self, and what the world is like. Bateson (1972) addresses this transformation that members of AA must undergo as a change in epistemology. We address it as a change in identity, that is, of self-understanding within a new figuration of the world.

As a cultural system, and one that no one is born into, this entire figured world of AA is new to neophytes. The propositions and interpretations of events and experiences, the appropriate behaviors and values of an AA alcoholic, and the appropriate placement of the alcoholic identity in the hierarchy of identities one holds must be learned. In short, an AA identity must be constructed and its moral and aesthetic distinctions made into personal knowledge. This cultural (and literal) information is communicated through the AA literature, and through talk in AA meetings and one-to-one interactions. One important vehicle for this communication is the personal story.

In personal stories, oldtimers in AA tell their own life stories or part of them—their drinking histories—and how they came to be involved in AA. These stories contribute to cultural production and reproduction in three ways. First, they objectify many cultural elements—the beliefs, propositions, and interpretations—that new or potential AA members learn through listening. Second, by virtue of their narrative forms, the stories realize a model of what alcoholism is and what it means to be an alcoholic. This model, in the absence of a well-defined, well-elaborated model shared by the wider culture, provides a basis for potential members to identify themselves as alcoholics, through comparing their lives to those in the stories. The storyline also provides a basis for labeling others, as others compare the lives of suspected alcoholics to the AA lives. Third, the AA story is a tool of subjectivity, a mediating device for self-understanding. As the AA member learns the AA story model, by listening to and telling stories, and comes to place the events and experiences of his own life into the model, he learns to understand his own life as an AA life, and himself as an AA alcoholic. The personal story is a cultural vehicle for identity formation.

In AA, personal stories are told for the explicit, stated purpose of providing an understanding of alcoholism, so that other drinkers may find so much of themselves in the lives of professed alcoholics that they cannot help asking whether they, too, are alcoholics. Since the definition of an alcoholic is not agreed upon in the wider society, arriving at this interpretation of events is a process negotiated between the drinker and those around her. AA stories provide a set of criteria by which the alcoholic can be identified. Like Ecuadorian illness stories or the stories told by the Ifaluk in recounting troublesome family situations (Price 1987; Lutz 1987), they provide a means of socially negotiating the interpretations of events. For potential members, who may have been labeled by others as alcoholic, listening to AA stories provides an alternative understanding for reinterpreting their own behaviors that more closely matches the interpretations others have made of them.

Simply learning the propositions about alcoholism and its nature is not enough. The drinker must apply them to his own life, and this application must be demonstrated. Scott (1969) notes that, for workers in blindness agencies, one key indicator of the success of rehabilitation is that the client comes to understand himself and his problem from the worker's perspective. Similarly, in AA, success or recovery requires coming to perceive oneself and one's problems from an AA perspective. AA members must learn to experience their problems as drinking problems, and themselves as alcoholics. This is why, as members often say, "AA is for those who want it, not for those who need it." AA members must agree to become tellers, as well as listeners, of AA stories.

Telling AA stories is a way of demonstrating that one has mastered, or at least has begun to gain facility with, the appropriate understandings. Telling an appropriate story is thus a means of gaining some validation from listeners for one's AA identity. But telling is an active process. It is a process of construction. Using the AA model and applying it to her own life, the drinker comes to understand better how and why she is an alcoholic. She locates herself within the figured world of AA. The stories are used in what is simultaneously a social and a cognitive and affective, personal process. In the process of identity formation, the AA member undergoes a kind of reorientation in her self-understandings, a detachment from identities subsisting in other figured worlds, followed by the reconstitution—a process not only of learning but also of valuation, indeed elevation—of an identity predicated within AA's world. She accomplishes this transition primarily by reinterpreting her life as an AA story.

The Process of Identity Formation

Arnold van Gennep, in *Rites of Passage* (1960), described the patterns of movement from one position within society to another. The ceremonies that take place at these points in an individual's life ritually express the transition from one status to another. The status movements in van Gennep's scheme are spatial and structural changes. Rites of separation, transition, and incorporation move the individual from one condition to another and cushion the disturbance in the equilibrium of both the individual and the group. Van Gennep's concern, reflecting the interests of the time in which he wrote, was with the impact of these rites on the social group—how the group marks the movement of individuals between subgroups. He did not ask how the rituals transform the individual's image of himself, his identity.

Schwartz and Merten (1968), in contrast, address the question of how an initiation ritual transforms the initiate's self-image and social identity. They develop a scheme for identity transformation in which the initiate undergoes what they term "identity diffusion" and "identity reconstitution." In their example of a high school sorority, identity diffusion takes place as hazing disrupts the initiate's perception of herself, raising doubts about the superior ability she had assumed made her "sorority material." This disruption opens her to the possibility of a radical reinterpretation of self. During a rite called "mock" the initiate is forced to take on exaggerated attributes of the morally devalued groups against which "socies" define themselves: "hoods" and "others." Highly stylized and stigmatized negative features of dress, hairstyle, and behavior associated with the "hood" and "other" identities are attached temporarily to the potential "socies," expressing what these girls fear are latent possibilities in their own character.

Reconstitution takes place as the negative is exorcized and the initiate is allowed to return to her normal state. This use of expressive, enacted symbols is more than a representation to the community of a transition. When the initiate attaches to all the negative possibilities she has feared in herself, and realizes that this attachment is a transient state, the resumption of normal dress is accompanied by a transformation in her image of herself: now she is forever cleansed of any possible latent moral impurities, and her identity as a "socie" is publicly confirmed. She is ready for induction (see Chapter 11 for more on this process of loosening oneself, or being loosened, from a figured world).

Schwartz and Merten's scheme for identity (trans)formation applies to cases in which the new self-understanding can develop only at the expense of an existing one. This is true for people who come into Alcoholics Anonymous: the old conception of self in relation to drinking is weakened through a process of discrediting not only the old identity as such but also the figured world that gives it meaning. We conceive this step as devaluation, rather than diffusion, as Schwartz and Merten call it. In the formation of a new identity an individual comes, with the social encouragement and insistence of others, to interpret the world in new ways, and to position herself and emotionally invest herself in that world. Individuals do this through participating in group activities, learning to produce and enact cultural forms particular to that world, and taking up these forms as devices for mediating their own conception of self and world.

For AA, the process of identity devaluation must begin before one enters the program. For a drinker to have reason to come to AA, she, or those around her, must realize that she is not what she thought she was, a "normal drinker." A normal drinker has no reason to go to AA. But if she has begun to suspect that she may have a drinking problem, or if those around her have begun to point out that drinking may be the source of problems, or even identify her as an alcoholic, then some disruption in the previous perception of herself as normal drinker has occurred. It may be that she does not yet understand or desire the identity of an alcoholic, but the disruption opens the possibility of this transformation in self-image.

Once the drinker makes contact with AA and begins to participate in meetings, she must come to understand drinking and alcoholism as AA understands them, and must come to see herself as a potential AA member. This involves making an appropriate connection between alcohol and the problems it has led to. She must replace her previous image of an alcoholic as a drunk or Skid Row bum with the AA definition of an ill person, learning to see the identity of an AA (non-drinking) alcoholic as desirable, and learning to see herself as like or potentially like those who hold this identity.

Making the appropriate connection between alcohol and the problems one is having requires seeing the problems as negative effects of drinking. This often leads the drinker to rethink who she is or why she drinks. Most of the personal stories told in AA include a segment in which the drinker justifies her drinking when people point out its negative effects. She blames her drinking on her problems, for example, rather than seeing her problems as the effects of drinking. This is one example of how the connection may be interpreted in ways inappropriate to AA. Other examples are given in published AA stories. Jim saw himself as a person for whom trouble was a natural part of his personality, and saw drinking as one aspect of that. When he joined AA he had to learn to understand himself as an alcoholic for whom trouble was an aspect of his drinking (AA 1979c). Similarly, a woman who understood drinking as "one more symbol of [her] neurosis" had to come to understand her neurosis as one more symptom of her alcoholism (AA 1968a).

Learning the appropriate storyline of an "alcoholic" is also represented in the AA stories. At first a potential member may reject the suggestion that he may be alcoholic, and that AA may be relevant to him. Typically, his conception of an alcoholic is someone who lives on the bowery and panhandles for a drink, and he believes this person arrived there because of a moral weakness or lack of willpower. He must learn that alcoholism is a disease that can happen to anyone (AA 1967, 1968b), and he must sensitize himself to the appropriate evidence for it. He must also see the identity of AA alcoholic as a desirable one. As expressed in AA literature and AA talk, the program cannot work unless a person wants to stop drinking, and this change usually occurs when a person "hits bottom." Finally, the drinker must see the identity of AA alcoholic as one that is possible for him to attain. Cain heard several members say that even after they admitted that they had drinking problems and that AA was relevant to them they still could not identify with AA oldtimers: "They had their lives so together, and I was so fucked up."

Personalization of the identity takes place as the initiate begins to identify with AA members. Through comparing his life to theirs, he sees that other members are like him and he is like them. As he becomes involved in AA, he learns to introduce himself as an alcoholic every time he speaks. The behaviors that mark progress in the AA program become subjective mediating devices; they become means by which the new member directs and evaluates his own behavior. At meetings he picks up colored chips, amid applause, to mark the amount of time he has been without a drink. If he has a "slip" and takes a drink, he must start over with a white chip, or "clean chip." He works his way through the Twelve Steps that guide, and mark one's progress in, sober living. The identity of alcoholic gains salience for him and takes a more central place in his conception of himself.

He becomes emotionally attached to the identity of AA alcoholic as he begins to care how others in the group perceive him. He comes to understand himself as a non-drinking alcoholic, and to reinterpret his past life as evidence. As he becomes an oldtimer in AA, he tells his personal story to newcomers to help them identify themselves as alcoholics. As Schwartz and Merten argue that identity reconstitution in sorority initiation takes place through the attaching and exorcizing of negative identities, we argue that identity reconstitution in AA takes place through reinterpretation of self and of one's life, and that the major vehicle for this reinterpretation is the AA personal story.

As mentioned earlier, there are two important dimensions to the identity of AA alcoholic. The first distinction AA makes is between alcoholic and non-alcoholic, where alcoholic refers to a state that, once attained, is not reversible. The second is between drinking and non-drinking, and refers to a potentially controllable activity. Normal drinkers, in the figured world of AA, can control their drinking, while alcoholic drinkers cannot; in order to stop drinking, AA members must turn their will and lives over to a Higher Power. Together these two dimensions divide people into four types, one of which is the AA alcoholic identity. For continuing membership in AA, one must qualify as an alcoholic, based on one's past, and make a continued effort at not drinking. The normative AA identity requires a behavior—not drinking—that is a negation of the behavior that originally qualified one for membership. One of the functions of the AA personal story is to establish both aspects of membership in an individual. This parallels Schwartz and Merten in that the AA story serves to attach what has now become understood as negative behavior—attributes of the active alcoholic—to the member, but demonstrates that these are in the past. In their place it attaches the attributes of the non-drinking alcoholic, as demonstrated in behaviors appropriate to AA and involvement in AA activities. Not the least of these activities is the telling of the personal story.

A Learned Form

AA dedicates a significant amount of meeting time and publishing space to the telling of personal stories. In these stories AA members relate their own drinking histories, how they came to understand that they are alcoholics, how they got into AA, and what their life has been like since they joined. From the founding of AA, the telling of personal stories has been both the major vehicle for "carrying the message to alcoholics who still suffer" (the Twelfth Step), and an important tool for maintaining sobriety.

Ever since Bill W. overcame the compulsion to drink by telling his own story to Dr. Bob in May 1935, these cofounders and those who have followed them in the program have claimed that telling their own stories to other alcoholics, and thus helping other alcoholics to achieve sobriety, is an important part of maintaining their own sobriety (AA 1976; Thomsen 1975). As one member told Cain, "We keep what we have by giving it away."

As a tool for carrying the message, the personal story helps alcoholics identify themselves as such. In a pamphlet directed at young people, Carmen says: "I heard a woman begin her story with her teenage drinking. It sounded familiar. Perhaps I might become an alcoholic, I thought.

Perhaps I might already be one" (AA 1979c: 20). The role of the personal story in helping others to identify is important because of the AA test for alcoholism. Evidence is found not in how much you drink, or how often, but in what alcohol has done to you (AA 1979b). The evidence for alcoholism must be found in one's entire life, and the personal story provides a prototypic alcoholic life for comparison with the potential member's own. Hearing AA stories, the drinking alcoholic thinks, "We've done the same things. This person is like me," and so, "Maybe I am an alcoholic."

This aspect of personal stories accounts for their widespread telling in AA. *Alcoholics Anonymous* (1976), the "Big Book," first published in 1939, includes twenty-nine personal stories of some of AA's earliest members, including Bill W. and Dr. Bob. These stories are prefaced by the hope "that many alcoholic men and women, desperately in need, will see these pages, and we believe that it is only by fully disclosing ourselves and our problems that they will be persuaded to say, 'Yes I am one of them too; I must have this thing'" (29). This early use of personal stories has been continued in much of the AA literature published since. Pamphlets written for specific audiences (young people, women, prison inmates, the elderly) devote considerable space to personal stories. Biographies of the cofounders and comic-book style publications are other forms the AA story takes.

AA members tell personal stories formally in "speakers meetings." In this type of meeting, speakers are prearranged, and, other than a short opening and closing, the meeting consists entirely of these tellings. These meetings are the most likely meetings for newcomers to attend, and often form the outsider's impression of what an AA meeting is like. Less formally, members tell shortened versions of their stories at discussion meetings. Sometimes, for example, when a newcomer is present, each oldtimer in the group will tell, in short form, how he or she got into AA.

Another important context for telling personal stories is "Twelfth Step calls." When AA members talk to outsiders who may be alcoholics in a one-to-one interaction, they are following the last of the Twelve Steps, "carrying the message to alcoholics who still suffer." When called, AA members will meet with nonmembers who are having problems related to drinking. Ideally, at these individual meetings, the member tells his story, describes the AA program, tries to help the drinker see herself as an alcoholic if she is "ready." The "Big Book" chapter entitled "Working with Others" provides instructions for telling the personal story in this context:

> See your man alone, if possible. At first engage in general conversation. After a while, turn the talk to some phase of drinking. Tell him enough about your drinking habits, symptoms, and experiences to encourage him to speak of himself. If he wishes to talk, let him do so. You will thus get a better idea of how you ought to proceed. If he is not communicative, give him a sketch of your drinking career up to the time you quit. But say nothing, for the moment, of how that was accomplished . . .
>
> When he sees you know all about the drinking game, commence to describe yourself as an alcoholic. Tell him how baffled you were, how you finally learned that you were sick. Give him an account of the struggles you made to stop. Show him the mental twist which leads to the first drink of a spree . . .
>
> If he is an alcoholic, he will understand you at once. He will match your mental inconsistencies with some of his own. If you are satisfied that he is a real alcoholic, begin to dwell on the hopeless feature of the malady . . . And be careful not to brand him an alcoholic. Let him draw his own conclusion . . .
>
> Continue to speak of alcoholism as a sickness, a fatal malady. Talk about the conditions of body and mind which accompany it. Keep his attention focused mainly on your personal experience. Explain that many are doomed who never realize their predicament . . . You will soon have your friend admitting that he has many, if not all, of the traits of the alcoholic . . . Even if your protégé may not have entirely admitted his condition, he has become very curious to know how you got well . . . *Tell him exactly what happened to you.* (1976: 91–93)

These instructions give an indication of the structure of the AA personal story. There is a general structure, in the form of a scenario in which the decision to join AA is made. This general structure is what we will call "the AA story." Apparently the story was consciously developed from the beginning as a vehicle for presenting an experience or person with whom the prospect could identify. Interviews published in 1980 show that Dr. Bob and early group members experimented with various explanations of alcoholism—including an "allergy" explanation and an analogy to diabetes—and methods of attracting prospects to their program. Members of the emerging group worked together to perfect their techniques: "We talked about how to get more members and how to handle them. Then we talked about the mistakes we had made in telling our stories. We didn't hesitate to criticize each other. We suggested certain words to leave out and certain words to add in order to make a more effective talk. It made a bunch of amateur psychologists and after-dinner speakers out of us" (AA 1980: 114). Since the time being described is before the writing of the "Big Book," it seems safe to conclude that the framework for the AA story and the AA word choice were worked out in practical presentations and critiques by emerging groups long before the "Big Book," with its personal stories, was published (John Peterson, personal communication).

The AA story usually begins with the teller categorizing his early drinking either as normal social drinking or as alcoholic from the start. He then describes how the drinking progressed, leading to negative effects such as loss of jobs, domestic problems, arrests, car accidents, or hospitalizations. Still, the drinking continues, even gets worse. The drinker justifies it by blaming it and its negative effects on circumstances or other people, or by explaining what drinking does for him. Perhaps drinking provides escape from pressures, or perhaps it makes him feel confident in situations in which he is usually insecure. People begin to point out that he may have a drinking problem, and perhaps they suggest that he try AA. He rejects the suggestion, though he may go to an AA meeting or talk to some AA members. He believes "alcoholics" are hopeless drunken bums, and since he is not that, he thinks AA has nothing to offer him.

His drinking continues, and with it the negative effects. His struggles to control it fail. Finally he "hits bottom," recognizes that he is powerless over alcohol, and gives AA an honest try. He finds out that members are really just like him. His definition of an alcoholic changes from the drunken bum to the everyday person afflicted with a disease. The story ends with a description of what AA has done for him and what his life is like now. A typical example from the pamphlet *Young People and AA* illustrates the structure. This is Al's personal story:

My drinking resulted in trouble from the very first. I was a sophomore in high school when I went to my first prom. We brought the girls home early and then went to one of the guy's homes. His parents happened to be away that weekend. We all did some very heavy drinking, finally winding up by taking it straight from the bottle. That night, at the age of 14, I experienced my first blackout.

The next seven years, my drinking and trouble got progressively worse. All through high school, I drank whenever the opportunity presented itself. I managed to secure phony proof of age when I was 15, so I could get served in bars. At 16, I bought my first car and began to mix drinking and driving, with the usual results.

I gained admission to a very good college. I knew why I was going to college—to have a good time and get a degree. If I got an education in the process, then that would be a fringe benefit. I got into the best fraternity on campus. Most of the brothers were athletes; the remainder, party boys. Since I had little athletic promise, I joined the ranks of the party boys.

Success in school was measured by the number of parties I went to, the dates I had, and the times I got drunk. I never did any more work than was necessary to stay in school. Anything more than just passing was wasted effort and could have been better spent on having a "good time." The blackouts were becoming more frequent. I never paid any attention to them except to note that they were probably a sign that I had enjoyed myself the night before.

At this point the proctor called me to his office. A friend and I had gone to a secretary's apartment after the bar closed, and had not been treated with the proper respect. Just to show her, we walked off with half her belongings. She reported us to the authorities, and we received a warning. This was in my freshman year.

My sophomore year, I brought a car to school. I could now have more dates, go away on weekends to other schools. In the spring, the president of the fraternity warned me that the brothers thought it was a good idea for me to cut down, as I was giving the fraternity a bad name on campus. It was none of his business, I told him; they were jealous because I was having all the fun, while they had to work to stay in school. Shortly thereafter, I was called to the proctor's office again.

My junior year was by far the worst. I started out by going back to school a week early, and for a week I never drew a sober breath. The progression had really set in. After school started, most days I made no attempt to attend classes.

In December, I was again called to the proctor's office, and sent to the mental-health clinic to see a psychiatrist and take some tests. The doctor told me that I would have to leave school to do something about my drinking problem. I was shocked. What drinking problem? I said I would stop drinking if they allowed me to stay, but he tried to impress upon me that I had lost control.

My bubble had burst. All of a sudden, the party had come to an abrupt halt. I left school that afternoon.

The day after Christmas, I was admitted to a psychiatric clinic in Manhattan. My condition could best be described as confused, about what had happened and what was going to happen. When someone tried to talk to me, my only response was to cry. As time went on, I was able to talk to the doctor quite freely about my drinking. The time came when I was finally able to admit that I *might* be an alcoholic.

After six months, I was discharged from the clinic. My father had gone to his first AA meeting years ago, in 1959, and my mother was a member of Al-Anon (for relatives and friends of alcoholics). I had attended many meetings in the past with my parents. Yet I made no attempt to contact AA when I left the hospital. I stayed sober for two months and then picked up the first drink, looking for the "good time" I was missing.

I drank for two months, and things got progressively worse. The day finally came when I was convinced alcohol had the best of me, and I needed help. I went to *my* first meeting that night, seeking an answer to *my* problem. That was over two years ago. I have not had a drink since, one day at a time. The understanding that people in AA showed was the first thing that impressed me. They were not shocked by my drinking history. They just nodded; they knew what I was talking about.

Two things that I caught on to right from the start were: constant attendance at meetings, and sticking with the winners. I went to meetings every night, and tried to attend midnight meetings as often as possible. After two months, I asked a man to be my sponsor. He proved to be the biggest help, providing the answers and encouragement necessary for me to make this program.

Being young bothered me at first. But the men who came in when they were old, and stayed with the program, gave me the incentive to do the same. I thought a man of 60 or more faced the same problem as I, only at the other end of the spectrum.

AA has given me my life and my sanity, two things I hold dear today. It has been a slow process of building a new life, one I never dreamed existed for me. I am the product of many people's devotion of time and effort, and I always welcome the chance to pass on what I have to someone else.

I am now back at the university, and will probably be on the dean's list this term. My concept of what a "good time" is has changed considerably. There is a balance in my life today between studies, AA, and doing other things I enjoy. All this is mine by staying away from one drink, one day at a time. I probably have one drunk left in me, but I'm not so sure I have another recovery left in me. (1979c: 10–13)

The AA story provides a general framework, of which the individual personal stories are specific examples. It is a learned structure, developed over time, and of course there are variations. One reason for variation is that any one personal story is created from the interaction of the learned AA story form, the actual events of an individual's life, and individual or group agendas. Many of the personal stories published in pamphlets include paragraphs or sections addressing such issues as being a teenage alcoholic or a female alcoholic. The point these stories make is that, while a person may be different from others in AA, the differences are unimportant in light of the similarities: all are alcoholics. The "Big Book" personal stories almost all address the issue of religious or spiritual beliefs.

There is also variation over time and situation. The personal stories in the "Big Book" are the earliest published AA stories. The "Big Book" stories tend to be longer than those in other literature, and they tend to give more autobiographical information. Some of the stories in the "Big Book" also seem more literary in style than those in other publications. Perhaps the shorter and more prototypic form of the published AA story has evolved since the publication of this book in 1939.

Stories also vary by whether they are told in speakers meetings or in discussion meetings. In speakers meetings a single person may talk for forty-five minutes to an hour. In discussion meetings, in contrast, nearly everyone takes part, and if personal stories are told they are abbreviated. Sometimes the teller concentrates on a single aspect of the story, such as what hitting bottom was like for him, or how he first heard about AA, or how he reacted to his first meeting. If a fuller story is told, recurring events, such as repeated negative effects of drinking, are condensed into generalized statements or illustrative episodes.

Other variation stems from differences in individual lives, and from differences in the extent to which individuals learn the model AA story and use it to organize self-understanding. In spite of all the possible variations, the personal stories told in AA are remarkably similar. Such similarity comes about through participation in AA, where members are supported in re-forming their life histories as AA stories. AA members come to fit the events and experiences of their own lives into the AA story structure and so to identify themselves in the figured world of AA.

Learning to Tell an AA Story

How to tell an AA story is not something one learns through explicit teaching. Newcomers are not *told* how to tell their stories, yet most people who remain in AA learn to do this. There are several ways in which an AA member is helped to tell an appropriate story. First, he is exposed to AA lives. The newcomer hears and reads personal stories from the time of early contact with the program—through meetings, literature, and talk with oldtimers. In addition to the structure of the AA story, the newcomer is also learning the figured world of alcoholism encoded in them, including AA propositions: "alcoholism is a progressive disease"; "the alcoholic is powerless over alcohol"; "the alcoholic drinker is out of control"; "AA is for those who want it, not for those who need it"; "AA is a program for living, not just for not drinking." These points enter, often verbatim, into stories as guidelines for describing the progression of drinking, the desire and inability to stop, the necessity of hitting bottom before the program can work, and the changes that take place in one's life after one joins AA.

Members also begin to view episodes of their lives as behavioral evidence of alcoholic drinking, and to supply the interpretations of these episodes sanctioned by AA. Thus blackouts, car accidents, loss of job, divorce, loss of friends, depression, involvement in illegal activities, hospitalization for mental illness or for detoxification enter into their stories as evidence. Drinking patterns taken to be alcoholic, such as morning drinking, bingeing, gulping drinks quickly, or hiding the amount drunk, are also taken as evidence.

In addition to learning from the stories and statements of others, new members begin to craft their own stories in social interaction. All members are encouraged to speak at discussion meetings and to maintain friendships with other AA members. In this social interaction the new member is called on to talk about her own life. As she does so a process of scaffolding occurs (Wood, Bruner, and Ross 1976). In scaffolding, individual skills originate in cooperative activity. In informal learning activities the teacher builds a "scaffold" around the limited abilities of the learner, as they cooperatively perform the task. The teacher begins with the skills the learner possesses, and builds on those, while taking responsibility for the aspects of the task the learner has not yet mastered. Over time the learner is given, and takes, responsibility for more of the task. "Scaffolding" is derived from the developmental psychology of Vygotsky, most particularly from his notion of the "zone of proximal development" (see Chapter 8). The scaffold that the teacher has built diminishes, and the skills that had been inter-individual in the cooperative task become intra-individual, personally produced and relied upon by the learner (Greenfield 1984).

Scaffolding of AA members who are beginning to tell their stories indicates that the AA identity is not natural or simple to develop. People do not describe themselves as alcoholics and their lives as alcoholic lives because this is natural and obvious; rather they learn to tell about themselves and their lives in this way, and the process of learning can take much effort and cooperation between the neophyte and other AA members.

Scaffolding occurs as the newcomer begins to talk about his life. For example, in discussion meetings the topic may be "admitting you are powerless," "making amends," "how to avoid the first drink," or shared experiences in dealing with common problems. Each person present usually relates some incident or insight. One speaker follows another by picking out certain pieces of what has previously been said, telling why it was relevant to him, and elaborating on it with some episode of his own. Sometimes a newcomer will say something that seems to parallel the episodes or comments of others, but will give an interpretation of it that is inappropriate according to AA beliefs. Sometimes the episode itself will seem to have little to do with those others are telling. Usually, unless the interpretation really runs counter to AA beliefs, the speaker is not corrected. Rather, other speakers take the appropriate parts of the newcomer's comments and build on them, giving parallel accounts with different interpretations, or expanding on parts of their own stories that are similar to parts of the newcomer's story while ignoring the inappropriate parts of his story.

At one discussion meeting members traded stories of how they had come to AA. A college athlete, a newcomer who had not yet quit drinking or using drugs, gave instrumental reasons for needing to quit—he had to undergo urine tests and would lose his athletic scholarship if drugs were detected. This was an inappropriate reason, since AA stresses that you must see yourself as an alcoholic, and must want to quit for yourself rather than for someone else. Most of the oldtimers who spoke after the newcomer focused on how they had realized they had a problem they couldn't control. Several of the stories had the themes of needing to see yourself as like other members of AA and needing to see getting sober as something desirable.

In another meeting Brad, who had just entered AA and had had his last drink three days before, said that he would still do pot except that he always drank when he did pot: "Pot is not a problem; I can give it up anytime." Steve, an oldtimer, said he had done a lot of different drugs that he could give up anytime . . . as long as he replaced them with a new drug. Mark said, "I experimented with pot . . . for twenty years." The implication of these comments was clearly that Brad was only kidding himself. In this way, members point out appropriate interpretations as they make jokes about their own past wrong interpretations. One night Gary told this tale: "One morning I woke up after a night of drinking, and I thought I'd had this bad dream about running into the side of a bridge at 55 miles an hour. Then I went outside. Three inches off the side of my car were gone. And I thought, 'Man, I've *got* to stop *driving*.'"

Members try to reinforce the appropriate parts of a story rather than point out the inappropriate. When called for, however, correction does occur. If someone says something that directly contradicts the basic AA propositions and interpretations, she will be called on it. Clair, who had been in the program for some time, said, "I thought I wasn't powerless over anything." William interrupted her: "You weren't powerless over *anything?*" She answered, "I *thought* I wasn't powerless over anything." On another night Eugene, who was fairly new to the program, was worried that he was about to lose his job because he believed his boss had found out that he was an alcoholic living in a halfway house. "It's not going to do me any good to be sober and not have a job," Eugene said. "I don't want to be sober with ragged underwear." An oldtimer answered, "If you're drinking, your underwear will get pretty ragged anyway."

At times, correct and incorrect interpretations are contrasted explicitly, as in these comments during a discussion on "honesty":

At least when I was drunk, and lying on the floor, if someone came by and asked me, "Hey, what's wrong with you?" at least I could say, "I'm drunk!" I might say, "It's that stinkin' rotten gin that did it to me," but I would say, "I'm drunk." I've seen a lot of people who would be lying on the floor—and there aren't that many reasons you would be there—and if you asked them what's wrong, they'd tell you, "Oh, I'm just tired, just resting." They'd tell themselves that. They just can't be honest. You don't see that kind of person get sober very often. At least if they can say, "I'm drunk," they might be able to get sober.

Sometimes members interpret newcomers' lives, more or less explicitly, according to AA principles. Patricia, a nonmember, spoke to Hank on the AA "hotline" and asked how she could know if she was an alcoholic. Hank brought her to a discussion meeting and suggested the topic "How we got into AA." Everyone gave an abbreviated personal story, focusing on the things that had led them to see themselves as alcoholics and to come to AA for help. After listening to these stories, Patricia spoke. She said she didn't think she was an alcoholic, but she did have a drinking problem. She often drank all day on weekends, and often didn't remember those days. She said she drank a lot, sometimes lied about the amount, and hid bottles. Sometimes she had blackouts. Her boyfriend was concerned about how much she drank, and he had talked her into contacting AA. Then she compared herself with her uncle, who was an alcoholic, and with the other members of the discussion group whose stories she had heard, and declared that she was not that bad: she had never wrecked a car or had DUIs; she had never been hospitalized, or had deep depressions, so she didn't think she was an alcoholic.

While she was speaking no one interrupted, but after she had finished several people spoke. Without actually telling her she was an alcoholic, they pointed out that the stories they told were their own, not hers, and the events they told about were not preconditions but symptoms. Gary, an oldtimer, said that just because he had never been "strung out in a hospital" like Elizabeth, he could not use that to say he was not an alcoholic any more than Elizabeth could say she was not one because she had never had DUIs as he had. "You don't have to get all the way to the bottom before you quit," Elizabeth told Patricia. "The only requirement for membership is a desire to stop drinking." At the end of the meeting Patricia picked up her white chip, indicating her intention to stop drinking and start the AA program. As another characteristic response to this form of denial, when newcomers state that they *haven't* done something, others will reply "yet."

Personal stories, as AA recognizes, are important in helping some drinkers identify themselves as alcoholics. Hearing or reading personal stories, potential members compare their lives to the alcoholic life, readjust their definition of "alcoholic," and say, "these people are like me." Telling an AA personal story also helps members construct the identity of AA alcoholic by signaling real membership and through transforming the members' self-understanding.

Telling AA personal stories also helps members identify with one another in ways that are harder to document. As a public event, one that is not only observable but material and co-participatory, the telling encompasses body practices, including vocalization, that realize structures of affect and disposition. Not only social theorists, from Durkheim and Mauss to Bourdieu, but any participant in such performances would tell you that the fellow-feeling born in these ceremonies is a powerful means of identification.

Telling a personal story, especially at a speakers meeting or on a Twelfth Step call, signals membership because this "is the time that they [members] feel that they belong enough to 'carry the message'" (Robinson 1979: 54). Twelfth Stepping and speaking at speakers meetings are often represented in the AA literature as the final evidence that the member's life has turned around from the drinking days to a life in which he helps others. The personal stories themselves are valued as the vehicles by which the member transforms his past experience into something useful.

Telling a personal story is also important as a process of self-understanding. The example of Patricia illustrates that, despite the hopes of AA members, drinking alcoholics do not always recognize themselves in the stories told at meetings and realize that they too must be alcoholics. The AA story structure has a stage in which the drinker rejects the suggestion that he might be an alcoholic, despite the negative effects of his drinking, because he does not match his own definition of "alcoholic." The drinker must learn an appropriate definition, and must learn the events and episodes that are evidence of alcoholism. As he learns the AA story structure, he must learn to see the events and experiences of his own life as evidence for alcoholism. He learns to put his own events and experiences into an AA story, and thus learns to tell, and to understand, his own life as an AA story. He reinterprets his own past, from the understanding he once had of himself as a normal drinker to the understanding he now has of himself as an alcoholic.

Reinterpreting the Past

The AA personal story is a cultural form that the teller learns to produce, and the process transforms her self-understanding from that of a drinker to that of an AA "recovering alcoholic." The stories encode the figuring of alcoholism held by AA, and this figuring organizes knowledge and guides inferences. As we argue in Chapter 5, identification with the world figured by a cultural model develops together with becoming an actor in that world.[4] As the newcomer learns to produce an AA story and identifies herself as an AA alcoholic, she comes to use the cultural model to direct her present actions and self-understanding and to reinterpret her past. The stories are tools for reinterpreting the past and putting the self into the figured world of AA. That is, the stories are cultural mediating devices, similar to the Nepalese rituals and songs that mediate the formation of gender identities (see Chapters 10 and 12).

In the course of my fieldwork with AA, I (Carole Cain) heard stories told in three settings: discussion meetings, speakers meetings, and interviews. In some cases I heard the same persons tell their personal stories, or parts of them, in more than one setting—in an interview and a discussion meeting, for example, or in a discussion meeting and a speakers meeting. It became clear that there were regularities in the stories each person told, even as they were adapted to the different settings. There also seemed to be a relationship between the way the stories were told and the extent to which the teller had made the AA identity and the AA model of the alcoholic life his own. The longer a person had been in AA, the closer his story was to the AA story structure. There were also markers incorporated into the stories that indicated a process of reinterpretation, continuing or complete.

Much of this section is based on stories collected during three interviews, although I occasionally refer to stories told in other settings. One advantage of the interviews is that they were tape-recorded and I have been able to work from transcriptions. Also, in the interviews the speakers clearly consented to my use of the information. Although AA members knew that I was attending meetings as part of my research, what was said at those meetings was intended for other members, not for the anthropologist, and much was sensitive in nature and private. I have edited out some material that I felt would be inappropriate to include.[5]

Interviews were done with people I met through AA meetings, and consisted of three parts (see Cain 1991). In the part presented here I asked for the individuals' accounts of their drinking experiences.

Before analyzing the interviews I collected personal stories published in AA literature: 29 from the "Big Book" (AA 1976) and 17 from two pamphlets (AA 1968a, 1979c). For these 46 accounts I did a careful analysis, for each paragraph noting main points, episodes and events included, and propositions made about alcohol, self, and AA. I sketched the overall structure of each story. I then did the same type of analysis (by frame) for two fictional stories presented in comic-book style (AA 1967, 1968b). Taking these two very similar stories, which I concluded were "typical" according to AA beliefs, as prototypes, and referring back to the 46 published personal accounts, I abstracted a general AA story structure. It included categories such as "first drink," "negative effects of drinking," "progression of drinking," "suggestion (by others) that drinking may be a problem," "denial," "attempts to control drinking," "entering AA," "giving AA an honest try," and "becoming sober." After I modified the structure to account for differences (for example, some sequences may be repeated; some categories are optional), the variation that remained could be accounted for as attempts to address specific issues, the agendas of particular publications. All the personal stories in the AA publication *Young People and AA* (1979) address the issue of being a young alcoholic; all the stories in *AA for the Woman* (1968a) address the issue of being a female alcoholic. The "Big Book" stories were all longer than those in the pamphlets and generally addressed the issue of religious or spiritual beliefs and AA (for more details about my analysis see Cain 1991).

I compared the stories I heard told in AA discussion and speakers meetings with those in the literature, and found that they fit the structure quite well, with two qualifications. First, some of the stories in the discussion meetings were short versions—either telescoped accounts of a drinking history or pieces of a drinking history used to make a particular point. Second, at the four speakers meetings I attended, three of the speakers told stories that closely followed the structure. The fourth story had events, episodes, and interpretations clearly matching AA beliefs, but the speaker did not present them in chronological order; rather he told episodes illustrating various points about his drinking and life. His interpretations and choice of events matched the AA model in all ways except the order in which they were told.

I applied the same analysis to the narratives recorded in interviews and compared these narratives to the stories told in meetings and published in the AA literature. The findings suggest that, over time, the individual develops his drinking history according to the AA structure, and as the AA identity is formed, the life story narrated comes to resemble the prototypical AA story more and more closely.

In the interviews I asked each person to tell me about her or his drinking experiences. Beyond this I tried not to direct the narrative until it reached what seemed to be a natural ending. Of the three people interviewed, two seemed to have a clear concept of a set of episodes that constituted a response to my request. The narrative told by Hank, who had been sober in AA for fourteen years at the time of the interview, most closely approximated the AA story structure. Ellen, who had been sober for two years, also told a narrative that closely resembled the AA story, but some of her interpretations differed from those heard most often in AA. While Hank seemed to have completed the process of placing his life into the AA story form, Ellen was well along in the process but had not yet completed it. The third informant, Andrew, did not have such a narrative. Andrew had been in and out of AA for over twenty years but had never stayed in the program for more than a few months at a time.

That the stories of Ellen and Hank were lengthy narratives requiring no prompting from me beyond the initial request, and that they paralleled the AA story in structure, indicates that Ellen and Hank are learning, or have learned, to tell their lives as AA personal stories. They proceeded from early drinking, through its progression and negative effects, to hitting bottom and getting into AA. Each of these narratives, excluding follow-up questions and an additional lengthy discussion of Hank's life now and his role in AA, lasted about forty-five minutes (which is also the approximate length of personal stories told in speakers meetings). Each seemed to form a unit that was a natural unit of discourse for the narrators. Both Hank and Ellen seemed to have a clear concept of a set of material that constituted such a story, and of how it should unfold.

The narrative of drinking experience as a bounded unit is named. AA calls it a personal story. Hank referred to his own narrative as a "drinking story" or a "drinking history," and indicated that there were some criteria for such a history: "I'm doing this more or less, I'm tryin' to keep this down to drinkin' and nothin' else. But you know, there was a life . . . And

I will say that, you know, all this time there is another life going on. And this, I think, is important . . . A lot of time drinkin' stories look like there's nothin' in life but drinkin', don't you see."

Neither Hank's nor Ellen's narrative matched the AA story structure perfectly, but both were very close. Both included a description of early drinking (or, for Ellen, drug use), the progression, the negative effects, others' reactions, hitting bottom, getting into AA, and life since starting AA. Interestingly, they did not say much about their first contact with AA, their impression of it, or their ability to identify with other members, a theme prominent in many of the published personal stories. This may be a result of differing agendas: the published stories have the purpose of trying to convince the reader to identify with the teller; in the interview situation this was not the purpose of the telling. But it may be that Hank and Ellen have not incorporated this part of the AA story structure into their own personal stories.

Andrew, the third AA member interviewed, seemed to have no such drinking experience story. My questions prompted only short answers about specific events rather than the progression of drinking that makes up the AA story. He spoke of himself as an alcoholic, but did not seem to understand this in AA terms. Alcoholism was not something he thought of as affecting all areas of his life. Similarly, he did not consider AA something he would have to remain in all the time, or for the rest of his life, in order to stay sober. Rather, he viewed coming to AA meetings, or "into the program," as a measure to take when things got bad. AA was where he went when he started to have DTs (delirium tremens).

Andrew seemed to understand the events of his life not the way other AA members would, as a progression of drinking and negative effects leading to a "bottom," but rather as a series of unrelated points where drinking was enough of a problem, based on its physical effects (DTs), that he had to do something about it. After a thirty-minute interview, the "drinking history" I had recorded resembled the sort of medical history that a doctor might collect, rather than an AA story. Andrew had accepted the label of alcoholic as applying to himself, but he had not accepted the identity of an AA alcoholic. He did not understand himself this way, and he did not present his life as an AA life.

In addition to evidence that AA members learn to tell their lives in the structure of the AA story, there are other indicators that they are reinterpreting their lives as they tell their stories. One of these is the incorporation of AA propositions into the stories. Propositions such as "alcohol-ism is a progressive disease," "the alcoholic drinker is out of control," and "to recover, the alcoholic drinker must admit that he is powerless over alcohol" appear in the narratives of Hank and Ellen.

> *Hank:* After my last drink, and coming back in, I realized that if I was gonna live, and live comfortable, and live happily, that I was gonna have to take the AA program, its directions, and *live it* . . . And it was rough at first . . . and so . . . I hadn't lived that way. The other two times that I was in, you know, it was something like, you know, making my own decisions and writing my own program. But this time, I decided that, you know, I was gonna do it . . . that way. And, and part of it is realizing that, you know, from the very beginning, that *I'm powerless over it, that there's nothing I can do about my drinking* . . .

> *Ellen:* So, everyone says, you know, *it's a progressive disease. And I can see the progression, how I went from bad to worse,* whenever I try to relate my story . . . I swear, from that day on, for the next two, almost three years, I was high every day. And after about a month I realized that *this is something that I couldn't stop. It's getting out of hand,* because I would wake up in the morning . . . I'd go to bed at night and I'd make sure I had the dope in the morning to get up with.

Ellen's narrative also includes sections interpreted in ways other than those common in AA, sometimes in opposition to certain AA proposi-tions. For example, she makes a distinction between different types of addiction, a distinction AA does not make: "And I know, I realize that marihuana is not physically addicting, but for me it was very psychologi-cally addicting." And she tells about a "slip" but minimizes its impor-tance, in opposition to the AA belief that a single drink (or joint) can lead to the previous level of drinking or using: "I told God and myself I would, if I ever get that baby back, I would never do anything like that . . . again. And so, I haven't. I, I smoked a joint at [a psychiatric hospital], but I haven't gotten back into that lifestyle that, that I was at that point. And I don't want to. When I smoked that joint, I think I did it mostly to see if I still got high, what it was like, and anything like that. It really didn't do much for me."

At some points Ellen seems to be working out her story, or at least the story she tells, as she tells it: "I was looking for a job. That's what I was doing. I was living with her and looking for a job. And . . . Except that I'd never look for a job. I'd just go out and get stoned." This quotation reflects a process that is recognized as necessary for progress in AA: that of "getting honest," or admitting that you have not been honest with yourself or others previously. "Well, they accused me of stealing money from the cash register at that job I had. And I said, 'No I didn't.' And they kept, and then, and then it would start. The lady, my boss lady said, well . . . you know, I just was real paranoid. I thought she thought I was stealing money from her, or something. So I quit. I got . . . I told my boyfriend that I couldn't take her telling me that I stole from her, 'cause I didn't steal anything from her."

These two quotations show that Ellen has not yet arrived at a finished version of her story. The second also reflects another important aspect of Ellen's life. Two years before this interview she was diagnosed as paranoid schizophrenic—the result, her doctors said, of her heavy drug use. In this passage she interprets her actions as the result of her paranoid thought system, although she seems unsure of this interpretation. The quotation illustrates a process she is still going through of choosing between two versions of events, posited within two different, if often related, figured worlds.

Ellen's and Hank's narratives also include verbal markers indicating that reinterpretation of the past has occurred. Hank's is the most fully reinterpreted life of the three interview narratives. He compares the way he now understands his past behavior with the way he understood it at the time.

> I *know now, what I have learned later,* that within two years of having my first drink, that I had trouble with alcohol. *I look back.* I did not drink like my peers. It affected me differently than others.

> Oh, I was a very, very sick man, *I know now,* before anyone ever recommended treatment.

> This was the first time I went to having serious problems with it. Two or three things . . . There was the separation, and then the other things. You know, these things, *I've learned later,* were perfectly normal. Divorce, separate and divorce. And the other things were perfectly normal.

> Well, *like a lot of the other recovering alcoholics, and like some I've heard about,* I wound up by my wife and myself getting back together. Oh,

outside of being something typical that a drunk would do, without any more thought than that . . . we did it.

Ellen has not reinterpreted all episodes she includes in her narrative as fully as Hank has reinterpreted his. Her markers of reinterpretation take the form of comparison of events in her life with events she has heard other AA members tell.

And it seems that to justify smoking dope and drinking, I would always say something about my parents. I'd say, like, "My parents don't love me," or "They don't understand me," or something, "So I'm gonna go get high." And that would get them. The other night I guess you heard Mark . . . talking about, you know, he was bored and didn't have anything to do. I think I used anger a lot instead.

And then starts a big period in my life where I was just depressed. I just was so depressed. And part of it, I was so depressed because I'd have periods where I'd be totally . . . And this can happen with drinking, too. *I've heard a lot of people say, you know, like, they, the blackouts, the insanity, that comes from a lot of drinking. About seeing hallucinations, and all that kind of thing. So it's not just the drugs that you can do that with.*

Other examples of marked reinterpretation of past events come from the personal stories told at speakers meetings:

I used to say, even after I got into AA, that I had never lost a job because of my drinking. And it's true that I was never fired with drinking given as a reason. But I *was* fired because I had not finished my thesis, and I had never finished my thesis because I was drinking. *Put two and two together . . .*

I used to say that prostitution was one thing I had never done to get money for drugs. *But I realize now* that I was prostituting myself to my husband. He would call [after she had left him] and say he had cocaine. I'd be there.

The stories change over time as the understanding of oneself and one's life changes. There seems to be a fairly strong relationship among the extent to which the AA identity has been formed, the extent to which the narrative of drinking experience resembles the AA story structure, and the salience of the AA identity to the individual. Hank had been in AA by far the longest time, and the identity of AA alcoholic was very prominent in his self-understanding: of 13 responses he gave to the question "Who am I?" 6 (46 percent), including the first 3, referred to his identity as an alcoholic or his participation in AA:[6] (1) "I am a recovering alcoholic"; (2) "14 years sober"; (3) "drinking history—twenty years or better"; (10) "spend quite a bit of time in AA service work"; (12) "love to talk to school and university classes [about alcoholism and AA]"; and (13) "man on AA hotline in my home (eight years)." His other 7 responses referred to family and career.

Ellen's responses to the question "Who am I?" indicated that she was not as far along as Hank in the process of incorporating the AA identity as a prominent self-understanding. Of 11 responses, 2 (18 percent) related directly to this identity, and these were within the first four responses: (3) "ex–drug addict"; and (4) "sober." Her other responses referred to social categories and personality traits, including (1) "woman," (2) "mother," (9) "bride," (5) "social," (7) "outgoing," and (8) "people pleaser."

In contrast, only one (5 percent) of Andrew's 20 responses to the question "Who am I?" related to the AA identity: (13) "non-drinker." The response preceding this was "non-smoker." His first response was his full name. The remainder dealt mainly with work and avocations— (2) "dishwasher," (3) "composer," (4) "performer," (5) "cook," (18) "writer"—and with his current living situation and his dissatisfaction with it: (7) "product of divorce," (8) "single," (9) "under-employed," (10) "unhappy with living arrangement," (11) "overweight," (14) "disappointed with locale," (15) "no children/wife," (20) "alone." These results support the conclusion that there is a relationship between the prominence of the AA alcoholic identity and the extent to which the narrative of drinking experience resembles the AA story structure.

Comparison of the stories told in various settings with one another and with the published AA stories indicates that the form of one's personal story changes over time as one develops and becomes emotionally attached to the AA identity. Ellen's and Hank's interviews suggest that these stories actually mediate self-understanding, by helping the tellers learn to interpret their lives in the same way other alcoholics interpret theirs. Episodes from one's life are grouped into a drinking experience story, or drinking history, that resembles the AA story in structure. One's understanding of the self and the past changes as AA propositions and interpretations are learned. As the AA member learns to place the events of his life into the structure of the AA story, he learns to tell his life as an AA story, and reinterprets his past in this way. He learns to understand himself as an AA person. By this same process, from the standpoint of the group, the neophyte is fully recruited, partaking both of AA's activities and of the imagined life, the figured world, that sustains AA's separate and recognizable sphere.

Members of Alcoholics Anonymous have found a particular definition of alcoholism and a particular way to deal with problem drinking. Their program for recovery requires accepting the idea of alcoholism as an incurable disease that affects all areas of one's life, and accepting the idea of oneself as an "alcoholic," one who is powerless over alcohol. The change that the men and women of AA undergo is more than one of behavior—from drinking to not drinking. It is a transformation of the meaning and the referability of behavior—that is, of identity, of how one understands oneself—from a drinking non-alcoholic to a non-drinking alcoholic.

Newcomers to AA must give up an old identity, that of normal drinker, and develop a new one. They go through a process of identity devaluation followed by a process of identity formation. This transformation takes place through reinterpretation, as members come to understand that their pasts have been a progression of alcoholic drinking and alcoholic behavior. They learn to cast their (drinking) lives in AA's distinctive way of figuring such a life. One way this reinterpretation takes place is through the AA personal story. The AA story is a genre, a cultural device, that newcomers can learn to produce and use to mediate self-understanding. As the newcomer learns the structure of the AA story, and learns the model of alcoholism encoded in the story, he begins to place the events and experiences of his own life into this form. He learns to tell his own life as an AA personal story, and through this, to understand his life as an AA life and himself as an AA person. He comes to understand why, and how, he is an alcoholic.

What happens when an AA member fails to compose this new understanding of himself and of his life? The example of Andrew suggests that such people may be those for whom AA does not work. Andrew has accepted the label of "alcoholic," and the idea of alcoholism as a disease, but has not accepted the AA identity, with its interpretation of what this means. He does not figure his life in AA's terms. He views AA as a measure to take when things get really bad. He does not share the set of values and distinctions that unites other AA members. The identity of "alcoholic" does not affect his actions, or his perceptions of self, beyond his drinking behavior. Andrew has never stayed in AA for more than one year, although he has been in treatment for alcoholism four times and in and out of AA at least three times.

A follow-up with Hank and Andrew further supported the importance of acquiring the AA identity. Two years after the original interviews, Hank remained sober and active in AA. Although a stroke had made him decrease his participation in activities, AA held a central and important place in his life. He talked at length about the role of speaking in AA and what speaking in meetings does for members.

Andrew had left the AA program within a month of the first interview. Two years later I spoke with him again at a community soup kitchen where he had come for lunch. He told me he had been "hitting it [the bottle] pretty hard" and was in bad shape. He said he had used the death of his mother as an excuse to go on a drinking binge, "though, if it's a disease, I guess you don't need an excuse." He had lost his job as a cab driver, partly because one night, while a customer went into a liquor store, he also went in and made a purchase. Now unemployed, he was about to be evicted from his apartment because he could not pay the rent. I asked him what plans he had. He said he would take a job as a dishwasher, but he thought he needed some time off to get "straightened out" before he took another job. He told me he planned either to check himself into a detoxification and treatment center or to get back into AA: "Anyway, I'm gonna go today and tomorrow . . . I'm gonna drink today and tomorrow. Sort of a binge, though I don't know if you'd call it a binge. Then after that, Saturday I'm gonna go back to the program, start meetings." Perhaps this time, this Saturday, Andrew would begin a journey toward what Hank had long ago reached, an enduring identity as an AA alcoholic.

5

How Figured Worlds of Romance Become Desire

"She took him to the prom . . . he was about 26 . . . he was with a whole lot of girls, it wasn't like he was just talking to her . . . she really didn't know what she was getting into." Americans often speak of romance as though it were a "natural" and intrinsically motivating activity that most people, by the time they reach a certain age, engage in at a reasonable level of competence. In the quotation a young woman named Cylene alludes to a much less common conception: that savoir faire in romantic pursuits is learned and that the motivating force of romance may not come about automatically, but may rather be formed in social life.

The larger issue here concerns how figured worlds come to engage people, to shape and be shaped by their actions. Not only the skills and competencies involved in cultural performances but also the meanings and salience of such activities and the desire to participate in them vary from person to person. As we saw in Chapter 4 with regard to Alcoholics Anonymous, participants develop an identification with a figured world in different degrees of engagement, and these "levels of identity" are products of people's social histories, lived as "history-in-person." These processes of identification are evident in the specialized world of AA and also in the more widespread activities of romance and attraction.

In a study of college student life (see Holland and Eisenhart 1990) we followed Cylene and twenty-two other women for a year and a half, through three semesters. The study was designed to investigate how women's peer groups affected their choice of career. As it turned out, much of the women's time and energy, much of what they said in their interviews, and much of what we observed in their peer activities had to do with romantic relationships. Because we interviewed the women again and again over the three semesters, we were able to follow their developing skills and ideas about the conduct of romantic affairs. Because we participated in some of their peer activities, we also were able to describe the social-interactional context in which these skills and ideas developed. The figured world of romance acquired motivating force as the women developed mastery of it, and their mastery, in turn, depended upon their development of a concept of themselves as actors in the world of romance. Although American culture tells us that the urge to romance is "natural," our findings suggest that the desire for romance is formed over time and in social life—in a process of recruitment and identification to action in a figured world.

The Directive Force of Figured Worlds

How do meaning systems "become desire"? In other words, how does a culturally constructed world encourage people to action? This question lies at the interface between the collective and the person and is implicated in any theory that gives weight to cultural logics. Parsons alluded to the importance of the issue; in his opinion the question of the relations of "social structure" and "personality" had been solved by a convergence between Freud's account of the ego, superego, and id and Durkheim's, Cooley's, and Mead's accounts of society. His excitement was evident: "This convergence is one of the few truly momentous developments of modern social science" (1961: 166).

Parsons's enthusiasm notwithstanding, there was and still is serious contention within the social sciences, and within anthropology in particular, over the proper conceptualization of the relationships among society, behavior, and the "presocial" nature of humans. In anthropological accounts the questions have often been phrased in terms of culture. To what extent does culture determine behavior? Is culture—defined as collective interpretations of social and material experience—merely an after-the-fact labeling of deep-seated human needs and interests stemming, say, from psychodynamic forces or from in-built materialist orientations? Or are cultural meaning systems influential to the point that they profoundly shape and define human needs? As Spiro (1982) points out, one's assumptions about this issue determine one's interpretation of the problem of the directive force of cultural systems.

If culture is assumed to define and determine individual human needs, then the challenge is to explicate the form and nature of a particular figured world and so its power to dictate action. The directive force is supplied by the figured world itself. Many anthropologists take culture to be a profoundly important determinant of human motivation and thus adopt this first approach.

If, in contrast, culture is conceived as a superficial labeling of deep-seated human needs, then questions about the directive force of cultural systems become questions about how a cultural system—the surface form—is harnessed to and so derives its power from underlying (psychodynamic) forces. This second approach can be found in the literature of anthropology as well. An anthropological position need not exclude the possibility that cross-culturally variable meaning systems are but gilt upon a more fundamental—psychodynamic, materialist, or even structuralist—substrate (see Quinn 1992; Hutchins 1987).

A third approach, one that emphasizes the formation of motivation during development, is less familiar in the anthropological literature. This third position is the one we take here.

In our neo-Vygotskian developmental approach, thoughts and feelings, will and motivation are *formed* as the individual develops. The individual comes, in the recurrent contexts of social interaction, to personalize cultural resources, such as figured worlds, languages, and symbols, as means to organize and modify thoughts and emotions. These personalized cultural devices enable and become part of the person's "higher mental functions," to use Vygotsky's terms.

Becker's (1963) analysis of the use of marijuana exemplifies the kind of study and conclusions implied by Vygotskian theory. Although Becker does not refer to Vygotsky's concepts, his study of how people become inveterate pot smokers clearly shows that motivation is developed within social process. Becker's findings challenged the then-prevalent idea that personality traits or the physiological effects of the drug motivated use. He found that the full measure of the motivation to smoke was neither brought by the individual to the activity nor compelled by the nature of the drug. Rather the compelling nature of the activity developed and was maintained in the context of interaction with others. The neophyte learned from others not only how to use the drug but also how to attend to and value the experience. Similarly, although we do not wish to draw parallels between using drugs and being involved in romance, our research suggests that the compelling nature of romantic pursuits comes about, or is constructed, in the process of learning the figured world.

The Study

Our study of college women covered a three-semester period in 1979–1981, from near the beginning of the informants' freshman year to the middle of their sophomore year. We interviewed the women monthly and joined in some of their campus activities. The "talking diary" interviews were designed to encourage the women to discuss their experiences and concerns in their own terms. A second type of interview, the "life history" interview, was conducted near the end of the study.

The participants were drawn from two universities in the southern United States—twelve from Bradford University, a historically black school, and eleven from Southern University (SU), a historically white school. Bradford draws students who are predominantly African-American and lower middle class; SU draws predominantly white, middle- and upper-middle-class students. Both are state universities. At both the ratio of women to men is about 60:40. (For details see Holland and Eisenhart 1981, 1990.)[1]

Romance and Attractiveness at the Two Schools

At both Bradford and SU, social activities were usually related to the conduct of romantic encounters and relationships. Going out with, or seeing, friends of the opposite sex ranked high on the list of valued activities, and places where one might meet new men and women—parties, mixers, or the local bars—were favored locations. The women and their friends spent a lot of time talking about potential romantic partners and their own and others' cross-gender relationships. Attractiveness—as validated by attention from a man or men—contributed in a major way to a woman's status in the peer system (Holland and Eisenhart 1990). The romantic sphere of life was especially important to the women of SU. Those who were less successful at coursework than they had expected began to emphasize romantic relationships even more than they once had. Relationships with women were subordinated to relationships with men; romantic relationships often interfered with relationships among women (Holland and Eisenhart 1990).

The themes of male/female relationships also dominated a vocabulary that the students used to talk about one another. Women knew hundreds of words for types of men, such as "jerks," "jocks," "cowboys," "frattybaggers," "brains," "pricks," and men knew hundreds for types of women (Holland and Skinner 1987). And romance figured profoundly in the semiotics of clothes and personal adornment.

An earlier study of the meaning of gender-marked terms and of descriptions of male/female encounters and relationships, also conducted at SU, had suggested that student discourse about romantic and close cross-gender friendships presupposed a "cultural model" or cultural narrative of how such relationships develop.[2] To understand the students' talk one had to know what they took for granted about these relationships (Holland and Skinner 1987).

As with other figured worlds, the cultural models of romance posited a simplified world populated by a set of agents (for example, attractive women, boyfriends, lovers, fiancés) who engage in a limited range of important acts or state changes (flirting with, falling in love with, dumping, having sex with) as moved by a specific set of forces (attractiveness, love). When the young adults talked about their acquaintances, friends, and (potential) romantic partners in terms of gender-marked types such as "hunks," "jerks," "Susie sororities," or "dumb broads," they were assuming that the talk would be understood in relation to a simplified world of cross-gender relationships. The typical progress of events posited in this figured world follows this course:

An attractive man ("guy") and an attractive woman ("girl") are
   drawn to each other.
The man learns and appreciates the woman's qualities and uniqueness as a person.
Sensitive to her desires, he shows his affection by treating her well:
   he buys things for her, takes her places she likes, and shows that
   he appreciates her and appreciates her uniqueness as a person.
She in turn shows her affection and interest and allows the relationship to become more intimate.

This standard scenario also presupposes the motives or purposes of such relationships:

> The relationship provides intimacy for both the man and the woman.
> The relationship validates the attractiveness of both the man and the woman.

And it allows and accounts for some exceptions:

> If the man's attractiveness or prestige is less than the woman's, he compensates by treating her especially well.
> If the woman's attractiveness is the lower of the two, she compensates by being satisfied with less good treatment from the man.

Most of the hundreds of gender-marked terms the students used designate problematic types of men and women—problematic in relation to the taken-for-granted progress of male/female relations posited by the cultural model. They are figures who cause such relations to go awry. "Jerk" names a typical problematic man. Our informants described jerks as "insensitive" and "stupid." But they did not fully spell out why a jerk was considered such a negative type or why women found jerks disgusting and irritating. The reason became clear when we considered the jerk as a relevant character in the figured world. A jerk is a type of man who is neither attractive nor sensitive to women. He cannot compensate for his low prestige by treating a woman especially well. He is too "out of it" to discern her special qualities and anticipate her desires. He cannot figure out the things he could do to make her feel well treated. He may be so insensitive that he cannot even tell she dislikes him. Because he cannot "take a hint," he will not leave her alone, and thus he becomes more and more irritating.[3]

Not only were the women expected to know these cultural assumptions about the "usual" romantic relationship and the many types who populated the world of romance, they also were constantly exposed to interpretations of their own behavior based upon this standard romantic scenario. In short, life among women students at both universities was dominated in large part—both socially and culturally—by romance. Social activities and relationships, including relationships between women, often revolved around romantic encounters or around talk about romantic relationships. Status was accorded, especially for women, in relation to attractiveness. The students shared ways of communicating about and conventions for interpreting romantic relationships. And one's goals, intentions, and qualities were likely to be interpreted according to these ideas about romance.

Differences in Romantic Expertise and Involvement

In the peer situation, with its constant enactments of and talk about romantic relationships, individual differences in expertise and involvement were obscured. Knowledgeability about the types of men and the ways romantic relationships worked was more or less assumed. Furthermore, as romance was assumed to be a natural activity, a basic level of competence in the conduct of relationships was presumed.

American culture does not generally treat romantic relationships as an area of expertise. The women did not usually talk about romance and romantic relationships as something at which one is good or bad, expert or inexpert. Love and romance were often talked about fatalistically, as something that happened to one, not something that one affected. Unsuccessful relationships were more often attributed to character flaws, luck, or mismatches of interests than to a lack of skill or savoir faire.

Nonetheless, some talk did turn upon questions of expertise and competence. The women sometimes saw themselves or others as having made mistakes. They had a sense of romantic situations that they were too inexperienced or too young to handle. They sometimes assessed themselves and others as more or less proficient at romantic activities.

Judging from the women in the study, this less often articulated view was the more accurate one. The more common notion that everyone has similar levels of competence in and involvement with romance did not hold up. Some women were quite ambivalent about romance (southern style) and had less-than-compelling images of themselves in romantic relationships. And the women differed in their facility with romantic situations. That is, they had been recruited to the figured world of romance, and they had rehearsed in the repertoire of activities, the scripts, of that world, but not all of them had rehearsed to the same level. They differed both in their degree of involvement with the world of romance and in their levels of expertise in conceiving and responding to romantic situations—that is, their skills as romantic actors and their "feeling" or sense (Bourdieu's *sens pratique*) for the game of romantic relations.

Involvement in the World of Romance

Romance was much more salient or present in the thoughts of some women. Apart from salience, but related to it, was another variable aspect of involvement: identification of self in the world of romance.

Salience of the World of Romance

Spiro (1982) has described five levels of "cognitive salience" of cultural systems. At the highest levels, a cultural system first guides and then instigates action. Some of the women in the study had apparently reached that degree of salience. They saw everyday life through the lens of the figured world of romance. Romantic involvements—actual or hoped for—occupied much of their time and thoughts. They spent far more of their time either with boyfriends, talking about boyfriends, looking for boyfriends, or adjusting their plans and activities to boyfriends than did others. Romance was less salient for others; they spent time instead on classes, clubs or committees, friends or family relationships.

For several women the salience of romance changed over the course of the study. For some, romantic activities became more important; for others, less so. These cases helped us tease out—as we shall show later—not only the concomitants of increasing and decreasing salience but also the factors that affected its rise and fall.

Experiences in nonromantic pursuits sometimes occasioned changes in a woman's emphasis on romance. Several of the women came to college proud of having done well in high school and then got upset when their university grades were not as good. They gradually became less involved with their schoolwork and switched their attention and time to romantic pursuits. Romance became an even more important world for them.

Friends were another impetus to romance. Peers generally encouraged the pursuit of romance. Sometimes, however, they stimulated opposition to this cultural system, and they may have figured in one woman's eventual loss of interest. For this woman, Sandy, the decrease in salience was dramatic.

At the beginning of the study Sandy seemed as interested as her dormmates in finding a male romantic partner ("You can have the blondes, I get the dark-haired . . . cute ones"). But as time went by she had trouble establishing the kind of relationships she wanted with men at college. She also learned that a potential boyfriend from back home did not feel equally attracted to her and was in fact involved with someone else. All her friends seemed to be having similarly unhappy romantic experiences. Sandy also began to feel that she did not fit in with the other students at SU: "In my hometown, I was pretty much respected in the community and accepted for what I am, or was, in that community. [I was] basically your nonconformist, and I dressed to suit me. But when I came down here I . . . got the impression that here I was a sloppy little girl and I didn't have any class or I didn't have any style."

She came to stress friendships more than she had before: "Friendships were . . . and probably still are one of the most important things to me. They were important to me not so very much socially. They were important to me as a person . . . I pride myself in my friendships."

Sandy formed a special friendship with one woman, Leslie. Despite the jealousy of other friends and the admonitions of her parents, who felt she was not availing herself of all the options at college, Sandy pursued her friendship with Leslie: "Our friendship is terrific . . . I just would like to spend more time . . . it's all been crammed into one semester . . . there's probably not gonna be another time in my life when I can just sit down and just be friends."

Sandy came to devote all her free time to Leslie. She had begun her freshman year with a professed interest in romantic relationships with men, but had dropped that interest altogether. Such romantic attachments became markedly less salient for her, and her identity as an attractive woman in the world of romance, as culturally construed, became unimportant.

Identification with the World of Romance

Not only the importance the women attributed to romance but also the nature of their stances toward it varied. Some seemed to have an idea of themselves as participants in the world of male/female relationships and to accept these romantic selves as real parts of themselves. Others either had an unclear image or sensed a discrepancy between themselves and the romantic role(s) they were acting out. At least one woman, Susan, explicitly contested the way romance was conceived and enacted in the student culture. Another, Natalie, devalued the importance of some taken-for-granted ideas of romance and marriage.

The women's process of identification with the romantic world took place in the context of constant social comment and action. Their peers, sometimes even their professors, cast them as romantic actors. Della's account provides a graphic example of such typecasting as a romantic/sexual character. One day she went to class dressed in a skirt and blouse:

> And I sits in front . . . of the class, and my teacher says, "What's this? What's this? Della, where's she at?" And I just sat there looking at him cause he looked dumb looking around me . . . and he said, "Oh, there's Della." He looked my legs up and down, up and down, and the whole class [was] looking at him. He said, "Oh, oh, I see. I see, Della, I see. Oh, oh." . . . I was so embarrassed; the whole class was looking at me.

Another woman, Karla, told about a seduction attempt by a former teacher. Her story consisted of the following episodes. She ran into a teacher from high school, one she had liked and respected and whose opinion she still valued highly. He gave her a book to read—a book by Freud—and they made plans to discuss it. Karla read the book and went to meet her teacher ready for an intellectual discussion. Instead she found out that he wanted to be her lover. Because he had a family, she had not thought of a romantic relationship with him and she disapproved of his invitation. She deflected his advances, but he persisted. When she finally made her reluctance clear, he became angry and told her that "intellectuals" were not concerned about whether their lovers were married or not.[4]

These two attempts to interpret or identify or position the women in certain sorts of romantic or sexual relationships were fairly explicit and direct, as were many such cases. We also observed an abundance of cases where the attributions were less direct. Even seemingly descriptive comments, such as "Oh, you're wearing your add-a-beads," could be abbreviated references to a romantic type. At the time of the study, "add-a-beads" were popular among sorority women. Such a comment on clothing, or even a pointed look, was sufficient to communicate an interpretation—in the add-a-bead case, that one was acting out a certain femininity and style of conducting romantic relationships.

The women sometimes accepted these interpretations of themselves as romantic types, sometimes explicitly rejected them, and sometimes ignored them. Della rejected her professor's casting of her in a sexual role. Karla ignored her former teacher's claim that intellectuals had different moral codes for extramarital affairs and that, if she wanted to prove herself an intellectual, she had to change her ideas about romantic relationships. Cylene, however, seemed to entertain the possibility that a characterization of her as a romantic type was true. Her father had told her that she wanted so many things—a house, a car, a boat—that she was going to "kill" her man. The gist of his comment was that she expected a boyfriend to treat her too well—to provide her with too many material possessions. She did not dispute his characterization and, in fact, considered it as a possibly valid interpretation.

The women seemed to winnow the possible interpretations, to accept some parts and reject others. Natalie talked explicitly about a vision of herself that she had formed as a young child and had since given up, at least in part: "'Marrying rich' is just a term for marrying the whole ideal guy . . . that's just a thing that most everybody thinks about . . . a good-looking rich man who loves me very much and won't let me cook . . . and lives in a big house." By the time of the study, Natalie had discarded a piece of this vision of herself as a married woman. For various reasons, particularly her sister's experience with a husband who could not hold a job, Natalie had decided to prepare herself to have a career, or at least a job that would free her from dependence upon a future husband's economic support.

Even though the women were bombarded with images of themselves in the world of romance, and even though many of their peers seemed to have sorted through these various interpretations and arrived at fairly stable views of themselves as actors in the romantic world, some of the women did not identify themselves as such. They had no clear idea of a "romantic" self—either a self to avoid or a self to realize.[5]

Susan, for example, had an extremely unsettled and ambivalent identification with romance. At one point she spoke of her trip out west, saying what a beautiful place it was for a romance. But she had not gotten involved with anyone because, she said, it was "too much trouble." Her boyfriend seemed more of an accommodation to peer demands than a reality. And she was openly critical of one of the motives for romantic relationships: the idea that boyfriends should be a source of prestige. She took the researcher to her dorm to show her how the girls brought their boyfriends to the lounge to "show them off." In Susan's opinion, boyfriends were not for showing off.

Susan spent much time thinking about the sort of life she wanted to have. Her dilemma seemed to be a choice between becoming a "socialite" and becoming a "hippie." She was inclined to reject the upwardly mobile, upper-middle-class lifestyle that she felt pressured—perhaps by her family—to embrace. This struggle was related to her ambivalence about her studies and about romantic relationships. The reliance upon boyfriends as a source of prestige enacted by women in the student culture seemed to remind her of the "socialite" women in her hometown. These women were typified, in Susan's mind, by frequent attendance at the country club, where they talked on and on about their rich husbands. Her feelings about socialites—and her distaste when she thought about herself as one—made identification with the world of romance at SU difficult for her.

There also were cases in which women—including Susan—participated in relationships without their hearts being totally in them, so to speak. These women told us of a distance between their "true" feelings and the ways they were acting. Cylene talked about having had a steady boyfriend in high school, but said that, looking back, she probably had had him as a "steady" not because she was particularly attached to him and did not want to date other men but because she was worried about people "talking."[6]

Susan most straightforwardly expressed the felt distance between her actions and her true feelings. Although some of the other women also had absentee boyfriends, who seemed primarily to be useful excuses for not going out with other men, Susan's way of talking about Howard, her boyfriend, clearly revealed her limited involvement in the relationship. She talked about their awkwardness when they did get together. She also talked about Howard in a sarcastic tone of voice that indicated she was not serious. Describing her feelings about his decision to attend a university halfway across the country, she said, "I don't know exactly when he's going but, um, I'm sure I'll see him sometime. So . . . heartbreak, sob and everything like that!" In another instance, when an older man from a nearby city tried to persuade her to go out with him, she told the interviewer: "But 30 years old, that's old. I mean I'm 18 years old. I don't want to go out with someone who's 30. It's not that bad but—shucks, I don't want to go out with anybody but Howard. He's worth the wait."[7]

Although she was less ambivalent than Susan, Natalie also seemed to participate only half-heartedly in activities where one might meet potential romantic partners. Natalie did attend many parties and mixers but seemingly only for appearance's sake. As she presented herself in the interviews, Natalie was much less involved in romantic endeavors than most of the other women, and much more invested in her schoolwork. She consistently talked not about boyfriends but about her schoolwork and her family. She appeared to be little identified with the world of romance. Her childhood vision of herself as a romantic partner (described earlier) had largely disintegrated as she watched her sister's marital troubles. She spoke positively of becoming, at some future time, romantically involved with a man, but her vision of this future relationship was vague and without detail.

As these cases suggest, although others continually cast the women as romantic actors, their involvement with the world of romance varied. Some resisted being identified as romantic participants; some opposed parts of the views of romance they associated with peers; some devised strategies for avoiding or circumscribing their romantic experiences; and many indicated that their feelings were at odds with the way they were acting out a relationship.

To reiterate, the women we studied were not equally involved with the world of romance, and the components of their involvement—salience and identification—proved to be interrelated. Talk about men, focus on men, and orientation toward romantic relationships correlated positively with how much the women talked about and treated themselves as actors in the world of romance. Cylene, Natalie, and Susan, in their different ways, were less involved in their romantic activities than many of the other women. Although they continued to participate, their comments conveyed a sense of distance. Correspondingly, they expressed less concern about romance in the interviews than women like Karla, who did identify with the world of romance and for whom romantic relationships and activities remained salient. The women's individual social situations and histories influenced their varying degrees of recruitment to this figured world.

The world of romance is a powerful element of the cultural life of college students, but, like any other frame of activity, it subsists in relation to other figured worlds. All such worlds are subject to social identifications, that is, associated with the people who conventionally participate in them, and these people in turn are subject to the social differentia of rank and prestige—class, gender, race, and any number of more local divisions of communities—that affect the evaluation, and thus the persuasiveness and authority, of the spheres they populate. This complex of social and cultural influence is realized personally, as in Susan's case, where a predisposition against "socialites" colored her relations to classmates she identified with the romantic world, and hence her vision of herself in that world. Only by moving between the institutional and the intimate, between history in its usual sense and history-in-person, can we do justice to social life. It is this same analytic movement that captures psychic life, because the two aspects are, according to Vygotsky and Bakhtin, transmutable and indissolubly related.

Romantic Savoir Faire

In concert with their varying degrees of involvement with the world of romance, the women also seemed more or less expert at, more or less agentic in, romantic relationships. They differed both in how much they relied upon the directions and motivations of others and in how they formulated and responded to problematic situations. Those who appeared to be less knowledgeable or less expert closely copied and took direction from others, attended to relatively circumscribed aspects of relationships, and had difficulty generating possible responses to romantic situations.

The women's ways of talking about men and relationships with men conveyed different degrees of facility with the cultural discourse. One woman had such proficiency with campus types that she was able to extract the "essences" of the types and put them together in a skit. She and some others were facile in talking about their own strategies for handling relationships. Karen talked about "keeping the upper hand" in a relationship, and Rosalind about "putting one man up front." Though Karen and Rosalind may not have invented these strategies, they seemed fully familiar with their use, reflecting upon and enacting them with ease. Susan, in contrast, seemed limited to repeating and attempting to carry out the directives of others.

To illustrate "getting the upper hand," Karen, a student at SU, described her behavior toward Hal, a man she had just met. She was trying to convince him that she was attractive—possibly more attractive than he was. A woman who is less attractive than a man she goes out with, according to the conventions of the figured world, compensates by settling for less attentive and sensitive treatment and by allowing the relationship to become physically intimate faster than she might wish. If she is more attractive than the man, he compensates by being especially sensitive and attentive to her. Karen tried to "get the upper hand" by convincing Hal that other men were interested in her. She tried to give him the impression that she was dating other men, that she had a boyfriend back home, and that she had a full social calendar.

For Rosalind, a student at Bradford, "putting one man up front" meant playing up her involvement with only one man. Romantic relationships at Bradford were complicated by the need to maintain integrity and self-control. One lost integrity and control if information about one's emotional investments became known to those who might use it to manipulate or interfere with one's relationships (Holland and Eisenhart 1990). Rosalind's idea was to mask the full range of her involvements by emphasizing one man as her primary romantic interest, thereby deflecting attention from all others.

Both "getting the upper hand" and "keeping one man up front" were strategies for achieving the valued outcomes of romantic involvements while avoiding the bad. These strategies were ones the women themselves had improvised or decided to use and could describe without much trouble.

Susan gave a quite different impression. During the first year and a half of her college career, she talked about gender relations in a variety of ways, most of which could be traced to her friends. Susan, like many new students, was seeking out a new group of friends. She struck up friendships with women who pursued a variety of lifestyles and orientations and had quite different ways of talking about men and gender relations. In the interviews she sometimes talked about her friends' relationships in terms that we knew were the same terms her friends used. Lee, a friend of Susan's, was having to fend off sexual advances from the owners of the restaurant where she worked. Susan said that a guy at the café had "pinched Lee on the buns and told her to loosen up." In another description of the same incident, Susan said that a "Greek was messing with her

[Lee]." "Buns" and "messing with her" were not the kind of words that Susan used in other interviews to describe similar situations.

For instance, Susan described her friend Patricia's relationships as being "open" or "not open": "It seems really good, the relationship they have, because they talk a whole lot, and it's a lot more open [than the] relationship that she had with George, as far as saying what she wants and feels." The "openness" of Lee's relationships was not something Susan talked about, presumably because Lee did not talk about them in those terms.

Susan used euphemisms to talk about sex, a topic she seemed not to discuss with her friends. For example, she said she had learned that a friend (and potential boyfriend) was "homosexual" and that she was "glad not to have to worry about that with him anymore." Knowing Patricia and some of Susan's other friends, we doubted that any of them would have referred to sex as "that."

Susan also seemed willing to be swayed by other people's arguments about her. She described a situation in which an "older" man was trying to persuade her to go out with him. The man had called Susan's dorm in search of a woman who no longer lived there. Susan answered the phone. They began to talk and he asked her out. She put him off first by saying that she had homework and then by telling him she had a boyfriend back home—Howard. The man was not so easily discouraged. As they continued to talk, Susan admitted to going out with someone other than Howard. The man retorted that if she went out with other people then she could go out with him. He almost had her persuaded. In her next interview Susan debated going out with him, although she eventually returned to her "boyfriend-back-home" position. Still she said, "But I guess I should meet him, you know, he seems like a pretty interesting person to meet."

By the end of the study Susan had settled upon one group as her primary set of friends, and her talk about men and gender relations had begun to conform to the way this group talked about such relationships.

Susan's motivation to participate in romance, as well as her words, seemed to be initially imparted by her friends. She did not find the culturally defined motives for romantic relationships—prestige and intimacy—sufficiently compelling to overcome her discomfort with romantic encounters. And, as mentioned earlier, she disputed whether one of the motives—prestige—was a proper motive for relationships.[8]

Nonetheless, in her sophomore year, Susan began to look for a boyfriend in earnest. Her efforts were spurred by the desire to participate in the same activities and talk that her friends did. She identified with them and their romantic practices. The following passage indicates the difficulty she had in her search and the support supplied by her friends. She had just said she wanted to find a boyfriend, and the interviewer had asked her how one goes about it: "You just scope out the crowd first . . . see, I found this guy that I'm interested in . . . But I never see this guy so that makes it difficult . . . I get all nervous and paranoid so I can't ever talk to him. It's pretty funny, all my friends are like: Go talk to the guy, Susan. Let's go talk to him. *I just can't.*"

Follow-up interviews, especially one conducted in 1987, showed that Susan had gained confidence in the world of romance and spoke more positively of her romantic experiences. But in 1980 her engagement with the figured world seemed to be borrowed from her friends.

The women varied not only in their facility with ways of talking—and presumably thinking—about romance but also in the breadth of their overviews of romantic relationships. Susan answered the interviewer's question about finding a boyfriend by outlining small-scale, step-by-step procedures that one could follow at a mixer or a party. In contrast, Karen's and Rosalind's strategies—getting the upper hand and keeping one man up front—paid attention to larger issues.

Paula, a woman at SU, became annoyed at starting relationships with men she met at parties only to find that they were also going out with her friends. After several such experiences, she decided that meeting men at parties did not work. In contrast, Aleisha, a woman at Bradford, who was having similar trouble with the men she was meeting, decided that the men behaved as they did because the women outnumbered the men at Bradford. Because they were in demand, she thought, the men became arrogant and expected more from the women than they were entitled to:

> At this school, it's about six girls to one guy . . . so the ugly [guys] . . . think they look like heaven and will try to [talk to you] all the time. It's really sick . . . Some of these guys have the cutest girlfriends, and I don't know how they got them . . . He must have the money. That's the reason why an ugly guy could get a fairly decent looking girl. He has one of two things: a car or he's got money . . . And most of the guys here that look good, they're real dumb and . . . as far as holding a conversation,

just forget it; I'd rather talk to a wall . . . But with so many girls to one guy, he gonna get somebody regardless of how he act.

This woman seemed to have developed a fairly broad overview of the relationship between men and women, while Paula seemed only to have learned by trial and error that relationships begun at parties did not work out. If she had formulated a more general assessment, a theory about the failure of these relationships, she never articulated it to us.

Besides these differences in the scope of their analysis of romantic situations, the women also varied in how rapidly and easily they devised responses in the world of romance. Della, in her encounter with the teacher who embarrassed her in class, was stymied and could not think of a response. The only solution she could reach to stop him from making similar remarks in the future was to avoid him.

Susan's manner of responding to romantic situations differed from Karla's. Recall Susan's thinking about how to respond to the older man who asked her out. Her representation showed no overview of the situation, no hypothesis about his actions. She thought about the man's arguments and her various reactions, such as her feeling that he was old, without piecing these incidents together into any kind of coherent account through which she could plan a response. She fell back upon the absentee boyfriend, Howard, and it was not clear how she might answer the man should he call again, since he already had countered her "Howard" excuse.

Karla's story about her former teacher's attempt to seduce her revealed a different sort of process. Karla seemed to form a hypothesis about the situation, on the basis of which she then devised a response. She had to change her hypothesis several times when events did not go as expected. Each time, however, she seemed to reformulate a new hypothesis and plan of response, without having to work through the situation piecemeal as Susan did. Her final response was to have a friend—a very large football player—call the teacher and warn him to leave her alone, "or else." After that the teacher no longer bothered her.

Agency in the World of Romance

The women we studied varied in their identifications with the culturally figured world of romance. Not all found it compelling or salient. They also varied in their apparent levels of expertise in romantic relationships. The less expert women tended to repeat the words and follow the directions of others. They had less of an overview of romantic relationships; they had to work harder to come up with responses to romantic situations. Not surprisingly, those who were less identified with the world of romance, and for whom it was less salient, also were less expert in managing relationships.

This suggests that involvement—the salience of and identification with the cultural system of romance—codeveloped with expertise. If a woman did not develop a clear identification of herself in the world of romance, then romance was not likely to be very salient for her and she was not likely to be much of an agent in conducting romantic relationships. Similarly, if she had not developed expertise, then she was unlikely to have formed much of a romantic identification. Salience, identification, and savoir faire appeared to develop together in an interrelated process—a process that was continually supported and shaped in the context of social interaction.

These connections among expertise, identification, and salience are foreshadowed and informed by the theoretical work of Spiro and Dreyfus. Though each of these authors explicitly focuses on only one dimension—Spiro with cognitive salience, Dreyfus with expert knowledge—both refer to the other dimensions, including identification.

Spiro (1982) is concerned above all with the "directive force" of cultural symbols and seeks to explain why symbols become more or less motivating for different individuals. He depicts five levels of the "cognitive salience" of cultural systems that form a kind of developmental progression. We will not recount the details here, but will limit ourselves to two remarks. First, Spiro points out that cultural systems may or may not reach a very high level of cognitive salience and so may or may not have anything to do with instigating or even guiding an individual's behavior. His postulation of variable cognitive salience certainly applies to our findings. Second, Spiro finds it necessary to refer to knowledge-ability in order to discuss salience. His first two stages are devoted to the individual's developing knowledge of the system. Individuals, his scheme implies, must develop at least a certain expertise with the cultural system before they will find it motivating. In our study salience appeared to codevelop with expertise (Spiro's knowledge).

Dreyfus (1984) is interested in the development of expert knowledge.

He too proposes five stages: (1) novice, (2) advanced beginner, (3) competency, (4) proficiency, and (5) expertise. He denies the usual idea that expertise develops through the formulation of more and more sophisticated rules or propositions from which inferences are more and more rapidly drawn. Instead he argues that it is primarily novices and advanced beginners—not experts—who rely upon rules. Those who advance further form a more comprehensive, "three-dimensional" understanding of the cultural system, be it a game such as chess, a sensorimotor skill such as driving, or a conventionalized, culturally interpreted system of relationships such as romance.

In the novice and advanced beginner stages, the individual's knowledge is mediated by (organized around) rules and maxims. These rules, which the learner has probably heard from others, address elements or aspects of the situation. They are like the steps in step-by-step recipes for winning the game, driving the car, or finding a boyfriend. Susan's rules about scoping out the crowd come to mind.

With competency, the various elements of the situation become organized into a gestalt. The individual learns to think in terms of broader components of the overall situation. Karen's concept of "getting the upper hand" in her relationship with Hal is an example of such a component.

Dreyfus's description recalls Vygotsky's understandings of learning. In the early stages of learning, cultural artifacts, whether objects, words, or figures, serve as obvious mediators of people's activity. We count our fingers, glance at diagrams, and recite rules to ourselves. After practice (and for the young, a degree of maturation), however, these means of mediation are taken into inner activity; words become inner speaking, and figures become forms of the imagination. We no longer need the obvious, external form, relying instead on inner means that we can reproduce at will. As our experience with the activity grows ever greater, as we grow in expertise, another change occurs. This Vygotsky called fossilization. The various parts or steps that we once learned as recognizable elements, and the cultural forms that mediated their learning even within inner speaking and imagination, lose their separability. The process, that is, the production of activity, falls from awareness, and all that is left is its product. We simply do something, no longer thinking how we do it.[9]

Dreyfus's explanation helps us graduate this process of fossilization and relate it to other features of Vygotsky's work. Following Dreyfus, we can conceive fossilization as a process of compression in which ever larger segments of activity become sequentially the elements of attention. This notion is directly analogous, and perhaps homologous, to Vygotsky's (and Bakhtin's) characterization of the developing syntax of inner speaking as a process of compression, where more and more grammatical elements are elided. It is this compression of inner speaking, of the imagination, that produces the markedly unconscious aspect of expert knowledge that Dreyfus emphasizes. At the competency stage one must still work consciously, that is, within inner speaking, to arrive at possible responses and assessments of those responses. At the more advanced stages of proficiency and expertise the experience of arriving at a response changes. The generation and assessment of responses becomes less conscious. Susan's process of thinking about her response to the older man who asked her out exemplifies a less proficient stage than that represented in Karla's account of her response to her former teacher's attempted seduction.

Just as Spiro cannot restrict his levels of salience to salience alone, Dreyfus does not confine his scheme to expertise alone. In describing the changes from advanced beginner and competency to more advanced stages, Dreyfus finds it necessary to refer to emotional involvement and a sense of responsibility in the system.

The shift between the advanced beginner stage and the later stages of competency, proficiency, and expertise is marked, says Dreyfus, by a qualitative change in the relationship between the individual and the system. The individual comes to experience herself not as following rules or maxims taught by others but as devising her own moves. Dreyfus describes this change as obtaining a sense of responsibility in the system. Perhaps a better phrasing would be that the individual gains a sense of being in the system—understanding herself in terms of the activity. She identifies herself in the cultural world:

> The novice and the advanced beginner applying rules and maxims feel little or no responsibility for the outcome of their acts. If they have made no mistakes, an unfortunate outcome is viewed as the result of inadequately specified elements or rules. The competent performer, on the other hand, after wrestling with the question of a choice of perspec-

tive or goal, feels responsible for, and thus emotionally involved in, the result of his choice. (1984: 30)

In play, as discussed by Vygotsky (see Chapter 4), the child suspends other possible interpretations of things in the environment and becomes caught up in a pretend world. Her desires become related to "a fictitious 'I,' to her role in the game and its rules" (1978: 100). Her motives become defined by the motives of the game. Here, according to Dreyfus, the individual gets caught up in a particular game or figured world and sees herself as an agent in it. As with play, the overall activity is emotionally engaging. Dreyfus argues that this sort of participation is necessary for greater mastery: "An outcome that is clearly successful is deeply satisfying and leaves a vivid memory of the situation encountered as seen from the goal or perspective finally chosen. Disasters, likewise, are not easily forgotten."

With competency the situation becomes "three-dimensional" and the individual is "gripped" by it:

> The competent performer, gripped by the situation that his decision has produced, experiences and therefore remembers the situation not only as foreground and background elements but also as senses of opportunity, risk, expectation, threat, etc. These gripping holistic memories cannot guide the competent performer since he fails to include them when he reflects on problematic situations as a detached observer . . . however, these memories become the basis of the competent performer's next advance in skill. (1984: 30)

Notice that the emotional involvement or identification comes only after a certain degree of competence is reached and that this degree of emotional involvement is necessary for further mastery. Dreyfus made this same point in a talk about the acquisition of expert knowledge in the game of chess: "It seems you can't acquire these skills [of having a complex view of the situation] unless you're taking the game very seriously; it won't help to just be reading book games. There's the story that Bobby Fisher, whenever he plays even a book game, says: 'Pow, got him, killed him that time!' even though there's nobody [no live opponent] there."

If Dreyfus's notions of the development of savoir faire are accurate, then identifying oneself as an agent in the system—an actor in the world as defined by the game—is a necessary precursor to mastering the system beyond a certain level.[10] One has to develop a concept of oneself in the activity and want either to realize that self or avoid it.

Spiro's and Dreyfus's schemes are interrelated. Dreyfus is discussing expert knowledge, but he finds emotional involvement necessary for the achievement of the stages of proficiency and expertise. Emotional involvement also figures in Spiro's account of the motivating force or cognitive salience of a cultural system. And Spiro's scheme implicates knowledgeability. His first two levels refer to the individual's knowledge of the system. Put together, the two schemes begin to describe an integrated process of the development of expertise and cognitive salience. Furthermore, both schemes predicate what we have interpreted as identification of self within the cultural world.

Dreyfus, for instance, vaguely notes a sense of responsibility as necessary for the development of expertise: he argues that one cannot go to the more advanced stages of proficiency and expertise without conceiving of oneself as devising one's own moves rather than relying upon rules and maxims learned from others. Spiro (1982: 48) calls the corresponding stage the stage of believing—when one comes to think of the system as being "true, correct, or right." He is attempting to explain why a supernatural world—patently impossible to a Western scientific mind—could seem true.

We believe this key transition that occurs in both schemes is best recast as identification—the formation of a concept of self as an actor in the culturally devised system. Spiro suggests that "belief" is crucial for advancement to higher levels of salience. Acceptance of the reality of the figured world probably is relevant, but it may not be sufficient. An assessment that a culturally interpreted world lacks validity, truth, correctness, or rightness may indeed affect whether an individual can conceptualize the system as relevant to herself. In our study, for example, Susan had trouble placing herself in the world of romance as interpreted by her peers. She disagreed with, and indeed was repelled by, the association between boyfriends and prestige. The world did not seem right to her. Sandy, in contrast, continued to "believe" that the world of romantic male/female relationships existed. She did not come to doubt the world; rather her concept of herself in such a relationship was uncompelling and became even less so in comparison with her valued conceptions of herself in other fields of relationship. Identification, as the more inclusive process, seems to capture better than Spiro's or Dreyfus's schemes the point where the figured world in which one has been acting according to the directions of others becomes a world that one uses to understand and organize aspects of one's self and at least some of one's own feelings and thoughts (see Quinn and Holland 1987).

How Figured Worlds Take Hold

Our study of young women's differential recruitment to and personalization of the figured world of romance revealed processes through which romance—as culturally construed in the southeastern United States—became (or did not become) compelling. The larger issues concern the directive force of cultural worlds and what the process of developing a self in a cultural world reveals about the motivating force of such figured worlds. The women in the study belied the commonsense notions that romance is naturally compelling, naturally salient, and an area in which competence is readily attained when one reaches a certain age. The commonsense notions imply a homogeneity of interest and competence that we did not find. The women varied in their expertise with romantic relationships and their interest in romantic activities. Furthermore, the commonsense notions underplay the pivotal significance of social intercourse in the formation of romantic interests and skills.

A close look at the women's courses in the world of romance suggests that savoir faire, salience, and identification with romance codevelop in a process that is integrally connected to social context. In accord with D'Andrade's (1992) point that cultural models (figured worlds) generate goals rather than provide a means to satisfy preexisting ones, we found that beginners may not know the assumed motives for romantic activity—prestige and intimacy—or may not find them especially enticing. Their knowledge of the conduct of romantic relationships may be rather piecemeal, their overviews of romantic situations rather vague, their responses to romantic situations rather labored, and they may not have developed any engaging visions of themselves as participants in the figured world described by the cultural system.

For the women we studied, the cultural interpretation of romance became salient and compelling as their expertise with romantic relationships increased and as they came to form an engaging interpretation of themselves in the world of romance. Women who were vague and unclear, or resistant to envisioning themselves in the world of romance, were the ones who remained less expert and who found romance relatively unimportant in their lives. Expert women were those who clearly identified with the world and for whom romance was highly salient.

Ethnographic case studies such as this one and Becker's (1963) make it clear that the social-interactional context of learning must be considered in any account of the formation of personal engagements. In our research the ubiquitous presence of peers—as participants in romantic relationships and talk about them, as coaches and motivators, and as targets of opposition—was marked. If the women were not all expert enough or engaged enough in the system of romance to find it compelling in and of itself, they were all propelled into the activities by the urgings of others. Further, those who resisted, rebelled, and did not form identifications with the romantic world did so, in part, in reaction to their peers.

If we are right that expertise, salience, and identification codevelop in an interrelated process, then descriptions of cultural worlds must become even more complicated than they are now. The manner of presenting the content of a cultural world—as if fully grasped by an expert—implies a level of savoir faire, a level of salience, and a level of identification that may apply only to a small subset of the people who are presumably participants in that world. The description may falsely imply a homogeneity of expertise, salience, and identification, as well as a homogeneity of content.

Unexamined assumptions of homogeneity are a problem not so much because they may be unjustified according to scientific canons as because they permit inattention to the social distribution of cultural knowledge and its role in power relations. Assumptions of homogeneity deflect attention from the social conflict, the social symbolism of knowledge, and individual appropriation and individual resistance, which are important even in an everyday activity like romance. Expertise with romance, the salience of romantic activities, and the formation of a view of oneself in the world of romance codevelop in a process that occurs within and is sensitive to the social-interactional context. Thus the directive force of romance—its compelling nature—integrally depends upon the realized world of social position, of hierarchy and power, as well as upon cultural forces.

III

Power and Privilege

6

Positional Identities

So far we have emphasized lived worlds as culturally constituted of conventional events, improvised but recognizable acts, and talked-about characters. Another facet of lived worlds, that of power, status, relative privilege, and their negotiation, and another facet of lived identities, that of one's self as entitled or as disqualified and inappropriate, must also receive theoretical attention. In order to highlight these facets, we make an analytic distinction between aspects of identities that have to do with figured worlds—storylines, narrativity, generic characters, and desire—and aspects that have to do with one's position relative to socially identified others, one's sense of social place, and entitlement. These figurative and positional aspects of identity interrelate in myriad ways. Sometimes they are completely coincident; sometimes one dominates over the other. Two incidents from our fieldwork in Nepal give a sense of the positional aspect of identity formation.

One day when Skinner was recording songs from three of the girls of Naudada, Tila Kumari, who owned the house Debra was renting, came storming onto Debra's porch and began to yell at the girls. She accused them of eating fruit and cutting fodder from her property:

> You stupid girls . . . Why do you cut grass from our fields? Are you not ashamed? . . . Everyone has seen the guavas here, but only you have eyes for them . . . Go to your husband's or father's field to eat. You have no fear to cut the grass in another's field. After telling your parents, I will weed your hair . . . I will complain like the daughter of Hari [a local adolescent notorious for her bad temper].[1]

All three girls were upset about this scolding. Muna, one of the three, said: "We hadn't done anything. I can't figure out why they made such a scandal out of it . . . I felt like crying. I couldn't retaliate. I do not do such things. I thought, who was she to tell someone like my mother such things? We did not get angry because we had not done anything wrong. That's why I felt bad and wanted to cry."

On another day, Shanta, Tila Kumari's six-year-old daughter, was berated because she ventured into an activity to which she had no right. Shanta was in the field where her older brother was plowing. As he steered the oxen past her, she reached out playfully and touched the plow. Immediately her brother began to hit and rebuke her. Her father and other brothers ran from the house to join in the scolding and beating, and her father told her it was a sin for a girl to touch a plow and threatened to beat her severely if she ever touched it again. Shanta cried and trembled for hours. When asked about the incident several weeks later, she remembered it well, repeating her father's words and promising never again to touch the plow. Although Shanta did not understand the wider moral universe in which her act was defined as a sin, she did learn in a dramatic way that, because she was a girl, she was restricted from acts that her brothers could freely perform.

Positional Identities in Figured Worlds

Shanta and the three girls had become embroiled in incidents in which their activity was constrained; they had encountered rebuffs to their freedom of movement and freedom of action, limitations of what we will call their social position. Others treated their actions as claims to social positions, positions that, on account of gender in Shanta's case and perhaps of relative caste position in the girls' case, they were denied. In Tila Kumari's eyes Muna and the other girls were appropriate targets for demeaning. By the acts she suspected they had committed—entering her yard and taking her fruit—they had claimed positions to which they were not entitled. The same fault could be found in Shanta's innocent intrusion into the male domain of the plow.

Sociolinguistics has long made much of the socially constitutive import of language choice (see Gumperz and Hymes 1972). One's choices of dialect, register, pronouns, and genre are not socially neutral. Such decisions partake of powerful systems that index claims to the social relationships between speaker and hearer and to the speaker's general social position. Linguistic choice is but one of these indexical systems. There are other systems of artifacts (returning to the language of Chapter 3) that carry with them a "theory of the person" who uses them. There could well be fields of sociosartorial studies, sociocognitive studies, even socioemotive studies, since styles of dress (Turner 1969), displays of knowledge (Gearing et al. 1979; McDermott 1974; Lutz 1995), and expressions of emotion (Lutz 1988, 1990) all index social categories of persons. Spaces, too, imbue and are imbued by the kinds of persons who frequent them; conventional forms of activity likewise become impersonated. The dialect we speak, the degree of formality we adopt in our speech, the deeds we do, the places we go, the emotions we express, and the clothes we wear are treated as indicators of claims to and identification with social categories and positions of privilege relative to those with whom we are interacting.

This is the stuff of positional or relational identities, and much research in anthropology and other fields shows that this aspect of identities is important. Relational identities have to do with behavior as indexical of claims to social relationships with others. They have to do with how one identifies one's position relative to others, mediated through the ways one feels comfortable or constrained, for example, to speak to another, to command another, to enter into the space of another, to touch the possessions of another, to dress for another, or, recalling Gyanumaya (Chapter 1), to enter the kitchen of another.

Hindu religious tenets posit a world of the sacred. In that extensively elaborated world, different castes are more or less intrinsically pure, and one's caste affects how polluting one can be to others. Perhaps Tila Kumari's reactions to the girls in her yard had to do with concerns about pollution. But her treatment of Muna and the other girls was not cast in these religious terms but rather in terms of forbidden territory and forbidden goods. It was more about what we will call positional identity than about what we have called figurative identity. Positional identities have to do with the day-to-day and on-the-ground relations of power, deference and entitlement, social affiliation and distance—with the social-interactional, social-relational structures of the lived world. Narrativized or figurative identities, in contrast, have to do with the stories, acts, and characters that make the world a cultural world. Positional identity, as we use the term, is a person's apprehension of her social position in a lived world: that is, depending on the others present, of her greater or lesser access to spaces, activities, genres, and, through those genres, authoritative voices, or any voice at all.

Bourdieu (1977b) makes some useful observations about the way the phenomenon that we are labeling positional identity manifests in different social situations. Here he extends his notion of habitus to speaking, to encompass one's sense of the value that is likely to be attributed to what one has to say in a particular situation. Bourdieu acknowledges, as did Bakhtin (1986), speakers' awareness of the differential social valuing of languages, genres, and styles of speaking, and he emphasizes the habitual, out-of-awareness assessments one makes before and during conversation: judgments of the linguistic forms that are likely to be valued, of one's command over those linguistic resources, and of the social privilege (or lack thereof) that a person of one's relative position has to employ such resources. The assessment reveals itself in the way speech is marked, leading the speaker to strained, self-conscious, "correct" speech or to effortless, unselfconscious speech; to comfort or to discomfort; to voice or to silence.[2]

We have already drawn an imperfect but helpful analogy between the two aspects of identity we are trying to distinguish and two aspects of linguistic utterances. Figurative identities are likened to propositionality, to the referential, semantic facet of speech; relational identities are likened to indexicality, to the pragmatic facet (see Irvine 1989). The import of a particular linguistic element, determined by its relationships with a system of other linguistic elements, is different from the import of the element defined in relation to its social situation of use. Understanding the difference between the meanings of "mother" and "father" is not the same as understanding the difference between the social relations indexed by calling the same person "Pop" rather than "Daddy" or "Father."

Likewise, understanding and identifying with the narrativized positions that allude to one's caste, as portrayed in some Hindu religious texts, is quite different from understanding and identifying with the indices of privilege, power, and entitlement that mark the relation of a Bahun to a Damai in Naudada—Tila Kumari to Muna—or the position of Shanta, a girl, vis-à-vis her brothers. Put perhaps too simply, figurative identities are about signs that evoke storylines or plots among generic characters; positional identities are about acts that constitute relations of hierarchy, distance, or perhaps affiliation.

Localized figured worlds have their own valued qualities, their own means of assessing social worth, their own "symbolic capital," to use Bourdieu's term. In the world of community relations figured among the Kabyle peasants (Bourdieu 1977a), men and families were ranked by honor. Men of high honor had more symbolic capital; what they did and said as men of honor was likely to be accorded more credence and more authority than the actions of men of low honor. Their word was more likely to be honored by others; a sort of social credit was more likely to be extended to them than to men of low honor. Likewise, relations among Kabyle men were generally figured in the idiom of honor. Gifts were a central cultural artifact, for example, that positioned the giver relative to the recipient in a script of reciprocity; if the recipient could not reciprocate he lost honor.

In the world of male-male relations in the Nicaraguan village studied by Lancaster (1992), *machismo* named an important calculus of social worth. Social position and relations among men and between men and women were often figured in this calculus. A man's relational position was played out in terms of the value accorded the active, penetrating role in intimate sexual activity, for example. A man who took the active role in sexual relations—whether with a man or woman—affirmed his masculinity.

In the world of romance we studied (see Chapters 5 and 7), "attractiveness" was an important form of symbolic capital. Relations between men and women were often cast into a calculus of relative attractiveness. Hence a man's treatment of a woman was taken as an index of his assessment of her attractiveness relative to his own, and vice versa. Relational/positional identities in the world of romance have to do with the assessment of one's attractiveness. In the taken-for-granted, unfolding script of developing intimacy and romantic love, a man and a woman are attracted to each other. He treats her well, and she permits the relationship to become more intimate. Actions index the development (or failure to develop) of an intimate relationship, but they also index the relative attractiveness of the parties to the romance and thus the entitlement of each party to the other's attention and support.

Positions and Markers That Cut across Figured Worlds

Relational identities and the cultural artifacts through which they are claimed may be specific to a figured world. They may have to do with one's honor in the Algerian peasant village Bourdieu tells us about, or one's attractiveness in the sphere of gender relations on college campuses in the United States, or one's machismo in the Nicaraguan village. Other positional identities and markers may, however, be less specific and cut across such worlds.

In the testimony of witnesses in court cases, O'Barr and Atkins (1980) identified several patterns of speech—such as the use of "hedges," locutions like "there may be" or "perhaps"—that experimental studies later showed to undermine the credibility of the testimony of any witness who exhibited them. There was a correlation between the use of these nonassertive patterns of speech and being female and/or of low "social power." O'Barr and Atkins see these speech behaviors as responses Americans use in formal situations that include people who are more powerful than the speaker. These speech behaviors are not peculiar to the figured world of law courts; instead, hedges, "intensifiers," and "hesitation forms," among others, communicate relative position in other figured worlds as well.[3] They are indices of relational identities that are not particular to any figured world.

In Naudada, too, there were cultural artifacts or resources for positioning self and other that crossed a number of figured worlds, those of domestic/household relations, school, and parma (reciprocal work groups). One important set concerned food. Taking certain kinds of food directly handled by another allows a kind of intimate contact that can be considered polluting if the handler is of lower status. To refuse food handled by another, then, is to claim greater moral worth and a higher social position. Conversely, accepting food indicates either one's affiliation and equality of status with its handler or one's deference to a higher-caste donor.[4]

Besides artifacts, social categories also can have meaning across many figured worlds. These categories are by and large associated with the major social divisions—gender, class, race, ethnicity—that separate those who are routinely privileged from those who are not. Cross-cutting markers tend to become stereotypically associated with these social categories, if not actually demanded of their members in practice. Studies in the United States have found that women use hedges, "tag questions," and other deferential forms more often than men (Lakoff 1975; O'Barr and Atkins 1980; Cameron et al. 1988). In Naudada, Bahuns were popularly stereotyped as greedy and maliciously clever, always looking to take advantage of others. These stereotypic associations between marker and category are the (practical) part and (cultural) parcel of the reproduction of social division, and of the categories that are its elements.

A controversy has raged in anthropological linguistics over women's styles of speaking in the United States and whether they should be viewed in the enduring, almost essentialist terms of "subculture" or in the relational terms of situated practice. Tannen (1990) and others take the former position, which we have called culturalist. Women grow up learning a set of values and ways of being in the world, which they translate into ways of speaking. McConnell-Ginet (1988, 1989; Eckert and McConnell-Ginet 1992), among others, takes a more constructivist position, arguing that women (and men) grow up learning how positions of relative power are communicated. Since women are often forced into positions of lesser power, they end up using deferential speech strategies more often than men.

Our approach does not automatically give us the answer to the controversy, but it does suggest that the situation is too complex to be settled by adopting either the culturalist or the constructivist position. It seems to us a double mistake to think of these cross-cutting relational identities as somehow cleanly separable from figured worlds. First, it is erroneous to believe that figured worlds all partake of these differentia in like manner. Rather, conventions of privileged access associated with gender, caste, or some other major social division may or may not have been taken up, elaborated, and made hegemonic in a particular figured world or field of power. In the schools of Naudada, the language of hierarchy communicated through the rules for exchanging food and water was being used to subvert the system of caste privilege; in the tea stalls, the same language was being used to maintain it.

A second mistake, the reverse of the first, is to think that styles of indicating relative social position can be cleanly separated from a figured world of moral meanings—that they are arbitrary indicators which evoke no figured world of their own.[5] In the world of academia, being verbally aggressive may be a sign of high status and position; but for a person who has formed an identity in a figured world where maintaining egalitarian relations is important, verbal aggressiveness has connotations of a moral failing.

Signithia Fordham (1993), drawing from a long-term study of Capital High School in Washington, D.C., provides an example of both of these points. She reveals the nuanced ways in which major social divisions may be elaborated and made crucial in a localized figured world. She describes some of the excruciating consequences of participating in social formations where the styles of one social category are taken as indices of quality and achievement for all people. She writes especially about African-American women and their disposition to silence themselves in the academic activities of the high school. Although Capital High's student body had, at the time of her study, an African-American majority, the space of its activities ideologically privileged styles that were white and male.[6] The school was oriented toward a particular style and way of being a student. Its model of the good student was one who behaved as did white men. The African-American women students, as a result, were in a place where the styles meaningful at home were considered signs of being a poor student.

That these styles of speaking and acting could not simply be put on or taken off at will is evident from Fordham's analysis as well. There were especially bleak results for the African-American women who tried to suppress their own styles and move toward the valued styles—who tried to "pass." By passing, Fordham means a more subtle and figurative kind of performance than the literal passing for white: "Passing implies impersonation, acting as if one is someone or something one is not. Hence, gender passing [for African-American women] suggests masquerading or presenting a persona or some personae that contradict the literal image of the marginalized or doubly refracted 'Other'" (1993: 3). Too much passing, she argues, drawing upon Said, can result in a potentially subversive self where the person can no longer speak or even think in his or her "native voice." Such persons lose their creativity: "because they are compelled to assume the identity of the 'Other'—in exchange for academic success—they cannot represent themselves; they are forced to masquerade as the authentic, idealized "Other" (26).

Taking Up Social Positions

What Fordham shows us in vivid detail are the results of a long process. Many of the women she studied had developed what we call a positional identity, a sense of their relative social position, which, among other things, led them to silence themselves within the figured world of school. Fordham also describes other young women who had developed an oppositional stance, rejecting the strategy of effacing themselves in order to conform to the model of a good student. How had the young women at Capital High arrived at these positional identities? What interests us is the processes of development over the long term. The long term, however, happens through day-to-day encounters and is built, again and again, by means of artifacts, or indices of positioning, that newcomers gradually learn to identify and then possibly to identify themselves with—either positively or negatively, through either acceptance or rejection.

In the groups that we studied, as in any group engaged in jointly creating and participating in a figured world, day-to-day practices always positioned the participants situationally, relative to one another. That is, participants in collaborative activities—be they staff members producing a treatment plan in a mental health clinic, old hands welcoming a newcomer to an AA meeting, or a romantically involved couple going out to see a film—engaged in conversation and interaction that invariably constructed their own social position and their social relations with one another.

As social constructivists emphasize, these "discourses" and the other forms of cultural artifacts used in everyday practices construct subjects and subject positions. These positions are, at least provisionally, imposed upon parties to the practice. The sociologist R. W. Connell provides an example of this idea when he sums up the argument that gender is more appropriately treated as a process or a practice than as a static attribute or an enduring characteristic. He suggests that "gender" would be more transparent if it were a verb rather than a noun: that its significant qualities would be clearer if we said, "I 'gender' you, you 'gender' me, she 'genders' him"; or, better yet, "I try to 'gender' you, you try to 'gender' me," and so on (Connell 1987: 140).

Entitled people speak, stand, dress, emote, hold the floor—they carry out privileged activities—in ways appropriate to both the situation of the activity and their position within it. Those who speak, stand, dress, hold the floor, emote, and carry out activities in these proper ways are seen to be making claims to being entitled. Speaking certain dialects, giving particular opinions, and holding the floor are indices of claims to privilege.

Examples of positional markers, and of the social work that goes on to maintain their value, abound in ethnographies. In the figured world of gender relations in a Mehinaku village in Brazil, described by Gregor

(1977), the men's house was an important part of the apparatus of male privilege. Men, especially when gathered together, protected the inviolability of that space. Women were threatened with gang rape should they enter the house and see the sacred flutes housed there. Men also engaged in taunting women as a group during certain festivals.[7] Helán Page (1994) details the ways in which public issues in the United States are defined in the public sphere from a "white" perspective, and how this guarded space preserves the system of race privilege. Hill (1995) shows how the speaking of "junk Spanish" by non–Spanish speakers in the United States works to debase the speaking of Spanish, keeping it an index of lower social position.

In Naudada, husbands usually addressed their wives with the less respectful pronominal form used to address children and animals. The respect and deference owed to superiors were communicated through other pronouns. Thus each time he used this form of address a husband afforded his wife a position inferior to his own. In reply, the usual, respectful forms of address that wives employed for husbands would accord him the greater deference. Their social relationship—his superordination, her subordination—was constantly reconstituted by the very media of this discursive practice.

Another example of the affording of a position comes from a practice in Naudada that depends upon the food etiquette of castes. The tea stall owners of Naudada served members of the Damai and other "untouchable" castes, but required them to wash their own cups and glasses. Because people of higher castes avoided food or utensils that had been touched by people of castes considered to be so impure as to pollute, tea stall owners, by enforcing this rule about washing, implicitly claimed to be, or positioned themselves as, pure, superior, and keepers of purity for others. They claimed the qualities of the higher castes, elaborated in relation to the figured world of caste relations, at the same time inviting customers of lower castes to enact a subject position of inferiority. For similar reasons, and with similar implications for the parties' relative positions, husbands refused to eat leftover food from their wives' plates, but it was not expected that wives would refuse their husbands' leftover food.

Viewed over the long term, these day-to-day practices are social work, acts of inclusion/exclusion, of allowing/compelling only certain people to evince the sign, that maintains positions and the value of artifacts as indices of position. Bourdieu (1977a) shows that maintaining one's relative position in the Kabyles' figured world of honor demanded such social work on a day-to-day basis. The value of relational indices and the relative right to use them are maintained through social work of the kind performed by Tila Kumari and Shanta's brothers. These valuations and the restrictions that enforce them have to be imposed, and the outcome of their imposition is uncertain. There is no guarantee that those upon whom they are imposed will not try to refuse the implicit positioning, as did Muna. There is no guarantee, in fact, that everyone will have been brought sufficiently "into" the "language" of the relational markers to understand the would-be impositions and take them seriously.

Much of the inclusionary/exclusionary work of sign restriction is done simply by the inclusion or exclusion of certain types of people from sites where the signing knowledge is interacted as a matter of course (see Rogoff 1990). Trosset (1986) describes the difficulties of a foreigner learning to speak Welsh in Wales. For various reasons, Welsh speakers invariably switch to English in the presence of a non–Welsh speaker, thus effectively limiting the signal means to their identity as Welsh, the ability to speak the everyday tongue.

Gearing and colleagues (1979) describe how processes of inclusion/exclusion work in the absence of clear control—that is, even when dialects can be overheard, or more privileged ways of acting can be directly observed and therefore imitated. They analyze the means by which children in school are kept from learning skills that are taken as indices of social position. They emphasize that knowledge (reading, knowledge of chemistry, skills in repairing machinery) is proprietary; that it is generally associated with, or belongs to, a recognized category of people; and that, by virtue of this relation, the use of knowledge signals identity.[8] Hence, even in situations where all students are admitted to the arena of learning, learning is likely to become unevenly distributed in its specifics. Teachers will take some students' groping claims to knowledge seriously on the basis of certain signs of identity. These students they will encourage and give informative feedback. Others, whom they regard as unlikely or even improper students of a particular subject (girls and shop skills, working-class students and philosophical essays), are less likely to receive their serious response.[9]

Bourdieu (1984, 1977a) addresses the issue of timing: the point in their development when children are given the opportunity to learn behavioral markers of privilege. He argues that many styles of acting and matters of taste that serve as indices of high social position are more easily learned in childhood. Those who learn activities in childhood perform them in a more natural, less self-conscious style, itself prestigious. Those who learn later usually retain an awkwardness, a more "mechanical" than "organic" sense of the activity. It is a complicated point for Bourdieu, one aspect of which concerns the proprioceptive acuity of childhood learning.

More to our purpose, late learners are impeded not only by their sense of inferior propriety or right to act, which their late access signals, but also by the withholding of aid and the acts of disapproval (such as sarcasm, practical jokes, and straight misinformation) through which knowledgeable associates enforce their superior claim. Many never overcome that awkwardness, which inevitably affects the acceptance of their claims and reproduces the situation of inferiority. They are always lesser than. And they may always feel self-conscious, linking durably in their persons the structures of privilege to the dispositions of silencing and acceptance that such structures demand. These are the dimensions of difference to which Lykes (1985) alludes when she argues that individuals have different senses of self because, senses of self being grounded in experiences of power, individuals have differential access to the positions of power that afford the experience. People develop different relational identities in different figured worlds because they are afforded different positions in those worlds.[10]

Bourdieu is careful to point out that the Kabyle man's protection of his status in honor, and of the indicators of honor itself, goes on in a largely automatic way; he does not mean to suggest, although he is often misinterpreted in this regard (Bourdieu 1990a), that consciously strategic maneuvers are the rule. Rather, just as Fordham focuses on the dispositions to silence and effacement that some of the women students at Capital High had developed in the school context, Bourdieu focuses on the embodied dispositions developed among Kabyle men to protect their honor. He details how adult men, in ways beyond their awareness, maintained a constant vigilance for slights to their honor. They noticed and were ever likely to react to social claims made by others of greater honor, and they worked indefatigably to refuse the positions of inferiority afforded them by those claims. Social positions, in other words, become dispositions through participation in, identification with, and development of expertise within the figured world.

How Social Position Becomes Disposition

Within the constructivist emphasis on the importance of discursive positioning—positioning by the cultural artifacts of discourse—there is also a counterpart open to those who, afforded positions, do not always take them up. Della and Karla, two students discussed in Chapter 5, provide contrasting examples of this kind of refusal.

Della rejected her professor's attempt to recast her as other than a student, his figuring of her as a type from the world of romance and attractiveness. But here we want to go beyond these ideas of positioning and resistance. Della was inexperienced with this sort of incident. Although she did not accept the position afforded her, her rejection was rather feeble. She showed her embarrassment and tried to forestall future incidents simply by eluding the teacher's notice.

Karla took stronger measures. For instance, during a period when she was ill, she felt neglected by her boyfriend and thought he was making excuses not to see her because he was afraid her illness was contagious. Generally, she felt he had begun to take her for granted. Finally she challenged him, claiming that he was treating her as though she were a "germ" (Holland and Skinner 1987).[11] In the incident described in Chapter 5, Karla was pursued by her former teacher, who saw her as a potential lover. Although he used various means—including trying to position her (against her own attraction to the intellectual life) as ignorant of the attitude of intellectuals toward adultery—none succeeded. Karla intensified her means of refusal with each new attempt, until she finally succeeded in warning off the teacher. Karla was one of the women in our study who were more determined, more active in the world of romance, more of an agent. She was adept at refusing positions that were afforded her and instead creating positions she liked.[12]

It is important, in understanding positioning, to pay attention to the fact that positional identities develop heuristically over time. The Vygotskian emphasis on semiotic mediation is helpful for understanding the process by which children, or neophytes to figured worlds of any age, develop the dispositions of relational identities. Semiotic mediation is also a means by which these dispositions can be countered and sometimes overcome.[13] People may develop a "sense" (in Bourdieu's terms) of their worlds, an expertise in the use of cultural artifacts, that may come to re-mediate their positions in them.

The development of social position into a positional identity—into

dispositions to voice opinions or to silence oneself, to enter into activities or to refrain and self-censor, depending on the social situation—
comes over the long term, in the course of social interaction. Relational
identities are publicly performed through perceptible signs. People "tell"
each other who they claim to be in society in myriad ways. In Naudada,
Skinner found, children learned early that a woman's marital status was
expressed by diverse signs: by the *tilhari* (a type of necklace) that married women wear, for example, or the vermilion powder worn in the
part of their hair. They learned that tea stall owners would not wash the
glasses of a lower-caste person, nor would high-caste persons allow
lower-caste persons to enter their homes. But much of this learning may
happen in a nonreflective way.

Embodiment versus Mediated Positional Identities

In the ordinary developmental sequence proposed by the sociohistorical
approach, the child first *interacts* the sign in concert with others. The
interaction of the sign, for the child, is part of a behavioral sequence that
may have no meaning in and of itself. It is likely that relational identities
are borne in a similar way, in what phenomenologists used to call the
natural attitude, the uninterrupted flow of everyday life, Bergson's *durée*.
The meaning of actions remains transparent or taken for granted in the
natural attitude, and response follows as a matter of course. The formation of identity in this posture is a byproduct of doing, of imitation and
correction, and is profoundly embodied. Positional identities inhabit the
landscape of Bourdieu's habitus.

Adults too can be drawn into a figured world and develop a relational
identity without much reflection upon the social claims carried in the
forms of their action. Kondo (1990) provides a telling illustration of the
effects of such embodied processes. Kondo, a Japanese American who
grew up in the United States, relates something that happened to her
after a period of fieldwork in Japan, a time in which she had immersed
herself in the daily lives of people in her neighborhood. She went shop-
ping one day:

> Promptly at four P.M., the hour when most Japanese housewives do
> their shopping for the evening meal, I lifted the baby into her stroller
> and pushed her along ahead of me as I inspected the fish, selected the

freshest looking vegetables, and mentally planned the meal for the evening. As I glanced into the shiny metal surface of the butcher's display case, I noticed someone who looked terribly familiar: a typical young housewife, clad in slip-on sandals and the loose, cotton shift called "home wear," a woman walking with a characteristically Japanese bend to the knees and a sliding of the feet. Suddenly, I clutched the handle of the stroller to steady myself as a wave of dizziness washed over me, for I realized I had caught a glimpse of nothing less than my own reflection. (16–17)

Kondo had acquired the dress, posture, and habits of a young Japanese housewife (or so she identified them) simply by immersing herself in social activity from the position that her gender and her associates assigned her. Her acquisition of the dispositions that marked a particular, gendered identity had occurred without her awareness, and the moment of recognition was disorienting. The image of herself in the butcher's display case and the image of herself in her mind's eye did not match, and that disparity led Kondo to distance herself from her fieldwork. Immersion gave way to a reticence in which she gauged her activity according to the recalled standards of her self-image.

No doubt many aspects of positional identities develop out of one's awareness, as Kondo's had before she caught a glimpse of herself. No doubt many behaviors develop out of awareness, unmediated by one's reflection upon them as claims to social position. One simply participates in the typical arrangements of people in houses, say, where one is more likely to find, in the United States, women in the kitchen and men in the workshop or yard; or in Naudada, women at the hearth, men at the tea shop. Or one simply takes part in everyday activities and finds young Japanese(-American) women walking about with sliding steps and slightly bent knees, pushing babies in strollers as they shop in the afternoon.

Occasionally a child may be admonished in a way that includes mention of social position. A mother may tell her daughter that girls don't do x. Shanta was certainly warned away from the plow in a dramatic and upsetting way, but perhaps the usual path to relational identity is through simple associations that pass unnoticed in any conscious way.[14] It may not be until later that the associations between social positions and entitlements become a matter of reflection. The child at first, and perhaps for a very long time, may not associate the access that she gains or does not gain to spaces and activities with the language of social claims. She may not consciously realize that her developing dispositions are caste-specific. Especially at first, she undoubtedly does not say to herself, "Tila Kumari is a Bahun. To go into her yard is to claim to be of higher caste than I am. If I go there, she is likely to mistreat me."

Other indices of positional identities, however, become conscious and available as tools that can be used to affect self and other. Muna interpreted Tila Kumari as accusing her and her friends of being morally bad. She defended herself, to herself and to Debra, as not deserving such an evaluation. In the lived world of Naudadan domestic and community relations, a woman's social worth was figured according to the life path of the good woman (described in Chapter 3). Girls of Muna's age had long been used to hearing and using terms such as *radi* (widow) to insult others. These were derogatory terms for women who had strayed from the life path of the good Hindu woman. They had even come to understand why radi was a negative term—a widow was a woman who had fallen from the life path by outliving her husband. Further, the girls cared about their own moral standing in the community and often constructed for Skinner representations of themselves as good daughters and sisters (see Chapter 10). Muna's emotional response to Tila Kumari's scoldings indicated her attachment to the understanding of herself as a good person.

In other words, some positional identities and their associated markers are clearly figured. In Naudada, good works and good behavior, when contrasted to the misbehavior that constitutes *pap* (sin), are noted and related to the script of the life path of a good person. In the world of romance of college students in the American South, attractiveness as a form of symbolic capital, a measure of one's social worth, was figured extensively, not only as a key element in the development of romantic relationships, but also as a motive for numerous projects, practices, and artifacts of beautification. Perhaps these figured aspects of relational identities become relatively conscious for anyone successfully recruited into the figured world where such qualities are deemed important. The everyday aspects of lived identities, in contrast, may be relatively unremarked, unfigured, out of awareness, and so unavailable as a tool for affecting one's own behavior.

We do not mean to imply that identities subsist in two exclusive forms, one type a pure product of imagination and the other of unreflected action. Rather, consider two orientations or attitudes to the production of social activity. Figured identities arise and are reproduced in the special attitude of play or, more precisely, imaginative framing. As we noted in Chapter 3, Vygotsky describes play as a special social form of activity, one in which the conditions and modes of action are not those of the "actual," that is, everyday setting, but of an imagined template cast over the everyday. He uses the simple example of a child's playing at riding a horse, when what the child rides is "merely" a broom. What counts in play, and what counts in the identities of figured worlds, is the cultural relations, the "rules," that govern the movements of a game. The meanings of play, like the meanings of *langue*, are only attached or assigned to the material tokens that instantiate them. Their source lies in the imaginative system.

Mundane activities, in contrast, have become a matter of habit. By differentiating between mundane activities and the more dramatic, re-marked activities singled out in figured worlds, we create not a dichotomy but a continuum. As Bakhtin maintained (Voloshinov 1986), even everyday behavior has an ideology, a cultural world. Hence the relation of play or life in a marked frame of imagination to everyday activity is more properly one of specificity (one that is marked) to generality (one that is unmarked). The two situations are convertible. Specific figured worlds—such as that of romantic love, which began as play in the courts of eleventh-century France (see Chapter 11)—can be made public over time to become more mundane genres of the everyday, and the generic figures of social life can become specialized, "survivals" in Edward Tylor's sense, and turned into the stuff of folklore and exotic ethnography.

Vygotsky called the process in which the historical sources and the distinctiveness of behavior are erased by its automation "fossilization." In a sense some imaginative frames become "fossilized" in mundane daily life. But fossilization is not irreversible. Ruptures of the taken-for-granted can remove these aspects of positional identities from automatic performance and recognition to commentary and re-cognition. (Kondo's experience is an excellent example.) This hermeneutic moment leads persons to specify the figured world that prefigures everyday activity.

This disruption happens on the collective level as well. Some signs of relational identity become objectified, and thus available to reflection and comment, in relation to the social category. Alternative figurings may be available for interpreting the everyday, and alternative ways of figuring systems of privilege may be developed in contestations over social arrangements. We heard in Naudada figurings of caste that differed from those given in Brahmanical texts. Schoolboys told Skinner that the blood of the lower castes was red, like that of the higher castes—members of different castes were at root the same, and not "naturally" different.

At some point the lower-caste child may begin to grasp consciously the emotional, evaluative nature of the signs that are used to position him as inferior, as a source of potential pollution for all those whose caste is higher than his own. By drinking from the glass at a tea stall, the Damai, the Sarki, the Kami pollutes it. At some point the child may begin to use the sign in relation to social category and in turn as a symbolization of how others experience him. Typically a child will reproduce the comments of adults in his own egocentric speech, that is, in the speech stream that frames, comments upon, and comes to manage action. Through continually objectifying or symbolizing himself enacting the sign, he becomes able to experience a version of himself as an object in a social world given meaning by these signs. Eventually this means of objectification, which is a form of self-management, becomes what Vygotsky and Bakhtin called inner speech (see Chapter 2), and what we consider an element of the imagination. One particular lower-caste boy so resented the position assigned him because of his caste that he dreamed of returning to Naudada as a doctor, a figure of such importance that higher-caste people would have to accept food and water that he had touched (Skinner and Holland 1996).

The women in Holland's study of romance often talked about such objectifications of themselves and ruminated upon them. Often these representations took the form of voices, of Bakhtin's (1981) vocal images, while others were visual images. Similar processes of objectification were evident for the children that Skinner followed in Nepal. These visions often seemed to motivate (plans for) action, sometimes even life-changing action.[15] Kondo suggests that for her, too, the image reflected in the display case became a mediating device; it allowed her to think about what she had become, and to attempt to change it.

Children in their development and neophytes entering into a figured world, then, acquire positional dispositions and identities. At some level of apprehension, they come to know these signs as claims to categorical and relational positions, to status. More important, they learn a feel for the game, as Bourdieu calls it, for how such claims on their part will be received.[16] They come to have relational identities in their most rudimentary form: a set of dispositions toward themselves in relation to where they can enter, what they can say, what emotions they can have, and what they can do in a given situation.

Explorations of the processes of these formations, followed in more depth in the next chapters, suggest that the associations children and neophytes form with different spaces and activities in their environment are, in fact, social positions that have become dispositions. Gendered dispositions to participate, or not, in given activities, develop in places where gender participation in activities is treated as a claim of gender specificity. Dispositions of lower-caste Naudadan individuals and groups to speak, or not to speak, with an authoritative voice in public gatherings where members of higher castes are present develop in places where speaking is treated as a claim to caste position.

Yet positional identities are not without their disruptions. The same semiotic mediators, adopted by people to guide their behavior, that may serve to reproduce structures of privilege and the identities, dominant and subordinate, defined within them, may also work as a potential for liberation from the social environment. We will see in the next chapters how people sometimes fix upon objectifications of themselves that they find unacceptable. These objectifications become the organizing basis of resentment and often of more active resistance. When individuals learn about figured worlds and come, in some sense, to identify themselves in those worlds, their participation may include reactions to the treatment they have received as occupants of the positions figured by the worlds.[17] Yet the "metapragmatic" capability to figure social practice—through narrative, drawing, singing, and other means of articulation—is at the same time a capability to figure it otherwise than it is. Its rehearsal is the opportunity to re-create dispositions to activities-in-mind that give shape to this dissatisfaction. The interchange or convertibility of the two contexts of identity provides opportunities to reform either by recourse to the other. In other words, symbols also enable the objectification of the treatment that women or lower-caste people receive, so that narrativized worlds are created around stories of these treatments and visions of better treatment.

7

The Sexual Auction Block

In our study of college women in the southern United States (see Chapter 5), the women's identification within the world of romance entailed that they form a sense of the social value of both self and others in that world.[1] Identification with that world meant taking, to varying degrees, what Bourdieu (1977a, 1977b; Bourdieu and Passeron, 1977) called "symbolic violence" into one's self and perpetrating (and perpetuating) it against others. Settling social position—the subtext of interaction and the stuff of positional identities—is a matter of struggle, often muted or even unrecognized, whose effects live on in personal and social history.

To illustrate the point, let us begin with Karen's description of things that had happened since her last interview:

> A friend of mine [Annette] invited us . . . to a party in the dorm. And she told us that there'd be . . . a couple of people there that she really liked a lot: guys, that is . . . and . . . when we got there . . . the main one she wanted to see . . . didn't even hardly acknowledge her presence. He practically didn't even speak to her . . . And it just sort of messed up the whole party—mainly for her, and because of that, it messed it up for all of us. I expected . . . some real nice guys. I thought they'd be really glad to see her. But . . . the one she wanted to see acted real stuck-up, as if she wasn't even there. . . . He ignored her . . . She'd be standing practically beside him, and he wouldn't say anything.

The interviewer asked why the man, Sam, had acted the way he did. "I don't know . . . maybe she just had it in her head that he liked her . . . and he was just trying to talk to this other girl or something. But he did act, he acted sort of too good for her, you know?"

Annette was upset. Karen explained that Annette was trying to reason out Sam's actions:

Interviewer: What were some of the ways she reasoned it out?

Karen: Um, well, she thought at first maybe because he was with that girl, he didn't want to talk to anybody else. And, but then, he was talking to other girls that were walking by, and um, then she was thinking, maybe he was mad at her, but she didn't know why, you know, she was just thinking of different stuff like that.

Interviewer: Did you think of any things like that too?

Karen: Uh, not really, I, I, it's gonna sound terrible. I thought, well he just didn't want to, didn't want to see her at all, 'cause he just didn't, I don't know, what I thought was that, he was like I said before, he was some big jock on campus, you know, and he just wanted the real, just certain girls around him, you know.

Interviewer: What . . . kinds?

Karen: Really pretty.

Karen's embarrassment in telling this story was palpable. Her discomfort draws our attention to the importance of attractiveness. Karen was clearly embarrassed to say explicitly that her friend was not pretty enough for Sam's tastes. It was as though Annette had something to be ashamed of, and Karen's speech marked that shame. And, even though Annette was obviously thinking over Sam's behavior, Karen did not try to save her time and worry by explaining. This incident underscored, for us, the pivotal aspect of attractiveness: Why should not being really pretty be something to be embarrassed about?

No doubt there was another source of Karen's embarrassment. Annette had publicly and boldly proclaimed her attraction to Sam, and, by approaching him, had in effect laid claim to a comparable attractiveness of her own, only to have it demolished by his lack of interest. In the student culture attractiveness was very important. It was at the heart of the gender status quo. Annette's claim to social worth among her peers had been proven false (for further analysis see Holland and Skinner 1987; Holland and Eisenhart 1990).

In Chapter 5 we noted that some women were more adept than others at claiming—and refusing—roles in romantic activities and that, as a matter of that same skill, some were more adept at claiming a high level of attractiveness. We want to pursue that clue and direct our attention to how these relational aspects of identity in the world of romance are negotiated actively within social interaction. Only by following this course can we understand Annette's vulnerability to the kind of insult she suffered and, the broader point, women's vulnerability to the symbolic violence that marks the ways romance is lived.

How were women developing their sense of place as gendered actors in the world of romance, and as more attractive or less attractive individuals? An important means is participation in the discursive practices described in the chapters on figured worlds and positionality. We noted in Chapter 6 the idea that gender is more appropriately treated as a process or a practice than as a static attribute or an enduring characteristic; that, in Connell's words, "'gender' would be more transparent if it were a verb rather than a noun" (1987: 84). We would argue analogously about the more specific, gendered quality of attractiveness. It would be more accurate to use a verb that meant "to make attractive": "I make you attractive," "you make me attractive," "she makes him attractive," and so on. This phrasing de-essentializes the quality by revealing its social-relational dynamics—the continually negotiated constructions and reconstructions that create "real" attractiveness and attractive people.

Because of its attention to everyday encounters and to the maneuvers and dilemmas of participants actively engaged in those encounters, the focus on practice, and on the constitution of images and statuses through interaction, is reminiscent of symbolic interactionism. Unlike most traditional forms of symbolic interactionism, however, practice theories go well beyond the encounters at hand. Bourdieu (1977a, 1990b), addressing practice in general, and Connell (1987), addressing practice in relation to gender, both build on symbolic interactionism, adding a critical step. They theorize about how systems of power and privilege render the participants of encounters more or less equal, more or less like agents, and more or less interpersonally powerful. Here too we must situate these interactions in a larger system, by recalling the cultural sources that give these discourses and practices their potency. One important source has already been introduced: the figured world of romance. Along with it, other figured and positional aspects of identities in the United States and the South—race, class, sexual orientation—evoke and give shape to what might be called the playing field of day-to-day romantic encounters.

When we submit identity to the rigors of practice, to this complicated field of play, an interesting thing happens. The figured world of romance predicates certain genres of gender relations and the acts and characters or positions that are meaningful in them. In encounters these generic worlds may be evoked through gestures, words, phrases, looks, and movements, and the relative positions of the parties to the encounter are constructed and counter-constructed.[2] Yet, in practice, these worlds are not everywhere the same and their instantiations are not automatic. Rather, the evocation is potentiated and differentiated by, first, the positional markers that constrain people's "fitness" for certain claims and rights of use, and, second, by evocations of other figured worlds, other ways to define the situation. The playing field is the space made of these possibilities. Southern discourses of romance, it turned out in practice, were double-edged. They provided for the pleasurable construction of desire, to be sure, but they also constructed a world in which the parties to desire could gain or lose attractiveness and prestige. These gendering discourses and practices were powerful vehicles for the playing out of romantic selves; they were also potential means of degradation.

In open-ended interviews, the women told us about many incidents involving actual or potential romantic/sexual partners, especially the upsetting ones, like the story of Annette, in which they or a friend had been mistreated and insulted by men. They also talked about incidents in which they or a friend had been, by their own assessment, inappropriately treated as a romantic/sexual partner by a professor or boss. Unlike Annette, who willingly sought Sam as a romantic partner, these women neither sought out nor desired romantic involvement with their bosses and teachers. Nor did the women in similar stories Holland has since been told, stories evoked by her lecturing on this material.[3] Whether the women invited the men's assessment or not, these instances involved insults, insults both to their attractiveness and (consequently) to their prestige.

Incidents of Symbolic Violence

The double-edged quality of romantic discourse can readily be discerned from such cases. It can also be discerned from a videotaped simulation of such an incident. Analysis of the videotape's transcript allows us to explicate aspects of the positionality of romantic identities in general and to explore what happens when these identities are evoked in the workplace. The video captures visually the importance of gestures and spatial positioning. It is useful in particular for understanding how the gendered identities of the world of romance are evoked clandestinely in the workplace—how the playing field becomes complicated by two figured worlds. In much of the incident, what is spoken stays in the realm of work. The world of sex and romance and the positioning of the participants in that world are evoked largely through nonverbal gestures and physical contacts.

The video clip we quote was part of a televised program on sexual harassment in the workplace. The simulated incident was arranged by a social psychologist, John Pryor, to illustrate his research on the conditions under which men are more likely to sexually harass women at work (Pryor et al. 1993). Our focus is not on the behavior of the men in the incident but rather on what this behavior can tell us about the readings of like incidents by the participants in our studies.

> *Narrator:* During a psychology class, Dr. Pryor re-created one of his more revealing studies.
> *Two men, John (the experimenter), and Mr. Williams (the subject), walk up to a desk on which is a computer; they shake hands.*
> *John:* What we're going to do here, I'm trying to evaluate a program I've developed for the Department of Office Management. Okay?
> *Mr. Williams sits down at the desk and John sits on the edge of the desk.*
> *Narrator:* In this scenario, a graduate student who is actually participating in the experiment leads the research subject to believe that he will be training undergraduate women to use a computer.
> *John:* What you're going to do is instruct the girl that's going to be coming in here on how to correct these mistakes. Okay? Now I don't know if you noticed the girl out in the hall, but the girls that are being sent down here by the Department of Office Management are real foxy.
> *Narrator:* In reality the real purpose of the experiment was to see if the research subject would harass given the opportunity.
> *John goes out and calls "Cindy." A woman comes in. Mr. Williams stands up.*

John: Cindy! It is Cindy, isn't it? I'm John. How are you?

They shake hands.

Cindy: I'm fine, thank you.

John: Don't I know you from somewhere? You look like an old girlfriend of mine. (*He still has her hand. Cindy laughs.*) I want you to come on over here. Cindy, this is Mr. Williams.

Cindy and Mr. Williams shake hands.

Mr. Williams: Hi, Cindy.

John: Mr. Williams will basically be your boss here for the next fifteen minutes. So all's you have to do is listen to what Mr. Williams has to say and follow his instructions. Okay? Okay?

Cindy sits down at the desk.

Narrator: By the design, the graduate student, who is really part of the research design, purposively harasses the woman—setting an example for the computer trainer to do the same.

John is standing behind Cindy. He puts his hands on her bare shoulders—she has on a "boat-top" sweater—and leaves them there as he speaks.

John: Make yourself comfortable, then just follow Mr. Williams's instructions and you'll be doing okay. Okay?

Cindy nods her head.

John (to Mr. Williams): And you remember that you're going to fill out an evaluation sheet?

Mr. Williams: Yeah. Okay.

John: Okay.

Mr. Williams: Okay, thanks a lot.

John leaves the room.

Narrator: Left alone, and left to believe that sexual harassment is permitted and even condoned, the computer trainer takes full advantage of the situation.

Mr. Williams: You want me to give you the sentence now?

He is standing behind the chair. He looks at his paper, then puts his right hand on the chair behind Cindy's right shoulder.

Cindy: Okay . . . What'd I . . .

Mr. Williams: It's number three. Just hit number three up here.

He reaches around her with his left hand and hits the key. When he removes his hand from the keyboard, he grasps her left shoulder.

Cindy: Do I have to hit return?

Narrator: Although this is a re-creation, similar behavior was observed during 90 percent of the experiments.

Mr. Williams: That's good.

Cindy: Okay. And?

Mr. Williams: Just use those. Those are fine.

Narrator: Shannon Hoffman, who participated in the real studies and has just played Cindy in the simulation, remembers feeling vulnerable because of the permissive situation created by the men in charge.

Mr. Williams kneels by Cindy's right side and leaves his left arm around her. A few seconds later he pats/rubs her back.

Mr. Williams: And that's all you really need to do. Just hit the letter and you'll be fine.

The scene changes to Shannon Hoffman being interviewed on camera.

Shannon Hoffman: It was very uncomfortable for me. I realized that, if it had been out of the experimental setting, as a woman I would have been very uncomfortable with someone that close to me and reaching around me like that. So, it really made me feel a little bit powerless because there was nothing much I could do. But I also realized that perhaps in a business setting, if this person really was my boss, then it would've been harder for me to send off the negative signals, or whatever, to try and fend off that kind of thing.

The simulation provides a vivid case of gendering, and a plausible example of the type of incidents described to us by our study's participants. We now want to read this incident according to the figured world of romance that we inferred from our studies. Through such interpretations, women and men live gender ideologies in day-to-day encounters. In order to avoid awkward, conditional phrasings, we will treat the participants of the simulation as though they were drawing upon the background knowledge we found common in our studies.

The Experimenter Genders Himself and the Other Man

The initial conversation between the two men set the stage for the incident. It drew upon the discourse of romance to construct the woman as an object of desire. Of equal importance, the experimenter, in the process of figuring the woman, gendered both himself and the other man. The experimenter, John, said to the subject, Mr. Williams, "Now I don't know if you noticed the girl out in the hall, but the girls that are being sent down here by the Department of Office Management are real foxy."

Here John drew upon a lexicon, comprising hundreds of gender-marked terms, that men in our studies had for talking about women as figures of romance.[4] This male lexicon provided many terms that ascribed value to different types of women and described the ways they were likely to behave in romantic relationships. The term "foxy" positioned the woman—relative to other culturally typed women, such as "broads," "babes," or "cows"—as one who was sexy, a companion with whom a man would want to be seen, and likable in that she was not likely to be overly demanding (Holland and Skinner 1987).

In our studies of the lexicons that men used to refer to women and women to men, it became abundantly clear that these vocabularies were not just tools of representation. The words were used to do social work as well. What stood out for many of the men and women we studied was less the semantics of these gender-marked lexicons than the ways in which the terms could be used. Their first remarks were often about the potential use of the words as insults. For example, some respondents grouped terms such as "bitch," "shrew," "dog," "dumb blonde," and "airhead" together because they could all be used to insult a woman. (Other terms, such as "sweetheart," were said to be endearments.) Against the conceptual horizon provided by the figured world of romance, terms such as "dog," "bitch," and the milder "women's libber" could be used to position, negatively, one woman relative to others. "Bitches" were women who in the man's view overvalued their own attractiveness and so demanded too much. A spurned lover would demean the woman who rejected him by telling friends that she had turned out to be a "bitch." Likewise, women had an arsenal of terms—such as "prick," "nerd," and "asshole"—that they used to claim that particular men were of little value.

The social work of the terms was even more complex. One's partners, or those to whom one was attracted, reflected back upon one's own attractiveness. In the taken-for-granted scenario, those who were equally attractive were attracted to one another.[5] "Hunks" were not attracted to "nags" or "dogs" but to "foxy girls" or "dolls," and likewise "foxy girls" were not attracted to "jerks," "nerds," "wimps," or "turkeys." Still, the attribution—exactly who was a "hunk" and who was a "creep"—varied by participant and was not carved in stone. There were no absolute measures of attractiveness; there was no authority that could definitively assess who was and who was not attractive. Instead, attractiveness was a symbolic capital attested to, aggrandized, or devalued by the attractiveness of those one approached and the treatment one received from them.

Both women and men read these words as making claims about their own attractiveness as well as that of others. The naming of others in the world of romance has a characteristic described by Boltanski and Thevenot (1983): social classification systems tend to classify the classifier as well as the classified. A woman who referred to a man as an "asshole" was implicitly claiming that he held no attraction for her at all, and thus that she was more attractive than he. By classifying a man as a "playboy," a woman admitted both his attractiveness and the possibility that he would try to treat her as though she were more attracted to him than he to her. In other words, she admitted the possibility that he was more attractive than she.

On their part, men used words such as "bitch" or "knockout" to make claims about particular women and, reflexively in the process, about themselves and the listener as well. Against the conceptual horizon provided by the world of romance, a man who referred to a woman as a "dog," a "bitch," or a "women's libber" was positioning not only the woman but also himself. He was claiming that the woman, as far as he was concerned, was unattractive, and therefore (the claim reflecting back upon him) that he was more attractive than the woman.[6]

In the case of attractiveness, the classifiers not only classified their targets and themselves, they also classified those who were intimately related to the classified. People of similar attractiveness became intimate in the taken-for-granted situation of the figured world. Thus a woman's boyfriend's attractiveness was a sign of her own attractiveness. If a woman's boyfriend was called a "nerd," her attractiveness also was impugned. If a man called another man's girlfriend a "dog," he also implied that her suitors were unattractive. The reflexivity of these categories enabled an individual to propose a hierarchical ranking of a number of people, including himself or herself, simply by labeling one person.

By labeling the women being sent down by the Department of Office Management as "foxy," the experimenter, John, evoked the world of romance and a comparison of the women according to their attractiveness. He construed Cindy, the woman who was there for computer training, as a prestigious object of desire, and thus when he later approached her in an intimate way he cast himself as an attractive, desirable man. Here was a "foxy" woman with whom he could be familiar. With his comment about foxiness, John also drew the subject, Mr. Williams, into the figured world of romance and sexuality. He gendered Mr. Williams by implying that Mr. Williams would participate—with John and from the same desirable perspective—in the world of male/female relations. He implied not only that he and Mr. Williams were heterosexual but also that they shared standards of taste in women and were roughly equal in attractiveness.

A Gendering Insult

In the two men's interactions with the woman, they used gestures that invoked the world of romance and sex. John said to Cindy, "Don't I know you from somewhere? You look like an old girlfriend of mine." He put his hands on her in an intimate manner, an intimacy that was unexplained by any prior history. His gestures and phrases, and the later physical intimacy of Mr. Williams, all invoked a clandestine discourse, a discourse that opened a space within the workplace that was ambiguously, if at all, governed by the work at hand, or the figured relations of occupational specialization and merit. The space was instead infused with gender relations, interpreted according to the model of romance, and peopled by types who were relevant to that world.

Yet the work went on, the computer trainer continued the training. The sexual world was always close to the surface, threatening to overwhelm the ostensible activity, but the discourse remained submerged, clandestine. Hence, here and in the incidents described to us, it was difficult for the women to refuse such a gendering. Especially in cases where gestures and innuendo were the language of choice, the evocation of the world of sex and romance could be counter-charged to the woman. Should she too blatantly or explicitly avoid the unwanted intimacies and communicate her refusal too forcefully, she could be accused of reading meaning into gestures inappropriately, of seeing something that no one else sees, or of fantasizing that she is attractive enough to be the object of a man's desire. She could be accused of purposefully evoking the world of romance herself. Her clothes, her makeup, her posture, and her movements could be scrutinized as cues, and put forward as evidence of her desire. Why was Cindy wearing a sweater that left the tops of her shoulders bare?[7]

When constantly invoked, despite a woman's wishes, the discourse of romance constituted a refusal to treat her as worker or student, on a par with other workers or students. It was a refusal to accord the woman any value other than that of her attractiveness. This is a general strategy of male resistance to the incorporation of women into traditionally male worksites (Weston 1990). The situation simulated in the video clip is more complex. The work went on; the computer trainer continued the training; but he did so in such a way that the world of romance and sexuality infiltrated the activity at hand, giving all acts a double significance. The incidents women described to us were similar. Sometimes they were even more blatant, and sometimes more ambiguous. We did not hear of situations in which male teachers or employers absolutely refused to treat a woman as a student or employee. Instead we heard of situations in which women were suddenly, without warning, removed from the context of work, treated as objects of desire, and positioned in the world of romance.

The women in our studies, most of whom were between eighteen and twenty-two, were shocked when such incidents happened to them or their friends. This was especially true of women who had been accustomed to deciding which men were and which were not in the group of potential romantic/sexual interests. Some of these bosses or teachers were considered too old to be appropriate partners, and their romantic approach was doubly troubling to the women. Especially distressing were those incidents that were observed by fellow students or employees. The women invariably described themselves as intensely embarrassed. They felt belittled and unable to counter-attack. (In none of the cases did the teller report that the audience came to her defense.)

Some of the women were learning through experience that their vulnerability to what we call the sexual auction block extended into the workplace and the classroom. They could be reconstituted, without their invitation or permission and before their fellows, from student or worker to object of desire and token of attractiveness. Some of the women experienced these incidents as revelations. One incident sufficed to make them realize that the clandestine discourse of romance and sexuality lay just under the surface in every classroom and workplace: that they might at any time be treated as a romantic or sexual object regardless of their absorption in the task at hand, regardless of their desire not to be so treated, and regardless of how inappropriate an arbiter of their attractiveness the man in question seemed to them to be. This subtext, once revealed, led to a more complex apprehension of men in positions of authority.

This shift in perspective was affectingly articulated by the young woman we call Karla. After the incident described in Chapter 5, in which one of her former teachers had approached her as a potential lover, she concluded somewhat sadly:

> But, you know, this has caused me to do a lot of thinking about the nature of the human male. Here is a man you would never suspect . . . upstanding member of the community, seemingly happily married. What more could he want? And trying to seduce an eighteen-year-old girl . . . and an intellectual seduction, too. It's made me a little leery of older male teachers who act incredibly friendly, because there have been a lot of them, that I always looked upon as just really nice people who were interested in their students. But now this whole other dimension has been added of, "Hey, wait a minute; maybe he's not interested in my intellectual development."

An Insulting Gendering

The woman in the video clip was exposed to a "gendering insult": without any invitation on her part and in a work situation where it was supposedly irrelevant, she was evaluated and treated according to her attractiveness. But there was more to the incident: not only was the gendering itself an insult; its substance or content was insulting as well. The discourse of romance evoked in the incident was double-edged. It constructed desire, but it also positioned the parties to the romantic encounter, ranking them according to their relative amounts of the symbolic capital, attractiveness.

Similarly, on the two college campuses we studied, the figured world of romance provided a means for creating gendered persons of more or less value, possessing more or less symbolic capital. Students used the lexicon of gender-marked terms to position themselves and others. Partners' treatment of each other was also read as claims about their relative amounts of symbolic capital.

Romantic and sexual activity were understood by the students to be about attraction. They were organized around the taken-for-granted unfolding of a romantic/sexual relationship that we presented in Chapter 5: Two equally attractive people were drawn to each other. The man treated the woman well: he appreciated her; he recognized her special qualities; he did nice things for her; and he was sensitive to her desires. The woman, in turn, showed her affection for him and allowed the relationship to become more intimate. Both were rewarded by the intimacy of the relationship and by the validation of their attractiveness.

In this figured world, attraction was the force that produced intimate cross-gender relationships, and the ability to attract was a crucial quality of those who would participate in the world of romance. Attractiveness determined how a woman would be treated by men. Attractive women received attention, gifts, and intimacy and gained access to whatever social and material amenities the men wished to share. Unattractive women either received ill treatment from attractive men or settled for relations with unattractive, less prestigious men. And it worked similarly in reverse: attractive men were admired and chosen as intimate partners by attractive women; unattractive men had to settle for less attractive women.

At first attractiveness seemed to be construed as an intrinsic characteristic of a person, a set of qualities that some had naturally, others cultivated, and many lacked. Closer examination, however, showed attractiveness to be less an enduring or essential quality than a product of one's relations and activities. It was drawn from the attractiveness of those who were attracted to one and how one fared in romantic/sexual encounters.[8] A man's attractiveness was affirmed, increased, or diminished by each of his encounters with women, according to the outcome. The same was true for a woman. Attractiveness was a form of symbolic capital: a putatively unchanging attribute of the person that actually fluctuated according to the treatment he or she received from others.[9]

There were ways to make up for mismatches in attractiveness. A relatively unattractive man could succeed with a relatively attractive woman if he treated her especially well. He could be exceptionally sensitive to her, especially creative and clever in pleasing her. In this way, expectations of good treatment became a language of claims to relative attractiveness. A woman who seemed to expect special treatment, with little demonstration of affection on her part, was interpreted as claiming to be more attractive than her partner. If a man felt a woman was demanding too much, overrating her own attractiveness relative to his, he could retaliate by calling her a "bitch." By the same token, if a man expected intimacy and affection from a woman and yet treated her badly, he was interpreted as claiming that she was less attractive than he. The woman too had the verbal means to counter this assessment, and many reasons to use them. For, in this only partly verbal language of claim and counterclaim, acquiescence demonstrated agreement. If a woman stayed with a man who treated her as less attractive than he, she enacted her lesser attractiveness.

In this figuring of sexual relations, rape constituted an ultimate form of ill-treatment. It was an acting out of the man's sense that the woman's prestige was negligible. And, as others have argued (Sanders 1980), because attractiveness was attested to by the treatment women received from men, the very act of rape *created* the victim's low prestige. Furthermore, in the logic of this system, women who "accepted" ill-treatment deserved that ill-treatment and relations with unattractive men. As one of the women in the study said, "The hall slut deserves the dullest guy around."

In the incident depicted in the video clip, both men continued to treat the woman in intimate ways, though she had given no indication that she desired intimacy with them. Except for John's fleeting acknowledgment that Cindy looked like the type of woman he was willing to have as girlfriend—an accolade that is more or less valuable depending on one's assessment of his attractiveness—neither man did anything for her that counted as good treatment in the world of romance. They gave no indication of sensitivity to her wishes. They gave no sign that they saw her as a special person. Nor did they do anything for her in the way of special favors. By the standards of the figured world of romance, they were claiming to be prestigious, desirable men whose attractiveness was so much greater than the woman's that she could expect no special treatment from them. They acted as though she would surely welcome, or at least allow, intimacy regardless of their relative disregard for her.

In short, they played out the entitlements of men possessing large amounts of symbolic capital, men of great attractiveness and high prestige. And in the process they devalued the woman's symbolic resources; they implied that her capital was less than theirs. The woman not only had to contend with a gendering insult but with an insulting gendering as well. She faced both the double-talk of romantic discourse, masked within the workplace, and its double-edged nature. The discourse can construct desire and pleasure, but it can also construct degradation.

Women in our study described many incidents in which they felt demeaned by men's treatment. The incidents had the themes just elucidated: their (potential) boyfriends and lovers enacted positions of greater entitlement and thus cast the women as relatively unattractive. The women complained of being treated as though they were only one of a crowd of women, many of whom would do just as well. They also objected to men's expectations that they would rush into intimate relations with little prelude. They disliked being made to feel as though they were simply props that men used to demonstrate their status to their buddies.

The incidents in the classroom or the workplace were similarly insulting and even harder to manage. At parties and social events, in dating relationships, a woman had ways to counter a man's view of his superior attractiveness. She could oppose him by trying to insult his attractiveness. She could publicly label him a "prick" or a "jerk" or a "nerd." Or she could simply leave, without much fear of damaging retaliation on his part.

Return for a moment to Karen's account of Sam, the big man on campus, and his treatment of Annette, the ordinary girl. Karen described her own reaction to Sam: "I didn't think he was attractive anymore." Her inclination was to demean him, to label him an unprestigious man, an unattractive type: "I wanted to tell him . . . he was acting like an ass."

The women had more trouble responding to such insults from bosses or instructors; they were not so ready to insult the symbolic capital of men in positions of authority. Potential retaliation from a boss or an instructor could be much more damaging. Compared with men of their peer groups, bosses and instructors had more power to impose "their vision of the divisions of the social world and their position within it" (Bourdieu 1985b: 732).[10] It was difficult, indeed dangerous, to resist because the boss or employer had an independent source of attractiveness/prestige as a result of his position. It was also difficult because of the double-talk nature of the clandestine discourse. Shannon Hoffman, who participated in Pryor's experiments, commented in the video that, even though the situation was artificial and sure to end quickly, she experienced a sense of powerlessness. She was being treated as a low-status object, a person of few entitlements, and placed in a position where she could be ridiculed if she protested.

The Buxom Woman in the Bikini

An incident from a paper written by one of Holland's students, a woman we will call Eva Haley, shows some of the same elements of the case portrayed in the video. The paper concerned the history of pinup calendars, and it included a brief tale of Haley's experience with such a calendar:

> In 1985, I was [the general] manager at a new car automobile dealer-ship . . . One day I entered the parts department for a consultation with the [parts] manager. As the door closed behind me I turned and with-out warning came face to face with a very large "pinup" calendar spon-sored by a tool company and displaying a bikini-clad, buxom woman whose exaggerated body positioning and seductive gaze infused the image with clear, culturally coded sexuality.

In this brief description this incident seems quite different from the one simulated in the video. The parts manager did not put his hands on Eva. He said nothing about his old girlfriends. He said nothing about bikinis, nor did he call attention to the bikini-clad woman on his door. There was no indication that he had put up the calendar in anticipation that Eva would see it. But Haley's reaction suggests a similarity: "I felt my face flush with anger and shame as the ground holding me on an equal level with my fellow manager shifted beneath my feet."

The same popular ideology of romance, the perceptible evocation of a figured world, made Eva Haley's situation as potent and insulting as the situation faced by the woman in the video. The pinup on the calendar recalled the world of romance and attractiveness. The space that was ostensibly a workplace was infused with gender relations. In that space, Haley's superior position as a manager of the car dealership, relative to her colleague, the parts manager, was rendered less potent. Instead, their positions in the world of romance and sexuality, that is, of a woman in relation to a man, were brought to the fore. To the extent that she had to occupy that position, the basis for her claim to superior status as a worker was vitiated. She experienced a gendering insult.

Furthermore, just as in the video, the gendering was an insulting one. The means of insult were different; the outcomes were similar. In the video simulation Cindy suffered an insulting gendering when the men treated her as being less attractive than they were. In order to understand how Eva Haley underwent an insulting gendering, recall that gender typing affects all those involved in the world of romance and attractiveness. Gender labeling redounds upon both the classifier and the person listening to the classification. In Haley's words, "the image defined a standard of beauty and a role by which to judge women, leaving me . . . physically substandard." The calendar's picture of the woman in the bikini evoked a ranking of women according to attractiveness—a ranking in which Eva felt devalued. Like gender typing by words—the use of "foxy" in the video—so too the image on the calendar reflected upon the person observing it.

We would extend Haley's analysis by adding that the parts manager was making a claim about his own tastes and attractiveness. He implied that he was attracted by handsome women, and so that he was a handsome man. The calendar evoked a three-way ranking of Eva, the woman in the bikini, and the man—a ranking in which the man was elevated as Eva was put down. The man had created a gendering space that offered him a claim to the symbolic capital of attractiveness.[11] Women entering the space were invited to feel disempowered.

Haley wrote that she was angry and ashamed. Yet, so far as we know, she did not try to retaliate against the man. Why might she have refrained? After all, she was the general manager and he was her subordinate. Again, the answer lies in the double-talk that conceals the discourse—or, in this case, the imagery—of romance and sexuality in the workplace. Had Eva confronted the man, she could have been accused of raising the specter of romance and sexuality herself and of being the sole author of any invidious comparisons between her and the bikini-clad woman. Again, note the double-edged nature of the talk. A pinup calendar can perhaps provide a shape for desire, but, in this case, it figured an act of degradation.

Privileging Spaces

Eva's response to the pinup calendar shows that her position as a woman in the figured world of romance has become disposition. She was very much affected by threats to her social worth, to her symbolic capital of attractiveness. Her disposition—to see herself through the figured world and to recognize her vulnerability to insults to her attractiveness, even in a situation that was supposedly divorced from romance—was also the disposition whose development the women in our study described. Recall such situations as the one where Della's looks were singled out for sexual innuendo by her professor (Chapter 5) and the encounter between Sam and Annette that Karen recounted.

Men, too, were vulnerable to having their attractiveness insulted by women, to having their social worth belittled, to bearing the brunt of symbolic violence. Women could accept their gifts, their attention, and their good treatment and still not reciprocate with any show of affection. They could refuse to allow the relationship to become more emotionally or physically intimate. Women could insult them verbally as well, referring to them as "pricks," "nerds," "creeps," and other unappealing names. Nonetheless, our studies showed that women's treatment by men had a greater impact upon evaluations of their social worth than the relationship reversed. That is, the gender ideology discussed here had more importance for women than for men.

On the face of it, the romantic/sexual relationship that constitutes the standard of meaning in the model—the pairing of attractive people who give and get equally, and the expected outcome of intimacy and prestige for both—seems to favor neither the woman nor the man. But, in the student world of the late 1970s and early 1980s, equality was not the rule. Women's attractiveness and prestige were far more dependent upon their relationships with men than vice versa. Men had diverse sources of symbolic capital. Men on the basketball team and men of (potential) wealth, for example, had sources of attractiveness and prestige that were largely independent of how women treated them.

There was no such alternative source for women. Participation on women's sports teams—no matter how many championships the teams won—added little to the athletes' attractiveness to male students; the same was true for women's participation in student government or university performance groups. The playing field for romantic encounters was not equal. When Sam snubbed her, Annette had little else to fall back on for validation of her social worth. Had she similarly snubbed him, Sam, a well-known athlete, would not have been as bereft.

It is clearly fairly easy to create spaces, figured by the world of romance, in which men are especially privileged. This easy access to privilege is a consequence of men's more numerous sources of symbolic capital. Yet other social and material contexts may affect the ways popular ideologies of romance are played out in particular sites. One woman in our study pointed out that women outnumbered men at her university. Consequently, in her view, all the men enjoyed an inflated sense of their attractiveness and prestige. Men who, in a larger market, would have been considered undesirable were treated as though they were attractive. Hence, for that time and on that campus at least, they *were* attractive.

Pryor's findings, reported in the video, could be interpreted along the same lines. The experimental conditions set up a situation in which simply being male gave all the men who participated symbolic capital and its attendant entitlements relative to the women. In the words of the video's narration, the experimental conditions established a "permissive situation." The men felt free to be intimate with the woman.

We would augment this analysis by drawing upon the ideology of romance and attractiveness. The experimental conditions established a "privileging" space with two characteristics. First, male/female relations were interpreted according to the figured world of romance and attractiveness. Through his comments and actions the person in authority, the experimenter, evoked this world. Second, the conditions created a space that automatically afforded the men greater symbolic capital than the women. The comments and actions of the experimenter, from his position of authority, not only evoked the world of romance but also positioned him and his male confederate as attractive/prestigious relative to the woman. That authoritative position gave the men reason to expect that the woman would treat them as attractive.

The most unsettling aspect of Pryor's findings, especially to those of us who are women living in this society, is how little effort it took to create a privileging space in which a high percentage of the men involved felt entitled to treat the woman as though her social worth were considerably less than theirs.[12] It sadly corroborates other evidence, such as the all too frequent occasions when male athletes, misusing the attractiveness and prestige attributed to them, act out their entitlement by mistreating women. The fraternity rape described by Sanday (1990) is an even more extreme case. Pryor's findings are also particularly distressing because the situation was putatively a workplace, where attractiveness should be irrelevant. His data confirm that many women in the United States are widely subject to evaluation, and potential degradation, in terms of the popular ideology of romance and attractiveness, no matter the context of activity.

That a high percentage of the men in the experiment engage in harassment does not lead us to think of the men, or men in general, as intrinsically or essentially sexual harassers. It does lead us to think of the way the popular ideology of romance and attractiveness empowers men in certain situations. It suggests that the ideology of romance was a potent part of these men's experience; the world of heterosexual romance and sexuality was very salient to them and very easily evoked. Pryor's experiment spells out how easily men may be induced to adopt the positional identity of an attractive man relating to a less attractive, less prestigious woman. The experimental conditions created a particular sort of gendering space, a particular privileging space, that was very potent not only for the woman but also for the men.

Many of the women in our studies had trouble handling such situations. Della, when her professor praised her attractiveness, felt embarrassed and subsequently tried to avoid him. Retreat was the only solution she could conceive that would not risk provoking his further comment. After Sam treated her badly, Annette was probably less quick to reveal her attraction to a man and perhaps less likely to pursue one of Sam's prestige. That the women struggled to manage such situations tells us not that they were intrinsically victims but rather that the playing field of the encounters was unequal. The women had relatively few resources for contesting such genderings.

The Discourse of Sexual Harassment

Since the time of our studies of romance on college campuses, there have been organized efforts by individuals and groups to use legal and quasilegal means to stop unwanted sexual advances. Now there are discourses of sexual harassment and other sources of remedy beyond the individual woman's attempts to counter-insult or dissuade a man from involving her in unwanted relations. The language of these policies and laws, and the debates over what precisely constitutes sexual harassment, have informed the relatively new discourse. They have at least created some new categories—beyond "prick," "jerk," and the like—for interpreting and naming the parties to the type of gendering insults analyzed in this chapter.[13] Were we to return to the same campuses today and interview students about the incident simulated in the video, we would no doubt find reference to this discourse. Perhaps women would tell us about incidents in which they did not respond with embarrassment, unex-

pressed anger, or guilt, but instead rebuked the man for sexually harass-
ing them. Perhaps we would hear, in other words, about cases where the
discourse of harassment was brought into the incidents themselves.

The availability of this discourse certainly does not eviscerate the
popular ideology of romance and attractiveness. Nor does it save women
from the type of gendering insults discussed here. The Anita
Hill/Clarence Thomas hearings were one potent testimony to women's
continuing vulnerability, even in the process of pressing claims of sexual
harassment, to degradation through discourses of desire (see Eisenhart
and Lawrence 1994). Nonetheless, there is little doubt that legal and
quasi-legal remedies for sexual harassment have altered the resources
available for contesting this form of sexism.[14] The ideology of romance
and attractiveness has the force of a cultural inertia, born especially from
its potential for constructing pleasure and desire, but it cannot be assumed that inertia grants it an automatic monopoly on meaning. Instead
its place must be held or dislodged through social effort and struggle.
Women now have an alternative discourse, and sometimes the backing
of an enforcement apparatus, through which they may try to refuse or
defuse situations of the type we have described.

The discourse of sexual harassment affords a woman a new resource to
turn the playing field to her advantage, redefining the incident from one
of her inappropriate and degrading gendering into one of *his* negative
gendering, of outlawing and ostracizing the man. A woman in a situation
like Cindy's could now try to alter the computer trainer's actions by
threatening to denounce him as a sexual harasser. The emerging discourse of sexual harassment gives women a resource for disrupting the
construction of spaces that give the privileged positions to men. They
can try to convert these spaces into ones where men are reminded of
their liability to sanctions by university hearing boards, corporate committees, and government agencies. Had Eva Haley's encounter with the
bikini-clad pinup happened in the late 1990s, not in 1985, she might
have been moved to counter-attack. Instead of feeling devalued because
she failed to meet certain standards of physical appearance, she might
have tried to turn the parts manager's office into a place that discomforted him, because the space *he* had created did not meet standards of
acceptability.[15] She might have hung an anti–sexual harassment poster
over his pinup calendar.

How useful these resources will turn out to be—how effectively they will aid women to defuse insulting genderings and disrupt gendering spaces—remains to be seen. Besides the dangers of insult to the victims of sexual harassment in hearings, there is intense struggle over the very discourse itself.

David Mamet's play *Oleanna* provides an instructive example. The play, a drama with only two actors, takes place in a professor's office. In the first scene an anxious undergraduate, a student in one of the professor's courses, arrives for an appointment. She is confused about her grade and generally insecure about her educational progress. She wants suggestions for improvement. The egocentric male professor, absorbed in contemplating his successful career and in buying a house, virtually ignores her wishes. He takes the opportunity, instead, to instruct her on his "quasi-radical" academic analyses of the failures of American higher education.

In the next scene the student returns for another appointment, this time armed with a more authoritative way of figuring the conflict between them. She has in the interim joined a women's group on campus, and she has learned not only that she has rights but also ways of asserting those rights. The communication between student and professor worsens, and she eventually makes a charge that sets in motion the college apparatus for investigating sexual harassment. The originally ambiguous tension between them has become socially clarified in the terms of a gendered conflict, not limited to his office, but grown campus-wide. He is (re)positioned, cast as a suspected sexual harasser, and eventually he loses his tenure, his job, his new house, and even his wife's support.

Mamet's play not only shows how sexual harassment might intervene between a woman and the "insults" of her position but also illustrates a contestation of the discourse of sexual harassment and the identities it affords. Audience discussions, which followed the performances we saw and those we read about, often denigrated the woman student for evoking the specter of sexual harassment and falsely accusing the professor. The discussants had the idea—though it was more often implied than made explicit—that recourse to charges of sexual harassment is both unfair and counterproductive because it is too easily abused. Our concern here is not to debate Mamet's play but rather to let it dramatize the simple point that these discourses are still under heavy dispute. Whether and how they will survive is still in question.

Equally intriguing is the question of just how salient the discourse of sexual harassment will become in the construal of gender relations. Could it become even more salient than the ideology of romance and sex? A world of gender relations figured on a central narrative of men as predators who use their power to exploit women sexually is imaginable and indeed has already been imagined. It is the emerging and monstrous world, the panic-world, portrayed in the writings of such controversial and self-proclaimed feminists as Roiphe (1993).

Romance and Attractiveness and Other Fields of Power

The popular ideology of romance is thoroughly entangled with other important collective structures that affect and effect gendering. The discourse of sexual harassment may offer an additional means of interpreting male/female encounters and relations, but it sheds little light on and gives little relief from a veritable obsession that some of us have with our own attractiveness. Capitalism has stimulated the fetishization of attractiveness, this central notion in the popular model of romance, and encouraged the commodification of gender itself (Haug 1986; Willis 1991). The advertisements of the cosmetics and apparel industries alone, not to mention the ways attractiveness, romance, and sexuality are harnessed to sell other products, clearly intensify and shape—and are intensified and shaped by—the pivotal role accorded attractiveness in the figured world of romance.[16]

Romantic practices are ever confounded with other powerful systems of privilege that affect the playing field of cross-gender relations. Clearly women and men are differentially advantaged as participants in the world of romantic and sexual relations according to race, class, age, and sexual orientation. How is it, for example, that some forms of appearance and ways of acting have come to be considered more attractive than others? How is it that the media represent images of attractiveness that are ageist, constructing younger forms as beautiful; racist, putting a premium on white features; and classist, promoting those forms of beauty that depend upon wealth? These race, class, and age privileges are not determined by the figured world of romance and attractiveness, but are mediated and potentiated by it.

IV

The Space of Authoring

8

Authoring Selves

Bakhtin's vision of self-fashioning, which we call the "space of author-ing," resonates with what the case studies have told us about identity formation. The cases belie any simplistic notion that identities are inter-nalized in a sort of faxing process that unproblematically reproduces the collective upon the individual, the social upon the body.[1] Bakhtin's con-cepts allow us to put words to an alternative vision, organized around the conflictual, continuing dialogic of an inner speech where active iden-tities are ever forming.

Dialogism

In explicating the interconnections of Bakhtin's seminal contributions to literary analysis and criticism, to linguistics, and to anthropology, Mi-chael Holquist (1990) draws out a central organizing principle, which he names "dialogism." The figured world of dialogism is one in which sentient beings always exist in a state of being "addressed" and in the process of "answering."[2] People coexist, always in mutual orientation moving to action; there is no human action which is singularly expres-sive. Holquist provides a helpful exposition:

> Dialogism begins by visualizing existence as an event, the event of being responsible for (and to) the particular situation existence as-sumes as it unfolds in the unique (and constantly changing) place I occupy in it. Existence is addressed to me as a riot of inchoate potential messages, which at this level of abstraction may be said to come to

individual persons much as stimuli from the natural environment come to individual organisms. Some of the potential messages come to me in the form of primitive physiological stimuli, some in the form of natural language, and some in social codes, or ideologies. So long as I am in existence, I am in a particular place, and must respond to all these stimuli either by ignoring them or in a response that takes the form of making sense, of producing—for it is a form of work—*meaning* out of such utterances. (1990: 47)

In the making of meaning, we "author" the world. But the "I" is by no means a freewheeling agent, authoring worlds from creative springs within. Rather, the "I" is more like Lévi-Strauss's (1966) *bricoleur,* who builds with preexisting materials. In authoring the world, in putting words to the world that addresses her, the "I" draws upon the languages, the dialects, the words of others to which she has been exposed. One is more or less condemned, in the work of expression, to choices because "heteroglossia," the simultaneity of different languages and of their associated values and presuppositions, is the rule in social life. In Bakhtin's words:

Language—like the living concrete environment in which the consciousness of the verbal artist lives—is never unitary. It is unitary only as an abstract grammatical system of normative forms, taken in isolation from the concrete, ideological conceptualizations that fill it, and in isolation from the uninterrupted process of historical becoming that is a characteristic of all living language. Actual social life and historical becoming create within an abstractly unitary national language a multitude of concrete worlds, a multitude of bounded verbal-ideological and social belief systems; within these various systems (identical in the abstract) are elements of language filled with various semantic and axiological content and each with its own different sound. (1981: 288)

It is important to remember that languages are, for Bakhtin, not only abstract semiotic systems but inevitably and inextricably also ideological and lived perspectives on the world:

all languages of heteroglossia, whatever the principle underlying them and making each unique, are specific points of view on the world, forms for conceptualizing the world in words, specific world views, each characterized by its own objects, meanings and values. As such they all may be juxtaposed to one another, mutually supplement one another, contradict one another and be interrelated dialogically. As such they encounter one another and coexist in the consciousness of real people . . . As such, these languages live a real life, they struggle and evolve in an environment of social heteroglossia . . . They may all be drawn in by the novelist for the orchestration of his themes and for the refracted (indirect) expression of his intentions and values. (Bakhtin 1981: 291–292)

In such a diverse and contentious social world, the author, in everyday life as in artistic work, creates by orchestration, by arranging overheard elements, themes, and forms, not by some outpouring of an ineffable and central source. That is, the author works within, or at least against, a set of constraints that are also a set of possibilities for utterance. These are the social forms of language that Bakhtin summarized: dialects, registers, accents, and "speech genres." We discuss speech and other expressive genres in more detail later, for they embody Bakhtin's closest analogue to what we call figured worlds. For the time being, we will gloss speech genres as conventional styles of speaking whose performances presume and depend (for their very meaningfulness) upon a figured world, which Bakhtin (1981) called a "chronotope."[3]

Dialogic Selves

In the figured world of dialogism the vantage point rests within the "I" and authoring comes from the I, but the words come from collective experience. Words come already articulated by others:

As a result of the work done by all these stratifying forces in language, there are no "neutral" words and forms—words and forms that belong to "no one"; language has been completely taken over, shot through with intentions and accents. For any individual consciousness living in it, language is not an abstract system of normative forms but rather a concrete heteroglot conception of the world. All words have the "taste" of a profession, a genre, a tendency, a party, a particular work, a particular person, a generation, an age group, the day and hour. Each word tastes of the context and contexts in which it has lived its socially charged life; all words and forms are populated by intentions. Contextual overtones (generic, tendentious, individualistic) are inevitable in the word.

As a living, socio-ideological concrete thing, as heteroglot opinion, language, for the individual consciousness, lies on the borderline between oneself and the other. The word in language is half someone else's. It becomes "one's own" only when the speaker populates it with his own intention, his own accent, when he appropriates the word, adapting it to his own semantic and expressive intention. Prior to this moment of appropriation, the word does not exist in a neutral and impersonal language (it is not after all out of a dictionary that the speaker gets his words!), but rather it exists in other people's mouths, in other people's contexts, serving other people's intentions: it is from there that one must take the word, and make it one's own. (Bakhtin 1981: 293–294)

The mixture of the perspective of the "I" and the words of others creates the contours of Bakhtin's contribution to our ideas of selves and identities. Here again,

an active understanding . . . establishes a series of complex interrelationships, consonances and dissonances with the word and enriches it with new elements. It is precisely such an understanding that the speaker counts on. Therefore his orientation toward the listener is an orientation toward a specific conceptual horizon, toward the specific world of the listener; it introduces totally new elements into his discourse; it is in this way, after all, that various different points of view, conceptual horizons, systems for providing expressive accents, various social "languages" come to interact with one another. The speaker strives to get a reading on his own word, and on his own conceptual system that determines this word, within the alien conceptual system of the understanding receiver; he enters into dialogical relationships with certain aspects of this system. The speaker breaks through the alien conceptual horizon of the listener, constructs his own utterance on alien territory, against his, the listener's, apperceptive background. (Bakhtin 1981: 282)

It is not only being addressed, receiving others' words, but the act of responding, which is already necessarily addressed, that informs our world through others. Identity, as the expressible relationship to others, is dialogical at both moments of expression, listening and speaking.

Reminiscent of Mead (1934), Bakhtin insists that we also represent ourselves to ourselves from the vantage point (the words) of others, and that those representations are significant to our experience of ourselves. In Holquist's rendition of Bakhtin's views:

It will be remembered that the time of the self is always open, unfinished, as opposed to the time we assume for others, which is (relative to our own) closed, finalizable. And yet, in order to be known, to be perceived as a figure that can be "seen," a person or thing *must* be put into the categories of the other, categories that reduce, finish, consummate. We see not only our selves, but the world, in the finalizing categories of the other. In other words, we see the world by authoring it. (Holquist 1990: 84)

The meaning that we make of ourselves is, in Bakhtin's terms, "authoring the self," and the site at which this authoring occurs is a space defined by the interrelationship of differentiated "vocal" perspectives on the social world. In Bakhtin's vision, the self is to existence as the pronoun "I" is to language. Both the self and "I" designate pivotal positions in the stream of (language) activity that goes on always.[4] In explaining what an "I" is, position, rather than content, is important. Suppose one tries to define "I" by summarizing the characteristics of everybody one has heard use the term in the past week. One can imagine a prototypical tree, but can one imagine a prototypical I? In Bakhtin's system the self is somewhat analogous to "I." The self is a position from which meaning is made, a position that is "addressed" by and "answers" others and the "world" (the physical and cultural environment). In answering (which is the stuff of existence), the self "authors" the world—including itself and others.

The authoring self is invisible to itself. The phenomenology of the self is, in Bakhtin's terms, characterized by "openendedness." Because the self is the nexus of a continuing flow of activity and is participating in this activity, it cannot be finalized. It cannot step outside of activity as "itself"; the self as it reflects upon its activity is different from the self that acts. In Bakhtin's view, the self-process must be dialogic. It consists, as told by Holquist (1990: 22, 28), in relating, orchestrating, the "I-for-itself" (the center) and the "not-I-in-me" (the noncenter). The other is authored, captured, and finalized in language as though the other were not a subject just as open-ended as the self. And, by the same token, in answering the other as its necessary counterpart, the self represents (and thereby finalizes) "itself" through a collective language. Reiterating Holquist: "And yet, in order to be known, to be perceived as a figure that can be 'seen,' a person or thing *must* be put into the categories of the other, categories that reduce, finish, consummate." The self authors itself, and is thus made knowable, in the words of others.

If, to be perceptible by others, we cast ourselves in terms of the other, then we do that by seeing ourselves from the outside. That is, we assume a position which Bakhtin names "outsideness" or "transgredience" (Bakhtin 1981, 1990; Holquist 1990). In earlier chapters we described selves authored via cultural resources, such as the life stories of Alcoholics Anonymous, that have become aspects of history-in-person. Putting one's self in the texts, the genres, of AA achieves "outsideness." Coming to realize how they can be read as romantic figures, the women described in Chapters 5 and 7, in effect, achieved outsideness.

Bakhtin and Vygotsky

Wertsch (1985a, 1991) and others (Emerson 1983b; Holquist 1981, 1990) have argued that Bakhtin's work complements that of the sociohistorical school of psychology and that it in fact remedies serious lacunae in that school's treatment, especially of the social conformation of activity.[5] We, too, see such an integration as productive, indeed necessary to the kinds of study we outline here.

Vygotsky's vision of psychology, seventy years later, remains one of the few to attempt a true integration of culture and mental life. What Bakhtin has to offer this still revolutionary psychology is a much keener appreciation of the ties of cultural forms to social others and to the fundamentally social nature of dialogism. By looking carefully, one can discern a philosophy of dialogism in Vygotsky—especially if one pays attention to his recognition that consciousness forms and re-forms in activity—but the theme is dim and underdeveloped (see Wertsch 1985b). Vygotsky attended much more to the issues of human *development* and, in particular, to the role of cultural forms in that development. Again, one can discern in Bakhtin aspects of change and development and the importance of cultural forms in mediating those changes—Bakhtin writes of the development of an "authorial stance" and of art and literature as providing possibilities for reorchestrating the self—but the theme is dimmer and less developed than in Vygotsky's work. Development and dialogism are the critical themes to be intertwined here.

Inner Speech as a Site of Subjectivity

Vygotsky and Bakhtin figured language, words, speech as the key means of subjectivity and consciousness, and both held "inner speech" to be the key intra-mental node, where social speech penetrated the body and became the premiere building block of thought and feeling. Vygotsky put forward a "law": "every function in the child's cultural development appears twice: first, on the social level, and later, on the individual level; first, between people (interpsychological) and then inside the child (intrapsychological)" (Vygotsky 1978: 57).

This maxim entails that inner speech is preceded in ontogeny by external speech, where children talk as though speaking were simply part of an activity, repeating words and gestures they have heard from others (see Chapter 3). Vygotsky thus reversed the Piagetian formulation (that speech begins for oneself), and argued that speech begins for others and then eventually is directed toward oneself. Speech directed toward oneself begins out loud (as so-called egocentric speech), but eventually becomes silent, inner speech, a speech whose formal characteristics (such as ellipsis, deletion of the subject, focus on sense rather than meaning) become differentiated from those of social speech (Vygotsky 1986; Voloshinov 1986). The possibility of directing speech to oneself is equally, for Vygotsky, the possibility of achieving at least a modicum of control over one's own behavior. One can at least have a voice in directing one's own actions.

As we discussed in Chapter 3, Vygotsky emphasized the ability of humans to use mediating devices, especially symbols, to modify their own mental environment and so direct their own behavior. These devices were generally first taken up in interaction with others, and then only gradually taken into one's self-activity. The resulting complex (device plus behavior—not forgetting context) could eventually become habitual or "fossilized," in Vygotsky's term (1978: 68), be moved out of awareness, possibly with no observable trace of the mediating means; "the" act, subsuming its exterior development, became seemingly an essential characteristic of the person.[6]

Vygotsky's attention to the achievement of freedom via discipline, that is freedom from the random stimuli of the environment and discipline by the direction of oneself through signs, emphasized the significance of cultural forms. Cultural forms were the creation of the collective, and through these forms a second world could be articulated. By constructing an unseen, a spoken if not imaginary, world for its agents—which as scientific concepts could achieve maximum distance from the directly experienced physical stimuli—humans vitiated external exigency.

Vygotsky's appreciation of the collective dimensions of human life also extended to the social. Individuals have access to the cultural legacy of the collective through others. Social interaction is the context in which cultural forms come to individuals and individuals come to use cultural forms. Learning is "situated," to use the term of scholars such as Lave and Wenger (1991); the cultural forms that come to inhabit the individual depend upon the place, the social position, from which the individual engages with others in activities, in practice. At least at first, and, we suspect, in many cases later on as well, others support or censure use of particular cultural forms in practice. With the helpful encouragement and gentle rephrasings of oldtimers, newcomers to Alcoholics Anonymous meetings gradually begin to tell their stories. In the interchange that surrounds the telling, they are softly directed toward the generic forms of the organization.

Vygotsky's theories of education and pedagogy made explicit his ideas about the distribution of neophytes' activities, even their thinking and feeling, over those with whom they interacted. Vygotsky summed up this absolutely social character of human learning through his concept of the zone of proximal development, the ZOPED. In most U.S. schools, students are measured for acquired and inherited skills and abilities by tests in which help from others is considered cheating. The ZOPED seeks to determine what the individual can do with the support of others, in the social context of learning. Perhaps an AA member can/will tell the story of her life as an alcoholic only with the support of other AA members. The story lies within her zone of proximal development, if not yet within her sole capacity.

Yet Vygotsky was himself guilty (as are we all, more often than not) of focusing too exclusively upon the *facilitation* of skills and abilities that took place in the ZOPED.[7] He often omitted its negative aspect—both the censuring and "extinction" of behaviors irrelevant to the learning task and the shaping and inculcation of only those skills and actions "fit" for the social position the neophyte was accorded. To reverse the title of Foucault's famous book, the ZOPED was also a place to punish and discipline.

While the social was clearly important to Vygotsky, we miss the elements of power, status, stratification, and ownership that Bakhtin emphasized. In Vygotsky's vision cultural forms became fused with mental life within social interaction, but he avoided attention to the conflictual in social life or to the oppressive nature of many institutions in which humans interact these cultural forms (Wertsch, Minick, and Arns 1984). And so we miss the social struggles and conflicts that drive aspects of inner speech. Vygotsky recognized differences between inner speech (speech for one's self), and social speech (speech for others), and he thus recognized a tension, for example, in moving from inner to social speech. But the tension lay in such contrasts as those between the "sense" of a word or phrase for one's self, the connotations and memories of the contexts of the word's use, and the "meaning" of a word or phrase for generalized others. Bakhtin's view of the social and the fusion of the social with cultural forms was much more complex.

Bakhtin was keenly aware that speech forms—social languages, speech genres—were neither neutral with regard to values and world views nor a simple means of expressing thoughts, leaving off the subtexts of power and stratification. Vygotsky quite appropriately emphasized the potential of words as tools, as "bootstraps" by which one could pull oneself up to another form of behavior,[8] but he ignored the conflicts and struggles, the whole history of contested practices now emblematized and brought along with the tools. Vygotsky's tools, according to Bakhtin's vision of human expression, came marked with social division and the often incompatible perspectives attached to them.

To appreciate the difference between the two it is also necessary to recall Bakhtin's insistence on dialogism, addressivity and answerability. Vygotskian psychology, especially its development by the Kharkov line of the sociohistorical school now referred to as "activity theory," emphasized the situatedness of thought and feeling and their developmental courses over the lifetime. But, where Bakhtin emphasized the always-continuing activity of producing meaning in dialogue, "activity" in the sociohistorical school refers to any historically specific, collectively developed or conventionalized, social endeavor such as work. Where Bakhtin emphasized a global self-fashioning, or authoring of the self, the tasks that Vygotsky considered, such as remembering to do something (Vygotsky 1978) or controlling one's emotions in a particular situation (Vygotsky 1987b), were more varied and more everyday.

It is true that, writing with and against the formalists, Vygotsky (1986) did discuss monologic versus dialogic forms of (inner) speech, but he simply did not give inner speech the dialogic quality that Bakhtin did. Inner speech was, for Vygotsky, only possible because of social speech, and thus dialogical in its developmental origins. But Vygotsky gave more emphasis to the semantic, representational potential of mature linguistic practice and its potential for semiotic mediation, and thus gave less attention to what Bakhtin continued to emphasize, the pragmatic aspects of language—how it was used, how it communicated power and authority, how it was inscribed with status and influence.[9]

Authoring the Self, Orchestrating Voices

Vygotsky wrote little about the self, at least as far as we are aware. If we extrapolate from his position, especially his emphasis on semiotic mediation, however, we find no incompatibilities with the writings of Bakhtin on the subject.[10] In fact, the implications of Vygotsky's work seem to complement Bakhtin's position. In Bakhtin's account of "self-authoring," the "I-for-myself" realizes itself explicitly in words and categories, naming the "I-for-others" and the "other-in-myself." As we have argued, following Vygotsky, such symbols for self may become important in attempts to control or modify one's behavior. The AA member who comes to identify herself as a non-drinking alcoholic may use the tokens of that identity, such as the number of colored chips she has collected, to tell herself parts of her personal story, to keep herself from taking a drink. The categories of the other not only finalize the self, putting closure on what is actually open-ended, but also guide the future self in its activity. They direct the trajectory of the self-process, becoming part of what we call history-in-person.

Bakhtin has more to offer. For him, the voices, the symbols, are socially inscribed and heteroglossic. Often the voices are in conflict. The AA member may hear the voices of other members, but she also hears the voices of her friends who still drink: "Oh, come on, have a drink." And it is unlikely that the member will be able to avoid situations in which these voices, which are reminders of earlier selves, promote divergent actions. These voices will have to be put together in some way. The orchestration of such voices, which Bakhtin calls self-authoring, thus is a complicated matter indeed. Or, in Vygotsky's terms, semiotic mediation, made over into a matter of voice, looks less like a smooth steering mechanism and more like a self-contest.

Consider Sandy, one of the college women introduced in Chapter 5. In her "talking diary" interviews we discern several voices, some of which Sandy identified with and others with which she was at odds, the voices of critics. Sandy was upset by the critical talk. She had come to the university from another part of the country and, from what she said, found her fellow students' ideas of attractiveness unfamiliar:

> In my hometown, I was pretty much respected in the community and accepted for what I am, or was, in that community. [I was] basically your nonconformist, and I dressed to suit me. But when I came down here I . . . got the impression that here I was a sloppy little girl and I didn't have any class or I didn't have any style . . . I have some preppie clothes, and sometimes I wear them but I don't feel that what you wear puts you in a certain circle, and all of a sudden I felt that I was put either to one side or to the other side . . . and I didn't have a choice because it was all around me . . . and I didn't like that . . . And it really really bothered me.

Sandy went on to say that the same forces made her feel that she was not a "lady" just because she cursed when she got angry. As she reported her thoughts and feelings, the criticisms were remembered in (took on) the voices of her peers. She seemed to reexperience the comparison of herself to an ideal through the questions and criticisms of her peers. These critics had become an "internal interlocutor," which invidiously compared her to the ideal and to whose charges she formulated answers and defenses (Holland 1988).[11]

Much of Bakhtin's most fascinating work is devoted to styles of authorship in literary genres. It was characteristic of the novel, as Bakhtin conceived it, that the author's position was articulated not through explicit statements but through the juxtaposition, the orchestration, of the voices and performances of the novel's characters:

> The author does not speak in a given language (from which he distances himself to a greater or lesser degree), but he speaks, as it were, *through* language, a language that has somehow more or less materialized, become objectivized, that he merely ventriloquates.
>
> The prose writer as a novelist does not strip away the intentions of others from the heteroglot language of his works, he does not violate those socio-ideological cultural horizons (big and little worlds) that open up behind heteroglot languages—rather he welcomes them into his work. The prose writer makes use of words that are already populated with the social intentions of others and compels them to serve his own new intentions, to serve a second master. Therefore the intentions of the prose writer are refracted, and refracted at different angles, de-

pending on the degree to which the refracted, heteroglot languages he deals with are socio-ideologically alien, already embodied and already objectivized. (Bakhtin 1981: 299–300)

We see this same sort of authoring in inner speech.

An excerpt from Lachicotte's interviews with psychiatrists and other mental health workers provides an example. Public mental health care is a profession involving at least four vocations: the medical or psychiatric, the psychological or psychotherapeutic, the sociological or social work, and the administrative or managerial. Because people are trained in at least the rudiments of each vocation, and because they work in teams drawn from these vocations, each professional learns and personalizes the discourse (and, as Bakhtin would say, the "volitional-emotional" content) appropriate to all the vocations. That is, the vocations become "voices," situated vocal-images within inner speech, and thus possible ideological standpoints for responding to the problems that confront practitioners. The authoring of mental health care, as an activity and an understanding that are one's own, is composed, in Bakhtin's terms, by the relations among these situated voices.

In order to elicit accounts that might retrieve that process of authorship, our interview confronted each professional with a hypothetical case summary, a description of a woman's psychiatric problems in the context of her life. We asked how the professional would plan treatment of such a case. As we will explain in Chapter 9, mental health workers have trouble treating the type of mental patient represented in the case summary. The following excerpt from an interview shows how a particularly articulate therapist tried to create an authorial position for herself in relation to the hypothetical character. Each ideological-linguistic voice available to the therapist is noted in brackets.

> [social] Find out what her resources are. A girl like this is going to need outside resources. Does she have any? A lot of times, surprisingly enough, they have. Surprisingly enough, they very often may have friends that you're unaware of, that they're unaware of!
>
> [therapeutic] But, work out with her, again, trying to get her to take as much control as she can of her life. "What are we going to do?" and, again, set up the rules. Set up the consistency and rules. Try to understand that just because her illness, her manifestation of illness

tends to be less pleasant than your chronic schiz's, doesn't make her any less safe.

So what does she want to do about the divorce? Does she want to divorce this guy? [social] Usually, right off, they don't have any money. Where is she going to live? So, with her, I would start off with much more practical considerations. "Where are you going to live? What are we going to do? What are the options? Where can you go? Can you go to your family?" [and administrative] Because if she's going to go to South Carolina to live with her family, then we're not going to do anything with this lady except get her to South Carolina.

[medical/therapeutic] So a patient like this, she's very easily depressed and very unstable. She's going to need stability before she needs anything else, so my first priority with her would be to find some way to get her stabilized.

[social] I don't mean psychiatrically stabilized, I mean socially stabilized. [medical/therapeutic] This is somebody who, you're not going to fix the psychiatric problems, for the next fifteen years, at least, even if she's cooperative. And I don't mean that in a mean way, but that the reason she's unstable is that obviously—her mom spent the last year in a hospital suffering from psychotic depression—[and social] basic lack of security. Husband losing a job; she's going to bounce off the walls and be dead.

For virtually all the people interviewed, the woman's case was a hard problem. Few expressed confidence that any treatment they could devise would prove effective, and most accounts reflect that diffidence. Many lack an authorial center, wandering substantially from task to task and discursively crossing the vocations conventionally responsible for these tasks. Others take an authorial stance that directly reports, without adopting or valuing any one interrelationship, the steps each vocation might take and the reasons for their failure.

The therapist quoted was an exception, and it is not surprising that she was considered an expert with borderlines—the diagnosis most often evoked by the hypothetical case. Throughout the case recitation she relates the vocations with little commentary. She presents each with respect, as a serious participant, but gives clear weight to the sociological standpoint. She begins and ends from that perspective, she interrupts speaking from the other vocations to return to social concerns, and, at times, she mixes (in Bakhtin's term, hybridizes) the other vocations' discourse with the social. The formal ways of relating social languages, evident in this therapist's speech, provide a powerful means to "outsideness"—a way of standing apart from immediate experience that yet defines it as ours by the very arrangement that relates it. It is utterly characteristic of self-identification under a regime of heteroglossia.

Mental health workers have long been exposed to heteroglossia, a cacophony of different languages and perspectives. They are faced with the choice of either taking on these different languages and perspectives willy-nilly or developing a more or less stable "authorial stance," a voice that over time speaks categorically and/or orchestrates the different voices in roughly comparable ways. A first step toward an authorial stance, one already mastered by this therapist, is the creation of internally persuasive discourses—external or authoritative speech that has been married to one's own:

> Internally persuasive discourse—as opposed to one that is externally authoritative—is, as it is affirmed through assimilation, tightly interwoven with "one's own word." In the everyday rounds of our consciousness, the internally persuasive word is half-ours and half-someone else's. Its creativity and productiveness consist precisely in the fact that such a word awakens new and independent words, that it organizes masses of our words from within, and does not remain in an isolated and static condition. It is not so much interpreted by us as it is further, that is, freely, developed, applied to new material, new conditions; it enters into interanimating relationships with new contexts. More than that, it enters into an intense interaction, a *struggle* with other internally persuasive discourses. Our ideological development is just such an intense struggle within us for hegemony among various available verbal and ideological points of view, approaches, directions and values. The semantic structure of an internally persuasive discourse is *not finite,* it is *open;* in each of the new contexts that dialogize it, this discourse is able to reveal ever newer *ways to mean.* (Bakhtin 1981: 345–346)

Here one sees a close approach in Bakhtin's thought to Vygotsky's notion of mediation. The creation of an internally persuasive discourse mediates the reorganization and extension of social speech into new forms of inner speaking. It changes the nature of subjectification.

In a situation of heteroglossia different languages and perspectives come inscribed with differing amounts of authority, which suggest how they might be orchestrated. Nonetheless, especially in situations where the usual authorities are unsettled (see Chapter 9), there is little agreement about how to orchestrate these various voices. As the case of Susan in Chapter 5 shows, the development of an authorial stance, in any figured world, can take a long time. Sandy, as well, struggled with the criticisms she encountered from her peers. Sorting out and orchestrating voices is much more than sorting out neutral perspectives in some rationalist's argument; the voices, after all, are associated with socially marked and ranked groups ("the in-crowd," one's sorority sisters) and even with particularly potent individuals (Mom, one's brother, a hated classmate).

A Bakhtinian "space of authoring" is then very much a particular "zone of proximal development," and one that is extremely important in an explication of the development of identities as aspects of history-in-person. Bakhtin does not take development as the center of his concerns, as does Vygotsky. Yet he does write about differences between the neophyte, given over to a voice of authority, and the person of greater experience, who begins to rearrange, reword, rephrase, reorchestrate different voices and, by this process, develops her own "authorial stance."[12] Again, in Bakhtin's words:

> This process—experimenting by turning persuasive discourse into speaking persons—becomes especially important in those cases where a struggle against such images has already begun, where someone is striving to liberate himself from the influence of such an image and its discourse by means of objectification, or is striving to expose the limitations of both image and discourse. The importance of struggling with another's discourse, its influence in the history of an individual's coming to ideological consciousness, is enormous. One's own discourse and one's own voice, although born of another or dynamically stimulated by another, will sooner or later begin to liberate themselves from the authority of the other's discourse. This process is made more complex by the fact that a variety of alien voices enter into the struggle for influence within an individual's consciousness (just as they struggle with one another in surrounding social reality). (Bakhtin 1981: 348)

Brown and colleagues (1993) provide a fascinating glimpse of this process in their examination of how American girls (ages 11–15) use the media's representations of sexuality. They describe three different styles of usage, three different dispositions toward the discourse presented in the popular media: uninterested, intrigued, and resisting. Members of the first, and youngest, subgroup remain uninterested in sexual content and avoid reference to it. Girls of the second, and largest, subgroup are intrigued by the representations of sexuality. They readily take up the media's images into their own talk, but in a relatively naive manner. The discourse provides a model for their own experimentation with sexual activity, but the model is still idealized, and provides a kind of retreat, a place of safety unfreighted with the contest of real partners. It is this attachment of identified others to the images and voices of the media that distinguishes the third, and oldest, subgroup, which the authors call "resisting."

The critical stance of these older girls toward depictions of sexuality developed within social interaction, with the realization of heterosexual activity: "at least for some, as more personal experience is gained, the fantasy painted by the media is tarnished by the reality of imperfect bodies, distant boys, and lack of control, and the media image is resisted" (Brown et al. 1993: 180).

Bakhtin (1981) described how one makes the authority of discourse into one's own word (into "internally persuasive speech") by first personifying the "alien word," attaching to it the real limitations of specific others. As one girl said: "Guys I know are so afraid of getting it [AIDS] . . . because they're so scared, they're more likely to use rubbers—that helps with the pregnancy problem—could it be a blessing in disguise?" (192). Far from the tepid waters of *Blue Lagoon!* The girls have used this technique to authorize their own understandings of sexuality, opposing to the idealized blandishments of television and magazine not only the boys of their own acquaintance but the foibles of people in the news: "First it's Jim Baker and recently Gary Hart. All some stupid sex scandals that no one really pays attention to. It's all been one bore after another" (189). It is not that girls find a voice independent of the media's discourse; they make a voice by taking a stance toward the variety of media and personal voices in their worlds.

From Inner Speech to Social Speech

We can now continue our argument about joining Bakhtin's dialogism to Vygotsky's developmentalism. To reiterate, Bakhtin brings to Vygotsky's rather abstract concern with the social roots of psychological activity a differentiated conception of sociality, both of its cultural means (sociolects and speech genres) and of its actual, localized articulation (the sociolinguistics of utterance). Vygotsky highlighted the ways in which language and other cultural forms are socially interacted and, in many cases, taken in and made into personal tools for affecting one's own behavior. Bakhtin reminded us that these forms are by no means taken in as socially neutral:

> It might be said . . . that in the makeup of almost every utterance spoken by a social person—from a brief response in a casual dialogue to major verbal-ideological works (literary, scholarly and others)—a significant number of words can be identified that are implicitly or explicitly admitted as someone else's, and that are transmitted by a variety of different means. Within the arena of almost every utterance an intense interaction and struggle between one's own and another's word is being waged, a process in which they oppose or dialogically interanimate each other. The utterance so conceived is a considerably more complex and dynamic organism than it appears when construed simply as a thing that articulates the intention of the person uttering it, which is to see the utterance as a direct, single-voiced vehicle for expression. (Bakhtin 1981: 354–355)

Vygotsky saw the escape from the tyranny of environmental and internal stimuli as coming through the gift of collective symbols wielded toward the self. In Bakhtin, escape from being ventriloquated by first one and then another authoritative voice comes through the orchestration of and adoption of stances toward these voices, arrangements that are themselves suggested (perhaps) by texts. Indeed, the complementarity is apparent here. Had he studied Alcoholics Anonymous, Vygotsky might have emphasized the life story as a sign by which an AA member comes to turn himself from drinking and eventually toward a new habitual way of responding to messages inviting him to drink. Bakhtin would have weighted the life story more as a text that provides the AA member with a model for responding to the multiple and conflicting voices that speak to him about drinking and what it means that he is drawn to drink. Both enable us to see that consciousness and subjectivity are thoroughgoing products of the collective life, but their paths to that vision take us to different vantages on self-fashioning. Vygotsky leads us to look at a more asocial, developmental effect of cultural forms, as mediating devices of consciousness. Bakhtin leads us to capture the ongoing social struggles, and the continuous social demands, the responsibility of "answering," that follow along with the symbolic gift.

The task of "answering" can be understood in the relation between inner and social speech. Both Vygotsky and Bakhtin (Voloshinov 1986) conceive inner speech as the major site where social speech and other aspects of day-to-day existence are brought into history-in-person, into bodily reactions and responses. Yet we have seen that subjectification, the traffic of social speech to inner speech, is not a simple or direct process. It does not result in a facsimile of the social reproduced upon the body. Inner speech, though parented by social speech, is not a clone of social speech.[13] Nor does the translation of bodily reactions and responses into social speech belie the difference between the two. The constraints of "answering" are not so stringent that sameness is produced and dialogue superseded.

The social shaping of objectification, that is, the social responsiveness of the movement from inner speech to social speech, is given more significance and reported more vividly by Bakhtin than by Vygotsky. Vygotsky approached the issue of "objectification" mainly through his distinction between the "sense" of words and symbols and their "meaning." Inner speech works primarily through the "sense" of words and events; social speech depends more upon "meaning."

Vygotsky argued that children first learn to use words and, by implication, other symbols in interactive contexts. They develop a "sense" of a word that is bound up with these contexts of its use. Over time, from comparison of the various contexts in which the word is used, they gradually infer the "meaning" or cross-contextual referents of the word. Meaning is a part of sense, the stable or systematic aspect, the signification, of a word or symbol. Sense is contextualized, connotational; meaning is decontextualized, denotational. Vygotsky put the distinction in this way:

> A word's sense is the aggregate of all the psychological facts that arise in our consciousness as a result of the word. Sense is a dynamic, fluid, and complex formation which has several zones that vary in their stability. Meaning is only one of these zones of the sense that the word acquires in the context of speech. It is the most stable, unified, and precise of these zones. In different contexts, a word's sense changes. In contrast, meaning is a comparatively fixed and stable point, one that remains constant with all the changes of the word's sense associated with its use in various contexts . . . Isolated in the lexicon, the word has only one

meaning. However, this meaning is nothing more than a potential that can only be realized in living speech, and in living speech meaning is only a cornerstone in the edifice of sense. (1987c: 275–276)

Luria provides a concrete example of this distinction:

The Russian word "ugol'" (coal, charcoal) has a definite and clear meaning. It involves a black substance, most often having its origin in wood, that is derived from the carbonization of trees. It involves a substance having a definite chemical composition, the chief constituent of which is the element C (carbon). However, the sense of the word "ugol'" can vary greatly for different people in different situations. For the housewife, "ugol'" is associated with something used for heating the samovar or something used for heating the stove . . . For the artist who wishes to use "ugol'" (charcoal) for making a sketch, it is associated with the means he/she has for outlining a picture. And for the little girl who has smudged her dress with coal, the word "ugol'" carries an unpleasant sense. It is something that has spoiled her dress, something that evokes an affective feeling. (1981: 45)

Vygotsky implied that the process of moving from inner speech to social speech reverses the proportional weight given sense over meaning. One may (indeed must) personalize symbols, using them to direct one's own behavior, but to affect others—whose histories of usage undoubtedly diverge widely—meaning must predominate. Thus Vygotsky tended to reestablish a kind of gulf between the social/meaningful and the personal/sensible.

Voloshinov (1986), Bakhtin's collaborator, made the fusion of the social and the personal far more complete:

Psychic experience is something inner that becomes outer and the ideological sign, something outer that becomes inner. The psyche enjoys extraterritorial status in the organism. It is a social entity that penetrates inside the organism of the individual person. Everything ideological is likewise extraterritorial in the socioeconomic sphere, since the ideological sign, whose locus is outside the organism, must enter the inner world in order to implement its meaning as sign. (1986: 39)

Or, more briefly: "there is no such thing as experience outside of embodiment in signs . . . It is not experience that organizes expression, but the other way around—*expression organizes experience*" (85).[14]

Not only does the speaker depend upon the words of others to author his "own" experience, he also must answer to, respond to, the social relations between himself and his addressee in speaking socially:

> Even if a word is not entirely his, constituting, as it were, the border zone between himself and his addressee—still, it does in part belong to him . . . If . . . we take the implementation of word as sign, then the question of proprietorship becomes extremely complicated. Aside from the fact that word as sign is a borrowing on the speaker's part from the social stock of available signs, the very individual manipulation of this social sign in a concrete utterance is wholly determined by social relations. (1986: 86)

> . . . expression-utterance is determined by the actual conditions of the given utterance—above all by its *immediate social situation.* (85)

> The *word is oriented toward an addressee,* toward *who* that addressee might be: a fellow-member or not of the same social group, of higher or lower standing (the addressee's hierarchical status), someone connected with the speaker by close social ties . . . or not. (85)

> *The immediate social situation and the broader social milieu wholly determine—and determine from within, so to speak—the structure of an utterance.* (86)

Utterances, that is, are constructed between socially related and thus positioned persons. Since utterances organize experience (as the source of the psyche itself), we are strongly affected by the position we are cast into within interactions. Voloshinov (1986: 87) gives an example of hunger and its expression. How hunger is expressed and therefore experienced depends upon one's social group and position, and upon the immediate situation. Suppose you are a guest in an expensive hotel (here we modify Voloshinov's example somewhat). Imagine that you enter hungry and are kept waiting for your dinner order. Imagine how you might express/experience the hunger. Or imagine yourself a political protester, jailed and deprived of food long past mealtime. Would the expression/experience of hunger be different from that in the expensive hotel? Or imagine you are a host, deferring your own meal in order to provide food for your guests. How would you express/experience your own hunger in that situation? For Bakhtin and Voloshinov, moving from inner to outer speech is a process in which the immediate social situation profoundly shapes the experience from within. Their position is reminiscent of the situational determinacy we discussed in Chapter 1. We see people's behavior/experience/expression conforming (in the sense of being created together) with the social situation.

In short, the task of "answering to" others is a significant one. Bakhtin's insistence on dialogism, the always present, always operating, always demanding job of being in dialogue with others, with one's environment, forces attention to the present situation and entails its importance in the space of authoring. We are reminded how unlikely it is that one's identities are ever settled, once and for all. Dialogism makes clear that what we call identities remain dependent upon social relations and material conditions. If these relations and material conditions change, they must be "answered," and old "answers" about who one is may be undone.

Development

It is not just the present condition of dialogue that is important to Bakhtin. There is history in the person, which also significantly shapes social activity. Voloshinov emphasizes, perhaps overemphasizes, the determination of utterance by the social situation. But he also postulates a feature of inner speech that he calls a "stabilized social audience": "Each person's inner word and thought has its stabilized *social audience* that comprises the environment in which reasons, motives, values, and so on are fashioned" (1986: 86).[15] This stabilized social audience can be specific persons or more idealized ones.[16] It is in this sense of an idealized audience (like Mead's generalized other) that Bakhtin and Voloshinov speak of ideology: "any cognitive thought whatever, even one in my consciousness, in my psyche, comes into existence . . . with an orientation toward an ideological system of knowledge where that thought will find its place. My thought, in this sense, from the very start belongs to an ideological system and is governed by its set of laws" (1986: 35).

Ideology is not, however, an abstractum, held in the mind as a set of propositions or in habit as a set of tropisms. It is instead a habituated, figured world. So, though Bakhtin does not often speak to the point,[17] there must be periods (and these periods may even be the majority) during which one's authorial stance becomes stable, or, in our terms, an identity becomes habituated, usual, common. These topics return us to

Vygotsky's concerns with development, consciousness, and control. The "space of self-authoring" can be illuminated by Vygotsky's concept of the zone of proximal development.

For Joas (1985), resuming Mead's position in terms of voices, voices that are very alive in inner speech may, at some point, fade in their insistence on being answered. The authorial stance that one takes, the orchestration that one makes, may become stabilized. The behavior that was meaningful or indexical with respect to the identity has become habituated, fossilized in Vygotsky's terms, automatic. The complexes of behavior associated with and mediated by the identity have become second nature, and their production has moved out of awareness. The relation of the self to a significant audience (which is the identity's reference) has become stabilized and the orchestration is one that has endured.[18]

Development of Identity as Problematic

Yet, despite the ordinary force of habituation, a developmental perspective must problematize development. As our ethnographic studies have made clear, identity formation should not be taken for granted. As we have seen, many actors are not sufficiently engaged by the world of romance, say, or that of Alcoholics Anonymous that they ever form much of "an" identity relevant to the particular figured world, at least not for a long time. Sandy's concern with her peers' remarks about her anomalous behavior and lack of attractiveness faded with time. Instead, her life became focused around a particular friend. She and the friend moved away from campus life, and Sandy eventually quit school. Years later, in the follow-up interview, we discovered that she had only recently returned to the university and to the world of romance and attractiveness that she had eschewed.

Similarly, some participants in AA never identified enough to attend meetings faithfully or to produce an interpretation of their lives that accorded with the genre performed in the meetings. It is folly to assume that members of a voluntary group, or even members of an "involuntary"—an ethnic or racial—group are uniform in their identities (see Rouse 1995). There may be far less to participation than meets the eye.

In other cases there is more to participation than might be suspected. As we shall see in Chapters 10 and 12, many of the Naudadan women who participated in the Tij festival developed identities and senses of themselves that were important to them. Nonetheless, those aspects of identity associated with the critical commentary voiced at Tij and with the social world figured by Tij songs were dependent upon the recognition of others. Since Tij was only a day-long festival, confined to a small space in the year, it might seem that these women's identities had little importance to the broader public world. In fact, the identifications founded in Tij readily turned the women to new forms of action and combined with other figures of femininity to produce a broader realm of social and political activity. The "subterranean" (re)production of identities, within inner speech or first in the putatively closeted venues of specialized practices, the force of history-in-person, may erupt in social interaction with surprising and powerful results.

We conceive the space of authoring, then, as a broad venue, where social languages meet, generically and accentually, semantically and indexically, freighted with the valences of power, position, and privilege.[19] Such a large concept is needed if we are to understand more particularly the places each of us occupies, and if we are to develop notions of authorship, of social and personal agency, that do justice both to Vygotsky's keen sense of persons-in-history and to Bakhtin's heteroglossic (and, we might add, heteropraxic) social worlds. Such a concept is needed to do justice to the complexities of self-fashioning in everyday worlds.

9

Mental Disorder, Identity, and Professional Discourse

Identity is produced socially and culturally from the generic personae and scenery of our figured worlds as they are positioned in the hierarchies of power and privilege that relate fields of activity. In these landscapes, or rather in the movement across them, are wrought the bodily and mindful impersonations of the people, ourselves included, whom we come to know in our lived worlds. That is to say, identity responds to both the imaginary and the embodied communities in which we live. My Hamlet is not *Hamlet,* nor Olivier's Hamlet, though it has much to do with both. Identity is mediated, a product of both dis-stance and in-stance, just as, Voloshinov and Bakhtin argued, human utterance (and we extend this to all activity) is somehow generic (it is language) and somehow specific (it is talking) and is realized as meaningful action only to the extent that it is both.

Let us continue our consideration of the intricacies of mediation through which human agency produces itself. The capacity of self-management, Vygotsky's great concern, is the paradoxical and final mediation of human experience. Through its development "within" people, in their inner speaking and proactivity, the power of language and image to suspend the immediate and thus resituate persons finds its own locus of reflection. In the commentaries of inner speaking, one's own activity is represented and reenacted (or pre-presented and pre-enacted) and thus becomes the object of evaluation and manipulation.

Yet this autonomy of the self, or self-agency, depends upon one's capacity to produce the means that organize one's activity. There is a second half-step of "personalization" hidden here. It is not enough merely to direct one's behavior intimately. Rather, one must be able to produce the means of signification personally as well. The relevant situation of semiotic mediation must be freed from its domination by discourse; others' words must become "internally persuasive speech." This feat, however, is itself a kind of social product and a form of social location created by the encounter of manifold discursive practices. This place is Bakhtin's space of authorship. It is not simply a natural artifact of people's invariant self-consciousness, but an achievement of different degrees in practice.

The power of discourse to define persons, Foucault's notion of subjectification, had its first articulation in his works on madness (1965, 1979). We will return to it to show the pertinence of his rendition to any human agent and also to diversify its intentions for that agent. We will try to recover from Foucault a social world whose various practices, professional disciplines, and everyday congeries are not so regimented—whose forms of power, though surrendering none of their formative primacy, produce something less than an "epistemic" totality. Rather, they work often at cross-purposes, in what Engeström (1987) calls, in straightforwardly Marxian terms, contradiction. We will try to show how one person plays and is played within these diverse fields—within a space of authoring, to make at last a repertory of potential identities and, from that repertory, something more than Foucault's subject—though less than an imperial self.

The Project

The Triangle Mental Health Survey, from which the case we report here is drawn, had two purposes.[1] The first was to reconstruct the ways in which people who suffer from severe and persistent mental disorders learn to survive economically and socially. It was a study of subsistence strategies, of personal economies—something familiar to many anthropologists (such as Spradley 1970). We recruited people who were, so to speak, early in the career of their illness, those to whom the potentially damaging effects of mental illness were yet new. We followed each participant for two years, doing a formal interview every six months.

The first, third, and fifth of these interviews were broad and long survey instruments. We collected information on employment history, the everyday experience of work, job seeking, working and financial relationships, and the context of financial decisions. We also collected extensive information on broader social network and interpersonal relationships, psychiatric status, and dealings with the mental health system. This information was compiled for analysis by multivariate statistical techniques, particularly by a method called event history analysis. Again, the objective was to weigh the conditions that influence the choices people make and the changes in their lives after those choices.

Still, the interpretable models, both of measurement and of the social world, that make statistical analysis possible derive from ethnographic inquiry, from rigorous, naturalistic description, and from the professional, critical discourse that is its commentary. Hence the real core of the inquiry concerned our descriptive, "narrated" understanding of our participants' economic and social lives. We devoted the second and fourth interviews and parts of the surveys to what may best be called discussion. We sought a picture of subsistence more complete than fixed-format items could elicit, a picture that would take account of our informants' own conceptions of the events of their socioeconomic and sociomedical worlds.

We also interviewed persons important in our informants' lives ("significant others"), staff members of the local mental health centers, and hospital social workers who dealt with the centers. With significant others, who were usually family members, the interviews centered on the informant. With staff, rules of confidentiality often precluded our speaking of the informant. Instead, these interviews plumbed the usual practice and conception of treatment of mental illness in the local area. Both these types of interview included extensive discussion. Our purpose was to re-create the perspective of representatives of groups that play important roles in the process by which the social career of a "mentally ill" person is constructed.

In order to recruit our participants, to follow them in their peregrinations, and to prepare for the interviews, we had to do much observation and much "natural" as opposed to "interview" talk. We spent hours in the hospitals, in the mental health centers, in people's homes, neighborhoods, and communities.

The information we collected from all these sources was vital to the second objective of the study: to understand how participants created new identities in the face of illness often thought to be destructive of the self. This objective is tied to economic adaptation, especially in a society that so emphasizes work. The making of identity is the precondition, the context, an outcome, and a means to evaluate the facts of subsistence. It is what we as social beings are about.

I want to bring all these sources of information to bear upon a single case, to answer not the project's question but the more complicated one posed earlier: How do we understand a person's "subjectivity" and his agency? The case is that of the man we have called Roger Kelly. Over two and one-half years I interviewed Roger six times and talked with him much more frequently. I also interviewed his wife and his psychiatrist. I will briefly describe how Roger tried to refigure his life in the face of its massive disruption by mental disorder. Mental disorder creates conditions that approximate what Vygotsky would call an experiment, albeit a natural one: situations in which the ordinary courses of activity and the forms of psychological functioning are disrupted. Under such conditions, the arrangements of self-management, the social constituents of identity, are revealed.

Disorders and Persons

Psychiatric practice is a kind of subworld, a demimonde, with many kinds of activities and many differing characters who perform them, all brought together to manage the social disorders of mental illness. It refers to more than what psychiatrists do about illness. Instead "psychiatric" practice encompasses all that psychiatrists and allied health professionals, social service administrators, police and social workers, patients, and their friends and families do about mental illness. Here I will focus mainly on one range of activity, diagnosis, and one aspect of the figured world, psychiatric classification or nosology. There are several traditions and vocations for managing mental disorder, some medical, some psychological, and some sociological. The efforts to unite these traditions under the hegemony of medical psychiatry—what is sometimes called medicalization—have not yet erased their differences. The field is still strongly contested at certain points. Moreover, American psychiatry differs from European and other ethnopsychiatries.[2] Let us begin, however, as if psychiatric classification were a simple thing.

Four broad groups of mental disorders listed by the fourth edition of the Diagnostic and Statistical Manual of Mental Disorders, or DSM-IV for short (APA 1994), were represented among the participants in our study:[3] (1) the schizophrenias and other psychotic disorders, (2) major affective disorders, (3) anxiety disorders, and (4) personality disorders. The first category, schizophrenias, designates severe disturbances of cognition, especially social cognition, and of perception. The extreme or "florid" manifestations of schizophrenia, once called hebephrenia and now simply "disorganized" schizophrenia, are the prototypic figures of the mad person. This group is also known as *thought* disorders, in contrast with the second large category, *affective* disorders. Affective disorder is characterized by severe disturbances of mood or emotionality, and the most important variants are major depressive disorder (major depression) and bipolar affective disorder (manic-depression).

There is considerable overlap between these two categories when they are attributed to people by diagnosis on the basis of symptoms. Persons with schizophrenia have frequent (and even characteristic) disturbances of emotional expression, called "inappropriate" (silly) or "flat" (monotonous or uninflected) affect. Similarly, persons with affective disorders often exhibit some "psychotic" behaviors: delusions, hallucinations, and confused thinking. Psychiatrists distinguish the two by judging the relative pervasiveness and often the persistence of the two symptomatic types. It is not uncommon, as we shall see in Roger's case, for a person to receive a diagnosis of thought disorder on one occasion and affective disorder on another, especially when different diagnosticians weigh the evidence.

The last two groups differ from the first two by the presumed severity of their effects and by their causes, their etiology. Anxiety disorders (in which for convenience I also include dissociative, somatoform, and adjustment disorders) and personality disorders are widely conceived to be less disabling and often less enduring conditions. They are also thought to arise more from psychological and social (situational) causes than from physiological dysfunction. Experience and learning, especially under conditions of extreme psychological stress or trauma, are at the root of these disorders;[4] they are simply secondary or contingent to schizophrenias and affective disorders, whose causes are ordinarily thought to be neurological.

Anxiety disorders span much of what used to be termed *neuroses* in the psychodynamic literature. Persons with anxiety disorders often respond favorably to certain medications, the widely used anxiolytics or "minor" tranquilizers (distinguished from the antipsychotics or "major" tranquilizers, like Thorazine), of which Xanax and Valium are the best known. Hence, and despite the larger role accorded to environmental factors in their etiology, anxiety disorders are considered to have a neurological substrate, to involve a physiological impairment. They are arrayed as specific, limited or episodic, clinical syndromes with the thought and affective disorders on what is called Axis I in the DSM.

Personality disorders are yet again different. They are stable but maladaptive patterns of relation to one's environment (and oneself) whose etiology is regarded to be primarily developmental in the psychological sense, a matter of learning during infancy and early childhood. They are global disorders of people's cognitive, affective, and practical organizations, that is, their "personalities" as this discourse defines them. Their formation precedes, coexists with, and may outlast the various clinical disorders. Beginning with the third edition of the DSM, the personality disorders were assigned to a second axis, affirming their distinction from other disorders. They are figured, in the abstract form of the diagnostic space, to vary independently of the "clinical" disorders of Axis I.

Ideally, any diagnosed person should be described along both axes. Practically, however, psychiatrists focus on one aspect or the other and accord one or the other precedence in treatment. It is unusual for a person with schizophrenia to be diagnosed with a personality disorder, and rarer still for such a disorder to be given much time in treatment. Schizophrenia is taken to be the more important problem because it is the more serious illness. In contrast, an anxiety disorder that coexists with one of the severe personality disorders may receive little attention beyond a drug prescription.[5]

This system of psychiatric classification is a phenomenological or descriptive system. The types of disorder are differentiated according to observed constellations of symptoms called syndromes. The ideology of psychiatry maintains that people are distinct from their illnesses, insofar as the illnesses are presumed to originate from somatic *dysfunctions,* that is, diseases of the brain. Still, because the illnesses are noticeable from the ways people behave, psychiatric categories inevitably identify "personae," recognizable modes of activity—what I call signatures of practice. There is an understandable confusion, an elision, that pervades not only popular discourse but also the practical and informal discourse of professionals. Persons diagnosed with schizophrenia become "schizophrenics"; those diagnosed with borderline personality disorder, "borderlines."[6]

Each diagnostic type has instructions, so to speak, for the making of a kind of person, and these instructions are communicated within the interchange of staff members and their charges. It is not usually direct transmission, though that may occur when therapists teach clients about symptoms and their interrelations in order to encourage self-monitoring and to minimize, by early detection, the effects of "exacerbations" (active episodes of chronic illness). It is more strongly the unspoken concerns, the ways questions are posed, and the themes of psychological "instruments," that is, the expectations embedded in the means of gathering information, that allow people to infer the symptomatic activities that constitute the therapeutic identity.

Only prejudice and misunderstanding make us think that persons we consider mentally ill are not as aware of and attentive to the social framing of communication as "normal" people. We attune to one another by voicing, inflection, and accent, by spatial orientation and arrangement, by timing, rhythm, and pace, through the contexts and intertexts of speech and gesture. All the mechanics of practical communication apply to convey a sense of one's own position. Moreover, there is a growing popular literature on psychiatric disorders in which people may read about the basics of (disordered) behavior that constitute such "therapeutic" identities. Roger, whose life we consider here, made frequent use of both therapeutic and popular resources to understand and, I believe, to produce the forms of his own behavior and their place within a world of related figures.

Roger has had many diagnoses in his psychiatric history, but has finally received the one that is almost characteristic of debatable cases: borderline personality disorder. The name of this disorder describes it accurately. Something that is borderline exists between more settled or more clearly defined things. Borderline personality disorder is a most unusual category, whose history includes a wide range of earlier diagnoses—odd forms of schizophrenia, affective disorders, and earlier personality disorders—which are preserved in its diverse symptomatic profile. Its historical course records the attempt to assimilate what was originally a psychotherapeutic identity into a medical discourse. The notion of the "borderline" comes from the psychoanalytic or Freudian tradition, where it designated those people whose volatile cognitive and interpersonal behaviors fell between the recognized psychotic and neurotic forms of organization. Even today, professionals can largely agree about the ways borderlines behave in therapy. Yet, as American psychiatry moved from its largely psychodynamic orientation of the 1950s to a "medical" or somatic model of illness and treatment in the 1960s and 1970s, this psychotherapeutic understanding of the borderline came into contact with ambiguous or intermediate forms of thought and mood disorder that derive from the medical psychiatric tradition (for more on borderline disorders see Lachicotte 1992; Stone 1986).

What "borderline" behavior signified was thoroughly unsettled by this mixture, and new hierarchy, of discourses. What kind of disease or disorder produces the "borderline" syndrome, and what therapeutic forms best treat it, are still undecided paradigmatic questions, in Kuhn's sense (1962). They refer to broad differences in the ways the object world of the discipline is construed. Professionals talk about borderlines far more than any other kind of disorder, and their mixed feelings about the people called borderlines reflect in part the uncertain status of psychiatric diagnosis. This uncertainty is not limited to borderline disorders; it is general to the entire nosology. Psychiatry has a descriptive system, but the discipline wants something more. It wants to connect its various categories by a general theory of neurological causation, or etiology, but cannot do so. Hence, odd categories like borderline personality disorder persist. The very uncertainty epitomized by this diagnosis gives the people who hold it a kind of power, a freedom, in dealing with professionals.

The Case

Roger at our first meeting was a rather short and rotund man of thirty-three. He looked the part of a prosperous middle-class salaried worker. He was well kempt and well dressed and showed few of the irregularities of self-care that were apparent among other patients. Roger did not have obvious thought disorders, behavioral abnormalities, or disturbances of mood. His "affect"—emotional tone of speech and activity—seemed, on observation, full and appropriate to his situations. It was hard to see why Roger was on the ward at all—until you spoke with him. Roger had a bad case of alien voice. He spoke loudly, with little inflection, yet with a force and speed that intimated agitation or excitement. His tone of voice often did not match his other means of expression, either gestural or facial.

There was something "at odds" about Roger. Although a college graduate, he had been consistently underemployed during the ten years he had
worked. He was married, throughout the time I met with him, to a
psychiatric nurse. I first interviewed him during his fourth psychiatric
hospitalization.

The previous year had been a hard one for Roger. He had suffered
several setbacks at work, including a transfer that he regarded as a demo-
tion. His marriage had gone through a shaky period after four years of
relative tranquillity. According to his own assessment, Roger turned suicidal because he could not handle the stress of his job, of his and other
people's expectations:

> Yeah, I just—racing thoughts and fearful thoughts and you feel closed
> in and "I can't do this job another minute," and yeah they had me on
> something called the mini-stacker. And these big boxes would come
> down with hundreds of parts in them. I had to count all the parts;
> they're in bags, some of them weren't in bags. Then I had to put them
> on another conveyer belt, punch in a few things, and it would take
> them to the racks and stick them up in stock. But some days you'd
> stand around an hour. Your technician is looking at you the whole time.
> And I don't know what to do. And he'll give me some racks to fill and
> I've never done them before. And it just created a lot of tension, him
> looking at me all the time. You know, and other days you've got so
> much on that conveyer belt, it's backed up around the corner some-
> place. [It changes so much] and I like something steady.

Three times that year he made attempts on his own life and each time
was hospitalized on the psychiatric ward of the local hospital. These
were short stays. Once in the hospital Roger stabilized quickly and soon
left to return to work.

At our first interview Roger gave the impression of someone who had
found an explanation of his problems that he could accept: "It's a major
psychiatric illness . . . A sort of thinking and feeling disorder. I can't
always trust what I'm thinking and feeling." He remembered, in a gar-
bled way, the names the doctor had told him: "Obsessive-compulsive
disorder. Bipolar. Schizoid-affective personality disorder." But he pre-
ferred to call his illness "neurotic depression."

After this discharge Roger was placed on medical disability by his
employer. As time went on he bought into the therapeutic system in a big

way. He told me at our second interview: "Maybe I'm really sick. I'm trying not to face that fact, but it looks like I'm really sick, you know. I may have this disability for several years; I don't know." Each time I asked, he would say that his "meds" (medications) were the best regimen he had had so far. He took an active interest in "psychosocial" therapies as well, attending weekly sessions with his therapist, with his support group, and, from time to time, with his wife in couples therapy. He told me a year after we first met: "I have a 200-page notebook upstairs that has notes on sessions with every doctor, social worker I've ever seen. It helps."

It was as if Roger had taken on his recovery as a job, and he worked quite hard at it:

> I think all the time. You know, "How can I go back to work?" and "How can I be less fearful and less depressed?" and "Should I exercise more at the spa?" "Should I change vitamins?" "Should I eat different foods?" and "Should I talk to myself and be positive all the time?" You know, all the techniques I've read about, so I incorporate a few of them, but not all of them. There's so many ways that I don't know, you know, what I've read. I've read probably thirty, forty books, but I can't remember, you know, what was what. I probably should stop reading those things.

About the reading he confessed: "That's my major activity. Self-help books, trying to change my personality better, and things like that." But this therapeutic labor met with little success. Each of his attempts to complete the task—to return to "real" employment—ended quickly: "I don't know [what will happen]. I—the book store had four days open for a cashier job in January. I worked two days and I got very panicky attacks, fearful. I had to leave, so I only completed two days out of four. I'd like to go back to work part-time . . . but I don't know if I can last more than a couple of days."

Eventually Roger settled into a routine of television, volunteer work, and the rounds of therapy. He applied for federal income maintenance (SSDI), which he was granted after a year's wait. Two years from our first interview he told me: "I'm only 35. I mean I wi—kind of wish I was 60, and I was done with all . . . It would make things simpler, you know, 'I'm disabled. I'll just live out my last few years and do a little good works and try to enjoy my day.' But when you're only 35 there's pressure to get back in there and try it again. I've tried four or five times. I've been up in the hospital five times now. How many more times do I have to try?" When I last talked to Roger, eight months after he admitted this secret wish, to be older, he was still planning a return to college, a plan he had conceived over a year before. He was "better now" and thought once again that he could move back into a regular life.

Throughout our acquaintance Roger professed a mental illness without hesitation. His ideas about this illness, however, altered. Not only did he learn more about psychiatric illness in general; his conception of the nature of his own illness changed. By the second interview he had adopted "manic-depression," a combination of "racing thoughts" and enduring depression: "how about just a guy feels lousy and there's no known reason?" The lack of apparent reason for both his cognitive and affective states clinched the argument for him: "I'm starting to believe I'm very manic-depressive. Over the weekend I was quite suicidal, and there was no apparent reason. My wife was here—she's a psychiatric nurse, so that's as good as anything. And she said, 'You're recycling too fast or something. You need another antidepressant.'" It had to be something within him, not outside and visible. At this point Roger focused more upon his symptoms than upon any causal model of his illness. It was enough for him that his illness was a medical or somatic condition and not, as his parents seemed to suggest, a problem of character or will.

By the third interview, one year after the first, Roger had again modified his ideas about his psychological problems: "I've always thought they were mainly chemically related and I still think they are. But there is some personality. When you're growing up, I believe—that affected the way I . . . my behavior, my thinking patterns. That has not changed. It's a combination of personality and chemical, that's what I feel, more chemical though." After discharge from his baseline hospitalization Roger had begun working with a new psychiatrist. This doctor told me that he had changed Roger's diagnosis and the emphasis of his therapy. Previously Roger had carried a primary diagnosis of either bipolar disorder or schizoaffective disorder, depressed type.[7] His new psychiatrist decided, putatively on the basis of psychological testing, that Roger was basically "borderline," that is, personality disordered. He had told Roger his conclusion, and Roger had begun to take it to heart.

The next interview, six months later, found Roger still learning his roles. In fact he reverted to speaking about his "racing thoughts" and "twisted, negative thoughts," which he carefully referred to mania and depression and not to any character disorder. He was pleased about a new cognitive therapy he had begun to learn and a new support group for manic-depressives he was attending. His medication was once again effective, especially the Prozac recently prescribed for him. Roger was quite upbeat and full of plans to return to normal life. He spoke of a piece of land he and his wife had recently purchased in a resort area, of their thoughts of relocating there. He did not expect, nor had he for a long time expected, a cure. He told me, with a sophistication that bespoke his continual reading: "No, you're always a manic-depressive. You never recover. You have a chemical imbalance that's always there in your synapses and all that, your serotonin uptake. It's always got to be regulated." Still, at this time Roger was optimistic about his ability to manage the illness.

I encountered a chastened Roger six months later at our fifth interview. He had just returned from a three-day hospitalization instigated by a severe bout of "suicidal thoughts." When I asked about the cause of this incident, Roger, in his rather oddly earnest and naive way, began to report problems of character: "I would say . . . borderline personality disorder. That means a manipulator, a liar, social behavior is sometimes you get abnormal—things like that. I go to massage parlors occasionally. My wife knows about it. She's very upset. So part of my personality is like that." And, alongside the biochemical model of the previous interview, he recounted different causes: "My parents were highly critical of me growing up. I had to be perfect, get straight A's, so I was very hard on myself, so some aspects of my personality probably never developed as much as they should have. I stunt—stunted, stunted growth, that's what happened."

He sometimes mixed the two sorts of understandings: "My mother's some traits of it. I think it's genetic, a lot of that stuff. It's how you're raised, according to that book, by your parents. Whether they uh, reward you or punish you, they're critical or loving. They're there when you need them. Breastfed, too early, not enough—I mean there's lot of factors involved in that, sort of like chemistry. There's a lot of factors." Roger had been reading again and was attempting to piece his ideas together.

What amazed me, after the countless times I had heard staff complain about borderlines, was that he showed no resentment, shame, or anger at the dread label of borderline personality. To Roger, one psychiatric condition was equivalent to another. But, as he reminded me, "I'm not really a full blown borderline . . . No. No, I got a book on it. I let my doctor—my psychiatrist—he said it's a good book, but I haven't been sexually abused as a child, I remember, nothing like that."

In the two years from our first interview to our fifth, then, Roger consistently identified himself as a mentally ill participant in the world of mental health care. But his ideas of his illness had deepened and broadened in the ways predicated by an ever fuller involvement in that world. Roger's final report of the extent to which his illness affected his life is no surprise: "It permeates you. It's everything, like friendships . . . it's in me. It affects everything. Everything from my relationship to God, who won't heal me, to my wife—try to cheat on her, to my parents—call them twice a day. I mean my best friend, I told his girlfriend he was seeing somebody else, and, I mean I've really screwed up lately. I uh, it's just—it's in my life. It affects my thinking and feeling, and my behavior. It's me. I'm who I am."

Public and Private Politics

As Roger left the public world centered upon work and the day-to-day accounting of common interaction, he entered into different means for the making and interpretation of behavior. These psychiatric means are not completely alien to the everyday, so influential has medical practice become. But the more removed one becomes from the ordinary arenas of interaction, the more salient are these special "technologies of the self." Not all people who find themselves so secluded agree with, or even attend to, the psychiatric line. But their opposition or indifference leaves them in the same ambit as those, like Roger, who accept it wholeheartedly. The power of social circumscription, what has been called "role constriction," sets persons with psychiatric disorders apart, despite their wishes and sometimes considerable efforts to counteract it.[8]

There were other reasons for Roger's willingness to adopt psychiatric ideas. Roger's inability to work was the central fact of his predicament in the eyes of others. It was both the great puzzle and the great complication of his everyday life. Work is, in many social venues of the United States, the central claim to personal competency and personal worth. When work is denied us, that "failure" requires explanation, and the explanation comes to serve as defense for our endangered personhood. Roger devoted an inordinate amount of discursive labor to this subject, and his explanation reveals much about his local as well as our society's world.

His mental illness obviously entered into a longstanding interchange among Roger, his wife, and his family. His wife told me: "There's always been a big competition in the family. And he was the one that went to four years of college, and you know, everybody wanted him to be a lawyer, and here's his brother who didn't go to any college and took a few courses at IBM and has a very good position in IBM." Roger's failure required justification if he was to reclaim some place of value among his close associates. He received little help or understanding of his efforts, as he himself admitted: "I'm very closely tied to my parents. I don't know why. They never—I'm probably trying to get what I never got from them. I don't know—love and understanding. All I got was criticism and 'you can do better' . . . They wonder why I'm not at work now. They don't understand mental illness. They think, you know, if you get off the pills, get off this, everything'll be OK." This sense of competitiveness in economic achievement, the emphasis on self-control, the giving and withholding of affection as motivation toward achievement, are stereotypical features of American "middle-class" family life. Roger's quite obvious failure to meet these standards, and the consequent disapproval he met from his family, was a lasting dilemma in his social life and for his self-understanding.

If from his family Roger met expectations that he found hard to fulfill, he encountered an opposing pressure from his wife (and his psychiatrist). She told me:

> When he sees a job in the paper that he really would want, I have to think in my mind, is he really going to be able to perform that type of work, and yet I don't want to be the one to be the bad guy and say "Roger, I don't think you can really do that." You know, I think he ought to look into job opportunities as he's been doing, but I think there's some things that he's just never going to be able to do. And until he goes and applies for these jobs and realizes he's not qualified he's, you know, it's hard for him to accept that.

She saw her task as helping Roger lower his expectations about employment, in line with her notions of the functional impairment that mental disorders cause. From her stance as a psychiatric nurse, she had adopted in her domestic relations both the separation between Roger and his illness and the power of illness over person that is the popular way of figuring this separation. But this toleration too was a problem for Roger. With his family, the distress that mental disorder caused Roger disappeared in the disguise of Roger's defective will. With his wife, Roger's own thoughts, feelings, and interests disappeared within the manifestations of illness.

It is not illness itself but the interrelations of various fields of practice that determine the possibilities of self-expression. It is easy to guess what impelled Roger's conflation of identity work and work in its usual sense. How Roger used psychiatric notions strategically in his everyday relations is rather more interesting. From his local world, shaped by the counterpositions and alliances among his wife, psychiatrist, parents (and silently, his brother), and employer, Roger crafted a response, which was at once his identified place and his proper labor.

It was not a singular response. When speaking about his parents or his employers and co-workers, Roger usually emphasized his manic-depression. Both medical psychiatry and much of popular psychological discourse conceive this illness, bipolar affective disorder, to be primarily a somatic disorder, caused by a dysfunction of neurotransmission. Susceptibility to the illness is also thought to be genetically based. Thus having manic-depression is not one's own fault. Roger opposed its unwilled disruption of his own capacities to his parents' and co-workers' interpretation that he lacked the willpower or the energy to change his misbehavior. He borrowed the authority of medicine to answer other people's claims against him. At the same time, the persuasiveness of this psychiatric identity increased as it provided Roger with a way to legitimate his past activity and to maintain the relationships he valued. It is appropriate, when one is afflicted by a disease that incapacitates, for one's therapy to become one's entire work. So Roger justified his withdrawal from the world of employment by his identity as manic-depressive.

This construction drew authority from explicitly biological models of bipolar disorder to oppose Roger's parents' ethnopsychology of "will." Unlike the latter, which locates disorder as misbehavior, within the realm of self-control, Roger's adopted understanding blamed no person, only his neurophysiology. It both signaled and consequently encouraged the restitution of his relationships, with himself, his wife (who shared this assessment of his disorder), and even his parents. Moreover, it explained the propriety of Roger's disability and the promise of his (chemo)therapeutic regimen. In his discourse manic-depression came up commonly with talk of work, of disability, and (however paradoxically) of hope.

When speaking of his wife and his psychiatrist Roger usually took a different line. He emphasized his borderline persona. After all, Roger's wife did not doubt his incapacity or the necessity of his treatment. If anything she went too far: her fatalism and her obsession were even greater than Roger's. Roger's life apart from his illness—what he wanted to do and what he could do, not what he was made to do by disease—was nearly lost in their dealings. Hence Roger changed the terms of interpretation. The personality disorders, to the extent that they are learned, matters of experience, remain within the scope of will. We can unlearn what we have learned, if we want to. Roger drew upon this sense about personality disorders to oppose his wife's (or his psychiatrist's) reduction of him to his disease.

By becoming "borderline" at the proper times and places, Roger empowered a sense of his agency, his active self-expression, without letting go of the legitimate disabilities of illness. Borderline personality disorder is peculiarly adapted to this kind of double posture because of its undecided position in psychiatric knowledge. It carries still the signs of schizophrenia, of affective disorder, and of character disorder, in a continually rebalanced mix. And the powerfulness attributed to its volatility, the fact that its balance may come apart at any moment, served Roger well. It went far to ensure that he, the actor "Roger," would not be dismissed or overlooked. So Roger reproduced a sense of personal power through his borderline identity.

The association of willfulness that colors the personality disorders does two kinds of discursive work here. It differentiates and reasserts Roger's self-activity, his autonomy, in the face of his wife's presumption (and cultivation) of his debility, and yet it leaves that activity somehow unwilled, beyond everyday self-management, and hence in the realm of therapy. Personality disorders (like the classical neuroses) double the "self" through its division into impaired (misbehaving) and intact (help-seeking) parts. They thereby afford inculpable opportunities for strategic action—which Roger pursued.

This talk, like the actions it describes, is directed to his wife. When Roger addressed his parents through the notion of the borderline, he did so in a way that did not accede too much to their view of his problems as willful. Instead, he indirectly reassigned culpability for that ill-formed will to his parents, according to the developmental etiologies conventional to these personality disorders. Roger's control over his social misbehavior was thus vitiated, his actions recast into a reenactment of an originally pathological relation of parents to child. Work has little to do with this settling of personal relationships, and Roger's talk of it did not coincide with his borderline discourse. Its absence may also have been strategically significant—though such an attribution is always chancy. "Work" disability is ordinarily associated with only the most severe personality disorder, which Roger did not avow. His borderline identification could not serve him, and was not invoked by this crucial problematic.

Hence Roger's bipolar and borderline identities participated in different social and imaginative landscapes. They were differently addressed and differently answerable, in Bakhtin's terms, yet they were not thoroughly separable. A figure in the realm of popular psychology united them: the idea of stress: "[My doctor] said depression and borderline personality disorder. That's what he labeled it as. And I can't handle stress. We agree on that." Though Roger clearly described the conditions of his work and personal life in terms any reader would call stressful, he did not use the word itself until the third interview (just quoted). The context was one in which he was asked to represent his doctor's understanding of his illness. "Stress" provided the figurative grounds of their agreement. Over the next year Roger increasingly used the notion of stress as a point of interchange not only between the differing understandings afforded by his dialogue with psychiatry but also between his (ever more psychiatrically informed) conceptions and those of his parents and friends: "[My parents] say, 'You can't take . . .' well, they finally realized I can't take stress, and they think I'm a little lazy. That's what they think."

This usage is not idiosyncratic. Just as, in contemporary Euroamerican social life, a common medium for material interchanges has developed in the form of money, so too a common medium for "psychic" interchanges has developed under the rubric of "stress." The concept takes a negative mode, somewhat like impedance, resistance, or "load" in engineering, and it predicates a differential between inner and outer, personal and public economies. In the metaphorical world of architectonics (using Bakhtin's Kantian terminology) the "person" or "individual" is conceived as a integral system of balances among constituents, as conditioned by its environments. When changes of state occur, such as when an interchange with the environment takes place, the equilibrium of the system is necessarily disrupted.

In Roger's words: "And, like I said, you don't know what feeling is normal, so it's a little bit of both, really. But mainly irrational thinking. Then I get under stress. I'm thinking irrationally and feeling fearful. So it's really a combination that kicks in under stress." Stress is the (retrospective) measure of effort requisite to reestablish the (interior) balance of the person, the cost of living in alterable circumstances. Projectively, it is the measure of an environment's potential disequilibrating effect. The notion was popularized in psychology by Selye (1956), though it has been extended from its original and calculable physiological settings to less measurable, "qualitative" changes of psychological state.[9]

"Stress talk" is a genre of both popular and professional psychologies, whose chronotope—Bakhtin's phrase for the definitive figured world of a form of discourse—is the abstract landscape just described. Different persons, different identified systems, are presumed to have differing susceptibilities to stress. (Roger said: "My stress tolerance is very low. I don't know why my stress tolerance is so low. I've never figured that out.") This susceptibility may come from either genetic causes or historical (developmental) ones. Likewise, different environments predicate differing stresses, for any number of reasons. In order to calculate actual "stress," one must know both functional components: systemic capability and environmental energetics. At this abstract level, the figured world of stress unites first the biological and sociological conditions of mental illnesses and then the different forms of illness as so many products of these generic conditions. Stress warrants that, no matter what variant illnesses one has, there exists a common ground for them in the relation of body to social world. As Roger told me: "And the other thing is sensitivity to stress, and depression, and fear, and obsession. They're all tied in. When I get stressful, depression, fear, and obsessional thinking kick right in, so I can't take much stress." It also warrants, by extension, the integrity of a person—"I can't take much stress"—inhabited by the personae named by these illnesses.

Artifacts and Associates

Roger used various tools to revise and establish his new identifications and understandings of himself. These mediating devices included the various behavioral templates provided by accounts of diagnostic categories (borderline, manic-depressive, obsessive-compulsive, and so on), by therapeutic regimens (cognitive "chaining" and replacement, de-escalation), and by Roger's own rehearsals (the therapy book) and others' renditions (self-help and support groups). Apart from these specifics, there was the structure, the means of organization provided by the token of the activity itself. Performing therapy, attending self-help groups, reading both popular and professional treatises—these activities express, by their very sensibility, a dispositional lesson. They signal to ourselves as well as others where we are headed and with whom we travel. They are the means we use to reproduce the desire for particular identities. But there is a price.

Access to these activities and to the specific identities they produce is a matter of social situation and negotiation—of, in a word, politics. By participating one adopts specific affiliations, disaffiliations, and relations of self-production. Roger's course was not smooth. He did not settle on one psychiatric identity but maintained several versions of himself: as bipolar, as obsessive-compulsive, as borderline. These were tied to the activities and agents from which they were mastered. As either the situational or the institutional relations among these activities and agents changed, so did Roger's identifications (or at least the work needed to maintain them). The change of psychiatrists, of therapeutic groups, of the relations between wife and family, wife and psychiatrist, psychiatrist and group, even abstract changes in the authority of psychiatric diagnoses, all had "direct" effects upon Roger's self-conception. Bakhtin would say that, even as means of the imagination, semiotic devices remain others' words and acts, others' speaking, others' voices. By using them one gains the material toward identity because they come socially identified. At the same time that you inform yourself, you open yourself (even in your own thoughts and feelings) to the social world.

Yet the world of inner speaking, of the imagination and consciousness, is not a simple copy of the social world. We have neither the time nor the resources to do analytic justice to Roger's history of self, to how prior self-concepts and self-understandings shaped the course of his self-reformation. What Roger's case shows, however, is that one's personal agency is not the creation of a self that is always uniquely one's own. Rather, agency takes shape in what we call the space of authoring. This space is formed, both within us and outside us, by the very multiplicity of persons, who are identifiable positions in networks of social production, and of worlds of inner activity that are also scenes of consciousness. When we act, whether that act is instrumental or imaginative, we "move" through this space figuratively. None of us is occupied singularly: we are not possessed by one identity, one discourse, one subject-position. Each act is simultaneously a social dynamic, social work, a set of identifications and negations, an orchestration or arrangement of voices. And our sense of self comes from the history of our arrangements, our "styles" of saying and doing through others. The freedom that Bakhtin calls authorship comes from the ways differing identifications can be counterposed, brought to work against one another, to create a position, our own voice, from which we work.

Roger opposed several identities drawn from psychiatric discourse to those cast for him by his wife, family, co-workers, psychiatrists, even by himself. We believe he did not do so either to destroy or deny or to assert or take up any one identity—to say that he was truly one person or another. Rather, he orchestrated these differing identities, differing voices, to shape a place for his own activity. When speaking of his family and friends, and of work, Roger counterposed his manic-depression, and thus signally the authority of the persons, his wife and psychiatrist, and the situations of therapy that were its expressive source. When contesting the confines of these last associations, he drew upon his borderline persona, referring to the strong (though in this case negative) voices of psychiatrists and the popular psychological literature, to the disorder of everyday impulse that wrecks the discipline of therapy. His agency was no one personage but the ensemble of persons that lived around and within him.

It is therefore entirely conceivable that Roger saw no conflict between identities founded upon the two types of disorder, that they simply coexisted for him, manifest at different times in differing forms. The figure of stress, which is the popular and professional point of some resolution of these differences, seems, in Roger's case, an afterthought. Or, stress is not so much the reality as the possibility of unity; not so much the source, the original, from which different forms of personal disorder arise as the point of exhaustion into which they collapse. Hence it is not really the resolution, but rather the recognition of these different figurations of personhood, these "psychiatrized" identifications. Roger's case teaches us one final lesson: there is no necessary integrity to self-understanding, but there are degrees of relatedness among the partial selves that respond to sets of our associates, our multiple others (see Gergen 1994). That is a story we will have to leave to another time.

Michel Foucault has taught us that historical and political actions, on the grand scale, created first "insanity" and then "mental illness" from madness, a notion of behavioral and cognitive aberration hardly divorced from everyday life. We must begin to amend his vision at the point where it seems whole, at the point where the variety of the forms of life, which after all was one of Foucault's motives, becomes subsumed in the habitual ordering of these forms. When it is forgotten that such an order must be reproduced, when it is acknowledged that the reproductions themselves are identical, then one must think again. Foucault must always be brought to contend against himself.

It is also a mistake to concentrate too much upon the course of discipline, for example, of interchanges that move only from therapist to client, however fully explored. As Roger's and my other case studies show, people participate in several discourses and fields of activity relevant to their "psychological" identities. They attend, besides the formal therapeutic activities of hospitals and mental health centers, self-help, support, and advocacy groups that are more loosely connected to the institutional psychiatric apparatus. The mass media also provide a substantial and less regular means toward psychological self-formation. Self-help and popular psychological literature and televised talk shows and documentaries take the discursive and practical subjects of psychiatry and medicine into a realm where they associate and contend with forms of subjectivity and agency created and preserved under different social and cultural worlds.[10] And, while these means are one important vehicle of the medicalization of everyday life, they are also an opportunity for the transfiguration of the properly medical, for what Bakhtin called the carnivalization of authoritative discourse. We will return to this interplay of figured worlds in Chapter 11.

Finally, if one penetrates even further into the underlife (Goffman 1961) of psychiatry, one reaches "common parlance" and the cultural subworlds that persons with mental disorders create among themselves and with consociates of other practical fields. What we call the everyday, or everyday practice, is a reality that is everywhere diverse and at the same time substantially whole. That is to say, it is composed within the interrelations of many specific practices. Any one instance of the everyday is both peculiar in the practical arrangement of the moment and locale and generic in its dependence upon the institutional (extralocal) and historical conditions of the discursive and practical fields.[11] Roger's and all our worlds are local, as Bakhtin would insist, only to the extent that they seek the general, and vice versa. Our identities are formed within, and serve to mediate, this dialogic movement between extension and intention in social life, between worlds at play and ways of self-discipline.

10

Authoring Oneself as a
Woman in Nepal

In the spring of 1990 a people's pro-democracy movement overthrew the one-party panchayat system in Nepal, which had been in place for thirty years. Political parties again became legal, and in the spring of 1991 elections officially restored the multiparty or *bahudal* system of government. In the interval between these events, several remarkable incidents took place in Naudada, the Hindu mixed-caste hill community where Skinner and Holland did ethnographic research.[1] Before the elections, women from one of the eastern hamlets *(gaon)* began a procession toward Tarara Gaon, the administrative center and gathering place of the community, a place renowned for its tea shops where men came to drink and gamble. Along the way women from other gaons joined them, and together they marched, shouting their demands: "Men, stop your drinking and gambling! Let women inherit property! Give women equal rights! Don't marry off your daughters so young!" In another incident, a group of women brandishing sticks entered some of the local teashops to break drinking glasses, bottles of distilled alcohol *(raksi)*, and the equipment used to make the homemade brew. A third incident took place after a woman was beaten by her drunken husband. A group of about fifteen women, armed with sticks, descended on him and threatened to beat him if he ever again abused his wife.

Both the women's banding together to voice demands at odds with patriarchal power and their retaliatory acts against men were unusual, perhaps unprecedented, events for this area of Nepal. On the surface they were surprising because, in Naudada, women as well as men voiced notions of the "good woman" that resonated with Brahmanical teachings about how women should be and act.[2] Women enacted this figured world and its identity of the good Hindu woman in many ways in their everyday lives.

But a closer look suggested that women also felt anger and resentment toward the ways this narrativized world defined them as women. Disrupting currents were also evident in relational aspects of identity. Skinner's research showed how young girls and women developed a sense of their position relative to others in the social world, a sense that as women they were entitled to, or denied, access to certain spaces and activities. There were movements into, and thus contestations with, the positional identity associated with the "good Hindu woman." The women's protests exemplified these contestations of self and of gender relations. The women's complex and contested self-understandings developed and were produced in particular social, historical, and cultural sites or activities, and their development allowed "good" Naudadan women to rapidly transform into angry, active protesters who called their treatment into question through their words and deeds.

Growing Up Female in Hindu Nepal

Skinner's research in Naudada focused on children's roles in the coproduction and reproduction of gender and caste identities and relations. Skinner examined the organization, contexts, and content of socialization activities in which children participated and the words and actions of thirty boys and girls, aged eight to eighteen, as they responded to and co-created these structures, activities, and cultural knowledge. We will concentrate here on the ten girls she followed most closely, and on what they conveyed to her about their lives in daily encounters, tape-recorded interviews, and, for the literate ones, written accounts.

The girls often portrayed themselves as good workers, good girls, and obedient and honorable daughters. These identities relevant to work, gender, and family were central ones for females in Naudada, and were figured by the Brahmanical model of the expected life path for women. When Skinner asked them to describe themselves, most girls recited the good habits they had and the bad ones they avoided. A typical response included most of the following characteristics and behaviors: "I am a good girl. I love those who are smaller than me. I obey my parents. I never tell a lie; I always speak the truth. I get along with others. I don't talk unnecessarily with boys, and I don't quarrel or scold others. I don't steal from others' fields. I stay in the house and do my work. I do my studies. I only get angry if someone scolds me."

Parbati, a thirteen-year-old Damai girl (Damai is a lower caste considered "untouchable"),[3] described herself this way: "I am a very good girl. I don't fool around with others . . . I am very good . . . I don't speak that much also. I will say *"Namaskar, didi"* ("Greetings, older sister") on the spot when I meet you. I am like that. I am very good. I don't even like to fool around much. In my being, I am very good. I do my own work by myself." And Muna, a Damai girl of fourteen, said: "I don't speak lies, and when somebody speaks a lie against me, I get furious, but I don't try to pick fights . . . I don't get angry . . . I have lesser quarrels and I don't speak nonsense." These self-descriptions did not vary much by caste or socioeconomic status. Here is Maiya, an eleven-year-old Chetri girl: "I am a good, nice girl. I don't get mad at anyone. I don't fight. I don't steal . . . I don't deceive anyone and don't lie."

The girls' responses had a certain canned quality. They were recitations that varied little in content or format. In these self-descriptions the girls were rehearsing themselves in relation to the figured world of the expected life path of the "good Hindu woman." In daily life and in rituals experienced in childhood and beyond, girls were presented with a variety of messages related to what was expected of them as women. Most socialization contexts promoted the notion of a "good woman," one who follows the ideal life path as set out in Brahmanical writings and teachings—the dominant ideology of gender identities, roles, and relationships in Naudada as in other Hindu areas of Nepal and India. The model presumed that Hindu women, except in cases of bad luck or bad morals, would follow a particular life path (see Bennett 1976, 1983; Caplan 1985; Das 1979; Skinner 1989, 1990; Stone 1978). The generic woman's roles in this figured world were family-centered, and the favored characteristics were those which supported the patriarchal family.

In the storyline envisioned in this world, a girl is first a daughter and a sister. She grows up surrounded by relatives who urge her to cultivate the habits that will mark her as a good daughter, wife, and daughter-in-law. From their teachings and scoldings she learns to be a hard worker, obedient and respectful to elders, and shy, gentle, and virtuous. In the next stage of the life path she is married soon after she reaches puberty. With marriage she becomes a daughter-in-law, a wife, and eventually a mother. She is hard-working, faithful and devoted to her husband, obedient and helpful to her mother-in-law, and a respectable woman in the community. With the birth of children, especially sons, she acquires a valued identity—what some have called the central or prototypical identity of women: that of mother (Stone 1978). A woman who bears sons proves herself to be a good woman with a good fate. Finally, as a mother-in-law, a position accorded higher status than other female roles in the family, she can direct and control the lives of her daughters-in-law. At the end of the life path, ideally, a woman never becomes a widow. A good and virtuous woman, through ritual observance and daily practice, ensures the health and long life of her husband and dies before him.

Women in Naudada were interpreted and evaluated against this narrativized world with its ideal woman and her life course. Those who deviated from the life path of the good woman were judged to be aberrant and problematic in some way. Women who withheld their labor from domestic and agricultural tasks, who gossiped about their husbands' shortcomings, committed adultery, contradicted their mothers-in-law, did not give birth to sons, or were widowed were the subjects of gossip. Good women labored for the benefit of their households. Good women never talked unnecessarily or wandered about to malinger, gossip, or flirt.

Within this figured world, women who deviated from the life path did so because they were intrinsically bad or the victims of bad luck. A woman who did not have children, for example, was presumed to be barren, and this condition was seen as a punishment for her misdeeds in a previous life. Widows, too, had fallen off the expected life path. They had the bad fate to outlive their husbands. Widows were to be pitied, but they were sometimes feared as witches.

Talk about "bad" or "sinful" women was part of daily conversation, a great deal of which included evaluations of self and others in relation to this figured world. Devi, a Chetri woman in her late twenties, talking with Skinner about women they both knew, explained that one was a *nathi* (a flirt or a woman who goes with men other than her husband). Another was a *papini* (female sinner) because she did not feed her grandchildren while her daughter-in-law was working long days in the fields. One of Devi's neighbors was a bad woman (*naramro aimai*) because she was very jealous of others and mistreated her father, who lived with her. The many negative types that commonly figured in such conversations—the *boksi* (witch), *radi* (widow—with the connotation of bitch and whore), *aputri* (barren woman), *alacchini* (a woman who brings bad luck to her household), *sande aimai* (a woman who acts masculine, like a bull)—were all characters who had gone awry in the figured world of good women's lives.

By the age of four or five, and in some cases even younger, girls knew the meaning of *chori* (daughter), *sasu* (mother-in-law), *sauta* (co-wife), and other terms that designated kin roles and relations. By seven or eight, they also knew words for women who had deviated or threatened to deviate from the expected life path and could begin to elaborate the meaning of these words in relation to this figured world (Skinner 1990): they knew these types were considered bad, and they knew why they were bad.

The appropriation of these terms began very early, especially in cases where the words were used as insults. Even children of four or five knew that *radi* (widow) was not a good word to say. It was one of the most common insults used for any female regardless of her age (and *radiko chora*, or widow's son, was often used as a term of abuse for males). It was used often in scolding and cursing. While the younger girls knew only that a radi was a bad thing to be called, the girls of eight or so knew why a radi was bad. They knew it was bad for a woman to outlive her husband. Likewise, from scoldings the younger girls knew only what behaviors they were supposed to avoid, whereas the older girls had acquired a broader understanding of the proper comportment of daughters in relation to the figured world. The older girls also talked frequently of life as a daughter-in-law and wife and knew the codes of behavior they would be expected to follow and the characteristics they would be expected to exhibit in these roles.

These evaluative terms for women indexed a moral universe, a figured world, and served as cultural resources in the process of identity formation (Skinner 1989, 1990). Girls developed understandings of gender-related terms and the discourse of evaluation in specific sites and activities such as everyday events of gossiping and scolding; and they used these terms to identify themselves and others as particular kinds of moral actors in the figured world of domestic relations in Naudada. They scrutinized their own and other women's behavior through the lens of this discourse. They described themselves, both to themselves and others, in ways that defined them as good daughters or good women, and they attempted to avoid or dispute the negative labels.

This evaluative discourse created an inner voice of censure and divided women from one another. Aruna, a Damai girl of fourteen, reported that anyone, even a close girlfriend, would say a girl was bad if she went to a boy's house. Kamala, a fourteen-year-old Chetri girl, complained that she could not show her anger because others would say, "How angry that daughter seems to be." Tika, a Damai girl of fifteen, described herself as being on a "straight line." Then she talked about a woman who had run away with her husband's brother: "It is better to take a straight line than to do such a scandalous thing. A good wife stays with her husband; a bad one leaves and goes with another." Kamala, talking about the same event, said others were saying that this woman was a *kukurni* (female dog) and had spoiled the prestige/honor *(ijjat)* of her family.

It appears that these girls not only knew the expected life path and the behaviors that counted as those of a good woman but also embraced these concepts and behaviors as ways to define themselves. They were figured by this world, valuing themselves and others in its terms. They desired to be and be seen by others as good selves. Their appreciation of the figured world was not a product of its intrinsic persuasiveness, however. It was not so much that they were drawn to the image of the good woman as that they were "backing into" it to avoid negative evaluations. For example, Kamala and her friends experienced many scoldings in which they heard evaluations of themselves and others. They cared about what other people thought of them, and they did not wish to dishonor their families. They tried to avoid behaviors that would categorize them as a bad type. In self-censoring their actions this way, they backed into attachments to good and valued identities, and developed claims to being good daughters and future daughters-in-law. Kamala said she and her friends often heard women talking about what made a good wife and daughter-in-law:

A good wife never criticizes her husband, and she never complains about her husband to other people . . . A good daughter-in-law always gets up early in the morning, and she does all the work she has to and obeys her mother-in-law. She obeys her husband. She does not run away to her natal home. She never steals to eat, and she does not steal corn that grows in another's field. Daughters-in-law are not good if they do not obey their mothers-in-law or if they move about here and there. They do whatever they like. They steal, and they spend their time at others' houses. They go to festivals sometimes.

Kamala thought that, if she had to get married, she would be a good daughter-in-law, but she recognized that it would be very difficult: "One has to work very hard. We all have to act good. We are not supposed to quarrel, lie, or steal. At home, we may not obey our parents all the time, but we must obey at our mother-in-law's." A friend of Kamala's added that women whose husbands beat them "should just take it."

As portrayed so far, the Naudadan girls seem to have been totally absorbed in all that the figured world promoted for women in their domestic life path. The reproduction of patterns of gender relations practiced by previous generations seemed assured. From the comments we have quoted, we might assume the girls accepted the life path and were committed to its views of marriage and their roles as daughters-in-law and wives, or, at least, that they acquiesced to their fate and silently complied with the dominant ideology, as some authors have suggested South Asian Hindu women do (see Dhruvarajan 1989). Their identities as figured by this world seem to be their only views of self.

This picture of their self-understandings becomes more complex, however, when we consider other things the girls said and did. Although they laid claim to being good girls and good daughters and said that if they married they would try to be good daughters-in-law and wives, they also questioned the expected life path, were critical of the unequal treatment of men and women, expressed anger and sadness about the way they were treated because they were female, and schemed to avoid marriage. They were gaining a sense of their position vis-à-vis others, noting their relative lack of privilege and power. They were developing relational identities along with the figured identities.

Maiya, like many of the other girls, compared her life to that of her brothers. In her first interview, in response to the question "Are you happy to be a girl?" Maiya replied that she would rather be a boy because "sons don't have to work hard. Girls have to carry water and cut grass, while the sons can just sit and eat." Sunita, a ten-year-old Bahun, said she had argued with her parents against the idea that only boys should go to school. She told her parents, "You are sending boys [to school], why not send girls?" Tika also complained: "If I were a son, I would have been allowed to study. Since I am a daughter, I did not get to study."

Muna, when asked what she thought about the future, replied: "In the future, now when I see others get married and have fights in their new home, um . . . why do we give daughters to another's house? These thoughts play in my mind. I think about it . . . If I am not able to study and not able to work, um, if I am not treated well after I am married in my new house. When I think that this may happen to me in the future, I fear it and am very worried." In trying to express her sadness and sense of injustice, Muna sang a song that included these lines:

> You are forced to leave your father's house,
> Stars floating in the sky . . .
> The stream of tears has floated the stars in the sky.
> Why do we have to wash the walls of others?
> Mother's lap of love is empty.
> Stars floating in the sky.

In her song Muna voiced her dread and sadness over having to leave her natal home and the mother she loved. In her husband's home she would be the servant of her in-laws and work for them. Muna's singing in response to a question about her life was not unusual. The girls frequently resorted to song to express some sense of their lives, often a sense that reflected a critical view of their position as women in a patriarchal society. A particularly strong example is a song sung by Naudadan schoolgirls in 1986 at the annual cultural performance at the local high school:

> Being enslaved and repressed, don't remain in isolation.
> We have to tear and throw out this web of exploitation.
> If the husband keeps a co-wife, it is all right.
> But if a woman takes another man, she must pay a price.
> Even to eat, you have to fight hard.
> Even to survive, you have to sell your very life.
> Wake up, oh sister, and recognize this sinner man.
> Let's unite to destroy this tradition.

Naudadan girls' accounts, evaluations, narratives, and actions revealed images, understandings, and feelings about themselves that varied within and across contexts. The ways girls talked about themselves and their lives and the ways they presented and represented themselves were not consistent.[4] Sometimes girls and women gave voice to culturally dominant notions of what the proper Hindu woman should be, portraying themselves in terms of the ideal Hindu woman who accepts her submissive and relatively powerless role vis-à-vis men. But they also, at least in some contexts, took another stance; they authored different senses of themselves through an emotional commentary of sadness, anger, and resistance about the position that the figured world put them in as women.

They were aware of the hardships and injustices that came with being a "good woman," and they gave extensive reflective and critical commentaries, both in discourse and in song, on the relative lack of status and privilege of that position. They denounced the treatment women received at the hands of some men (and sometimes other women such as mothers-in-law) and castigated the legal system that gave men inheritance and marital rights that women were not granted. The girls Skinner interviewed were at times critical of the expected life path; they sometimes rejected it or tried to find acceptable alternatives to it. In the interviews all but two stated that they did not want to get married, and a number had plans—usually involving going to school and becoming a teacher or office worker—for avoiding or delaying marriage.

The evaluative discourse used in everyday activities of Naudadan life—in scolding and gossiping, in the telling of hardship tales—gradually had been appropriated by the girls; at the same time they had inferred the figured world of the expected life path and women's domestic lives (construed in these activities of everyday evaluation). Words such as *alacchini* (a woman who brings bad luck to her family) and *naramro chori* (bad daughter), and behaviors such as doing household chores and avoiding being with boys evoked for them the figured world and the meaning of being a good daughter, daughter-in-law, and wife as defined within it.

But the words and behaviors also evoked memories of the actual episodes of scolding, gossiping, and hardship that the girls had experienced. The expected life path that was symbolized in ritual and indexed in everyday discourse was constituted as natural, as ahistorical and timeless. It was the path for the generic woman. Attention to the grounding of this figured world in historically particular conditions and in the various social spaces of Naudada was not invited. The girls had been encouraged almost daily by their parents and others to develop a view of themselves as traveling along the taken-for-granted life path and as accountable in that figured world. They had clearly developed such an identification, one readily expressed in certain contexts, but they also retained a definite sense of injustice. Girls often told of situations in which they were shamed, hurt, angered. While developing an understanding of the meanings underlying the Brahmanical cultural model of women's lives, the Naudadan girls were also developing a sense of the hardships *(dukha)* associated with the actions required of them in this figured world. How had they arrived at the point where they both embraced and rejected the expected life path?

Here Bakhtin and the sociohistorical school of psychology are helpful. Its theory does not insist upon a coherent and integrated self. Instead it guides us to look at the sites and practices in which identities and selves are formed and to consider that the existence of a transcendent self—a self that is independent of content—is contingent upon the existence of cultural resources, such as the AA personal story (Chapter 4) or the means of accounting oneself a good woman, for creating that self and for the continuing social work that reminds one of one's self.[5] It leads us to specific spaces of authoring; it also recognizes what we observed in Naudada. Children appropriated conventions of meaning—to interpret and evaluate their own behavior and that of others, but their sense of the contexts or sites in which those more abstract meanings were being distilled was distinct from those conventions. The girls seemed to have developed a salient identification with the figured world of women's lives: a desire to be a "good girl," a "good daughter," a "good woman." Yet they were also developing a sense of gender as entitlement, a knowledge of their gendered position and how it limited their access to certain spaces, activities, and resources.

Naudadan girls distilled the common, public meanings associated with specific sites and activities and identified with them, (re)producing subjectifications of these figured worlds in inner speech. At the same time, they were developing embodied senses associated with their positionality in these sites and activities. In the realm of inner speech, these different senses of self intersected and, at times, conflicted. From this internal and heteroglossic dialogical process, girls developed both good selves and oppositional, angry selves.

Sites and Activities of Identity Formation

In Naudada there were a number of activities in which gender-marked terms and gender-specific rules were expressed: scoldings that children overheard, received, or gave; gossip sessions that they overheard and sometimes contributed to; exchanges of complaints and worries about one's life, often in the form of *dukha* stories (stories of hardships and suffering); domestic scenes in which girls observed and heard women's problems; the telling of their worries for the future; the singing of songs about women's lives; and the conduct of rituals that marked girls' transition from one status to another (see Skinner 1989). Most of these activities were fairly common, occurring almost daily, and they, more than the less frequent rituals, were what the girls talked about in the interviews.[6] We will discuss three activities: scolding, domestic scenes, and the annual Tij festival.

Scolding Activities

Scolding and cursing others were ubiquitous, everyday activities. Children were the frequent targets of scolding for transgressions and for problems they caused their parents, other adults, and one another. Such scolding generally began with an insult. *Radi*—one term for widow— was a common insult to hurl at any female, even a toddler. *Nathi*, loose woman, was another. "Radi!" the scolder would scream. Then the girl would be told the rules that she had violated. A typical scolding might run as follows: "Radi! What a daughter you are! After we have given you food, this is all the work you have done! What have you done the whole day? Why are you sitting there when the cattle need fodder and there's no water in the house? Did I raise a lazy daughter?"

Aruna, a Damai girl of thirteen, said her mother always scolded her, saying "radi" when she did not do her work.[7] Kamala, a Chetri girl of fourteen, related that mothers sometimes called their daughters nathi, scolding them, saying, "Don't walk with boys this way." Muna said: "I feel very sad . . . when my father and mother scold me when I am not doing any work, and get angry with me, when they say something and scold, I feel very sad and unhappy. I feel sad when they scold my friends."

The incident that opens Chapter 6 presents a dramatic example of scolding and its effects. To recapitulate, Skinner was recording songs one day when three girls who were visiting her ran afoul of Tila Kumari, the Bahun woman who lived in the house above hers. Tila Kumari walked down to Skinner's porch and yelled at the three Damai girls for eating fruit and cutting fodder from her property:

> You stupid girls. You are joking with us. Why do you cut grass from our fields? Are you not ashamed? . . . Everyone has seen the guavas here,

but only you have eyes for them . . . Go to your husband's or father's field to eat. You have no fear to cut the grass in another's field. After telling your parents, I will weed your hair. You have no shame to show those teeth of yours. I will take your molar teeth out. I will complain like the daughter of Hari. Do not do unnecessary things here.

The girls were upset and angry, particularly since Tila Kumari also went to their houses and berated them and their families. They brought up the scolding in a number of later interviews. As quoted earlier, Muna said this about the scolding: "We hadn't done anything. I can't figure out why they made such a scandal out of it . . . I felt like crying. I couldn't retaliate. I do not do such things. I thought, who was she to tell someone like my mother such things? We did not get angry because we had not done anything wrong. That's why I felt bad and wanted to cry."

Evidently Muna heard implications about behavior she should avoid, but she also heard and felt other things. For her, the *context* of the knowledge was highly charged. If we can judge by her interviews, Muna thought of the episode not only in terms of the content—the do's and don'ts of how to act—but also in terms of her own feelings about the scolding. Muna recounted her process of reacting to the scolding. She rehearsed seeing and hearing Tila Kumari, and she composed arguments to defend her actions. She described feelings of pain, sadness, and a sense of being unjustly accused. Tila Kumari became a dialogic other, envisioned and heard as a particular person, but also perhaps as a representative of the higher-caste Bahuns, who sometimes accused and insulted the lower castes.[8] By replaying this event Muna was forming a notion of her liability to the public meaning of certain acts, but at the same time she was developing a sense of mistreatment and a sense of her positioning as a lower-caste woman by a higher-caste woman.

Another example of the distinction between a developing knowledge of the meaning of acts in the figured world and a personalized sense of one's own positional identity can be seen in the way girls attained an understanding of *radi*. Girls heard mothers-in-law and husbands call daughters-in-law and wives radi for a variety of perceived offenses. Often the girls themselves were the targets of scoldings in which *radi* was the insult or epithet. Over time they abstracted the common meaning of the term and came to know that a radi was a deviant type, one who had left the life path and failed to be a good woman. *Radi* evoked and was understood in relation to the Brahmanical cultural world of the expected life path. But the girls also embodied personal senses of the word that were more contextualized.[9] When they heard the term *radi* they remembered lived situations in which they were scolded unjustly by parents, humiliated by boys, screamed at by Tila Kumari, or saddened by the taunts and insults of strangers.

Scolding involved the expression of generic concepts, meanings, and evaluations commonly applied to women's behavior in Naudada. The activity of scolding was a potential source not only of the public meanings that the girls were appropriating to talk about their own and other women's behaviors in Naudada but also of their embodied *sense* of the treatment they received in the positions afforded women. On the one hand, they were developing an understanding of themselves as participants in a narrativized, figured world organized around the life trajectory of a good woman. They were developing the disciplines and characteristics that could earn them praise for being good daughters—disciplines and characteristics naturalized to stand outside of history, outside of time, and in isolation from caste or other local social groupings in Naudada. On the other hand, they retained vivid memories of abrupt encounters with these expectations—memories of the particular people who scolded them, of their feelings of shame and anger, of bodily sensations associated with their sense of having been unjustly accused. Where their parents were involved, they retained a question of how their mother or father could treat them like this: "Why am I expected to do all of this work and my brother is not?" Thus subsequent reminders could evoke for them both the cultural meaning and a sense of injustice, anger, or other emotions not accounted for in the figured world of the good Hindu woman.

Domestic Scenes and Their Telling

Girls also witnessed scenes from everyday life that centered about gender and kin relations. They were admonished as they went about their household and agricultural chores to be good, obedient, hardworking, and honorable daughters. At the same time, as daughters in the natal home, they were given fewer rights and privileges than their brothers; they saw their brothers getting more and better food and clothes, and they often had to work in the fields while their brothers went to school.

They were teased by their parents and others about being married away "beyond nine mountains," while their brothers, they knew, would stay at home. They observed cases in which parents were in such a rush to marry off their daughter that they chose a man who would cause her many problems. They saw that an incoming daughter-in-law was expected to work long days at arduous tasks without complaint while the mother-in-law sat idle or went out of her way to scold the newcomer.

They heard daily the expectations for wives: be respectful, virtuous, and hardworking. The reward for all this servitude was supposed to be the husband's affection and support for the wife and her children and the wife's increasing status in the household. But girls knew of numerous cases in the community in which women were abused or forsaken by their husbands. They talked of marriage as an uncertain fate. A woman's husband might turn out to beat her and lose the family property through drinking and gambling. If the wife scolded him, he might bring in a co-wife, who would take away not only his affection but also scarce resources.

Devi, a Chetri woman, often told her life story to the girls of Naudada. Devi's husband once had a good job with a local development agency. He owned land, a house, and other wealth. But he drank the locally brewed liquor to excess and gambled away all of the money and property. Devi was powerless to stop him. He sold not only his wife's gold jewelry but her pots and pans as well. He would drink until late at night, then come home and beat her. Finally he deserted her and had not been seen for years. But Devi still told her story, recounting to attentive girls the times she would hide with a baby at her breast in the terraces below her house until her drunken and enraged husband fell asleep.

While bad treatment was not the norm in Naudada, a girl heard about and witnessed enough of it to make her worry that her own future might include similar hardships. Everyday exhortations and evaluations of women's behavior directed her to accept her roles without complaint and to strive to obtain the favor of kin in both her parents' and her husband's home, but her observations provided her with images of the pain possibly awaiting her on this life path. The expected life path may have given her one means of envisioning her life, but it did not address all the ways she thought and felt about her position as a female.

The Naudadan girls had clearly developed an identification with the ideal woman of the figured world of women's lives; yet they also retained senses from their experiences of what it meant to be a girl. These individual senses were figured publicly and objectified in critical commentary that was produced and passed on by groups of women. This commentary, as a cultural resource, provided an alternative meaning and a means of both expressing and understanding one's gender identity.

Songs and Activities of the Tij Festival

In Naudada and elsewhere in South Asia (see Raheja and Gold 1994; Skinner et al. 1991, 1994), songs have been a primary way for women to express their experiences and their awareness of their positioning within the figured world of domestic life. The Tij festival is part of a larger ritual complex called Tij–Rishi Pancami, during which women fast, do *puja* (worship), and ritually bathe to protect their husbands' health and life and to purify themselves from sins connected with menstruation (see Bennett 1983). What interests us here is not the ritual complex but the songs that the women compose and perform for the festival.[10]

Tij songs are a specialized genre of folksong that extends women's critical commentary from inner speech and private conversations among two or three women to a public setting where hundreds of people gather to observe the women sing and dance. Tij songs portray and comment upon the shared feelings of women in their sometimes problematic positions as wives, daughters, and daughters-in-law. A *dukha* (hardship) Tij song composed and performed by Naudadan girls in 1991 resounds with a daughter's sense of the favored treatment her brothers receive:

> [Daughter:]
> I rose in the morning to pick flowers,
> But did not pick them because they were covered with dew.
> Parents just keep the daughters to do work at home,
> But not even a small piece of the courtyard is given [to daughters].
> [Parents:]
> The small piece of courtyard is needed to dry the paddy,
> Go, daughter, to your husband's house to get your property.
> [Daughter:]
> We have to go empty-handed [to our husband's home],
> The brothers fence in their property.

> Brothers' clothes are so many that they rot away in a box,
> But when they have to give us a single cloth, tears come to their
> eyes.

These verses give voice to a daughter's resentment that she has no rights to inherit her parents' property. Other Tij songs expressed girls' fear of marriage and the treatment they might receive at the hands of their future husbands and in-laws, their criticism of their parents for marrying them far away or into a poor or bad family, and their feelings toward mothers-in-law who mistreat them.

Many songs were about the husband-wife relationship. Women sang of their own hardships in marriage and those of their friends and sisters. One song that moved Devi to tears recalled her own experience with a drunken husband:

> Whatever money he has, he runs to the bazaar,
> He searches for a place to drink alcohol.
> If he has five or ten rupees, he goes to the bazaar.
> He forgets his family and household and drinks alcohol.
> Waiting in the kitchen the rice becomes cold,
> Waiting for the husband the night is almost gone.
> How much rotten alcohol is there in Thakali's hotel![11]
> The husband came with a stick at midnight.
> If I say, "Do not drink alcohol," he threatens to bring a co-wife.
> The new wife will give [him wine] and pleasure,
> And she will give orders, and bring the water to wash his feet.

A second type of Tij songs, political (*rajniti*) songs, became predominant in Naudada following the people's movement against the one-party panchayat system. Rajniti songs thoroughly dominated the Tij festival of 1991. In them girls and women criticized various political parties and government officials, chronicled their abuse and exploitation of women and the poor, and demanded equal rights for women and the poor. In 1986 Naudadan girls composed the following song verses, which represented a more explicit critical commentary and call for equal rights:

> You [parents] compel the daughter to work hard.
> How can we abolish this exploitation?
> When the daughter is educated, they call her a prostitute.
> They believe such matters.
> Our society won't allow women to be educated.

When we think of this, it makes us angry.
They not only select the husband,
And donate us to him like the gift of a cow.
We have no right to select a boy whom we like.
No money is in our hand to spend.
Even when we are sick, we women have to work.
They say we are lazy and trying to cheat them.
A minor mistake they blow out of proportion.
We women have to live like animals.
How long can we tolerate this kind of custom?
We must become determined to abolish this condition!

In the 1991 Tij festival one group of singers took on the problem of alcohol, urging men to stop drinking the local brew (*raksi*). They took an active political stance, asserting that only with communism would liquor cease to flow and women get equal rights and better treatment:

Our brothers of Ward 2,
It is our request that you don't drink raksi.
In Ward 2 of our village,
Don't drink raksi in this area.
Brothers, keep this in your mind,
Remove raksi and gambling from here.
Drunkards are treated like animals,
People give them grass to eat.
The dignity of our village is gone,
You're not allowed to sell raksi in the shops.
If you do, you'll not be allowed to keep a shop.
After drinking raksi, you people walk around talking nonsense.
The oxen [the drunkards] are used to plow the fields.
From now on, you stop playing cards and drinking.
Move forward to bring the revolution.
You wasted grain making raksi.
You killed the poor people.
Raksi was free in the panchayat period.
Star Beer was started in the Congress period.
Communism is needed to stop raksi,
We can get rights only when communism comes.

In Tij, women's experiential and personal senses of being female, developed in other contexts, were expressed publicly, cast into a critical, cultural form. These songs provided a cultural resource and an alternative perspective on women's lives, an alternative way of understanding the life path and oneself as female.[12] Women who had experienced the problems associated with being daughters, daughters-in-law, and wives joined together in Tij to censure those who had created difficulties for them (the mother-in-law, husband, father) and, increasingly, to criticize the social and political system that allowed or brought about these abuses.

In day-to-day situations Naudadan women were constrained in what they could say and do. Because of power relations in Naudada, the groups of women who composed Tij songs were a restricted group, circumscribed to meet within a brief period, once a year. But in the context of Tij they came together and drew upon their individual experiences to evoke, through song, strong, shared feelings. As individuals they had little power to change others' ideas, but as a collectivity, even for a brief time, they could create new songs, develop alternative perspectives, and express usually outlawed meanings of what it was to be female.

These critical Tij songs, composed and sung as long as the oldest women could remember, acted as cultural resources to organize more strident opposition to the patriarchal aspects of society in Nepal and helped create a potentially resistant group. Rituals can overflow their boundaries (Bakhtin 1984b), and this happened in the Naudadan situation. The events chronicled at the beginning of this chapter—the women's procession for equal rights and the "posse" that threatened local distillers and wife-beaters—were the stuff of Tij songs. The understandings of women's lives developed through the critical commentary voiced at the Tij festival were being pushed forward into more and more public venues and were thus gaining significance for a re-visioning of selves and a reshaping of figured worlds.[13]

Naudadan girls' participation in the sites and activities we have discussed gave rise to emotionally charged visions of and rehearsed dialogues about themselves as women. These selves were contradictory and contested, selves that Bakhtin (1981, 1984a) would have called "heteroglossic." The girls were developing a nuanced understanding of the figured world of Hindu women's lives and an emotional attachment to an identification of themselves in that world. The girls were also developing an embodied personal sense of themselves in their position as female, as the victims of frequently unfair treatment. Though left unaccounted for by the public meanings associated with the expected life path of Hindu women, these personal senses were of concern to the girls.

At the annual Tij festival, women expressed a critical commentary on their position in the world of domestic relations of Naudada, and, in 1991, after the country's first multiparty election for many years, on the mistreatment of women by the government. These Tij songs, especially the ones addressed to relatives, echoed girls' reactions to the scoldings they were receiving and the domestic scenes they were witnessing. Unsurprisingly, some of the girls used these songs as a cultural resource to express their sense of their lives.

This case study from Naudada reveals ways in which women not only appropriated the identity afforded to them by the figured world but also formed personal senses and, especially in practices related to the Tij festival, personal perspectives that contested the expected life path. Women's selves in this formulation were part of a dialogic process, emerging in social interactions and sites where different voices coexisted, and part of dynamic, changing social formations tied to competing interests in the sociohistorical context of their emergence. We will return to this case in Chapter 12 to examine both the new world of gender relations created in Tij songs and the tentative acting out of that emerging world by some of the women's groups.

V

Making Worlds

11

Play Worlds, Liberatory Worlds, and Fantasy Resources

Specialized discourses and practices, each predicating a figured world and each realized in a variety of positional identities, exist in all societies—though they are especially profuse in large-scale societies. These discourses and practices lead to a great diversity of options for, as well as constraints on, people's activity. People's lives take shape among the identifications, figured and relational, that are arranged within the space of their activity. We have argued, following Vygotsky, that these social forms, these discourses and practices, are not simply the context but the content of inner life, albeit in some way transformed. The interpersonal becomes the intrapersonal in a literal way; the forms of speaking and interacting inhabit us to make "inner" speech and "inner" action. They are the mediating devices of our thinking, feeling, and willing.

We have extended Bakhtin's notion of "voices," that is, of the social identification and valuation of these cultural resources and artifacts. Dialects, genres, styles of dress, ways of holding and moving the body—all are socially inflected forms that have both substantive and indexical value, telling our social category, our relational position, and our group affiliations. These social forms and cultural resources become personal in the arrangement or orchestration of these voices. Within this arrangement exists whatever reality there is to the self, as a collocation of social "persons" (Harré 1984) that endures, at least for a time. Concurrently, social interactivity becomes personified, so that its forms assimilate the "character" of the people from and by whom they are reproduced.[1] This process itself is a kind of dynamic, uniting the intimate and the social sites of cultural production, and it is within this double-sided context, set within a larger historical and institutional context, that new figured worlds and new identities—both figured and positional—emerge.

Play Worlds and Artifacts of Fantasy

Play occupies a central place in Vygotsky's theories; it constitutes ontogenetically the completion within the organism of the capacity for symbolic mediation (Vygotsky 1978, 1987a). All games are *jeux d'esprit*. In play, more than in other human activity, aspects of the natural world, and by extension, of social worlds that have come to seem natural, are suspended and made subject to pretense. Play is the form of activity that proceeds in ignorance of any constitutive condition other than a cultural and conventional design. It draws upon recognized genres of speech and activity, but it takes the player beyond the immediate setting. Play happens "through" the world in which it is observably set. Its real setting is imaginary; it answers only to a figured world. Each generation, however, comes to play historically and socially; one learns the bounds of play, the scaffolding, from one's predecessors and fellows and passes them on to one's successors. It cannot be otherwise for Vygotsky, for it is play that, by its use of collectively produced artifacts, realizes what is only a species competence. Each of us learns to inhabit the cultural world through play when it is instituted within us. The social practices of "acting otherwise" become the grounds for our "thinking otherwise." The mastery we gain over our play is mastery over our imagination (see Lachicotte 1992).

Play is also the medium of mastery, indeed of creation, of ourselves as human actors. Without the capacity to formulate other social scenes in imagination, there can be little force to a sense of self, little agency. In play we experiment with the force of our acting otherwise, of our projectivity rather than our objectivity. And through play imagination becomes embodied, proprioception as much as conception, experienced in activity, moved as much as mapped. Through play our fancied selves become material.

It is the opening out of thought within the activity of play, what we might call the cultural production of virtualities, that allows for the emergence of new figured worlds, of refigured worlds that come eventually to reshape selves and lives in all seriousness. Vygotsky and Bakhtin both attended to this process, but Bakhtin was especially alert to its place in larger social structures.[2] He showed that genres and other forms of specialized practice, informal and formal, come to inhabit one's speech and thought on an everyday basis (Voloshinov 1986; Bakhtin 1981, 1984a). Within the relation of interplay that defines and partially suspends specific activity from the everyday (what Bakhtin called "behavioral ideology"), people are subject to the regulation, which we call the figuring, that governs the practice. They learn to act as roles in play; they are inhabited by the discourse so that, as Foucault demonstrated, the instituted relations of the practice are disseminated "within." This inhabitation is the hallmark of Foucault's disciplines (1979), of Habermas's colonization of the life-world (1984). But it is only half the story.

The work of Foucault, Habermas, and other contemporary students of agency and subjectivity can be reconceived as the development of Weber's (1978) category of traditional or habitual action.[3] We find the "habitual" a useful touchstone for understanding what these social theorists have contributed and so, too, what they have missed. Habit or habituation forcefully communicates the bodily aspect of activity and thinking, yet it overlooks our ability to fantasize, to envision other worlds, to create other worlds by recombining elements from those we know. In Chapter 6 we characterized positional identities as more or less conscious, more or less habitual, moving sometimes out of awareness, toward fossilization, and at other times toward consciousness and susceptibility to manipulation. As we see it, play, especially socially organized play, works in both directions of this process. Were this not the case, were inhabitation the *only* means of reproducing practices and practitioners, then we would have Weber's iron cage not only around us but within us.

Bakhtin had another word to say, which he took, most appropriately, from the author of the word made flesh, François Rabelais. He directed attention to the ways play frees people from the generic forms that govern their actions. This moment of freeing is at the heart of his famous notion of the carnival, or better of the process itself, carnivalization (Bakhtin 1984b).[4] From its very abstraction and mimicry, which make representation itself thematic and thus ironize everyday usage, play moves these identities and the figured worlds in which they are embedded closer to consciousness. Only in its second moment, through the continued rehearsal of its activities, does play that has been popularized move, with its figures and their contexts, toward habituation.

We can use Bakhtin's notion of dialogism (discussed in Chapter 8) to understand how carnivalization becomes a real force. Dialogism pictures social and cultural activity as a manifold phenomenon, of a variety shaped by the juxtaposition of incommensurate voices not only within but also between figured worlds. Bakhtin's dialogism sets everyday social life in what might be called an "inter-world." This postmodernesque phrase describes the condition of a sociality whose generality derives from the convention of many figured worlds. (The model of a language, composed within its dialects and other sociolects, is the one Bakhtin most often used to represent this condition.) In our everyday lives we encounter and enter into many specialized practices, and these practices exist in various degrees of interrelation. Activity predicated upon a figured world is never quite single, never quite pure. It is dialogized, figured against other possible positions, other possible worlds. Our habitual identities bump up against one another. And this is just Bakhtin's point. The space of freedom that is the space of play between these vocations is the space of the author.

Each person constitutes a potential convocation of numerous practitioners, that is, each of us has a repertory. In the heart of inner speech, according to Bakhtin, these socially identified, vocal images are orchestrated. They are played out. It is not imaginatively necessary to accommodate all voices at any given time. Under most situations ordinary relations of authority prevail and establish that one (or several) vocations arrest the dialogue. There are situations, however, whether they be scenes of practice or scenes of consciousness, in which conventional relations are disturbed. Other sources of social valuation abide where realms of interaction—games, arts, rituals—are established in the partial suspension of the ordinary course of events.

These arenas of play, the power of carnival, have much to do with social experimentation as well as social reproduction (see Bakhtin 1984b; Vygotsky 1978, 1987b; Huizinga 1955, 1956). Here people create new orchestrations from the play of inner speaking and seek to convert them interactively to new imagined practices, new virtualities. If inhabitation is the one moment of social reproduction when one figured world, one set of active identities, comes to dominate us as authors, then dishabitation is its complement. We unlearn bodily in the remove from dominant to emerging world, so that we return to the everyday, perhaps, with an altered subjectivity, an altered sense of who we are. The art of play has a spectrum of effects: new genres are created and recorded in the durable media, old ones are refigured, and new worlds and new identities are created.

Or it can have such effects. It is the irony of play that its freedom is as contained as its discipline. Both depend upon the authority and power which establish the possibility that is also the boundary, the space of possibilities, that holds play apart from ordinary life. It is no automatic thing, either the inscription or the dissemination, either discipline or novelization (as Bakhtin would have it). We must turn once again to the life of communities, to their institutional and historical coproduction—with the persons who populate them and the cultural forms that express them—to understand both how play worlds are realized and how real worlds are played out. The media through which new worlds are envisioned have no life of their own, and the people have no "own" to their life apart from one another. A particular historical case—the medieval genre and practice called courtly love—will illustrate the large social movements that create new figurations of human life. It will show how a play world may be taken, ultimately and profoundly, into the "real world," to shape the sites of everyday activity.

Courtly Love

In the area of southern France that was called Languedoc, or more broadly the Occitans, there arose during the eleventh century a new form of poetry and of entertainment.[5] It was fostered by the upper nobility and practiced by them, their retainers, and their courtiers. The poets were called the troubadours—after one name for their verbal arts, the *trobar*—and the entertainment was known, if it had any one name, as *fin amors*. The genre has been intensively explored by medievalists, and its status is still intensely debated (Newman 1968; Boase 1977; Kay 1990; Bloch 1991). Its reality, as a way of behavior and even as a literary phenomenon, has been questioned (Robertson 1962, 1968; Donaldson 1965; Benton 1968). The balance of opinion today holds that courtly love (as it has come to be known) was indeed a specific form of both artistic performance and courtly behavior (Frappier 1972; Boase 1977; Paterson 1993). It was an activity of social life in the courts whose participants included the poets, other members of the retinue, and the principals, lord and lady. Indeed, there was seemingly little separation between performers and audience, for the poet could be a court follower, or the lord himself—the first well-known troubadour was Guilhem IX, Duke of Aquitaine—or even the lady (Paden 1989). Courtly love was a convivial pastime, a genre of fanciful conversation and play-acting, or at least of diversion (Huizinga 1956; Stevens 1973).

Much of the skepticism directed toward courtly love as a social phenomenon with real effect derives from its pretense, its status as a kind of game (Howard 1966) played by the powerful after their serious work of oppression had concluded for the day. What difference could such after-hours ephemera make in the materially hard and often brutal life of those desperate ages? Our answer reveals much about the processes by which new figured worlds emerge and the kinds of effects their emergence brings. Cultural historians have traced the slow dissemination and transformation of courtly love (see Rougemont 1956; Smith and Snow 1980), which amounts to a domestication, from medieval court practice into the "ordinary" world of contemporary romance, where it is part of the lives of, for example, the college women discussed in Chapters 5 and 7. We live today a figured world of heterosexuality that owes much of its interpretation to the casual spectacles of old courtship.

The scene of courtly love is a familiar one. The principal characters were two: a lover and his beloved.[6] The lovers inhabited their own special world, apart from the social realities that ordinarily defined them. In some versions this displacement was taken to extremes, as in the cave where Tristan lived with Iseult, free in their fantastic and solitary absorption with each other. All acts within this exhaustively meaningful world carried emotional charge. Each lover addressed and focused upon the other. Predisposition and proaction, the movements of the passions and the essence of emotion, united them. So much is romantic love, then and now, the figure of rapture.

To make this supercharged fantasy manifest, obstacles to love were taken as the very precondition of it. Only by overt movement, the deeds achieved to overcome impediments, could love be securely signified. The private world had to become articulate; talk was the necessary service of adoration. Yet talk was also cheap, indeed speech was seen as the very bed of falsehood. The false lover and the talebearer, the maledictor, were the greatest villains in the figured world of courtly love.[7] Love had to be proved in ways that surpassed speech. Hence great travail—the body's sacrifice and truth, the constant striving of lover to lover, their continuous attraction—proved and sanctified the bond. In the play world that was courtly love, this rule held: the greater the effort, the more dire the obstacle, the nearer to surety and revealed truth—and the greater the reward. It was preeminently the part of the beloved, the lady, to set obstacles of her own, though there would be plenty set by the world outside, because intimacy with her was the reward given.

Inevitably romantic love was also about prestige. Each lover was the token of the other. But all this exertion was not entirely other-directed. From the accomplishments that proved love also accrued the authority that enforced belief. Each lover remade his or her life in front of the audience and was valued accordingly, for courage, for sincerity, for that gift of self which required return, and above all for competence. All other things being equal, the greater one's prestige, the greater were one's chances of attaining a "fitting" lover.

But that statement must be qualified. For one thing, love was about gaining elevation through learning and instruction. The woman employed her desirability toward this goal, that her lover become worthy of her. Here again is a reason for all those trials of love, dragons slain, competitors bested. The man did not simply instance an already worthy character. Rather he acquired that character, spurred by his love, informed by his lover's care and cleverness, and tempered through action. In that achievement the beloved gained her glory. How much more telling was the skill that created worth than the lesser wisdom that only recognized it. Thus the beloved, for all her seeming passivity, had the power in courtly love. She was exalted and served, yet that service was only the realization of her subtle action and the proof of her love for her courtier.

Courtly love turned the public world of medieval Occitania outside in, as does modern romantic love the contemporary world of work. Worth and power subsisted there in the attractions and the stations of the private, after-hours court, not in the acts and offices of the day's work. But what sort of vision was this inverted world? What relation did the play world of courtly love bear to the political-economic, social, and cultural forms of life in the Occitans of the eleventh and twelfth centuries, or in the western medieval communities that later became acquainted with the traditions of courtly love? Historical research (Duby 1983, 1994; Jaeger 1985) suggests that the scene fantasized through the artifacts of courtly love—the poetry, performances, contests, and ceremonies—had an ambivalent relation to the "real" worlds of its participants. For instance, many writers have remarked that the relation of the male lover to the female beloved inflected and therefore satirized the relation of servant (courtier) to lord. It has been read both ways, as elevating the beloved to a kind of potentate and as derogating the lordly power by giving it feminine form.

The beloved was called *domna*, literally a feminized form of lord (*domnus*), a title that signified a kind of political power, a sovereignty over those pledged to her. This fact has led several scholars (for example, Jackson 1960) to propose that courtly love was fostered, if not created, by the powerful women who sometimes ruled lands in the Occitans. Eleanor of Aquitaine, the granddaughter of Guilhem IX and wife of Henry Plantagenet, the Angevin king of England, is the prototypical case: several writers have suggested that her courts at Poitiers were havens for troubadours and home to the entertainments called "courts of love."[8] Although there is little evidence that Eleanor actively promoted courtly love—there were other powerful, though less grand, *domnae* whose sponsorship is better attested (see Paterson 1993). Nonetheless, most of the supporters of courtly love were men, and it was their wives (as much as any other actual beloved) who were being addressed in the poems. What are we to make of their support?

The support of the male nobility was essential, and not simply for the place and sustenance they gave the poets. Courtly love was a double profanation, first of feudal forms of authority and second of the religious teachings on relations between men and women. Its elevation of women to higher position, even if in play, made powerful enemies among the clergy, and therefore needed, all the more, the protection of power.

In the Occitans the cultural elements that shaped the generic forms of the courtly arts—Moorish lyric poetry; erotic Latin poetry along the model of Ovid; the secular poetry of peripatetic monks, ex-religious and peri-religious court followers, clerks; and perhaps other elements as well—were brought together with social conditions that allowed them to flourish.[9] There existed in the Occitans, first, a "feudalism" founded upon alliance between lords and fee-for-service between lord and retinue, which was less rigid and hierarchical than a vassalage system founded upon the control of land and labor bound to land; second, a polity where provincial magnates played off the contending interests of great dynasts—kings of France, England, Castile, and Aragon, the German emperor—to build their own substantial realms; third, a contentious and diverse, sometimes heretical, religious life and establishment; and fourth, a relatively open and egalitarian tradition of gender relations, at least among the nobility and perhaps among the bourgeois as well (Paterson 1993). These political and social conditions became motive, means, and occasion to create the new practice.

It was in the interest of the Occitanian nobility to recruit people to their retinue and offices, and, for that purpose, to foster the arts that both provided the enticements and accrued the courtly prestige that attracted followers and allies. The troubadours spread praise of the lord's largess as widely as praise of their lady's beauty. They echoed a double entreaty and a hope of paired reward, material and intimate, that bound the household together. In this regard, though the lord acted more by his license and even his absence, he was as much a principal of courtly love as his lady. Conversely, the lady, though she often stayed in the domestic sphere, became a full partner in a realized, intimate polity: the household as court of power and affect (see Duby 1994; Paterson 1993). It is small wonder that the poems seem to address each patron in the guise of the other.

Courtly love, then, was first a game of etiquette, and also a discipline of politicized personal relations. It dramatized for its devotees (members of the retinue and allied lesser nobility) the hope of advancement through service, and for its patrons (the higher nobility) the means of fidelity and allegiance. Its rehearsal established the common dispositions, the inner activity proper to a house of its kind.

The Publicization of Courtly Love

If proponents of courtly love used it as a kind of propaganda, to spread news of the pleasures and rewards available to those who would support them, they faced strong opposition to and even co-optation of these means of political persuasion. This counteraction came from many fronts. The French, adherents of the Capetian kings whose land bordered Occitania to the north, ridiculed the effete character of this courtly diversion and boasted of their own prowess in arms and of the code of chivalry told in the great Carolingian epics. They were forced to share their inheritance of that imperial glory with the Hohenstaufen rulers in Germany, who now held the imperial seat of Rome, the so-called Holy Roman Empire. The Angevins, who under Henry II held not only the crown of England but, through his marriage to Eleanor, the Duchy of Aquitaine itself, adopted the Arthurian heritage for their own. The kings of Castile and Aragon laid claims to the deeds of the Reconquista, the long struggle against the Moors, and these "Spanish" kingdoms shared much economic, linguistic and demographic interchange with the Occitans. Indeed it is hard to separate the two regions, especially at the Catalonian and Pyrenean "boundaries." All these powers were active in Occitania, seeking dominion or hegemony in alliance. And all were actively moving against the others toward that end.

Perhaps for this reason, though not for it alone, their respective court apparatuses began to adapt courtly love to their own purposes (Heer 1963). In the twelfth-century Arthurian cycles, especially the tales of Chrétien de Troyes, the precepts of the courtly lover reached in the figure of Lancelot a union with the peerless man of arms. So potent did the Arthurian tradition become, reworked by the new courtliness, and so capacious did its imagined realm of Arthur become, that French and Imperial courts too discovered their own part in it. Of the great thirteenth-century Arthurian romances, those in prose are mainly of French sources, and the epics, Parzival and Tristan, are German. These works realized the conjunction of the courtier and the warrior that was the idiom of later chivalry (see Painter 1967; Duby 1983; Jaeger 1985). Even the Spanish works took on this chivalrous manner, though they remained involved in the Reconquista, not in Arthur.

Oddly, the Occitanian world remained unmoved by the new chivalry. Its vision of the court remained more urbane and everyday, almost academic in its devotion to the arts. There persisted a lyric tradition of courtly love, appropriate to the quiet times at court, to an everyday evening's entertainment. It too spread out from Occitania, sometimes with troubadours attached to the retinues of heiresses who married foreign powers. Two daughters of Eleanor of Aquitaine exemplify this means of transplantation. One, Eleanor (Leonora), married Alfonso VIII, king of Castile, and their court hosted many troubadours. The custom was already established in Castile, though that land was at the edge of the troubadours' ambit (Paterson 1993). With the advent of Leonora the Castilean court became a much more popular stop on the circuit traveled by poets who were not attached to a single patron. The second, Marie, married the "French" Count of Champagne and, on his early death, attained some power in that rich county. Her court at Troyes (where

Chrétien wrote) became the most famous center of courtly love in the north.

The north of Europe remade and learned courtliness in the warlike dress of imperial dreams. Of foreign lands, Italy best absorbed the amusements and manners of courtly love. What is now the west of Italy, along the Provence/Savoy border, was then the eastern reach of Occitanian society and culture. The *trobar* was well known there from the early twelfth century (Paterson 1993), adopted by a nobility that was to become ever more urban and ever more commercial. In the following centuries the great poets of the Lombard coast and plain, Dante, Petrarch, and Boccaccio, were sophisticates, and sometimes critics and satirists, of the art of love. Still, they were its heirs and their works, vehicles of its devices. It was a woman transplanted from this urbane Italy to the courts of Paris, Christine de Pizan, who would at the end of the fourteenth century present a new model of courtly behavior, a modified etiquette for gender relations, that sought to counter a misuse of courtly love (see McLeod 1976; Willard 1984).

During its adaptation and dissemination beyond Occitania to the north, especially in its marriage to chivalry, courtliness took on a decidedly masculine bent. Even in its earliest forms courtly love was produced largely by men, and it had only one female character of note. But that character was central, her token (the woman addressed) was near at hand, and the image of her power differed greatly from the customary lot of even the noblest women found in other contemporary ideologies (Paterson 1993). However, as the domestic court of the troubadours was transformed, replaced by the grand courts of kingdom and legend, the presence of the domna faded. Her customage became less important, and her station, not her person, became the thing. Epics have small place for idiosyncrasy. One consequence of courtly love, or rather its transmuted appropriation, is the woman on the pedestal, the woman whose only realization lies in the activity of her lover (Kay 1990; Bloch 1991). Another is her opposite, the figure of lechery known from later and cynical romances. Ironically, this veneration of the abstract beloved—who thus displaced Jesus or Mary as object of worship—offended the church as much as the taste for pleasures of the body (Denomy 1947).

To be sure, the church had opposed courtly love from its inception, for its vanity and frivolousness, its celebration of worldly merit, and its parody of male and religious authority. Given the often strained relations between church and nobility, clerical condemnation may have only added to the attractiveness of this most secular of doctrines. The teachings of love were countered by clerical treatises (Jaeger 1985), to little effect. Churchmen, who were the lettered people of the day, even played a role in memorializing and disseminating the troubadours' folderol. Andreas Capellanus, author of the treatise *De Arte Honeste Amandi,* was reputedly a chaplain at Marie's court of Troyes.[10]

Only with the crusades against the Cathars (1209), known as the Albigensian crusades, was the church able to move against the troubadours and their patrons and followers in Occitania. The crusaders and their propagandists claimed that the worldly, frivolous, and blasphemous pursuits of love reflected, and brought the innocent to acceptance of, a heresy they painted as lost to the devil and the world of the flesh. That portrait was hardly true of Catharism, or of courtly love. The heresy was actually world-renouncing, and its effects on courtly love, if negligible, were to make it more ideal (Rougemont 1956; Boase 1977). Catharist love would replace the domna with a "perfect" (the Catharist ascetic), a woman to adore, certainly, but one definitively removed from worldly pleasures and the promise of worldly reward. Yet that replacement too was blasphemous, and only condemned the practice more deeply.

The crusades were an effective campaign, if one (intentionally) erroneous in its interpretation of Occitanian culture. Occitanian courts and sovereignty were terribly disrupted, lands were usurped by the crusaders (mostly northern French), and the inquisition was established. A living for the troubadours became harder to procure. Poetry became more ideal, more orthodox, or at least more obscure (Boase 1977).[11] Occitanian courtliness, as a living, not literate, practice, necessarily changed. The play of *fin amors* ended.

The death of a lived world—an embodied, that is, socially enacted way of realizing figured worlds in practice—is not necessarily the end of the figured worlds that developed within it. Court life in Occitania was irreparably disrupted during the crusades. Courtly love moved on, becoming a literary project or a performance to be attended, ever more a spectacle and ever less a mode of conversation and conviviality. It became the stuff of manuals and treatises, manuscripts and later books.

Considering English only, it was part of Chaucer, Gower, Malory, and Spenser. It was played out in the Forest of Arden and on the streets of Shakespearean Italy. Jacobean, Restoration, Augustan, and Georgian; romance, lyric, epic, and epistolary—the image of love changing somewhat, but always remaining, whatever the tradition or form, the service of a courtier to win the favor of a lady. The Victorians, aristocracy and middle classes, were fascinated by it, by the cult of Arthurian chivalry, by a medievalism in which courtliness was the nostalgic centerpiece. Today the figures of the troubadours live in high literature and the most mundane and banal romances, in soap operas and grand opera, in advertisements, and in the talk and dispositions of college students. Courtly love, albeit in modified form, has been absorbed into the contemporary figured world of romance. It participates in a lived world far removed from the noble households of High Medieval Occitania.

Imagined Communities

Benedict Anderson, in his book *Imagined Communities* (1983), provides a second example of the development and proliferation of a figured world—that of modern nationalism. He emphasizes not so much the figured world of nationalism as the "imagined community" created in relation to that world. His work has important implications for the possibilities for positional as well as figured identities that are dependent upon the mass circulation of cultural resources.

By an imagined community Anderson means a potent and effective sense of commonality, of membership in a categorical social body—a social body that exists despite the absence of direct or even indirect social intercourse among its (putative) members. Such an imagined community is developed and continued through common participation in activities that figure for people their identification with others who also, elsewhere or nearby, perform similar acts. The sense of abstract community is acquired and maintained through the use of common cultural artifacts that have acquired indexical value. Anderson is clearly not talking about actual cooperation or conjoint work, where people are involved in a face-to-face community of practice. Rather he is talking about solitary or "modular" activities, which most individuals or small groups perform separately.

Anderson's classic example is reading the newspaper, and the lesson of it is less what happens during the activity than the notion of a readership that accrues from it. The common information, convened in the single medium whose use becomes emblematic, creates for those for whom it has become a marker an index of relational identity, a sort of kinship with others imagined to be reading the same stories in the same paper in similar places. Particular newspapers, the *New York Times,* say, or the *Nation,* come to realize a theory of (and thus to signify) the persons who read them. And so is formed, of this common perception, an imagined community. The media mark, in their users' minds, those who use them with a particular relational identity.

Anderson is not particularly concerned with the figured world of nationalism. He speaks mostly of the "meta-effect" of a manufactured and generic (and to that extent formless) sense of community. However, the media do carry specific instructions, scripts, or guidelines for the enactment of the various figures of a specific nationalist world: they provide narratives for potential adherents. Many of the stock characters of these nationalist dramas are the stuff of school primers and songs, folktales of the state-to-be. Though the writings of the more serious and quotidian media, newspapers and journals, make mostly ironic or condescending reference to this mythos, still it is the touchstone, the root knowledge of political culture. (The greater the sense of a trial of state, during periods of war or political dissension, the closer will the quotidian prescript approach the mythic model.)

American versions of these narratives include revolutionary heroes (Washington, Marion), lesser but exemplary martyrs (Nathan Hale) and patriots (Paul Revere, Patrick Henry), revered statesmen (Franklin, Jefferson, Madison), followers whose devotion gives them a collective grandeur (the soldiers at Valley Forge, the Minutemen), and worthy allies (Lafayette, Grasse). In opposition to these are the traitors (Benedict Arnold), the loyalists caught in blind servitude to colonial masters, the colonizers themselves (King George, Pitt), and the occupying troops (Cornwallis and so on) and foreign minions (the Hessians), who inevitably commit brutal acts of oppression. There are the activities performed by these iconographs, repeated locally and largely: the Tea Parties and Midnight Rides, the Resolves and Declarations, Crossings and Camps. These are the origin myths; they are followed by stories of the new country's institution, its early history and trials of statehood and its ultimate salvation by second-, third-, and later-generation patriots and citizens.

Alongside these political figures, and sometimes in the same character (such as Franklin), exist "culture heroes," who emblematize the populace as a nation, an ethnos distinct from (though attached to) the governing apparatus. American mythohistory is also replete with such figures, heroes and antiheroes, from founding fathers to latter-day personages figured according to such narratives—Sacco and Vanzetti, Rosa Luxemburg, the suspected Communists pursued by McCarthy in the 1950s, and, as contemporary conservatives might have it, "liberals" and other advocates of "political correctness" in today's politics. All combine to provide the forms for emulation or rejection, so that an action, such as voting for a particular candidate or physically attacking immigrants, can be figured to protect the country from Communist traitors or to make sensible one's identity as a patriot.[12]

Calhoun (1991) relates Anderson's imagined communities to the general condition of sociality in modern society, to the fact that many relationships we moderns have with one another are *indirect*, conducted at a distance by means of generalized media. He also reiterates an important caution: it is important not to get too enamored of "the media" as the tutelary spirits of postmodern societies. The stories and images they provide are learned, retold, analyzed, and revalued in the contexts of our everyday communities. There exist embodied traditions of use—commentaries, practical guides, rules of thumb, and outright regulations—that make the effect of the figured worlds of our mass media anything but automatic or axiomatic. The social practice of the public houses, salons, clubs, and associations that fostered "newspaper literacy" cannot be erased from the story of nationalisms. Calhoun argues, and we concur, that there is also no necessary fascination with these imaginary worlds, just as there need be no *necessary* alienation from our embodied lives as the social power of such "imaginaries" grows. From the sociological or social psychological vantage, it is a mistake to rely upon some universalistic, usually psychodynamic, apparatus to explain the impact of cultural forms on personal life. It is better by far to attend to the social history of their use and to the specific identities that form in relation to them.

Nationalism and courtly love, to the extent that they are popularized, are locally figured worlds—imagined or play worlds of a sort—that have come of age. Their specific visions have been publicized, moved from the local, highly circumscribed, conditions of their original production to a broader purview, their audience grown from a coterie to a true public. (By this standard, it is harder to imagine a more successful figured world

than courtly love.) Imagined worlds are then potentiary, cultural resources that help us envision new identities that could give shape to the
affiliations and disaffiliations we live by day to day. Like courtly love for
Occitanian courts, looking outward, they can oppose the positions assigned to us by other powers. Or, looking inward, they give content and
form to the positions we seek for ourselves.

Counter-Worlds

The movement from play world to figured world, from a world without
a public to a world with communities, imagined or otherwise, is often
accomplished by the figuring of "the opposition" to this publicization.
Our brief accounts of courtly love and nationalism revealed glimpses of
opposition and barriers to the emergence of these worlds, and of the
development of tools of insult and derogation for threatening or mobiliz-
ing action against those who supposedly endanger the course of emergence. Often these villains are imagined as allied with an opposing
figured world. In that counter-world, motives are askew and actions are
opposed to the course of events appropriate to the world's topos. For
courtly love the counter-world was that of the illiberal court, whose
lord closets the lady and keeps a retinue of maledictors, talebearers,
and opportunists. For the nationalism of the twentieth-century United
States, the counter-world, as construed by conservative talk-show hosts,
is one of secular humanists and multiculturalists whose liberal social
and economic policies dilute and weaken the family and undercut the
country itself. These are portraits given to struggle and mobilization,
scenarios to fear, worlds into whose mismaking all of us will be condemned.

These counter-worlds, though undoubtedly "figured" as we have used
the term, rarely posit what a lived world should be. Instead they show us
what should not be, what threatens us, and they position the persons
presumed to inhabit them as relationally inferior and perhaps beyond the
pale of any imagined community we would ever want to join. The portrayal of these counter-identities, transgressors of "principles" and "values," often becomes a genre itself, a concatenation of powerful artifacts
left to suggest an awful specter. Typically one figure, say Stalin, or one
transmogrified event, the making of the Gulag, becomes a metonym for

the entirety. Their rhetorical use is, first, to censure activities by claiming they lead to the nightmare world and, second, to motivate an amorphous support for the activities of the propagandists, which are presented as the antidote to the actions of those censured.[13] Villainy, however, is also in the eye of the beholder, and so persuasion must be sought elsewhere. Influential persons or associations may be recruited to perform or endorse performance of the vision; the figured world will be allied to those forms of life already known to be popular. And the opposite views will be linked to despised people or to already established negatives. These tactics are familiar in the material churned out daily in the conduct of modern politics.

Codevelopment

This political-cultural "process," however, is less a matter of choice, of the "marketplace of ideas," than a matter of production, the labor of constituting Bourdieu's habitus. The contention of figured worlds is not one that simply presumes its audience. Instead a public is located, cultivated, created from a cultural system become desire. At this point again the notions of Vygotsky and Bakhtin are important. Figured worlds move through us as spoken discourse and embodied practice. By continual rehearsal they are transfigured within the activity of inner speech into the vocal images, the virtual voices that are the resources of pro(to)action. The interplay of a person's identities is thus open to and dependent upon a field of continuing social discourse and everyday interaction. The realities of "countercultures" and movements of resistance remind us that the "negotiation" of authority is not a matter of pure power or rank. Yet the person inside is always political, in the sense that the persuasion of a voice, the valence of identification through it, must alter as the social position of its speakers moves relative to the other member voices in the ensemble, the repertory of intimate actors.

But, by the same circuit that social production takes "through us," into inner speaking and activity, the political itself becomes personal. That is the inevitable conclusion toward which Bakhtin and Vygotsky draw us. The "pathetic fallacy" of romanticism, that human mood and thought are mirrored in the external world, here has a kind of realization. The cultural production of virtualities, of new figured worlds, is thus simultaneously a new personification, a repopulating of the cultural media through which humans associate. Whether it is Kabyle houses, Occitanian court life, or the songcraft of Hindu women in rural Nepal, a figured world enters the very landscape of social life. Only so can the public constituency of its practice, the imagined community, be stably reproduced.

12

Making Alternative Worlds in Nepal

The imagined communities discussed in Chapter 11 are often the outcomes of large-scale, spectacular social movements. Anderson (1983) takes us through the colonial revolutions of South and Central America on the way to modern nationalism, and surely other historical dramas could be added to that story. But there also exist quieter means of social reconstitution, where a public and its habitus take shape together before the great events happen. E. P. Thompson's great history of the English working class (1963) showed that seemingly ordinary forms of communal life can produce the grounds for large social upheaval. Another example of the quiet formation of a new public and the realization of an alternative vision of social and political life is the cultural production of the Tij festival in rural Nepal.

In 1990 we (Skinner and Holland) went to Naudada, Nepal, for Tij, an annual festival for women that takes place in late August or early September.[1] We were struck, as Skinner had been in 1986, by the incongruities between the public part of the festival and the rituals that preceded and followed it. The portions of the ritual complex that called for women's fasting for the health of their husbands or bathing to cleanse away the pollution of menstruation were in accord with Brahmanical texts and the patriarchal ideologies and practices that shaped life in large parts of Nepal. Other portions did not: as noted in Chapter 10, the women's groups that sang and danced in public on the day of Tij had composed songs that explicitly criticized male privilege in the family.

In 1991, when we returned to continue our research, our appreciation of the significance of Tij grew. The 1991 celebration differed markedly

253

from those of 1990 and 1986. The songs of the Tij groups had shifted from criticism of women's positions in the family to criticism of the government and its treatment of women. Songs that identified women's problems in terms of abusive husbands, vulnerability to sharing resources with a co-wife, or parents' favoring of sons over daughters had given way to songs that blamed women's troubles on the former government and on the political party that had recently come to power.[2] Increasingly strident verses called for equal rights for women, lower castes, and the poor.

In addition to an important space of authoring gendered identities (discussed in Chapter 10), Tij contained, or rather opened up, an imagined space where women envisioned and rehearsed, at least for several weeks of the year, a figured world that rearranged gender relations. Through the medium of Tij songs and the collective activity of their song groups, the Naudadan women brought to life an atmosphere of possibility. In the "play" of Tij, women's groups composed and performed songs through which alternative worlds were imagined and experienced, through which alternative femininities were given shape.[3]

The Tij Festival

In some older literature the Tij festival is described as a part of the Tij–Rishi Pancami complex (Bennett 1983; Bouillier 1982; Goodman 1981; but see Bista 1969). Such accounts emphasize the relation of the rituals to Brahmanical cosmology and ideology. They include the dancing and singing on Tij Day, but contextualize these activities within the religious observances—fasting, performing *puja* (worship), and ritual bathing—that, in addition to the feast on the night before Tij, take place over a four-day period.

Interpreted in light of Hindu religious texts, the rituals call for an emulation of the ideals of womanhood—represented by the devotion of Parvati to her husband, Shiva, and of the acts of atonement performed by the wives of a group of Hindu holy men called the Rishi. By fasting on Tij Day and dedicating the fast on the following day to their husbands, women act to ensure long lives for their husbands. By ritually bathing on the day of Rishi Pancami, they act to absolve themselves of sins associated with menstruation.

Bennett (1983) described the Tij portion of Tij–Rishi Pancami as a time of license—a complete reversal of what is expected during the rest of the year, a deviation from the "Hindu ideal of womanly behavior" (225). Women are supposed to be shy and embarrassed, yet the dancing they do on Tij Day, representing Parvati's seduction of Shiva, is considered erotic and highly suggestive. Bennett interpreted the sexuality expressed at the festival as being licensed by the ascetic rituals (the fasting before and during and the ritual bathing after) that bracket the performance and therefore regulate it. She argued that these rituals, done on behalf of husbands, could be viewed as controlling women's sexuality and reaffirming patrilineal principles. She suggested that the village women who perform Tij–Rishi Pancami rituals "have accepted the restrictions placed on them by the dominant ascetic and patrilineal ideology of Hinduism" (234). The ritual complex including Tij was reproducing a femininity valued in the world figured by Brahmanical doctrine.

In our research, we found that religious observances provided only a part of the picture (see Holland and Skinner 1995a). Bennett's research was conducted in the 1970s in Narikot, an area much closer to Kathmandu. It is possible that the women of Narikot were more subject to the guidance and supervision of Bahun priests than were those of Naudada. In Naudada the women were not constrained to adopt or even to hear the priests' renditions of the ritual complex, and many were, according to the most learned priest in Naudada, at least partially ignorant of the textual interpretation of the fasting and the ritual bathing.[4]

For the women who sang at Tij, the emotional and attentive center of the festival we witnessed was not in the rituals. It was in the bringing together of groups of women, and it was in the making of the songs. Song composition and rehearsals began long before Tij Day. Several weeks before the public events of the festival and before any of the other rituals, groups of girls and young women gathered at night to compose new songs, sing old ones, and dance. Traveling about at night and getting together with women friends, especially to dance, were unusual activities for women in Naudada. At times other than Tij a woman who engaged in such activities risked being labeled immoral. On the day of Tij itself the women adopted a more serious and composed demeanor, but at the rehearsals they took the opportunity to engage in a little bawdiness and playfulness.

The girls and young women in the Tij groups, particularly the eight to twelve core singers and composers, referred and related to one another according to kinship ties, usually glossed by the terms *didi* (older sister) and *bahini* (younger sister). Although friends from other *gaons* (hamlets, neighborhoods) sometimes joined in, as well as mothers and in-married women, the members of a given group were mostly of the same gaon, related by consanguineal ties, and between ten and twenty-five years old. Often they were also members of the same *parma*, or cooperative labor exchange group. Women organized and carried out much of the agricultural work in Naudada. They accomplished this work through labor exchange with a set of more or less permanent partners.[5] The groups of didi/bahini produced songs at the nighttime rehearsals and also in their parma groups as they worked in the fields.

In the rehearsal sessions there was, in addition to the somewhat carnivalesque atmosphere, an edge of anticipated competition. Tij groups knew that their songs and dancing would be compared to those of other groups that performed on the day of Tij. They had a sense of which songs would be of interest to the audience and which would not. "God" songs, for example, were said to be uninteresting.[6] Although the upcoming performance did not overshadow the rehearsal sessions, which were enjoyed in their own right, the anticipation of having their songs and dancing appreciated lent excitement to the groups' preparations.

Another emotional ingredient of the festival was extremely powerful in shaping the atmosphere of Tij. It came from the return to Naudada of women who had recently married out. Women from Naudada were usually married to men unknown to them, whose homes took hours or even days of walking to reach. At Tij the young married women got a respite from the work and tension in their husbands' homes; they were permitted to return to their natal homes.[7] Before the roads to Gorkha and Pokhara were finished and before bridges spanned the larger rivers, trips home were especially formidable. Then, as well as during the period of our fieldwork, Tij might be the only time the married didi/bahini were able to make the difficult journey back home.[8] And only then were they able to tell anyone about the situation they faced in their husband's household. At their *maita* (natal home) they found some relief from the constant work and the strains of being a daughter-in-law. Among their didi/bahini they could find listeners sympathetic to their ordeals.[9] Coming home was a strong emotional event for both the women who returned and their didi/bahini who remained in the gaon.

The returning women's stories often became the inspiration for new songs. Their news of incidents outside of Naudada—for example, homicides in their husbands' communities—became the events reported upon in *ghatana* (incident) Tij songs.[10] And, even more strikingly, their ordeals in their husbands' homes supplied images for *dukha* songs (songs of sadness, hardship, and suffering). The dukha songs sung on Tij Day resonated with the special atmosphere created by the return of the married sisters.

Tij commentators—that is, practically every person in Nepal to whom we expressed our interest in Tij—called the festival a time of license. But they differed from Bennett in their emphasis on the songs rather than the dancing. Many told us the festival is a time when women can pour out their thoughts and feelings in Tij songs. They likened Tij to Gai Jatra, a festival in which men put on skits that satirize unusual people—such as holy men and tourists—as well as government officials, development workers, and doctors. Tij is a time, they said, when women can express sentiments and ideas that they usually keep hidden. Dukha songs were said to spring from experience, from the *man* (the seat of thought and emotion, located in the chest).

Together, then, the groups of girls and women in Naudada made up new songs and rehearsed old ones that they wanted to sing again. Their excitement mounted as the day of performance drew near. On Tij Day the women and older girls spent most of the morning bathing and making themselves their most beautiful. They put on their best saris, preferably red or pink (colors associated with auspiciousness and fertility), and adorned themselves with jewelry and makeup. The married women wore all the markers of that status: the red vermilion powder in the part of their hair, a red hair braid, red glass bangles, and a style of necklace worn only by married women. They then gathered at the political and religious center of Naudada where there was a *tati* (gathering place) big enough to accommodate the people attending the festival.

In the early afternoon the women constituting the core of the performing group paraded in as a team. They spent a few minutes listening to other singers who had already established themselves at the tati. They then situated themselves in the best unclaimed space and began to sing and dance. One member of the group danced in the center while her friends sang and clapped along with her. Other women and girls surrounded the core groups and joined in the verses and clapping. Since each verse was repeated twice, onlookers could sing the repeated verse even if they had not heard the song before. Contemporary songs were all sung to the same tune and cadence, and the movements and gestures of the dancer evoked the meaning of the lyrics. As many as four groups performed simultaneously.

People of all ages and castes came from the surrounding hamlets to view the performance. Men encircled the women's groups or stood on the periphery of the crowd, watching, listening, and sometimes tape-recording the songs. They commented on the beauty of the women and the quality of the songs. The women of each group hoped that their singing and dancing would draw the largest crowd, a sign that their lyrics had been judged the best. The dukha songs were especially moving. Women both young and old nodded their heads and exclaimed in agreement with the sentiments expressed by the singer, and sometimes even wept as the images evoked memories of sad events in their own lives or the lives of their friends. A woman who became visibly agitated while listening to one song about a drunken husband's mistreatment of his wife told us later that her *man* started churning when she heard the verses. They brought back vivid memories of her own husband, who would often come home drunk late at night and beat her.

The Tij–Rishi Pancami complex, we learned, did collectively represent the feminine ideals figured by the Hindu stories that priests read and reread to families throughout the year in Naudada. Yet it also did something else in the rehearsal and performance of Tij songs, replete as these were with women's feelings about their lives and their friendships with one another. Tij provided, for a brief period each year, a space for the gathering of the didi/bahini groups and a time for them to reflect, through song, upon their lives as daughters, daughters-in-law, and wives, and increasingly as political actors. The Tij festival and the month-long preparation for it provided a space for "play"; in their production of Tij songs women could represent themselves as kinds of actors in social scenes other than those figured by Brahmanical texts and rituals. They could together think and act "otherwise." As we shall see, in envisioning a novel world of gender relations where women were not the social and ritual inferiors of men, they were agents in bringing about this world and agents in reshaping themselves.

Imagining Alternative Worlds and Alternative Femininities

As the two Tij dukha songs we presented in Chapter 10 show, Tij lyrics provided a perspective on women's difficulties, hardships, and problems.

The actors in the world of domestic relations envisioned in Tij songs were women and their unkind and sometimes abusive husbands, mothers-in-law, fathers, and co-wives. These dukha songs portrayed—poignantly, if we may judge by the tears of listeners—the unhappy situations of their female protagonists. But the songs did more than portray suffering: they implied and often stated that these women deserved a better lot in life. Through the verses they jointly produced, women assessed their status and their relative worth within the world of domestic relations. They often included in their dukha songs a more general social and political analysis, to the effect that women were unfairly underprivileged. The songs criticized differences in the treatment of sons versus daughters and husbands versus wives. They opposed the gender privilege instituted in Nepalese law, carried out in social practice, and interpreted through religious texts and teachings. They criticized women's limited right to inherit land, women's lesser access to education, and women's constant vulnerability, under polygyny, to the division of their husband's resources and affections with a co-wife.

Through the cultural form of Tij songs and the atmosphere created around the festival, a figured world and subjectivity were developing together. Girls and women were producing a figured world in which women's modes of being and acting differed significantly from those promoted by Brahmanical texts and Hindu religious rites, and they were developing identities meaningful in this alternative world: not as the passive and submissive "good" Hindu woman, but as an aggrieved and wronged character vis-à-vis others in the domestic sphere.

Renu, a member of the Chetri caste (one of the two highest castes in Naudada), who was in her mid-twenties in 1991, provides an example of these dual processes. Renu lived in her *maita* in one of the hamlets that made up the community of Naudada. She had never attended school, but her parents arranged for her to marry an educated man. According to Renu, her husband soon came to have contempt for her because she was uneducated. This, coupled with his attraction to drink, forced her to leave her husband's home and return to her maita to live and find support. After her return she composed several songs for Tij, which she, her friends, and her female relatives performed for the festival. Her songs seemed to be a medium she deftly used to objectify her thoughts and emotions. The following song is one Renu composed for the 1991 Tij festival:

I worked all day on the flat lands of Salyantar.
On that long road, no one was there.
Though I say no one, my husband was walking with me.
He didn't say a single word on this long road.
I walked ahead and my husband walked behind.
My husband did not scold me.
If he didn't like me, why did he marry me?
If I walk ahead and behind, why did he turn his eyes away from me?
When I went inside and out, my mother-in-law didn't want to see me.
Though it was a time of drought, my tears created a lake.
You knead flour in a plate and [separate] oil from water.
If my husband doesn't like me, he will return the *sidur.*
By fate, you are [as] the brother and I am [as] the sister.
Then I'll say I'm unmarried and go to the river.

These lines expressed Renu's distress at her husband's and mother-in-law's contempt for her. Her husband was so angry he would not speak to her, not even to scold; her mother-in-law could not bear to look at her. She worried that her husband would take away the vermilion powder (*sidur*) that women wear in their hair as a symbol of being married. If he did this, she threatened to "go to the river," a very literal reference to suicide: over the period of Skinner's research several Naudadan women had committed suicide by throwing themselves in rivers swollen by monsoon rains.

In a song Renu composed the year before, in 1990, she sang of a drunkard husband who squandered the family's wealth and property on alcohol. She criticized the inheritance system that keeps property in the patriline and relegates women to being "outsiders" in both their husband's house and their maita.

. . .
Listen to the description of the drunken husband.
Rising in the morning, he goes down to the hotel.
Who will do the household chores?
The hotel girl has probably made the tea.
The raksi has finished all the money.
The household wealth has all gone to the *hironi* [a cinema role—here, the hotel girl].

The most fertile land is all finished because of his drinking
raksi.
Whatever money you have, it is not enough,
Two or even four bottles of raksi is not enough for you.
If I say, "Don't drink," he replies, "I'm not drinking your father's
[property]."
The most fertile land is gone and still he does not know.
The best land is gone because of the drunkard husband.
How will we spend our lives?
The whole day the husband king drinks a jar,
You don't need to return home after drinking there in the
evening.
In Pokhara bazaar [there is] an electricity line,
The household property is not mine.
The housewife is an outsider,
All the household property is needed [for raksi].
If this wife is not enough, you can get another,
The head of the cock will be caught [that is, with two wives
he'll have problems].
Why do you hold your head? Go sell the buffalo and pigs,
If you don't have enough money, you will even sell your wife.
After selling his wife, he'll become a *jogi* [here: a beggar
without a wife].
I, the daughter, will go stay at my maita.
If I want a man, I can find one just like you,
For my parents' reputation, I have to stay with you.

Renu had become expert at producing dukha songs of a certain type,
and her two songs chronicled and criticized the suffering and difficulties
she had experienced. By her account, these songs flowed forth from her
man. She transfigured the thoughts and feelings "stored" and "churning"
in her *man* in these vocal images, which in turn were taken up by other
women as a way of shaping and evoking their thoughts and feelings
about their own lives.

Renu, like other women in Naudada (Skinner 1989, 1990), had made
Tij songs a tool for authoring herself as a woman in this society. The
songs provided a perspective on her life, an understanding of herself as
female. These songs, these cultural forms, and the way they were produced and used in women's interaction with one another in the Tij song
groups affected women's understanding of themselves in the lived world

of family and domestic relations among Hindu caste groups in central Nepal. The women became, through the medium of Tij songs, critical commentators on their lives in families and their various roles as daughters, sisters, daughters-in-law, and wives.

Over the course of our research (Skinner first attended Tij sessions in Naudada in 1986), we watched young girls first hover on the periphery of the composition and practice sessions and then gradually take on a larger role. Over the years they became proficient in (re)producing critical commentaries, and they developed, or so we infer from their descriptions of their concerns and choices in life, identities or self-understandings informed by this critical stance on women's positions within the family (see Holland and Skinner 1995a). During the same years the groups underwent a heuristic development as well.

Our understanding of the Tij festival as a ground for play, as a creative space for envisioning other worlds and subjectivities, deepened in our 1991 research. We realized that Tij was even more dynamic than we had imagined. We learned that the Tij groups could compose another type of song in addition to the dukha songs and that the previous boundaries on the time and space of Tij groups were being breached. In 1991 those members of Tij groups who identified themselves as students and educated women moved their groups to sing about the world of political parties and of antigovernment activity. These songs were not considered dukha songs but rather *rajniti* (political) songs.

In 1990, as mentioned in Chapter 10, a people's movement for democracy succeeded in abolishing the panchayat, or one-party, system of government. Under the new constitution Nepal's government was transformed from an absolute to a constitutional monarchy. Political parties became legal and gained strength. These changes ushered in a feeling of freedom in political expression and a call for human rights. Beginning in 1990, after the revolution, and especially in 1991, after the establishment of the multiparty system and general elections, rajniti songs were much more widely sung in the Tij festivals.

In 1990 a majority of the songs in Naudada's festival referred to the world of family relations. In these songs the didi/bahini attributed women's suffering to their bad treatment in the family. They disparagingly compared the treatment of daughters with that of sons; they called attention to the harsh treatment of daughters-in-law and wives by mothers-in-law and husbands. In contrast, a majority of the songs in 1991 criticized the government, old and new, for policies and practices that harmed women and other groups. Although complaints about the lot of women were similar to those of the earlier dukha songs, the 1991 rajniti songs were sung against party politicians and members of the ruling class, not against mothers-in-law, husbands, brothers, and other kin.[11]

We learned that these rajniti songs were not new. Several people, mostly men from Gorkha, Chitwan, Lamjung, Pokhara, and Naudada, told us of composing or of hearing women sing antigovernment songs at Tij festivals decades before the pro-democracy movement of 1990. These earlier songs told of corrupt practices, brutality, and exploitation encouraged by those in power during the panchayat period. A few people even remembered critical songs that might have been sung during the earlier Rana regime. Our own recordings from 1990 included an antigovernment song, and Skinner's collection from 1986 revealed several songs critical of local politics. It became clear that this kind of song, abundant in 1991, had been sung, though sparingly, for a long time. After the political changes it was less dangerous to sing them, and they proliferated in great number.

Although the Tij groups remained the same in 1991, we found a different set of participants stepping forward to lead the composition of rajniti songs. Kamala, a thirteen-year-old, belonged to the same caste as Renu, but unlike Renu she attended school. In 1991 she was in the eighth grade. Kamala strongly identified herself as a student and was clearly developing, as were many of her school-going friends, a view of herself as an educated and a politically active person. Like Renu she was recognized as an expert at song composition, but her songs were oriented to a different field of action than Renu's songs. Kamala composed political Tij songs that were critical of regional and national politics and that called for equal rights for women and the poor. The following song, produced and performed by Kamala and her Tij group, condemns the old political system for exploiting women and calls for a new political party that will give women equal rights under the law:

> Oh, dominated sisters of Nepal,
> We have so much tyranny.
> The panchas ate the flesh and also the blood,
> At last we have the multiparty system.
> The thirty-year panchayat reign gave so much trouble to women,
> They drank liquor by selling unmarried girls.
> They sold our innocent sisters,

And filled their bellies with liquor and chicken.
For even a small thing, they call a meeting,
Panchas took bribes, their reign is like this.
The administration was like this,
The panchas dominated women.
Now this type of rule cannot be tolerated.
Women will no longer tolerate what they did in the past.
Understanding these things, we moved forward,
We fought in the people's movement.
Rise up, women, now we don't have to fear,
Clapping cannot be done by a single hand.
On the day of Baishak 29, 2048,
There will be a general election.
There are so many parties in the multiparty system,
At last we need the party that benefits us.
A party called the Democratic party was established,
It deleted the name panchayat and deceived the people.
If this party wins, it will be the same as before,
Women will not have rights and they will have to weep all of
their life.
There is a party called Congress,
If this party wins, women will have to suffer more.
There is another party called Communist,
If this party wins, women will get rights.
The symbol of Communists is the sickle and hammer,
Women, let's publicize the Communist symbol.
Though I want to stop my pen, it doesn't stop,
Goodbye to my respected listeners.

In song, officials of the former panchayat system (the panchas) were accused of selling women as prostitutes to India, taking bribes, and exploiting the people. The singers assailed two political parties as abusers of women's rights, and promoted the Communist party as the only one that would bring justice to women.

Also in 1991, another group of women in Naudada combined some lines from a published Tij song with some they had written themselves to create a song entitled "Tij Is Our Festival," which compared their status as Nepalese women with that of other women in the world:

Tij is our festival, Tij is celebrated in a gathering,
This is the time to tell our heart's happiness and sadness.

> This happiness and sadness are pressing fully on our hearts,
> I have to stay with my eyes full of tears.
> Other countries' women have accomplished so much,
> Our country's women are involved in dancing.
> We only do household work.
> Why did you panchas walk about wearing wristwatches?
> Women have reached the moon and climbed Mt. Everest.
> What have women not done in this world!
> They go to school and also to the battlefield,
> If they get the chance women can do anything.
> The girl child grows by mother's love,
> Another child cries upstairs.
> Until the mother's love goes to the daughter,
> This heart won't have any peace.

This rajniti song recognizes Tij as a time when women can sing about their heartfelt feelings. But instead of focusing on the domestic problems and relationships portrayed in dukha songs, it orients its performers toward national political parties and the international arena of economic development and it takes up the question of women's roles in this broader world.

In 1993 Kamala told Skinner about a song she and her group had performed for the 1992 festival. In this song, which Kamala and her group called "Tyranny over Women," women demanded equal access to education and jobs and a recognition that women are as capable as men in developing the country:

> Listen sisters, listen society,
> Today I am going to speak about tyranny over women.
> The male and female born from the same womb,
> Do not have equal rights.
> The son gets the ancestral property at the age of fourteen,
> Whereas the daughter has to get married when she is only twelve.
> Parents engage in great trickery,
> Sending their daughter weeping to her husband's house.
> Parents send the son to school,
> Whereas they are afraid to provide education to the daughter.
> Father bought books and pens for my younger brother,
> Whereas he wove a basket for me, the daughter.
> My name is Kamala, who has studied only to the eighth grade,

But who has a great desire for further education.
Parents, don't take me out of school,
See if I can study well or not.
Parents, if you provide me with an education, I won't fail,
And after study, I can live by myself.
Parents, provide me with an education at any cost,
And later when I hold a job, I will repay you.
We women are also energetic and want justice,
We also have the right to hold a job.
A red ribbon tied around black hair,
We women are always deprived in Nepal.
Women have even climbed Mt. Everest and reached the moon,
Women have done so many things in this world.
Women of other countries are pilots,
We Nepalese women will be happy if we get the chance to be
great women.
Therefore, women of Nepal, this is not the time to be silent,
Let's fight to obtain our rights.

This song is a clear example of what Bakhtin (1981) would call a hybridization—a mixture of two voices within a single utterance. Kamala as author combined the voice of dukha songs with themes of the rajniti songs. Her verses draw from the figured world of dukha songs, criticizing family relations that fashion inequalities between sons and daughters. But mixed with this voice from the domestic realm is a voice from the world of politics, and explicit talk about fighting to obtain equal rights. Through her hybridized form, which brings different worlds into contact with each other, Kamala illuminates a potential link between the worlds imagined by the dukha and rajniti songs. The voice of the dukha songs frames the move into the world of politics and offers a vision of how the figured world of dukha songs could lead to a world outside the household, a world of politics, and to new positions for women. From Bakhtin's perspective it is possible to view all rajniti Tij songs and the political world of gender relations they embody as a hybridized discourse, drawing from the figured world of dukha songs and from the discourse of politics spoken and practiced among the educated in their world of schools and party-affiliated groups (see Skinner and Holland 1996).[12]

Political Tij songs thus were involved in constructing yet another figured world in which women act, one different from both the Brahmanical world and the world envisioned by the dukha songs. Through symbols used in song composition, women created stories and visions of better treatment, and in turn, the narrativized world in which their visions had meaning. Through the play allowed in Tij, women were producing new imagined priorities and relationships. They were suspending the "natural" world, where women were subordinate to men, to envision a world where women were powerful and educated, equal to men, capable of achieving any feat, and deserving of the same opportunities as men. The actors in the social scenes depicted in political Tij songs were educated women, political activists, rebels, revolutionaries.

The women in Naudada, over the course of scores of Tij festivals, built a vision of an alternative world. Through both dukha and rajniti songs, they constructed counter-worlds to the ones they knew. They imagined other figured worlds in which there was a possibility, and a moral valuing, of equal rights for women. In the Brahmanical world depicted in Rishi Pancami, a ritual bathing that occurs two days after the Tij festival, women are a problem. They menstruate, and their menstrual blood is polluting. In the dukha songs of the Tij festival, women are portrayed not as being problems but as having problems; wives are unjustly underprivileged relative to husbands, and daughters unfairly disadvantaged relative to sons. In the rajniti songs, women (and women's problems) are redeployed in a broader political arena, where corrupt government officials and unjust laws keep them from having equal rights and opportunities in work, education, and politics. In the special atmosphere and space of the Tij festival and the rehearsal sessions preceding it, the women created and participated in imagined worlds where injustice against women was recognized and deplored.

The Tij festival has been a site where women, through symbolic mediation and play, have been able collectively to envision a world in which women deserve better treatment, rights to inherit land, more say in decisions about family resources, and greater access to education. The pivot of the songs enables them to enter a different place and become a different "I."[13] The Tij groups of Naudada were composing and performing songs that had become a means of symbolic bootstrapping, a medium through which a different world could be envisioned and experienced, and new dispositions and new sensibilities could be formed. These novelties were not so much the results of "free play" as the outcomes of situated cultural production. It is not only women's increasing participation in education but also an emergent form of song production, in which Tij songs are written down (often by individual authors) for rehearsals and for publication, that has opened up the space of Tij to the world of the educated and vice versa—making possible the revolution of rajniti songs.

The years and years of Tij songs have been important at both the individual and collective levels. During some period in the past, perhaps from their inception, Tij songs became a medium for describing women's worlds and the position of women in those worlds. At some point women's Tij groups began to articulate a critical commentary on the world of domestic relations and, much less frequently until the people's movement, on the world of the state. Although Tij was time-bound—the practice sessions constrained to a few weeks, the public performance lasting only one day—the festivals provided a space for women to objectify, and thus the possibility to "disinhabit," the familiar domestic world and, if only for a brief time, inhabit a new one. To relegate Tij to the category of "rituals of rebellion" or "rituals of reversal," in which people are portrayed as stepping outside the boundaries of everyday life then returning unchanged with the boundaries reaffirmed, is to miss the power of play-worlds like Tij to transform selves and boundaries. After Tij, though women returned to the domestic world, they re-created, by rehearsing the Tij songs to themselves, the altered subjectivities and the sense of the unnaturalness of the social and political relations that kept them unequal to men.

Over the period of our research this time-bounded world began to expand. Tij groups became less circumscribed in time, their compositions less controllable. Their songs became available both in handwritten versions and in published songbooks, outside the time and locale of the festival (earlier, singing Tij songs after the festival had been labeled a sin). The relations between women in many Tij groups also became more multi-stranded: some of the women began to relate to one another not just as sisters and friends but also as political actors and, in one case, as a literacy teacher promoting equal rights. Women in these groups also expanded the scope of their agency in the worlds of domestic relations and political action. For instance, the women who participated in the march and the posse described in Chapter 10 cast their demands and sought redress in ways novel to both the world of political action and the world of domestic relations. The influence of these Tij groups has grown apace, extended beyond Tij Day by songbooks that have carried their songs to other arenas of activity and broader expanses of time.

In the space of the Tij festival, women were authoring new worlds and, in turn, new selves. Different constructions of being female were evolving along with novel imagined worlds. As they appropriated political song texts as tools of self-identification, Kamala and the other women producing these songs were developing ways of conceptualizing themselves as politically aware actors and activists in a political world. Through the medium of the festival, alternative worlds, identities, cultural forms, and senses of agency were codeveloping. This was a path toward a new world of gender relations and gendered identities in Naudada.

13

Identity in Practice

We have attempted to articulate the relation of person and society in a way that makes light of neither social life nor the world of the psyche. At the same time, we reject a dichotomy between the sociological and the psychological. "Person" and "society" are alike as sites, or moments, of the production and reproduction of social practices. But there is a substantiality to both sites. We object to an anti-essentialism that rotely rejects any sense of durability or predisposition in social life. Forms of personhood and forms of society are historical products, intimate and public, that situate the interactivity of social practices. It is in this doubly historical landscape that we place human identities. We take identity to be a central means by which selves, and the sets of actions they organize, form and re-form over personal lifetimes and in the histories of social collectivities.

Identity is one way of naming the dense interconnections between the intimate and public venues of social practice. In the cultural studies of the person described by Hall (1996), these connections are understood as a "suturing" of the person to social position, via psychodynamic processes of identification. We move toward a different metaphor, that of codevelopment. Improvisational responses to social and cultural openings and impositions elaborate identities on intimate terrain, even as these identities are worked and reworked on the social landscape. In order to set forth our own figuring of this connection between the social and the intimate, we have followed closely Vygotsky (and the sociohistorical school), Bakhtin, and Bourdieu. We have often set aside the voluminous literature on "identity"; instead of arriving at our point about identity after another lengthy critique of extant versions, we provide an alternative formulation, one grounded in practice and activity theories, to be sure, but also in our own fieldwork. Our focus is on what we call, in homage to Bakhtin, the space of authoring, and it directs our effort to understand *identity in practice.*

"Practiced identities" are constructs that can be described by reference to several contexts of activity. The first context of identity is the *figured world.* The notions of "cultural," "intentional," "virtual," or "imaginary" worlds are quite common across the disciplines of contemporary social science. They are the frames of meaning in which interpretations of human actions are negotiated. What we add is the peculiarly "practical" notion that such worlds are also socially identified. Their "figures" are not figures of speech or expression as these are ordinarily conceived: as disembodied conveyances, or neutral media, of interchange. Rather the parts of figured worlds are figures in Bakhtin's sense; they carry disposition, social identification, and even personification just as surely as they carry meaning. Thinking, speaking, gesturing, cultural exchange are forms of social as well as cultural work. When we do these things we not only send messages (to ourselves and others) but also place "ourselves" in social fields, in degrees of relation to—affiliation with, opposition to, and distance from—identifiable others.

The second context of identity, then, is *positionality.* It is less a separate "second context" than a (separable) counterpart of figuration. Positionality has to do with more than division, the "hereness" and "thereness" of people; it is inextricably linked to power, status, and rank. Social position has to do with entitlement to social and material resources and so to the higher deference, respect, and legitimacy accorded to those genders, races, ethnic groups, castes, and sexualities privileged by society. It is the context of identity that was most developed by constructivism. But the activity of positioning refers back to the cultural lay of the land, to figured worlds, and not only to some species-given universal frame. It is true that people never inhabit only one figured world. It is true that the more durable social positions—such as gender, race, ethnicity, and class—have probably been cultivated in almost every frame of activity. Positions marked by these enduring divisions, and their expectations of privilege (or not), are features of the worlds we describe, whether that of

AA, of romance, or of mental disorder. But they are prominent features in some worlds, highlighted less in others, and figured differently in terms of the symbolic capitals particular to each world.

The third context of identity, the *space of authoring*, is Bakhtin's rendition of the normal world faced by any person or collective. The world must be answered—authorship is not a choice—but the form of the answer is not predetermined. It may be nearly automatic, as in strictly authoritative discourses and authoritarian practices (thus nearing Bakhtin's monology), or it may be a matter of great variability and most significant to a single person's address. In either case authorship is a matter of orchestration: of arranging the identifiable social discourses/practices that are one's resources (which Bakhtin glossed as "voices") in order to craft a response in a time and space defined by others' standpoints in activity, that is, in a social field conceived as the ground of responsiveness. Human agency comes through this art of improvisation; the space of authoring also includes Vygotsky's zone of proximal development. The "voices" that make up a space of authoring are to an "author" as Vygotsky's instructing adults are to the neophyte: they do not so much compel rote action as extend, through their support, the competencies, the "answerability," of persons to operate in such a diverse yet powerful social universe. The histories that give shape to spaces of authoring, besides being both personal and public, are thus also compulsory and liberatory, in degrees that vary greatly.

This vision of human activity makes a mockery of any notion of individual authorship, if that means a kind of independent or autonomous creativity. But it fills personal authorship with social efficacy, for identities take us back and forth from intimate to public spaces. The fourth context of identity is that of *making worlds:* through "serious play," new figured worlds may come about, in the peculiarly Bakhtinian way that feeds the personal activities of particular groups, their "signatures," into the media, the cultural genres, through which even distant others may construe their lives. Vygotsky's understanding of play is crucial to this argument. Just as children's play is instrumental in building their symbolic competencies, upon which adult life depends, so too social play—the activities of "free expression," the arts and rituals created on the margins of regulated space and time—develops new social competencies in newly imagined communities. These new "imaginaries" build in their rehearsal a structure of disposition, a habitus, that comes to imbue the cultural media, the means of expression, that are their legacy. The course of "publicization" is markedly complicated (as suggested by the "spectacularization" of courtly love, and by the new divisions of women signaled by *rajniti* songs), but this concretion of a novel figured world brings us back to the first of the four contexts.

Climbing Houses

In Chapter 1 we related an incident involving caste identities in Nepal that lent itself equally well to a cultural or culturalist interpretation of action and to a social or constructivist view. Now that we have joined aspects of the two perspectives, let us return to the incident to discuss a significant piece neglected by either framework alone.

Recall that Gyanumaya, a lower-caste woman, arrived at the house where Skinner was living in Naudada. Calling down from the second-floor balcony, Skinner invited her to come in through the kitchen and up the stairs to be interviewed. But instead Gyanumaya scaled the outside of the house and climbed through an opening in the railing that enclosed the balcony. Since neither Naudadans in general nor Gyanumaya in particular was accustomed to climbing the sides of houses to reach the second floor, something called for explanation.

In the world of human behavior figured by those we call culturalists, cultural conceptions or beliefs, in this case Hindu understandings of pollution and purity, move people. They are powerful enough to make a person go to great lengths to observe cultural tenets—even if she is disadvantaged or discomforted in the process. Hence a culturalist might propose the following reason for Gyanumaya's climb: subscribing to the religious tenets she absorbed in childhood, Gyanumaya may have seen herself as a moral actor who, because of her caste, carried an impurity that would pollute the household she was being invited to enter, especially as the route Skinner suggested led through the kitchen, taking her near the hearth. So Gyanumaya found a way to compromise between refusal of Skinner's invitation and pollution of a higher-caste household, and reached the balcony by another route.

In a constructivist interpretation, the events at Skinner's house would have been, first and foremost, social dramas in which participants commanding different levels of power and privilege in the local community were actively negotiating the idiom of social relations that was to predominate. A Chetri (higher-caste) woman was already seated on the balcony when Gyanumaya arrived. Perhaps a glance from that woman positioned Gyanumaya as one who had no right to enter the kitchen of a house clearly occupied by higher-caste persons. Gyanumaya would, in this account, be compelled by social power, not cultural "logic"; she would be constrained in her access to the house's space by her subordinate social position, not by her embrace of a cultural imperative that just happened to disadvantage her. Although the constructivist perspective includes the possibility of resistance to what Goffman called the "interaction order," in this incident Gyanumaya accepted (or at least chose not to contest openly) the position afforded her by the Chetri woman, did not enter through the kitchen, and so avoided making a social claim that she probably would not have been able to defend.

Research in Nepal, our own and that of others, leads us to appreciate both the culturalist and the constructivist perspectives on Gyanumaya's actions but to accept neither as sufficient or comprehensive. Caste identities in Nepal are extensively developed, both figuratively in talk and other forms of expression and relationally in practice. Cultural elaborations, many unmarked for the social position that they privilege, abound. Religious teachings, folk stories, images, rituals, and holy texts provide a wealth of interpretations in which caste is portrayed as a rightful ordering of the social world. Other figurings, less prevalent, objectify the caste system as wrong.

Someone like Gyanumaya would have had many experiences with the cultural resources, discourses and practices, that justify caste. She would have learned early in life to figure herself and others as inhabitants of a culturally constructed world of caste. She no doubt could interpret interactions between persons of different castes according to the discourses of caste and imagine herself and others inspired by the motives (such as maintaining purity) of this figured world. As a child she had probably also had many experiences in which particular castes were associated with the particular localities in Naudada that placed them and the particular activities and acts that marked their "presence": particular languages, ways of speaking, ways of carrying the body, ways of holding the body when in the presence of persons of different castes, ways of dressing, moral evaluations, and so on.

For her, her own caste identity no doubt was "embodied" and, as Bourdieu has insisted, powerfully affected her behavior through habitual associations that she might not have been able to verbalize. Her body carried a sense of caste, and of her caste position in respect to others about her, wherever she went. At the same time, she both knew and could generate figurings of caste and possessed an embodied sense of how caste was practiced in Naudada. She could probably tell herself (and others) about herself as a person of a particular caste, as well as consciously monitor and edit her own behavior to fit an image of proper caste behavior. She was, in sum, highly susceptible to figuring herself and being figured by others according to caste, and to positioning herself and being positioned as a lower-caste person—one prohibited from entering the kitchens of higher-caste persons. She lived in a web of constraints organized around caste and was probably propelled at times by purely ideological constructions; at other times by an almost purely "tactical" social reckoning of what it would cost her to refuse the caste position afforded her in a given situation; and, probably a majority of the time, by a mixture of the two.

Both a culturalist view, which credits an asocial emphasis on cultural logics, and a constructivist view, which emphasizes the calculus of social position by actors, make too little of the kind of agency we have seen throughout the cases described in this book. This is our major disagreement with both frames of interpretation. For us, the incident of the woman who climbed up the house became an invitation to consider not only the means by which her behavior was collectively orchestrated but also the ways in which creativity is collectively enabled. Even hemmed in by caste constraints, Gyanumaya managed, in a strikingly inventive way, to circumvent the obstacles to her participation in the interviewing. She improvised from the resources at hand a rather spectacular entry to the house. By focusing only on the social constraints, we would have missed the significance of her improvised departure from a routine path. By ignoring the constraints, we would have missed the forces that made the path obligatory and the pointedness of her deviation.

Or take the case of Roger (Chapter 9). Foucault has presented a compelling picture of scientific discourse, its contribution to a constructed behavioral normality, and the specifically modern impetus to discipline those who deviate from this norm. Roger was one such person, who had come under the purview of the medical establishment and was subjected to its categorization of mental disorders and to the treatments prescribed to manage these disorders. But Roger "twisted" the categories applied to his case. He used what his caregivers told him and popular texts about mental disorders as ways to figure an identity or rather identities, as ways to interpret and organize his actions in the social contexts important to him. He was having difficulties with both his parents and his wife; the histories of negotiations around his problems with them had created dilemmas that troubled him. Roger appropriated different diagnoses of his "mental problems" to create distinctive standpoints within these two dilemmas. With his parents, he elaborated an identity organized around manic-depression; with his wife, an identity around borderline personality disorder. Roger assimilated the textual artifacts and categories of psychiatry to an everyday part of his life, improvising several new identities through which he would craft new answers to his dilemmas and (concomitantly) new positions for his parents and his wife. He used these resources opportunistically, as a Lévi-Straussian *bricoleur* would, yet without regulation by an overarching cultural logic or an institutionally prescribed blueprint.

A more collaborative improvisation, and one of clear importance, was evident in the Tij festival in Naudada, Nepal (Chapter 12). A particular sort of Tij song, rajniti or political songs, predominated in the festival of 1991, virtually supplanting the dukha or suffering songs that had predominated in earlier festivals. Rajniti songs were responsive to the People's Movement of 1990 and the resulting change from the king's one-party system to a multiparty system. They were quite different in content from the dukha songs: instead of being about women's mistreatment by husbands and mothers-in-law, the songs of 1991 were more often about the atrocities of the former government and the ill-treatment of women and poor people by political parties. In one regard, however, rajniti songs were rather simple improvisations on a third, less frequent type of song. These *ghatana* or "event" songs typically described newsworthy incidents—suicides, landslides, plane and bus accidents. Formally, rajniti songs were mere variations, a type of ghatana song that took political events and incidents as its subject matter. The improvisation allowed women to redirect their critical commentary from the domestic hearth and field to the arena of government and party politics.

The Significance of Improvisation

Why celebrate these moments of resourcefulness? Why pay attention to these improvisations that piece together existing cultural resources opportunistically to address present conditions and problems? Why pay attention to them instead of analyzing the webs of constraints that limit people's activities and life possibilities? Webs like those imposed on Gyanumaya in the name of caste, on Hindu women in Naudada in the name of the life path of the good woman, or on Roger in the name of personal competence: surely they overpower these improvisational moves and reveal their feebleness and insignificance?

To put it simplistically, there are two answers. We attend to improvisation because we speak from a critical perspective, in a manner akin to that of Haraway (1988). We take an evaluative stand toward gross oppression, exploitation, and the small kinds of relentless and irredemptive strictures that Foucault detailed. Yet we neither anticipate an impending liberatory revolution nor favor schemes of intervention that would impose policies and programs that only a select few recognize as beneficial. The remaining option is to document and support those local openings and social movements which seem liberatory.

The second answer concerns theoretical comprehension. Improvisations command our attention because they may be excluded only at the risk of missing the back-and-forth of engagement. Even within grossly asymmetrical power relations, the powerful participants rarely control the weaker so completely that the latter's ability to improvise resistance becomes irrelevant. Tactics such as Roger's, for example, by which the terms for controlling "patients" and "clients" are taken up by their subject for his own purposes, are more than problematic for mental health practitioners. The "borderline" confounds both the ideology and the practice of psychiatry by refusing to accept the boundaries of the practitioner-client relationship (see Lachicotte 1992). The borderline diagnosis itself and the commentary produced around it are historical constructions responsive to the perturbations caused (in part) by the particular improvisations of a particular type of client that the practice has not learned to control.

A Second Form of Agency

If improvisations are significant means of renovation, which even the most powerful and hegemonic of social regimes cannot preclude, they are even more significant when paired with another form of human agency: agency through self-directed symbolizations. In developing our picture of identity in practice we drew upon two theorists: Bakhtin and

Vygotsky. Together they afford us a sober view of the possibilities for human agency. They tell us where—along the margins and interstices of collective cultural and social constructions—how, and with what difficulties human actors, individuals, and groups are able to redirect themselves. Though an overemphasis on social constraints leaves little room for human agency, many accounts make the opposite error: they neglect the cultural and social contexts that inform the "playing field" to which human action is directed and by which it is shaped. Vygotsky and Bakhtin explicitly addressed the issues of agency that were such a part of the intellectual field of post-revolutionary Russia. Yet, through the socially mediated ways in which they cast such forms of intimate action as inner speech and the dialogical interplay of self and others, they avoided the asocial and acultural figuring of the world of human action that still predominates among many of those who explore "psychological" processes.

Vygotsky and Bakhtin have allowed us to elaborate a theory of human action that also takes advantage of Bourdieu's shift to the study of culture in practice and his correlative appreciation of embodiment and rejection of the conception of culture as rules. The two Russian theorists' fascination with the relation of language and other means of expression to consciousness—taking into account both everyday genres and such specialized forms as literary and artistic works—led them to devise conceptual tools that we have used to augment practice theory's understanding of human action. Improvisations crafted in the moment are one of the margins of human agency. Self-directed symbolizations are a second means by which a modicum of agency is made possible.

In Bourdieu's work, identity seems principally embodied; he pays much less attention to objectifications of identity or self-understandings. For our work, the more interesting cases of identity are those which are objectified, for they are the ones more likely to mediate sustained "agentive" action. The positional aspects of identity, such as the discomfort a woman may feel on entering a space she has experienced before as for men only, are most often embodied, and may be unmediated by any linguistically realized apprehension. But to grasp the potential for ennoblement, for moving beyond such "mute" positioning, we must consider how the symbolization of identities can come about and be used to direct the behavior of others and oneself.

Bourdieu (1977a) makes improvisation the predominant form of agency. He argues conclusively that it is fruitless to make up a set of cultural rules to account for people's behavior. The material and social conditions of activity vary in a plenitude of ways; even in highly restrictive environments, it is difficult to avoid unusual combinations of people and things. Rules that handle "all possible combinations" in real-world settings are impossible to devise. Instead, Bourdieu suggests, our bodies are repositories of a complex set of associations—of actions (movements), figures (categories), and contexts (environments)—sedimented from experiencing concrete instances of their combination, their work together. More complicated experiences, sequences of joint action coordinated among actors as a relation to particular "qualities," such as honor, produce sensitivities toward a set of culturally devised games or contexts of action like our figured worlds, where there are general, dispositional motives and acts and ways of faring well and faring poorly. Agency lies in the improvisations that people create in response to particular situations, mediated by these senses and sensitivities. They opportunistically use whatever is at hand to affect their position in the cultural game in the experience of which they have formed these sets of dispositions.

Bakhtin and Vygotsky, too, emphasize that we have our existence not in repose but in practice. Bakhtin takes the culturally specific games that Bourdieu elucidates (which compare to Bakhtin's notion of speech genres), gives them voice, and directs them to a more general, even universal, condition of human activity. If we are alive, says Bakhtin, then we are engaged in answering what is directed to us. We are always engaged in the activity of making sense of what is happening as one who will respond. We are always authoring the meaning of action. If, for Bourdieu, we can best understand cultures and the people who enact them by considering behavior in the space of practice, then, for Bakhtin, we can best understand languages and the selves constructed in and through the words and voices of others by attending to the space of authoring. Improvisation using the resources at hand, and the limited agency improvisation entails, characterize both spaces. Furthermore, both spaces are shot through with the activity of social positioning. Bourdieu's action, Bakhtin's utterance, take place within an always present, partially durable construction of stratified social differences, positions, languages, and other cultural media of action.

Vygotsky's work, in comparison with that of Bourdieu and Bakhtin, often appears both socially naive and simplistic. Vygotsky neglected the social forms and constraints to which the others attend so carefully. He was nearly silent on the kinds of human domination that they reveal. He focused instead on a fantastic, seemingly utopian and liberatory power granted by symbols and the human ability to play with symbols: the power to create worlds, effective contexts of action, that may never exist apart from the pivot of imagination. Yet it is Vygotsky's focus that enables us to link Bourdieu's space of practice with Bakhtin's space of authoring and so helps us envision this second kind of agency.

Human life is inexplicable without our abilities to figure worlds, play at them, act them out, and then make them socially, culturally, and thus materially consequential. This collective ability to take imaginary worlds seriously—the sort of fetishization that makes certain pieces of paper over into "money"—is the magic that anthropologists as well as others have tried to capture in the concept of culture. Vygotsky was fascinated by the human ability to escape the immediate control of environmental stimuli and instead organize behaviors, thoughts, and feelings in relation to imagined stimuli. Children early in their lives exhibit the ability and the desire to enter into worlds that they imagine, to treat objects around them as (refigured) objects from those worlds, and to put aside, at least temporarily, feelings, interests, and concerns that are irrelevant to the play world. The play worlds that children create are akin to the more complex culturally constructed or figured worlds that they enter into as they grow older.

Human play, Vygotsky emphasized, develops the child's capacity for semiotic mediation and makes it a part of the child's intimate world. Through play people acquire the key cultural means by which they escape, or at least reduce, the buffeting of whatever stimuli they encounter as they go through their days. Vygotsky stressed that only part of the significance of language, signs, and symbols was caught by their representational potential or their capacity for stating rules. Like Austin, he believed that people do things with words, and that "representation" is only one action, albeit an important one, that words make possible. People *use* symbols: to organize and manage their own and others' behavior, to intervene in what Bakhtin would call the world's "addressivity," to objectify, or concretize even in their literal absence, other contexts of activity. This is the reason we find it important to think about how cultural resources are used; for example, how the life narratives described in Chapter 4 are used in Alcoholics Anonymous to evoke and shape members' conceptions of themselves as non-drinking alcoholics. Remembered stories, re-creations of one's own story, can be purposively used to redirect oneself away from the impulse to take a drink, to interpose new actions, and to cast oneself as a new actor in a new social play.

Bourdieu calls attention to the taken-for-granted or out-of-awareness associations between the important categories of social division and social spaces, body postures (hexis), the uses of colors, and so on. These connections are especially important for understanding how relational (positional) aspects of identity work. But worlds are figured through language and images as well, and these means of objectification make possible the kind of "re-cognition" that Kondo experienced when she saw her reflection (Chapter 6) and even the deliberate efforts of persons and groups to direct their own behavior. Through the transfiguration that commentary provides, people may even increase their awareness of, and thus their capability to inhibit, such "automatic" responses as the deferential body postures assumed in the presence of higher-status people. Vygotsky's formulations, in short, direct us to attend to people's collective ability to imagine themselves in worlds that may yet be scarcely realized, and to the modest ability of humans to manage their own behavior through signs directed at themselves. These important aspects of human agency need to be considered in tandem with the kinds of improvisation that Gyanumaya, Roger, or the Tij groups accomplished. They both enable the creation of new worlds and new identities and make us appreciate how figured (objectified) identities become important tools with which individuals and groups seek to manage one another and their own behavior.

The Social and Political Work of Identities

Vygotsky recognized that tools of self-management are not the products of personal invention. Instead they are cultural or collective resources first experienced by children and neophytes in social interaction. People learn to use these signs historically, first as parts of behavioral routines, then as signs meaningful to others, and finally signs for directing their own actions, managing their own feelings, and organizing their own thoughts.

This is a basic process in the intimate formation of an identity. One learns "the" identity of inscribed acts—the signs or markers of culturally constructed identity, whether they be the display of particular skills, the enactment of certain motives, the cultivation of ways of speaking, the use of certain expressions, the display of certain emotions, or the wearing of distinctive clothes—in like manner. They are first parts of an undistinguished behavioral routine, second a means to affect others, and third, if the identity forms to this extent and especially if objectified in the figured world, means to evoke one's own sense of who one is and so organize one's behavior. The process Vygotsky describes is a developmental one that proceeds by converting signs into what we have called heuristic devices: signal relations turned toward self-understanding. Identities have, to our minds, principally this import: they are social forms of organization, public and intimate, that mediate this development of human agency.

It is a process of personal formation that occurs via cultural resources enacted in a social context. The person "makes" herself over into an actor in a cultural world; she may even, over time, reach the point of being able to evoke the world and her sense of herself within it without the immediate presence of others. But the cultural figurings of selves, identities, and the figured worlds that constitute the horizon of their meaning against which they operate, are collective products. One can significantly reorient one's own behavior, and can even participate in the creation of new figured worlds and their possibilities for new selves, but one can engage in such play only as part of a collective. One can never inhabit a world without at least the figural presence of others, of a social history in person. The space of authoring, of self-fashioning, remains a social and cultural space, no matter how intimately held it may become. And, it remains, more often than not, a contested space, a space of struggle.[1]

The way in which identities take an intimate form (which we discussed in Chapter 8) is still a political process. As we have shown, the social value of various identities—the symbolic capital they command—is often contested interpersonally through the attempted denigration of the discourses that posit them or the acts that sign them. Even in the intimate venue of inner speaking and the imagination, however, the signs and tools of self-formation are themselves likely to be inscribed with social position. Bakhtin's inspired notion of a "dialogic self" predicates the condition of self-formation in that space of authoring where (re)forming senses of self are addressed, even challenged, by the socially inscribed voices that one (re)generates in inner speech. His notion of authorship, in other words, often depends upon personalizing the contestations of identity that mark social speech.

Our discussion of the beginnings of the figured world of romance in medieval Europe's "play world" of courtly love (Chapter 11) looked back to a collective or public space of authoring. Even though it was play, many of the powerful found courtly love objectionable and unacceptable. Among its many transgressions, courtly love modeled the relation of male lover to female beloved as the feudal tie of vassal to lord, an inversion of the prevailing gender hierarchy that also mocked the bonds of authority. Opponents wanted no space where gender and power relations were transfigured in such a radically different way. Some of the church hierarchy even attempted to brand proponents of courtly love as heretics. Other writers inveighed against the effeminacy of its practitioners, and all but called for their conquest. Both groups saw their dreams of eradication of this source of social heresy attempted (if not entirely realized) in the Albigensian crusades.

A more recent struggle over acts and discourses, recounted in Chapter 7, similarly disputes the value of the identities they organize and the standing of the people and groups of whom the identities are taken as a sign. Judging by the amount of energy and attention directed to the contestations over the discourse of sexual harassment, something must be collectively at stake. The rancor aroused by the testimony of Anita Hill in the Clarence Thomas hearings (Eisenhart and Lawrence 1994), and even the ink spilled over the lesser case of J. Donald Silva, a University of New Hampshire professor who was charged by female students with sexual harassment (Bernstein 1994), attest to the power of issues of sexual harassment. These are trials, whether of a metaphorical or literal variety, over the social positioning of specific acts and individuals. Silva was accused of sexual harassment for acts such as giving out in his classes the following example of a simile: "Belly dancing is like jello on a plate with a vibrator under the plate." He was at first unrepentant and defiant. Months later, he said on a radio talk show: "It makes one begin to think one might be all the things that these people say that you are. You begin to think of yourself as really a, you know, probably a . . . a . . . a . . . a very, you know, evil teacher . . . which is frightening."[2] And, as we pointed out with the example of Mamet's play *Oleanna*, there are also trials over the authority to be given to women who try to wield this new weapon and, thus by Bakhtin's rule, even to the discourse itself.

The critical discourses of Tij songs (see Chapters 10 and 12) provide another example of an "identity politics" that is both public and intimate (see Holland and Skinner, 1995a). Several of the songbooks published by various Communist parties around the time of the Tij festival of 1991 included forewords that invited readers to figure the world according to a Marxian analysis of gender relations espoused by the sponsoring parties. They did so in a manner that was not necessarily politic. They branded the analyses of gender relations given in the older *dukha* songs as correctly critical but as failing to understand the true source of women's oppression in class dynamics. The *rajniti* songs published in the books were designed to remedy that failed critique. The domestic world figured in dukha songs and the village women marked by that world were devalued, and a new division between them and their younger, more educated, and more politically active "sisters" was opened up.

Because Tij songs are such important resources of inner speaking, this division was felt and rehearsed personally and reproduced (in some parts of Nepal, though not in Naudada) in interpersonal relations among the group members. The feminist wings of the parties have grown sensitive to these ill effects, and now seek to disseminate songs that unite the communities that practice rajniti and dukha singing. These politics of identification concerning (types of) people, the cultural resources they produce, and the acts that are taken to signify particular identities characterize the social space of authoring. They provide generic and personified "models," the voices that are re-created in inner speech, for the complex interchange that makes up particular identities.

The social and political work of identification, in brief, reveals two closely interrelated lessons. First, identities and the acts attributed to them are always forming and re-forming in relation to historically specific contexts. They come to bear the marks of these contexts and their politics. Identities and their cultural resources, their semiotic tools in Vygotsky's terms, are constantly being generated, sometimes censored or suppressed. But they are responses to, develop in, and so include the dilemmas set by the struggles, personal crises, and social recruitment under which they form. The salience and authority of Roger's "psychiatric" identities grew as he refigured a place for himself in the web of familial and institutional relations disrupted by his mental disorder. Tij groups, especially the schoolgirls within them, responded to the new openings made by the people's movement of 1991 by expanding, in rajniti songs, the scope of women's social and political worlds and the identification of women's places in them. In doing so they inadvertently created a split within the groups and within each of the members.

The second lesson is that identities form on intimate and social landscapes through time. The distinction of particular acts as indexical of an identity, and the expansion of identities to include broader or different ranges of acts, depend upon the work of the groups involved in the relevant field of activity, and the work of their allies and opponents. The historical moment of this work—the conjuncture of the allied personal and social histories that determines whether the identities posited by any particular discourse become important and are worked into the everyday lives of people—cannot be simply dictated by the discourse, the cultural form itself.[3]

Forming an identity on intimate landscapes takes time, certainly months, often years. It takes (and makes) personal experience to organize a self around discourses and practices, with the aid of cultural resources and the behavioral prompting and verbal feedback of others. It takes the heuristic developments of disposition and savoir faire to imagine the world and to identify with the figured world. Conceiving oneself as an agent whose acts count in, and account for, the world cannot happen overnight.

Forming an identity on social landscapes also takes time—public and institutional time. The dim images of fantasy worlds and the actors that populate such worlds cannot be devised and translated into practice from one week to the next. The work of reproduction and regeneration of public life moves heuristically as well, through a kind of historically contingent "hybridization" (as Bakhtin might call it). Cultural resources take form from elements that may have been generated in other contexts and brought together in the mix of struggles that may lack any logical connection to the world being improvised in social play. Nor do these worlds necessarily endure the transfiguration beyond the local sites of their production. No constituency may coalesce to work them into different places, different landscapes of activity. Or an opposition may successfully choke them off. Just as an identity may never gain any prominence among a person's organizations of behavior, a fantasized world may never gain any purchase on the sociohistorical landscape. Its figurings and the identities afforded by them may simply not be taken up, as Andrew refused to learn the world according to Alcoholics Anonymous and to figure himself in the shapes of its narratives. Worlds and identities can be fleeting—a moment's play—or they can eventually become as central to personal and public life as the (once courtly) world of romance.

Subjectivities across Figured Worlds

If persons and figured worlds are in the making over months, years, decades, even centuries, then so must be the groups with which people affiliate. Critics of the concepts of culture successfully argued, during the period we call the critical disruption (see Chapter 2), that social positions cannot be disregarded in any cultural figuring of the world of human action. Accounts that conceived cultures as shared webs of meaning, in which all are equally suspended regardless of such structured social divisions as gender, class, and race, were called into serious question. This recognition of the importance of social position in shaping people's experience led to experiments in ethnography. This trend was marked, for example, in gender studies' descriptions of women's cultures and socialities, of gendered "worlds"; in British cultural studies' emphasis on subcultures, whether based on gender, race, class, or generation; and in Bourdieu's even more ambitious concepts of class (and potentially other forms of) habitus.

Yet, as proponents of these approaches have noted, perspectives predicating clearly differentiable arrays of social forces, even those privileging class dynamics as a definitive social and cultural divider, have proven too limiting. Social positions cut and cut again across one another. Women's experience in the social life of the United States is not only different for, say, black women and white women; each of these groups is further divided by class differences, by differences of sexual orientation, by ethnicities, by the gamut of social dividers that have become common in "postmodern" sociologies.

Our use of identities—informed by these two dependent, but noncoincident processes, figuring and positionality—leads to another way of conceptualizing personhood, culture, and their distributions over social groups. Figured worlds and their situated realizations, rendered collectively and personally as spaces of authoring, are socially animated by groupings that may not be reified as social groups. The politics of participation in figured worlds—for example, who may enter the activities of an AA chapter and how members gain or lose place among themselves— may not reproduce a group according to the categories of currency in social positioning. Furthermore, these same politics may bring together persons who share little else: few means of figuring common action and few of the common markers of social position. As Bourdieu's fields are meant to be, though in an even less structured and durable form, our spaces of authoring are games peculiar to themselves.[4] Yet, as the examples of courtly love and nationalisms attest, these spaces have the potential to expand, and their players may become social groupings and categories of newer currency.

Likewise persons may be stretched over times and spaces, fully active in some worlds, perhaps scarcely formed in others. Bakhtin's dialogism lives within this understanding. These fields and spaces of human activity work in the recognition of an otherness that reaches beyond their specific polities to other ways of figuring activity. The world's address is both generic and specific, and only in the transit between the two aspects can we craft an answer to it. So we cannot deny what we might call the power of culture. And this is as true for a single person as it is for the collective subjects; the sites of consciousness lie within a thoroughly social world. Figured worlds, the politics of social positioning, and spaces of authoring are our attempts to conceptualize collective and personal phenomena in ways that match the importance of culture in contextualizing human behavior with the situating power of social position. Identities are our way of figuring the interfaces among these dimensions of collective life; our way of naming the places where society organizes persons and persons in turn reorganize, albeit in modest steps, societies; the pivots of our lived worlds.

Notes

1. The Woman Who Climbed up the House

1. All persons' names and many place names are pseudonyms to preserve the anonymity of those who helped us in our research.
2. McCall and Simmons (1978) represent an important Meadean vein that inspired us originally. That literature now includes an expanded and elaborated vision of the social and cultural bases for possible identities. Besides social roles, cross-cutting "master statuses" of race, ethnicity, class, gender, and sexuality are important bases (McCall 1987; Stryker 1987), as are salient cultural conceptions of personality (e.g., an aggressive person).
3. In the United States, at least, the center of gravity of cultural studies is currently in the humanities. This book is part of an effort to extend cultural studies through more sociological and ethnographic work.
4. This tradition was centered at Marburg (see Holquist 1990). Bakhtin's early works (1990, 1993) developed a phenomenological aesthetics (or better, perhaps, an aesthetic phenomenology) through a technical, philosophical language and argument more or less faithful to the Marburg position (see Chapter 9).
5. "Self" and "identity" are loaded terms. In Chapter 2 we place our use of them in the context of the literature. For the present, let us borrow Harré's (1984) notion of the self as the (theoretical or presumptive) collocation of a personal repertory. The self is the place from which persons view or sense the world and reflect upon it. There is no presumption that a person has only one important sense of self; or an impetus to consistency across these different senses of self. We are not concerned here with the psychodynamic dilemmas that occupied Erikson but rather with the selves that are assembled from, and in relation to, cultural resources.
6. This book is a collective product, including the analyses of the experiences we describe, but from time to time we speak from the perspective of one person.
7. The incident happened in 1986. Note that, although Holland had already

289

read the convincing theoretical treatises of Bourdieu (1977a) arguing for a shift away from culturalist views in the field, she still first went through a culturalist interpretation.

8. Hegemony is a much debated concept. We refer here to something like the hegemonic practices discussed by R. W. Connell (1987: 183): "Hegemony means . . . a social ascendancy achieved in a play of social forces that extends beyond contests of brute power into the organization of private life and cultural processes. Ascendancy . . . achieved at the point of a gun, or by the threat of unemployment, is not hegemony. Ascendancy which is embedded in religious doctrine and practice, mass media content, wage structures, the design of housing, welfare/taxation policies and so forth, is." Hegemony is also not total domination. What is hegemonic is contested and variable according to situation.

9. One cannot, Lutz says, reduce the social claim to a contingent or secondary matter. Rather, social status is one of the things emotion *is about* among the Ifaluk.

10. The extent to which women's ways of speaking in the United States are characteristic of a women's culture or of women's position in society is disputed; see Chapter 7.

11. Here we have set up ideal types. Some constructivists emphasize positioning to the point that they convey a radical constructivist perspective (see, e.g., Davies and Harré 1990; Harré and Van Langenhove 1991).

12. The school was another such place (see Skinner and Holland 1996). Also, caste restrictions were not observed in the more illicit arenas of drinking and gambling.

13. Others have made similar arguments, e.g., Begoña Aretxaga (1993: 231): "As an anthropologist I am interested in cultural formations of meaning and their articulation through personal experience because it is at this intersection at which cultural constructions blend together with unique personal (or collective) experience that models of feeling are shaped and new meanings created."

2. A Practice Theory of Self and Identity

1. This definition is roughly built from characteristics shared by the many meanings of "self" in the anthropological literature. It alludes to a fuller definition given by Ito (1987): *Self* has (1) a reflexive quality, the ability to distinguish, evaluate, and objectify self and other; and (2) a dynamic quality, the apperceptive ability to understand, interpret, manipulate, and incorporate sensory judgments. Self is both executor and object of judgments, discriminations, creativity, and order. Besides Ito, Skinner (1990),

White (1992), Harris (1989), and Fogelson (1979) review the anthropological uses of "self," "identity," "person," and "individual."

2. Nepal is home to many groups, whose history and social position vary widely. Their cultural practices, including self-related discourses, also vary. Skinner's and Holland's research was carried out in a different area of Nepal with people who, for the most part, were not Newar.

3. Concepts that might be translated as "self" in South Asia, including Nepal, are complex. A Sanskrit term, *atma* or *atman*, is sometimes translated as "self" or "soul." This term, deriving from Hindu religious and philosophical texts and discourses, is sometimes used by nonspecialists to speak of an aspect of themselves that continued on in a cycle of death and rebirth. In Naudada, where Skinner and Holland did their research among mixed-caste Nepali speakers, people made more use of concepts having to do with what we will later define as "self-in-practice." Skinner (1990: 21) writes: "There is no noun I heard used to indicate this notion of an empirical self [self-in-action], but there are pronouns (e.g., *aphu*, which is used as a reflexive pronoun to refer to one's 'own self,' *mero* or 'my,' *ma* or 'I'), that an individual would use to refer to herself as an actor in the world and to reflect on her actions." *Man* was also an important concept in Naudada (see Chapter 12); it is often glossed as "heart/mind." The *man* is where thoughts and feelings are stored and churn about. It is located in the center of the chest. McHugh reported that Gurungs, an ethnic group living primarily in another region of the country, used the term *sae* to mean "the seat of will, memory, and emotion . . . conceived as a kind of entity located in the chest" (1989: 82). She found the concept to be an important one that individuals use to articulate their own will, thoughts, and emotions.

4. For reviews see Harris (1989); Marsella, DeVos, and Hsu (1985); Levine (1982); Shweder and Bourne (1984); White (1992).

5. The slight differences between the culturalist position we describe here and that set out in Chapter 1 are artifacts of the opposition of culturalists to constructivists, rather than to universalists. In Chapter 1 we assumed the effects of the "critical disruption" that gave birth to constructivism.

6. A proposition that psychologists such as Markus and Kitayama (1991), Kitayama, Markus, and Lieberman (1994), and Miller (1988) have set out to test through quasi-experimental designs.

7. This was why Hallowell argued that "self" was a better focus for cross-cultural research than "ego" or "personality": "The term 'self' . . . seem[s] to connote a concept that remains closer to the phenomenological facts that reflect man's self-awareness as a generic psychological attribute. It retains the reflexive connotation that is indicated when we say that a human

individual becomes an object to himself, that he identifies himself as an object among other objects in his world, that he can conceive himself, not only as a whole, but in terms of different parts, that he can converse with himself, and so on" (1955b: 80; see Skinner 1990).

8. He called these invariant characteristics orientations. In a manner similar to Neisser's (1988) delineation of different forms of self-knowledge, Hallowell (1955a) identified five such invariants: self-orientation, object-orientation, spatio-temporal orientation, motivational orientation, and normative or moral orientation.

9. Shweder (1991) muddies the universalist-culturalist waters by asking us to problematize what we consider natural. He proposes that demons and other constructions we deem unnatural may, in fact, be parts of the natural environment that we do not acknowledge because of our cultural lenses. He chides Obeyesekere for not considering the possibility that the malevolent ancestral spirits his informants tell him about "do exist and can get into one's body, . . . and that the cultural representation of their existence and a person's experience of their existence lights up an aspect of reality that has import for the management of the self" (346–347). Sahlins (1995) also takes Obeyesekere (1992) to task for a kind of ethnocentrism.

10. For a more hopeful vision see Haraway (1988), who disavows radical forms of the social-constructivist criticism of science and opts for a "successor science project that offers a more adequate, richer, better account of a world in order to live in it well," one that has "*simultaneously* an account of radical historical contingency for all knowledge claims and knowing subjects, a critical practice for recognizing our own 'semiotic technologies' for making meanings, *and* a no-nonsense commitment to faithful accounts of a 'real' world" (579).

11. Especially relevant here is the construction of the "psychological" in modernization theory. Such theories—of achievement motivation, "modernizing personalities," and the like—were complicit in rationalizing and depoliticizing processes of colonization.

12. They include, e.g., images of the other in *National Geographic* (Lutz and Collins 1993), life-story genres in Alcoholics Anonymous (Cain 1991 and Chapter 5), specialist discourses on the self in the anthropology and psychology of the 1950s, and performances such as the Balinese cockfight made famous by Geertz (1973a).

13. Kenneth Gergen, a social psychologist, pursues other aspects of social constructionism related to our work: "Narratives of the self are not personal impulses made social, but social processes realized on the site of the personal" (1994: 210). His point—about the figuring of self within social

relationships—is like Bakhtin's notion of dialogism, which we consider in Chapter 8.

14. Dennett (1988) argues that the self is an "abstractum," a fiction—but a convenient one. He suggests an analogy between selves and "centers of gravity." A chair, say, has no tangible, but only a virtual, center of gravity. Still, the figurative reification is useful in describing the behavior of chairs in many circumstances. Likewise, self is a popular fiction, a "figurative reification," by means of which we account for our and others' actions. Dennett's notion is in a sense constructivist, in that the self is a dependent figure of our ethnopsychological discourse. Yet it has a kind of persistence and a transitive, cross-situational quality, indeed almost an inevitable or natural aspect. It is difficult to imagine how to interact with, or speak about, people without such a fiction of integrity. Harré (1979, 1984) has presented the most extensive argument for a "fictive" notion of self, which is at the same time a virtually necessary consequence of the deictic character of social interactivity. See the discussion of Bakhtin in Chapter 8.

15. Studies critical of psychology and psychological anthropology are an obvious result of the critical disruption. Works by psychologists (such as Henriques et al. 1984 and Parker 1992) and the writings of the "critical psychologists" (Tolman and Maiers 1991) parallel "critical" works by anthropologists writing on psychological topics. Scheper-Hughes's (1992) analysis of the Brazilian folk idiom of "nervios" is an example, as are Lutz's (1988) critiques of scientific discourses on emotion and research (in press) on the effects of U.S. military funding in the 1950s on subsequent directions of psychological research. "Critical psychological anthropology," critical psychology, and critical social psychology (Wexler 1983; Gergen 1984, 1994) are important because they disallow innocent-seeming and apolitical views of the conceptual tools and discourses that researcher/practitioners use. They have a more specific import for theories of the self, suggesting a revised theoretical orientation that admits power relations.

16. Although, as Scheper-Hughes (1992) points out, such theory mostly awaits invention—a task we undertake in this book.

17. Reification of this sort not only creates an impression of immunity to social and historical change but also overlooks a crucial heterogeneity. Reification obviates the recognition that social conditions themselves may be changing. Markus and Kitayama (1991) point out that scientific terms for independent self-processes, such as self-disclosure, are recent. They interpret this as a matter of delayed discovery. Our guess is that the creation of more and more terms that assume independent selves is both

responsive to and creative of historical conditions (see Gergen 1991 for an analogous point about concepts of mental deficiency). The discourses and practices that construct selves as independent may be more powerful in the United States now than they were fifty years ago. Holland and Kipnis (1994) argue that *both* modes of self-organization, sociocentric and egocentric, are evident in American society. Perhaps independence is a more pervasive mode at present, but to read pervasiveness as essence obscures recognition that the relative salience of the two modes is a matter of tension, if not struggle.

18. Efforts to study members of the same social position simply defined—as women, say—have proven problematic. Social positions are multidimensional, and their context is too important to ignore. One solution has been to focus on historically and socially constituted groups relevant to the context in question, avoiding any assumptions about the groups' homogeneity (or representativeness).

19. Seminal examples are Rosaldo (1980) and Crapanzano (1980). Abu-Lughod (1986), Kondo (1990), and White (1991) extend (and criticize) these. A recent example is Holland and Skinner (1995a). For more discussion, see Holland (1997).

20. Others use this concept or emphasize a similar idea, e.g., Ewing (1990); McHugh (1989); Mines (1988); Parish (1991).

21. Whether the psychodynamic account of history-in-person, to which Hall alludes, and our sociohistorical account can contribute to each other remains to be seen. Bakhtin (see Voloshinov 1987) and Vygotsky had complex and complicated relations with psychodynamic theory, and kept their distance from it (van der Veer and Valsiner 1991). They give us little help with this question. But we have little reason to exclude the classic psychodynamic dilemmas as sources of contingencies with which the authoring self must contend.

22. See Wertsch (1985b) and Clark and Holquist (1984) for biographical sketches of Vygotsky and Bakhtin, respectively.

23. Bourdieu's emphasis on embodiment at the expense of symbols has helped move anthropologists away from the notion of culture as beliefs—as linguistically mediated, symbolically encoded conceptions and convictions about the world—and toward a notion of culture as dispositional, out-of-awareness orientations toward the world (see Strauss 1992). With "semiotic mediation," Bourdieu and the sociohistorical school diverge in emphasis. Bourdieu alludes to "symbolic mastery" in *Outline of a Theory of Practice* (1977a: 83), but does not develop the concept. In *The Logic of Practice* (1990b) he says enough to indicate that his idea of symbolic mastery is of a representational rather than a heuristic sort. His "symbolic

mastery" is a rationalist view of symbolic mediation and does not capture what Vygotsky was describing. For a Vygotskian semiotic mediator, the important fact is its investment within the pragmatics of communication, which includes its representation. Heuristic development is replete with symbolic forms—forms whose "meaning" is not solely, or even principally, representational.

24. "Training wheels" is Hubert Dreyfus's metaphor (personal communication).

25. By distributed over others we mean both that one's use of the tools depends upon the collaboration of others and that the ability to sustain one's own behavior under ordinary conditions is continually reconstituted by collectively produced practices. Becker's (1963) study of marijuana users in the early 1950s provides a good example: neophytes were often dependent upon collective interpretations to experience pot smoking as having a noticeable effect and as being pleasurable. And even the old hands, during "bad trips" or under intense social criticism, had to turn to their fellows for reinterpretations and reasons to continue (see Chapter 5).

26. There are major arguments regarding the relationship of Leontiev and Vygotsky (see van der Veer and Valsiner 1991; Kozulin 1986). Van der Veer and Valsiner (1994: 5) state that in the literature "interest in Leont'ev's activity theory spilt over to Vygotsky (as Leont'ev himself claimed direct heritage from Vygotsky's and Luria's cultural-historical theory—a claim much disputed and proven questionable . . .)." Though we recognize the need for accurate attributions of intellectual genealogy, we believe their conceptions are compatible and more usefully taken in tandem than alone.

27. Leontiev's position differs from the way we render culture. What is important here is his distinction between the necessity of three versus two terms in accounts of behavior.

28. Bourdieu develops ideas about specific practices less than activity theorists develop ideas about specific activities. Sometimes he writes of games (e.g., 1990b); "game" as he uses the term is somewhat equivalent to activity.

29. The relationship of Bakhtin's work to his associates in the "Bakhtin circle" is a matter of much debate (Clark and Holquist 1984; Todorov 1984; Titunik 1987; Holquist 1990; Morson and Emerson 1990). We follow Todorov (1984) and refer to Bakhtin-plural, that is, his circle inclusive, when we say Bakhtin. We agree with Todorov's defense of shared authorship as eminently Bakhtinian. Nonetheless, for purposes of citation, we list only the author under whose name the work was originally published.

30. Similar processes of development occur for groups; we primarily address persons here for convenience.

31. Although we use identity here as a cover term to refer to the senses and understandings that one has, no matter how symbolically (un)developed they are, it will later become clear that our prototypic identity is one that is symbolized.

32. Holland and Reeves (1994) describe perspective not only as the "angle" from which one views the world (through one's position in activity) but also as one's "take" on activity, the understanding one comes to have of activity (from one's position in it). They emphasize that the objectification and development of a perspective are collective, historical, and contingent achievements. In this view, perspectives are always at least an incipient, though often as yet inarticulate or unsymbolized, identity.

33. Especially in practice theory, these aims are conceived to take form out of awareness. They nonetheless constitute a point of view. See Bourdieu (1977a; 1990b).

34. For Bourdieu, social and material conditions can change rapidly, affecting the interrelations of positions in the field of production. Forms of behavior are modified in response to the altered conditions, but the habitus is slower to change and the lag between the two produces "hysteresis" (1977a: 78).

35. To what extent the various identities are organized coherently depends upon the collective resources that exist and the person's successful use of them. In the prototypical life stories of Alcoholics Anonymous, for example, participants are exposed to a symbolic means that orders the gamut of their different identities. They are encouraged to be, first and foremost, non-drinking alcoholics. This identification supersedes all others, even religious identities or potential identities as drug users.

3. Figured Worlds

1. The anthropological examples are vast: every ethnography tries to capture at least one significant figured world. Two fascinating examples are Luhrmann's work with witches in contemporary Great Britain (1989) and Lancaster's account of machismo and male sexualities in Nicaragua (1992).

2. Vygotsky and the sociohistorical school made much of the child's dependence upon social interaction as both the source of cultural symbols for imagination and the initial support for enacting the symbols.

3. An important pivot into figured worlds is through discourses. In any conversation or text a great deal of taken-for-granted information is omitted. This talk, the particular material and social conditions in which it is

being used (Holland and Cole 1995), and the more generalized notion of discourse are made more determinant in relation to an underlying cultural model (Quinn and Holland 1987). "Cultural model" directs attention to the ways in which individuals come to know and sense figured worlds. Defined cognitively, cultural models consist of schemas (mental/emotional knowledge structures) that guide attention to, draw inferences about, and evaluate experience. They also provide a framework for organizing and reconstructing memories of experience (D'Andrade 1995). The types of cultural models most closely related to figured worlds are what Leavitt (1996) calls prototypical social situations or scenarios. Lutz (1988) and Lutz and Abu-Lughod (1990) argue that emotions have meaning in relation to such simplified social "scenes," imagined courses of social interaction, or what Quinn and Holland (1987) and Holland and Kipnis (1994) call prototypical event sequences. We believe that types of people are identified and have meaning in relation to figured worlds.

4. D'Andrade (1981) calls this kind of abstraction, through which persons form (generalized) cultural knowledges, "guided discovery," and contrasts its slow and "natural" course with the "artificial" means of specialized and highly regulated knowledges. The latter are particularly dependent upon verbal commentary and formal instruction. Vygotsky's "zone of proximal development" casts a different light upon this distinction, since it takes the heart of instruction, the verbal commentary of "elders," right into everyday "discovery" in the form of inner speech.

5. Harré and others have used the concept of "storylines" in a way that is relevant to figured worlds. Storylines seem to be the taken-for-granted unfolding of particular activities such as instruction. There are many storylines associated with figured worlds. One might consider what we have called the central narratives in the world of romance and the world of domestic relations in Nepal storylines that are especially important.

6. These "arrests" recall what Bakhtin (1981) called "centripetal" social forces: those forms of (meta)practice (e.g., translinguistics) which asserted the presumptive unity of "language," in the face of an always overwhelming diversity of "speaking" practices. The point, for Bakhtin as for Crapanzano, is the dialogicality of social activity, the mutual interplay of specific instance and generic means, neither of which exists apart from the other.

7. This is not an unusual occurrence in anthropological research. Holland, in studying Shango in Trinidad, traveled around the island to many different feasts and celebrations, learning from participants about the African powers that manifested at the feasts. In the world of Shango, gaining knowledge of this sort was a meaningful act. To become expert in Shango it was necessary to enter into a reciprocal relationship with the powers.

Eventually, at one of the feasts, a power manifested and directed Holland to give a Thanksgiving (a celebration of lesser scale than a feast); that is, to enter into a more proper relationship with the powers. All of us were more or less drawn into the figured worlds we studied and began to form identities in those worlds.

8. In later chapters we describe women's resistance to the treatment they received and their criticisms of the world of romance.

9. These commonsensical exemplars of activities are reminiscent of Wittgenstein's chosen illustrations of "language games." In either case, the rhetorical point calls attention to the concept's scope—that it refers not to some specialized or technical form of life, but to the virtual worlds' entirety.

10. See also Wulff's (1995) concept of "microcultures." Other concepts we draw upon to explicate figured worlds—e.g., "fields," "activities," "power systems" (Lancaster 1992), "discourses," "communities of practice"— posit collective complexes of meaning and action. However, unlike older notions of culture indicated by such phrases as "American culture" or "Hindu culture," these concepts are partial and modest. Their proponents make no claim that such complexes of meaning and action are essential or ubiquitous, that they make up a "way of life" or are even necessarily tied to a particular (ethnic) group. Rejecting the earlier assumption that these complexes of conventions are equally accepted by all who participate in them (Amit-Talai and Wulff 1995), they place these conventions *in practice,* looking at the ways in which people use them to organize, dispute, negotiate, and often impose or resist sets of joint activities. These newer means for conceptualizing lived worlds attend to relations of power and control. They posit that cultural frames of interpretation and evaluation are seldom socially "neutral," and that, even if they were, such neutrality would itself be a historical (and potentially mutable) product of political life.

11. Engeström pays a great deal of attention to the social-theoretical dimension of activity theory. Wertsch has also developed and extended this perspective. He emphasizes ways in which broader systems of privilege enter into activities, such as reading groups in schools (1991). Many proponents of activity theory, however, omit these connections; see Holland and Reeves (1994).

12. As a field is partly a "space of possibles," against which actual social positions are matched and valued, it also explicitly includes the imaginative, as-if character of figured worlds.

13. Bourdieu (1985a) acknowledges Weber's concept as suggestive in his thinking.

14. We have Americanized references to the academic world.
15. For the sake of contrasting "field" and "figured world," we downplay one of Bourdieu's main points: that status is multidimensional, the value of its various dimensions itself constituting a source of struggle.
16. Field, as Bourdieu has used it in his sociological studies of French intellectual production, encompasses the interconnections among related figured worlds. Bourdieu is careful to point out that semi-autonomous fields—of academic and artistic production, e.g.—are embedded and limited in social space by the field of power and the political-economic system of class relations (see esp. Bourdieu 1993). The embedding notion is important for us as well. We are suggesting that figured worlds could be described as nodes that together make up the fields that Bourdieu analyzes.
17. Bourdieu in other works attends to the effects of fields of power on life in the figured worlds embedded in them. He attends, for instance, to the ways day-to-day school activities (e.g., grading exams) transmute signs of privilege or elite background into "intelligence" and thus into a symbolic capital that figures in the reproduction of elite status and access to power and wealth (see Bourdieu and Saint-Martin 1974). He also offers a powerful commentary on the ways status pervades linguistic practice—such as how one's sense of the (lesser) value attributed to one's dialect or style of speaking can lead to silences in, or withdrawal from, interpersonal encounters (Bourdieu 1977b).
18. Bourdieu's writings on fields (collected in Bourdieu 1993) are also suggestive for figured worlds in other ways. They remind us that the lived worlds of romance, Alcoholics Anonymous, or gender relations in Naudada—as only somewhat independent sites of cultural production—intersect with and are affected by social actions carried out in the name of other lived worlds. Holland and Skinner (1995a) reveal the intersection between the lived worlds of domestic gender relations and political activity in a community in Nepal; Holland and Reeves (1994) argue that students' perspectives on classroom activities were not formed by what the teacher said but by discourses coming from outside the classroom.
19. It is worth reiterating how "figured world" departs from the older concept of a group's culture. It adheres more specifically to activity and therefore does not imply that the works and persons created and re-created by a particular group will exhibit the same principles across all settings. Nor does it imply that a particular figured world incites the same level of participation from all people of a country or an area. With today's transportation and communication, participants from many places can mingle in a number of activities that realize figured worlds across many notional,

social, and political boundaries. Moreover, participants in these worlds are identified with and knowledgeable about them to greater and lesser degrees (see Chapter 5) and develop different perspectives on them (see Chapter 7).

20. This discussion of cultural artifacts resonates with the approach to cultural forms taken in cultural studies. There the focus has shifted from "culture" as some sort of whole to "cultural texts"—where "text" is a term with a very broad meaning. The "texts" of cultural studies still include written representations, but they also encompass films, television programs, travel advertisements, and popular song genres. For example, in Lutz and Collins's (1993) analysis of photographs of non-Westerners in *National Geographic* or Schade-Poulson's (1995) work on *rai* music in Algeria, cultural forms are analyzed for the "theory of the task" (their purpose) and "theory of the person" (who will "read" them) that they embed. See Johnson (1986–87) for a critique of those who analyze "texts" (cultural forms) without regard for their collective history and present use.

21. The properties of artifacts apply equally whether one is considering language and genres of speech and action or the more usually noted forms of artifacts such as tables and knives. What differentiates a word such as "table" or a social routine such as "setting the table" from a table is the relative prominence of their material and conceptual aspects. The difference remains relative, however, and not essential to the artifact. The word "table" has no existence apart from its material instantiation (as a configuration of sound waves, hand movements, or writing), and every table, in addition to its duration over time as a physical object, has, equally indicative of its artifactuality, a past embedded in collective memory so that it embodies an order imposed by thinking human beings.

22. On this model of cognition in psychology, especially educational psychology, see Lave (1988).

23. "Words themselves do not carry meaning" (Davies and Harré 1990: 57). They must be related to a conceptual frame, or in our terms, a figured world.

24. As Inden (1990: 23) called the three "orientations" of persons in practices.

4. Personal Stories in Alcoholics Anonymous

1. For this fieldwork, Cain attended open meetings of three separate AA groups in a small city in North Carolina in 1985 and 1986. All names have been changed and identifying information disguised or omitted.

2. As we shall see, personal knowledge of this sort, gained in the absence of an identification with a figured world, is both superficial, poorly attached affectively and conatively to one's actions, and mechanically and laboriously produced, step by step, from rules and maxims.

3. These two aspects are analytical distinctions, not requirements for membership. Officially, the only requirement for membership is a desire to stop drinking.

4. Here "cultural model" is used in the sense of the taken-for-granted "standard scenarios," what Bakhtin calls "chronotopes" (time-spaces), that inform the narrative possibilities within a figured world.

5. To protect the confidentiality of the AA members Cain spoke with, we have avoided including information from which outsiders might be able to recognize them. Preventing other AA members from recognizing them is more difficult. Much of the information is known to other members already, but some of the information from the interviews may not be. Where we suspect this may be the case, we have omitted the information.

6. In the first part of the interview Cain asked the "Who am I?" questions of Kuhn and McPartland (1954).

5. How Figured Worlds of Romance Become Desire

1. The names of the universities and all personal names are pseudonyms. Some potentially identifying details in the quotes have been changed. Although we sometimes use the term "American," the sample is small and from the Southeast. There were differences between the black and white women's interpretations of romantic relationships, but they are not relevant here (see Holland and Eisenhart 1990).

2. See Chapter 3 on the concept of cultural model and its relation to the notion of a figured world. Here, as in Chapter 4, we sometimes use "cultural model" in the more specific sense of the taken-for-granted "standard social scenarios" that form backdrops of meaning for a figured world.

3. Because few men were interviewed in the earlier study at SU, we describe the model as one held by women. Women at Bradford used similar sorts of terms and seemed to rely upon similar ideas about attractiveness and the respective roles of men and women, but were more likely to emphasize self-determination and self-protection in their interpretation of male/female relationships (see Holland and Eisenhart 1990). We did not happen to have any women in our study who identified themselves as lesbian. Later studies of the world of romance for gay and lesbian couples on one of the campuses suggest both similarities with and differences from the one we describe (Reidel, personal communication).

4. Both Della and Karla were embarrassed and offended by being cast into the world of gender relations in what they considered to be inappropriate situations by men they considered inappropriate partners. While most of the interpretations of them as potential romantic/sexual partners were not taken amiss, these were. The women were learning of their vulnerability to romantic/sexual typing regardless of their wishes to be so typed (see Holland and Eisenhart 1990).

5. Markus and Nurius (1987) argue that individuals form personalized images of themselves in various situations—e.g., visions of themselves receiving a Nobel Prize. These visions motivate actions that seek to realize these possible selves. There also is evidence that some images of possible selves are negatively evaluated, so that one works to avoid their realization.

6. As mentioned earlier, the African-American women at Bradford were concerned about maintaining self-determination and control. Since knowledge about one's behavior and feelings can be used by others to manipulate one, having a steady boyfriend—as opposed to going out with a number of boyfriends—becomes a way to control information.

7. Susan's implied commentary, carried partly through her sarcastic tone, calls to mind the "space of authoring selves" (see Chapter 8).

8. Susan's process of learning is a good example of the appropriation and personalization of social discourse (see Chapter 8).

9. This notion of fossilization as habituation is also pertinent to Bourdieu's conception of the habitus, and of the processes of embodiment that ground learning in the habitus. It suggests, for instance, that nonverbal (proprioceptive) forms of practice interact with verbally mediated practice in the reproduction of the habitus more intimately, and perhaps more convertibly, than Bourdieu seems to think.

10. In other words, expertise is far more than cognition. It involves emotions that are, in Rosaldo's (1984: 143) words, "embodied thoughts, thoughts seeped with the apprehension that 'I am involved.'"

6. Positional Identities

1. One reader of this chapter, a man who'd grown up in Nepal, remarked that this sort of extreme scolding is unusual in his part of the country. Part of Tila Kumari's anger and willingness to express it seemed to relate to her higher-caste status (Bahun) relative to the girls (Damai).

2. Harré and van Langenhove (1991) and Davies and Harré (1990) propose a framework that intersects in some regards with ours. Their concept of "positionings" does not analytically separate the figurative from the positional as we do. Nonetheless, Harré and von Langenhove briefly discuss

people's relative power to position themselves and others. Their "conversational dominance" and "conversational charisma" relate to our notion of positionality.

3. Brown (1980) comes to a similar conclusion about Tenejapa Maya women. Women tend to use linguistic patterns of negative politeness (as Brown calls strategies such as indirection, formality, and deference) more frequently than men in many different situations. Brown concludes that women, because of their position of lesser privilege than men, often take special care not to cause offense. Their sense of their social position is evidently important across several figured worlds.

4. Skinner learned that, in the schools of Naudada, students who thought of themselves as progressive indicated their rejection of the hierarchy of castes by accepting food and water from one another regardless of caste.

5. Others who picture social and cultural life as organized around semi-independent spheres include, besides Bourdieu (1993), Connell (1987), whose idea of gender "regimes" combines development in local institutions and settings, themselves intricately related, with their ties to state interventions, to make up a "gender order."

6. Fordham primarily emphasizes race and gender. She does say that race "undercuts" class in African-American communities, so that two dissimilar class structures, Euro- and African-American, are created.

7. Gregor tells of a woman who taunted the men back; she became the target of a rumor that she had entered the men's house. Although the men, individually, were reluctant to carry out the threat of gang rape, they persuaded one another that the act was necessary and carried it out.

8. Lave and Wenger (1991) argue that social position specifies knowledge in what they call communities of practice. Knowledge differs for the different positions of such communities and must, in a sense, be reconstructed when one moves from one position to another. For instance, knowledge of an academic topic must be reconfigured when one moves from student to teacher, because the social claims that one makes in the expression of knowledge cannot be extricated from its "content" to create any invariant form of "meaning."

9. Knowledge display is not the only skill with signing import that is learned in exclusive activities. Brenneis (1990) makes the point that emotional experiences are also collectively developed in certain activities. Those who are barred from these activities are unlikely to develop the emotional experiences to the same degree of facility as those who fully participate. If expressing a certain emotion competently is treated as a claim to a certain positional identity, then one is unlikely to be able to claim that identity if one has been barred from the formative activity.

10. The situation is more complex and fluid than we have indicated. The

relationship between index and position is to some extent a transitive one. Signs and people "rub off" on one another. The sign mediates who the person is, and the person mediates the meaning of the sign. In U.S. high schools, for example, clothing styles worn by popular people attain the aura of the popular people.

11. One benefit of analyzing conversations according to the social actions of positioning that are taking place is the illumination of the social scientist's own conversations with people in her study. Our interviews with Karla, Della, and the other women were subject to the same processes we describe here. Thus, in Karla's case, the interview situation was such that an image of her was produced, a representation of a woman who was active in structuring her romantic relationships. See Crapanzano (1980), who describes a common process in which the persona collaboratively produced in interaction is attributed to the other as essential characteristics.

12. While it is more convenient at this point to pose these arguments in relation to individuals, it is perhaps even more significant that counterpositionings are also produced collectively. Willis (1981), in his ethnography of working-class boys in an English school in the 1970s, describes the cultural practices they produced, practices that created subject positions different from those offered them by the discourses of the school. In Chapter 12 we look at this process in relation to the women's groups of Naudada who produced songs for an annual women's festival.

13. That is, if we ignore the way Vygotskian ideas have been appropriated into educational work in the United States. As van der Veer and Valsiner (1994: 6) put it, "in the educational applications of Vygotsky, a very curious oversight can be observed—the *role of the 'social other'* (teacher, more capable peer, parent, etc.) *is presented as always helpful,* concerned about the future advancement of the child, etc. The (very real) possibility that under some circumstances educational interference . . . might be purposefully harmful, promote ignorance and be potentially detrimental in other ways, is not considered."

14. See Lederman's account of women in Mendi, highland Papua New Guinea, who explain by rote why they fail to attend public meetings: "That's men's business," "I had garden work to do" (1984: 100). Even women who were active leaders of public opinion—one, in particular, who stayed near her husband in public discussions and told him what to say—seemed to have little reaction to being disqualified, because of gender, from taking the floor themselves.

15. In William Faulkner's *Absalom Absalom!* Thomas Sutpen spends a lifetime reacting to a scene that objectified how others saw him. As an adolescent Sutpen travels with his family from his native western Virginia to resettle

in the eastern area of the state. Though he feels superior to the black slaves who work the plantations of the region, he finds out—in a scene that epitomizes for him the relations of power defining (and confining) his place in the Antebellum South—that he, a poor white, is not regarded as very different from them. He goes to the "big house" of the plantation for which his father works, to deliver a message to the owner. The black butler who responds to his knock denies the positional claim he has innocently made by going to the front door and sends him, in a condescending manner, to the back. From this revelatory experience, a moment of recognition like Kondo's glimpse in the butcher's case, Sutpen determines a lifelong course of action that he follows with singleness of purpose (to tragedy).

16. This mutually constitutive relationship between the semiotic mediator and the target of the mediation can also be more complex. Kulick (1993) describes a highland Papuan man who used a genre usually associated with women to mediate, in fact to accentuate, an understanding of his message.

17. In effect, this statement repeats in more personal terms Bakhtin's point about the social valuation of language-images, "voices," and other media of figuration (see Chapter 8). It is not simply that people's activity is motivated and shaped by the social valuation of the forms of its expression. It is equally that the real activity of people changes the forms' valuation. There is no abstract process of reproduction, like a psychologized notion of "generalizability," which removes the form from its social context of use. There are only real iterations in specific instances.

7. The Sexual Auction Block

1. In this chapter first-person pronouns refer to Holland and her associates.

2. Here we focus on discourses of romance. Other gendering discourses are those of parenting, reproductive medicine, and any culturally constructed world in which gendered types have taken-for-granted interrelations and greater or lesser value.

3. Many of the tellers had a vivid, seemingly emblematic, memory of at least one such experience, a memory still evocative of mixed and unresolved feelings—anger, embarrassment, guilt, and helplessness. Their stories, like those of the women in the study, were "readings" of incidents according to the figured world of romance and attractiveness. More recent ones often refer to the incidents as possible cases of sexual harassment.

4. Although the main portion of our studies focused on women, our studies of gendered marked terms included men (Holland and Skinner 1987).

5. By taken-for-granted scenario we mean the situation that constituted the standard of meaning. Participants to a discussion assumed that particular cases fit the taken-for-granted case. Unless faced with explicit indication to the contrary, students assumed that they and their compatriots would be attracted to romantic and sexual partners who were of roughly equivalent attractiveness.

6. Harré and Van Langenhove (1991) point out that subject positions in discourses are generally interrelated, such that the claiming of position for oneself or another suggests a distribution of positions to all who are party to the field of interaction.

7. The very description of the woman as "foxy," with its overtones of approachability and sexual invitation, colluded in the double-edged construal of the situation. "Plausible deniability" is built into the men's prologue, and is a presumption of their power to define the gender regime of the situation.

8. See Holland (1988) on "essentialized" and "enacted" attractiveness. The idea that attractiveness is "in" the person is much fostered by the industries that benefit from people's anxiety about social worth, as figured according to appearance.

9. As with the symbolic capital of honor among the Kabyle, attractiveness is claimed and validated through face-to-face interaction (Bourdieu 1977a). Its reification as "physical attribute" is a characteristic form of misrecognition (méconnaissance).

10. Bourdieu contrasts the insult, in which individuals try to impose their point of view of the divisions of the social world and their position within it, with "official nomination." An insult is made by an individual who takes the risk of reciprocation. An official nomination is backed up by force (Bourdieu 1985b).

11. Here we are dealing only with cross-gender relations. Such images also have powerful, and somewhat independent, effects upon male-male transactions.

12. The 90 percent figure given by the narrator is misleading when compared to the statistics given by Pryor et al. (1993). A large group of men was assessed by a scale designed to measure attitudes toward women and likelihood to harass. Two subgroups, those who scored high and low on the scale, were selected for the experiment; 90 percent of those who scored high engaged in harassment in the experiment—not 90 percent of the whole sample. Of those scoring low on the scale, 36 percent engaged in harassment.

13. On the campuses we studied, other changes have occurred as well: women's studies programs have been instituted and expanded, and gay rights activists have become much more visible.

14. Alarm and retaliation over sexual harassment charges belie this point. See Richard Bernstein's (1994) "Guilty If Charged" in the *New York Review of Books*. Bernstein is not reviewing a book, but rather ridiculing sexual harassment charges and their prosecution at the University of New Hampshire (see Chapter 13).

15. Michael Lynch (1991) makes a similar point regarding laboratories and the spaces where science is done. Space, in the way he uses it, is not simply a neutral place on some ideal geophysical (or even psychological) grid. Rather space is haunted by the activities that take place in it, and hence by the dispositions and emotional "tones" of their performers.

16. These processes of commodification are surely implicated in the degree to which attractiveness is thought of as an essential characteristic of a person.

8. Authoring Selves

1. The fax metaphor comes from Strauss (1992).

2. Bourdieu's (1977a, 1990b) practice theory and a stream of the cultural-historical school, activity theory, also reflect this conception; see Chapter 3.

3. James Wertsch (1991) has employed Bakhtin's notion of speech genres to build a social developmental understanding of mind and consciousness. Our accounts have a similar intent. Wertsch too wants to combine Bakhtin and Vygotsky in order to develop an account of human activity as mediated by specific sociocultural "tools" and contexts. He too emphasizes the interconnection of social and psychological activity through the conceptual means of dialogue, inner speech, and "voices." Our accounts diverge, however, at several points, as we shall see.

4. Lee and Hickman (1983) also remind us that the deictic position that is the "I" is meaningless without a counterpart, the "you" or other.

5. Vygotsky's ideas also have been grafted to Bakhtin's, to expand Bakhtin's vision of literature and art. See, e.g., Holquist's (1990) appropriation of Vygotsky's "zone of proximal development."

6. Vygotsky's insistence on a genetic method was motivated by his conceptualization of this process of development. A simple focus on outcome was insufficient, for outcome was likely to be a fossilization of a complex built around a mediating device, not an essential characteristic.

7. Van der Veer and Valsiner (1994) argue that Vygotsky's apparent disregard for conflict and the possibility that mentors can be harmful or have negative influences on their charges is a product of the selective translation and appropriation of his work.

8. In trying to find a microcosm within mental life on a par with Marx's

identification of the commodity within economic life, Vygotsky (1986) settled upon the word. Wertsch (1985a) spells out why this choice, even though "word" for Vygotsky also included phrases, was an unfortunate one. Too bad Vygotsky evidently did not read the arguments of Bakhtin and his circle that identified utterances as just such an element of analysis (Voloshinov 1986).

9. Around these differences we also diverge from Wertsch (1991). Wertsch addresses the variety of social languages primarily through speech genres rather than other, traditional sociolects: dialects, registers, accents. He details the differing ways speech genres divide the world—its objects, relationships, and transformations—and examines how actors (children) come to apprehend and accord these differing world views place and time by the activity pertinent to them. His account is well tailored to his primary topic, the development of cognitive resources and skills from the appropriation of differentiated social forms, but it neglects (relatively) what we wish to emphasize, processes of self-identification. When speakers appropriate social languages, they address themselves not just to the object-world conceived there, nor just to the other speakers present, but to the socially identified "voice" of the genre itself. Voice expresses a social position, a politics by affiliation or disaffiliation that moves toward or away from forms of agency.

10. Lee and Hickman (1983) extrapolate from Vygotsky's insistence on the psychological importance of language to build a Vygotskian view of the emergence of self through the metapragmatic functions of language. Despite the number of, as yet unconnected, steps to be taken between their extrapolation and Bakhtin's conceptualization, we do not discern any incompatibilities.

11. In his analysis of rebellious working-class schoolboys, Willis (1981) surmised that they had internalized the position of the school adults, and thus the larger society, as an "internal interlocutor" that questioned and criticized their behavior. Luttrell (1996) shows similar internalized dialog for women in adult literacy classes. They had developed images of themselves against others in the figured worlds of school and success.

12. He also, edging close to Vygotsky's notion of mediating devices, discusses the potential of literature and art to model different possibilities of orchestrations. Holquist (1990) elaborates this aspect of Bakhtin by incorporating Vygotsky's "zone of proximal development." Holquist applies the ZOPED concept not to the individual, as Vygotsky tended to do in reference to schooling, but to the collective. Artists, in this vision, are able to develop "outsideness," to the extreme position that Bakhtin labeled "transgredience," and by virtue of that advantage, are able to create a vision beyond what is currently understood. It is Bakhtin's version of the

avant-garde. Their visions become templates for possible futures; their art provides texts of possibilities. We shall take up this world-forming aspect of cultural expression in Chapters 11 and 12.

13. In Vygotsky's account inner speech becomes differentiated from social speech somewhere in the first decade of the lives of most of us. The person is not simply a robot of the collective in either Vygotsky's or Bakhtin's view. In the Vygotskian view even the total neophyte, the infant and subsequent child, is active. Valsiner (1993) describes the cross-generational transit of cultural forms not as a "cultural transmission," which makes the child simply the recipient of the lifeways of the parental generation, but rather as a bi-directional exchange, where the child is likely to produce behavior outside the cultural repertoire of the parent.

14. Voloshinov posits two extremes, or ideal types, of experience, which conform to the poles of expression (socioeconomy/organism). One, entirely shaped by common parlance and social speech and thus perfectly "ideological," he called "we" experiences. The second, "I" experiences, approaches the organismic, and is virtually unarticulated. "I" experiences, because they cannot be put into words, are chaotic, unorganized.

15. Reference to this stabilized audience sets Bakhtin apart from many of the social constructivists, such as Harré, who give no bases for people's durability despite multiple resistance to discursive positionings.

16. Here he specifies that we are always communicating in inner speech with an addressee—if no particular person, then "we assume as our addressee a contemporary of our literature, our science, our moral and legal codes" (1986: 86).

17. It can be argued, however, that Bakhtin's notion of monological or authoritative discourse implicitly requires a stable, even juridical or ritual, audience. This assertion would be partly the converse of Bakhtin's argument (1981) that heteroglossia arises and ramifies through the social division of labor.

18. Stability of social relations and material conditions is a necessary condition of the stability of the authorial stance.

19. Languages are not just verbal or scriptural. We have already discussed other means of communicating social relations, including spatial configurations, positions and decorations of the body, silence and nonsilence. Communication via these means need not coincide with the communication that proceeds linguistically, via choice of social language and dialect. Indeed, the force of social stratification, of social hierarchy, is often objectified in the disjunction across differing media of expression. Dialogues happen via these metacommunicative means as well, in ways that are important to the development of identity.

9. Mental Disorder, Identity, and Professional Discourse

1. Fieldwork for the study was done from 1986 to 1991 by a research team at the University of North Carolina School of Medicine headed by Sue E. Estroff. "I" in the account is Lachicotte; "we" in this section includes not only his coauthors but also his colleagues on the research team.
2. See, e.g., Siegler and Osmond (1974) on medicalization in psychiatry; Millon and Klerman (1986) on classification of psychopathology in the DSM; Grob (1973, 1983, 1991) for the classic histories of American mental health care; Stone (1986) on differences in European traditions; Szasz (1961, 1970) on the antipsychiatry movement.
3. The discussion adheres more to the language of the third edition, the one in use at the time of our study. The fourth edition, for instance, substitutes the term mood disorders for what we call affective disorders. The fact that psychiatry has its own manual says something about its peculiar history. All other medical specialties use the International Classification of Diseases, now in its tenth edition.
4. Two recent and excellent monographs examine the social and cultural constructions of traumatic disorders: Hacking's study (1995) of multiple personality and Young's work (1996) on post-traumatic stress disorder.
5. The nature of the personality disorders is perhaps the most debated topic of modern American medical psychiatry. See Millon (1981, 1985, 1990) for a comprehensive treatment. Nuckolls (1992a, 1992b) draws upon Millon in his own work on personality disorders.
6. It is unrealistic to call this confusion a kind of error, if by that we make the diagnosis the basic figure. The personae precede, in most cases, the formal diagnosis. It might be more appropriately called the medicalization of a psychological discourse. This cultural world is replete with discourses related in various degrees of sub- and superordination. Though medical psychiatry, ordained by the DSM-III and now IV, is hegemonic, it has itself a compilation of earlier and contemporary discourses, not all of which are well subsumed or even regulated (see Lachicotte 1992).
7. Schizoaffective disorder is a form of schizophrenia whose dominant symptomatic expression features mood disturbances—depression or mania or both. Schizoaffective disorder, like borderline personality, is a specific kind of intermediate or liminal category of the nosology.
8. The notion of role constriction comes from Kai Erikson (1957, 1962) and from the medical sociological tradition founded in role theory (Parsons 1951, 1972). The classic account of the social formation of "mental patients" is Goffman (1961). Labeling theory (Scheff 1966) was another limited but influential view of the social foundations of mental disorder; for criticism of it see Townsend (1976); Gove (1970, 1980).

9. For generalization of Selye's work see, e.g., Coelho, Hamburg, and Adams (1974); Monat and Lazarus (1977). According to Marsh (1992) this generalization entailed changing Selye's *pathogenic* model of stress to a *transactional* model. The latter describes the interrelations of organism and environment dynamically, so that the stress present in the local ecosystem is a function less of the nature of the components (such as a pathogen) than of their interactions. It is analogous to the change from pathogenic to ecoimmunological theories of disease. Hatfield (1987) calls this basic perspective a stress-diathesis model.

10. Cain (1995) studied patients undergoing treatment in mental health facilities in Costa Rica, where neither psychiatry nor alternative treatments (such as Neurotics Anonymous) have established authority to the same extent as in the United States. The persons she followed tacked back and forth, sometimes chaotically, among the explanations of these various "schools."

11. Compare Habermas's examinations (1975, 1984, 1987) of the general forms of communicative practice in relation to authoritative, often state-sponsored, discourses. Our view owes a more obvious debt to Bourdieu.

10. Authoring Oneself as a Woman in Nepal

1. Much of the material reported here comes from Skinner's fieldwork in Naudada in 1985–86. We also include some information from joint research by Skinner and Holland in 1986, 1990, and 1991.

2. We prefer to use the more specific "Brahmanical" instead of "Hindu" to refer to ideologies and practices promoted by Vedic literature and by most Bahun (that is, Brahman) priests. For aspects of the Brahmanical model for women's lives see Bennett (1976, 1983); Caplan (1985); Das (1979); Skinner (1989, 1990); Stone (1978).

3. The people of Naudada divided themselves into several *jat* (caste/ethnic groups): Bahun and Chetri, considered the two highest or "big" (*thulo*) castes and together constituting a slight majority of the population; Newar and Magar, ethnic groups in the middle of the caste hierarchy; and the lower or "small" caste (*sano jat*) groups, including Damai, Sunar, Kami, and Sarki. Only a minority of the members of the lower-caste groups seemed to support themselves primarily by the crafts and services conventionally associated with them (Kami, blacksmithing; Sunar, goldsmithing; Sarki, leatherworking; Damai, tailoring and music). Nonetheless, most families, especially among the Damai, still supplied the traditional services to particular Bahun or Chetri families in return for a portion of the upper-caste families' harvests.

4. We are not the first to notice seemingly inconsistent stances in what

people say and do; see Strauss (1990). Our interpretations are compatible with Strauss's position, but we add a temporal dimension by always considering people's acts and self-understandings within the context of heuristic development. For a psychoanalytic perspective see Ewing (1990) and Obeyesekere (1981).

5. The possibility that somewhere there exist the encompassing resources and consistently effective social work required to produce a single, transcendent self seems very small. As described in Chapter 4, the personal story of Alcoholics Anonymous posits a self for alcoholics that crosses many situations and contexts. Yet, as Hank says about his own story, "there was a life, too."

6. One important exception to the pattern of not talking much about rituals concerned Tij, which we discuss later in this chapter and in Chapter 12.

7. Two people from other areas of Nepal were appalled when they heard of this scolding, saying they had never been scolded in such a way when they were children and had never even heard it in their villages. They associated such scolding with poorer and lower-caste and lower-class families. In Naudada not all parents scolded their children this way, but parents from all castes did so. Some parents said they did not know how to scold, distinguishing themselves from those who did such things, but even they could be heard scolding their children in such a way when they were angry.

8. Holland (1988) describes these sorts of representations for oneself as "epitomized scenes." Willis (1981) writes of an "internal interlocutor." For other references on the dialogic self see Abu-Lughod (1990).

9. This notion of "sense" is, in Vygotsky's conception, the currency of "inner speaking." When extended to the embodiment of all means of expression (as "inner activity"), it becomes like Bourdieu's understanding of practical sense, *sens pratique* (see Chapter 8).

10. We have done extensive research on Tij songs as a form of women's critical commentary: see Holland and Skinner (1995a, 1995b, 1996); Skinner (1990); Skinner et al. (1994). For other accounts see Enslin (1992, 1998); Raheja and Gold (1994).

11. Thakali is an ethnic group whose members run tea shops and hotels where various kinds of liquor are available.

12. See Egnor (1986) and Raheja and Gold (1994) for other accounts of South Asian women's songs as expressions of alternative visions of femininity and as vehicles for the production of both selves and cultural meanings.

13. Sites and activities other than Tij, such as schools, literacy classes, the activities of political workers, and women's organizations, are also impor-

tant in this regard (see Enslin 1990, 1998; Skinner and Holland 1996; Skinner et al. 1998), but the development of this critical commentary in Tij antedates by far its development in these other sites (Skinner et al. 1994).

11. Play Worlds, Liberatory Worlds, and Fantasy Resources

1. In a way more convenient to the human sciences of today than the Hegelian dialectic of self-consciousness, Vygotsky and Bakhtin socialize the person and impersonate sociality. They have made "being thought through"—differentiating the "individuum" of inner speech in order to return to association more fully "held"—the way of being human. Those who fail to attend to this achievement may be lost in postmodernity.

2. Because he insisted on the original interpersonal, interactive context of all cultural forms that become intrapersonally significant, Vygotsky by no means closed off attention to social dynamics and structures. But, at least as his ideas have been transported to English-speaking academics (van der Veer and Valsiner 1994), he did not develop these aspects as did Bakhtin.

3. Perhaps it would be more accurate to say that such theorists combine habit and Wert-rationalität.

4. The play of carnival may at first appear chaotic—as if social order had been uprooted and dispelled. But as one continues to observe carnival, it becomes clear that its activity is more a counter- than an antigenre (see Lancaster 1996 for another view).

5. The term *amour courtois* was first used by Paris (1883). In this section we rely heavily on secondary sources, esp. Boase (1977) and Paterson (1993).

6. Our account follows Andreas Capellanus (1941), a late twelfth (or early thirteenth) century codification of the genre. The Occitanian poems included this kind of programmatic lover's world but also exhibited more varied and mundane romantic landscapes. Although virtually all lovers are depicted as male, there are a few exceptions. These may occur in poems composed by female troubadours, or male poets may have created female personae from which to speak. See Paden (1989); Kay (1990); Paterson (1993).

7. Courtly love was ordinarily adulterous love, the love of an already married woman. Hence the vulnerability of lovers to false, and sometimes true, witness (Lewis 1936; Boase 1977).

8. These were mock trials (of dubious authenticity) at which cases concerning breaches of the proper conduct of love were adjudicated (Neilson 1967). Eleanor's daughter Marie was said to sponsor such amusements

(Wilcox 1930; Lewis 1936; Kelly 1952). One of the more popular forms of the trobar, the *tenso,* did take the form of a debate over questions of love (or other topics).

9. Various literary and intellectual sources have been named as origins of courtly love. The "Hispano-arabic thesis" (Dawson 1935; Denomy 1947; Daniel 1975; see Boase 1977) is perhaps the best supported. Lewis (1936) championed Ovid; Denomy (1947), neoplatonism; Rougemont (1956), Catharist doctrine; and Briffault (1965), Marianism and older fertility cults.

10. In this treatise Capellanus goes so far as to discuss the love of nuns, which was to his mind the most chaste and unattainable of all such loves— though it was often not held in such high regard by popular reputation.

11. The cult of Mary, Mariolatry, may have benefited from this development, for, some have argued, the devices that live on in ecstatic religious poetry resemble the praise of the troubadours for their beloved.

12. Such figured worlds and their associated imagined communities are objects of controversy. The figured world of race relations is another extremely contested social venue in contemporary America. It has heroes and villains—Martin Luther King Jr. and Orville Faubus, Malcolm X and Lyndon Johnson, Stokely Carmichael and "Bull" Connor—and events evoked by the names of towns and cities—Little Rock, Montgomery, Selma, and so on. But who is villain and who is hero? What is the significance of these events? The accent, tone, and value of figure and scene vary according to the positions of the persons one asks.

13. In the cultural studies literature their propagations have been called "panics" (Hall et al. 1978).

12. Making Alternative Worlds in Nepal

1. Tij means "third day." The festival occurs on the third day of the bright fortnight of the Nepali month of Bhadra.

2. We collected verses from and/or information about roughly 1,000 songs. For 26 songs, in both English and Nepali, see Skinner, Holland, and Adhikari (1994). For more detailed analyses see that article and Holland and Skinner (1995a).

3. For more on the complexities of the Tij festival and its relationship to the larger social and political context see Holland and Skinner (1995a, 1995b); Skinner et al. (1994).

4. Women sometimes called upon priests to guide the *puja* that is part of the Tij–Rishi Pancami complex, but not to explain the meaning of the fasting and the ritual bathing as interpreted through the textual accounts of the

Hindu gods, goddesses, and holy men. The most learned priest said no one consulted him; they lacked interest.

5. Although men were invited to participate in *mela* (work parties), they were not usually permanent members of a parma group.

6. In spite of the religious themes of the ritual complex and its dedication to husbands' well-being, the overwhelming majority of Tij songs were neither about gods and goddesses (*deuta* songs) nor about devotion to husbands. Only a very small proportion of the songs we collected from older women and of those in two other collections of Tij songs that we saw were deuta songs (see Skinner et al. 1994). We heard no deuta songs on Tij Day.

7. Women with several children were less likely to return to their natal home for Tij. Those whose parents had died were especially unlikely to return.

8. Married women were also allowed to travel home during Tihar, for a ceremony in which the sister carries out rites that protect the brother from death in the coming year. When a sister was still residing in the natal home, however, the married sister was not always invited. There was not the same anticipation that all the younger married daughters would return home, nor was there license for women to gather together for singing and dancing. Unlike Tij, Tihar was a family affair, confined to each household, and not a matter of the didi/bahini of the gaon.

9. In the Tamang women's life narratives described by March (1988), women emphasized the right to speak in their natal family's home and the injunction to silence in their husband's family's home.

10. Tragic events that happened in the ten gaons nearest the *tati* (public space) where the Tij groups performed were not sung about on Tij Day. No group prepared a ghatana song, for example, about the deaths of Naudadans run over by a truck a few weeks before the 1991 festival. We were told that such songs would cause the relatives too much pain.

11. Holland and Skinner (1995a) detail how this shift from local, familial relations to the world of antigovernment activity and party politics was able to occur so rapidly.

12. Hybrid forms, as thoroughly dialogized speech, refract the voices that are juxtaposed. They not only create a novel social standpoint—here a distinctly "feminine" (perhaps even a feminist) political agent—but also change the social positions of the element voices. The articulation and reproduction of the hybrid refigures the space of authorship, multiplying the possible ways of identifying activity. The Tij songbooks that have proliferated in Nepal since 1990 recognize the changed shape of both women's authority and political opportunity.

13. The song pivot also exists in women's intimate activity: Skinner's inform-

ants not only sang to themselves, they even sang some of their answers to her questions in the words of Tij songs. The world of Tij has long transcended the temporal and spatial bounds of the festival.

13. Identity in Practice

1. Holland and Lave (forthcoming) collect a number of recent studies that explore local contestations as they relate both to long-term, historical struggles (as in Northern Ireland) and to the production of subjectivities in these histories of intense struggle.
2. Silva was interviewed in the fall of 1994 by Christopher Lydon, host of "The Connection," a show aired by WBUR, one of Boston's public radio affiliates. On Silva see Bernstein (1994).
3. One can assimilate this point, we suppose, to the fact of "intertextuality" among discourses. But, should we move to Bakhtin's language, and call it "multivocality" under the condition of "heteroglossia," we come closer to our point. Utterance and human expression are fully materialized, social actions, works whose shaping is open to the complex of political-economic, social, cultural, and psychological productions of any activity.
4. Of course these games are socially constrained. But cultural figurings need not form a transcendent logic that produces by its reductions only one figured world.

References

Abu-Lughod, Lila. 1986. *Veiled Sentiments: Honor and Poetry in a Bedouin Society.* Berkeley: University of California Press.

—— 1990. "The Romance of Resistance: Tracing Transformations of Power through Bedouin Women." *American Ethnologist* 17(1): 41–55.

Alcoholics Anonymous. 1967. *What Happened to Joe—and His Drinking Problem. . . .* New York: Alcoholics Anonymous World Services [hereafter AAWS].

—— 1968a. *AA for the Woman.* New York: AAWS.

—— 1968b. *It Happened to Alice! . . . How She Faced a Drinking Problem.* New York: AAWS.

—— 1976. *Alcoholics Anonymous: The Story of How Many Thousands of Men and Women Have Recovered from Alcoholism.* 3rd ed. New York: AAWS.

—— 1979a. *Time to Start Living: Stories of Those Who Came to AA in Their Later Years.* New York: AAWS.

—— 1979b. *Too Young? Teenagers and AA.* New York: AAWS.

—— 1979c. *Young People and AA.* New York: AAWS.

—— 1980. *Dr. Bob and the Good Oldtimers: A Biography with Recollections of Early AA in the Midwest.* New York: AAWS.

American Psychiatric Association. 1987. *Diagnostic and Statistical Manual of Mental Disorders.* 3rd ed. rev. [DSM-III-R]. Washington: APA.

—— 1994. *Diagnostic and Statistical Manual of Mental Disorders.* 4th ed. [DSM-IV]. Washington: APA.

Amit-Talai, Vered. 1995. "Conclusion: The 'Multi' Cultural of Youth." In Amit-Talai and Wulff, eds., 1995, 223–233.

Amit-Talai, Vered, and Helena Wulff, eds. 1995. *Youth Culture: A Cross-cultural Perspective.* New York: Routledge.

Anderson, Benedict. 1983. *Imagined Communities.* London: Verso.

Andreas Capellanus. 1941. *The Art of Courtly Love.* Trans. John J. Parry. New York: Columbia University Press.

317

Aretxaga, Begona. 1993. "Striking with Hunger: Cultural Meanings of Political Violence in Northern Ireland." In *The Violence Within: Cultural and Political Opposition in Divided Nations*, ed. K. Warren, 219-253. Boulder: Westview.

Asad, Talal, ed. 1973. *Anthropology and the Colonial Encounter.* London: Ithaca Press.

Bakhtin, Mikhail M. 1981. *The Dialogic Imagination: Four Essays by M. M. Bakhtin.* Ed. M. E. Holquist, trans. Caryl Emerson and Michael Holquist. Austin: University of Texas Press.

———— 1984a. *Problems of Dostoevsky's Poetics.* Ed. and trans. C. Emerson. Minneapolis: University of Minnesota Press.

———— 1984b. *Rabelais and His World.* Trans. Helene Iswolsky. Bloomington: Indiana University Press.

———— 1986. *Speech Genres and Other Late Essays.* Ed. Caryl Emerson and Michael Holquist, trans. Vern W. McGee. Austin: University of Texas Press.

———— 1990. *Art and Answerability.* Ed. Michael Holquist and Vadim Liapunov, trans. Vadim Liapunov. Austin: University of Texas Press.

———— 1993. *Toward a Philosophy of the Act.* Ed. Vadim Liapunov and Michael Holquist, trans. Vadim Liapunov. Austin: University of Texas Press.

Bateson, Gregory. 1972. "The Cybernetics of 'Self': A Theory of Alcoholism." In Bateson, *Steps to an Ecology of Mind*, 309–337. New York: Ballantine.

Becker, Howard S. 1963. *Outsiders: Studies in the Sociology of Deviance.* New York: Free Press.

Bennett, Lynn. 1976. "Sex and Motherhood among Brahmins and Chhetris of East-Central Nepal." *Contributions to Nepalese Studies* 3: 1–52.

———— 1983. *Dangerous Wives and Sacred Sisters: Social and Symbolic Roles of High-caste Women in Nepal.* New York: Columbia University Press.

Benton, John F. 1968. "Clio and Venus: An Historical View of Medieval Love." In Newman, ed., 1968, 19–42.

Bernstein, Richard. 1994. "Guilty If Charged." *New York Review of Books* 41(1 and 2): 11–14.

Bista, Khem Bahadur. 1969. "Tij ou la fête des femmes." *Objets et Mondes* 9: 7–18.

Bloch, Maurice. 1985. "From Cognition to Ideology." In *Power and Knowledge: Anthropological and Social Approaches*, ed. R. Fardon, 21–48. Edinburgh: Scottish Academic Press.

Bloch, R. H. 1991. *Medieval Misogyny and the Invention of Western Romantic Love.* Chicago: University of Chicago Press.

Boase, Roger. 1977. *The Origin and Meaning of Courtly Love: A Critical Study of European Scholarship.* Manchester: Manchester University Press.

Boltanski, L., and L. Thevenot. 1983. "Finding One's Way in Social Space: A Study Based on Games." *Social Science Information* 22(4/5): 631–680.

Bouillier, Véronique. 1982. "Si les femmes faisaient la fête: A propos des fêtes féminines dans les hautes castes Indo-Nepalaises." *L'Homme* 22: 91–118.

Bourdieu, Pierre. 1977a. *Outline of a Theory of Practice.* Trans. Richard Nice. Cambridge: Cambridge University Press.

———— 1977b. "The Economics of Linguistic Exchanges." *Social Science Information* 16(6): 645–668.

———— 1984. *Distinction: A Social Critique of the Judgement of Taste.* Trans. Richard Nice. Cambridge, Mass.: Harvard University Press.

———— 1985a. "The Genesis of the Concepts of 'Habitus' and 'Field.'" *Sociocriticism* 2(2): 11–24.

———— 1985b. "The Social Space and the Genesis of Groups." *Theory and Society* 14: 723–744.

———— 1988. *Homo Academicus.* Palo Alto: Stanford University Press.

———— 1990a. *In Other Words: Essays towards a Reflexive Sociology.* Trans. Matthew Adamson. Palo Alto: Stanford University Press.

———— 1990b. *The Logic of Practice.* Trans. Richard Nice. Palo Alto: Stanford University Press.

———— 1993. *The Field of Cultural Production: Essays on Art and Literature.* New York: Columbia University Press.

Bourdieu, P., and J. C. Passeron. 1977. *Reproduction in Education, Society and Culture.* Trans. Richard Nice. London: Sage.

Bourdieu, Pierre, and Monique de Saint-Martin. 1974. "Scholastic Excellence and the Values of the Educational System." In *Contemporary Research in the Sociology of Education,* ed. J. Eggleston, 338–371. London: Methuen.

Brenneis, Donald. 1990. "Shared and Solitary Sentiments: The Discourse of Friendship, Play, and Anger in Bhatgaon." In Lutz and Abu-Lughod, eds., 1990, 113–125.

Briffault, Robert. 1965. *The Troubadours.* Ed. L. F. Koons. Bloomington: Indiana University Press.

Brown, Jane D., A. B. White, and L. Nikopoulou. 1993. "Disinterest, Intrigue, Resistance: Early Adolescent Girls' Use of Sexual Media Content." In *Media, Sex and the Adolescent,* ed. B. S. Greenburg, J. D. Brown, and N. L. Buerkel-Rothfuss, 177–195. Cresskill, N.Y.: Hampton.

Brown, Penelope. 1980. "How and Why Are Women More Polite: Some Evidence from a Mayan Community." In *Women and Language in Literature and Society,* ed. Sally McConnell-Ginet, Ruth Borker, and Nelly Furman, 111–136. New York: Praeger.

Butler, Judith. 1993. *Bodies That Matter.* New York: Routledge.

Cain, Carole. 1991. "Personal Stories: Identity Acquisition and Self-understanding in Alcoholics Anonymous." *Ethos* 19: 210–253.

——— 1995. "Wandering the Streets without Direction: The Search for Meaning in Mental Illness in Costa Rica." Ph.D. diss., University of North Carolina at Chapel Hill.

Calhoun, Craig. 1991. "Indirect Relationships and Imagined Communities: Large-scale Social Integration and the Transformation of Everyday Life." In *Social Theory for a Changing Society,* ed. P. Bourdieu and J. S. Coleman, 95–121. Boulder: Westview.

Cameron, D., F. McAlindon, and K. O'Leary. 1988. "Lakoff in Context: The Social and Linguistic Function of Tag Questions." In *Women in Their Speech Communities: New Perspectives on Language and Sex,* ed. J. Coates and D. Cameron, 74–93. New York: Longman.

Caplan, Patricia. 1985. *Class and Gender in India: Women and Their Organizations in a South India City.* London and New York: Tavistock.

Caughey, John L. 1984. *Imaginary Social Worlds: A Cultural Approach.* Lincoln: University of Nebraska Press.

Clark, Katerina, and Michael Holquist. 1984. *Mikhail Bakhtin.* Cambridge, Mass.: Harvard University Press.

Clement, D. C. 1982. "Samoan Cultural Knowledge of Mental Disorders." In *Cultural Conceptions of Mental Health and Therapy,* ed. A. J. Marsella and G. M. White, 193–215. Dordrecht: D. Reidel.

Clifford, James. 1988. *The Predicament of Culture: Twentieth-century Ethnography, Literature and Art.* Cambridge, Mass.: Harvard University Press.

Coelho, George V., David A. Hamburg, and John E. Adams, eds. 1974. *Coping and Adaptation.* New York: Basic Books.

Cole, Michael. 1985. "The Zone of Proximal Development: Where Culture and Cognition Create Each Other." In Wertsch, ed., 1985, 146–161.

——— 1996. *Cultural Psychology: A Once and Future Discipline.* Cambridge, Mass.: Harvard University Press.

Connell, R. W. 1987. *Gender and Power: Society, the Person and Sexual Politics.* Palo Alto: Stanford University Press.

Conrad, Peter, and Joseph W. Schneider. 1980. *Deviance and Medicalization: From Badness to Sickness.* St. Louis: C. V. Mosby.

Crapanzano, Vincent. 1980. *Tuhami: Portrait of a Moroccan.* Chicago: University of Chicago Press.

——— 1990. "On Self Characterization." In *Cultural Psychology: Essays in Comparative Human Development,* ed. J. W. Stigler, R. A. Shweder, and G. Herdt, 401–423. Cambridge: Cambridge University Press.

Csordas, Thomas. 1994. *The Sacred Self.* Berkeley: University of California Press.

D'Andrade, Roy. 1981. "The Cultural Part of Cognition." *Cognitive Science* 5: 179–195.

——— 1992. "Schemas and Motivation." In *Human Motives and Cultural Models,* ed. R. G. D'Andrade and C. Strauss, 23–44. Cambridge: Cambridge University Press.

———— 1995. *The Development of Cognitive Anthropology.* New York: Cambridge University Press.

Daniel, Norman. 1975. *The Arabs and Medieval Europe.* London: Longman.

Das, Veena. 1979. "Reflections on the Social Construction of Adulthood." In *Identity and Adulthood,* ed. S. Kakar, 89–104. Oxford: Oxford University Press.

Davies, B., and Harré, R. 1990. "Positioning: The Discursive Production of Selves." *Journal for the Theory of Social Behavior* 20: 43–63.

Dawson, Christopher. 1935. "The Origins of the Romantic Tradition." In Dawson, *Medieval Religion and Other Essays,* 121–154. London: Sheed and Ward.

Dennett, Daniel. 1988. "Why Everyone Is a Novelist." *Times Literary Supplement* (16 Sept.): 1016, 1028–1029.

Denomy, Alexander J. 1947. *The Heresy of Courtly Love.* New York: MacMullan.

Dhruvarajan, Vanaja. 1989. *Hindu Women and the Power of Ideology.* Granby, Mass.: Bergin and Garvey.

Donaldson, E. T. 1965. "The Myth of Courtly Love." *Ventures* 5: 16–23.

Dreyfus, Hubert. 1984. "What Expert Systems Can't Do." *Raritan* 3(4): 22–36.

Duby, Georges. 1983. *The Knight, the Lady and the Priest: The Making of Modern Marriage in Medieval France.* Trans. B. Bray. New York: Pantheon.

———— 1994. *Love and Marriage in the Middle Ages.* Trans. Jane Dunnett. Cambridge: Polity.

Dumont, L. 1980. *Homo Hierarchicus: The Caste System and Its Implications.* Chicago: University of Chicago Press.

Eckert, P., and S. McConnell-Ginet. 1992. "Think Practically and Look Locally: Language and Gender as Community-based Practice." *Annual Review of Anthropology* 21: 461–490.

Edgerton, Robert B. 1967. *The Cloak of Competence: Stigma in the Lives of the Mentally Retarded.* Berkeley: University of California Press.

Egnor, Margaret T. 1986. "Internal Iconicity in Paraiyar 'Crying Songs.'" In *Another Harmony: New Essays on the Folklore of India,* ed. Stuart Blackburn and A. K. Ramanujan, 294–344. Berkeley: University of California Press.

Eisenhart, Margaret, and Nancy Lawrence. 1994. "Anita Hill, Clarence Thomas, and the Culture of Romance." *Genders* 19: 94–121.

Emerson, Caryl. 1983a. "Bakhtin and Vygotsky on Internalization of Language." *Quarterly Newsletter of the Laboratory of Comparative Human Cognition* 5(1): 9–13.

———— 1983b. "The Outer Word and Inner Speech: Bakhtin, Vygotsky, and the Internalization of Language." *Critical Inquiry* 10(2): 245–264.

Engels, Frederick. 1968. "The Part Played by Labor in the Transition from Ape to Man." In *The Origins of the Family, Private Property and the State*, ed. Eleanor Leacock, 251–264. New York: New World Books.

Engeström, Yrjo. 1987. *Learning by Expanding: An Activity Theoretical Approach to Developmental Research*. Helsinki: Orienta-Konsultit Oy.

————— 1990. *Learning, Working and Imagining: Twelve Studies in Activity Theory*. Helsinki: Proemta-Konsultit.

————— 1992. "Interactive Expertise: Studies in Distributed Working Intelligence." Dept. of Education, Research Bulletin 83. Helsinki: University of Helsinki.

Enslin, Elizabeth. 1990. "The Dynamics of Gender, Class, and Caste in a Women's Movement in Rural Nepal." Ph.D. diss., Stanford University.

————— 1992. "Collective Powers in Common Places: The Politics of Gender and Space in a Woman's Struggle for a Meeting Center in Chitwan, Nepal." *Himalayan Research Bulletin* 12: 11–26.

————— 1998. "Imagined Sisters: The Ambiguities of Women's Poetics and Collective Actions." In *Selves in Time and Place: Identities, Experience, and History in Nepal*, ed. Debra Skinner, Alfred Pach III, and Dorothy Holland, 269–299. Lanham, Md.: Rowman and Littlefield.

Erikson, Erik. 1963. *Childhood and Society*. 2nd ed. New York: Norton.

————— 1968. *Identity: Youth and Crisis*. New York: Norton.

Erikson, Kai T. 1957. "Patient Role and Social Uncertainty: A Dilemma of the Mentally Ill." *Psychiatry* 20: 263–272.

————— 1962. "Notes on the Sociology of Deviance." *Social Problems* 9: 307–314.

Ewing, Katherine P. 1990. "The Illusion of Wholeness: Culture, Self, and the Experience of Inconsistency." *Ethos* 18(3): 251–278.

Fabian, Johannes. 1983. *Time and the Other: How Anthropology Makes Its Object*. New York: Columbia University Press.

Faulkner, William. 1936. *Absalom, Absalom!* New York: Modern Library.

Favret-Saada, J. 1980. *Deadly Words: Witchcraft in the Bocage*. Trans. C. Cullen. Cambridge: Cambridge University Press.

Fillmore, Charles. 1975. "An Alternative to Checklist Theories of Meaning." In *Proceedings of the First Annual Meeting of the Berkeley Linguistics Society*, ed. C. Cogne et al., 123–131. Berkeley: University of California Press.

————— 1982. "Towards a Descriptive Framework for Spatial Deixis." In *Speech, Place, and Action*, ed. R. J. Jarvella and W. Klein, 31–59. New York: Wiley.

Fogelson, R. D. 1979. "Person, Self, and Identity: Some Anthropological Retrospects, Circumspects, and Prospects." In *Psychosocial Theories of the Self*, ed. B. Lee, 67–109. New York: Plenum.

Fordham, Signithia. 1993 "'Those Loud Black Girls': (Black) Women, Silence, and Gender 'Passing' in the Academy." *Anthropology and Education Quarterly* 24(1): 3–32.

Foucault, Michel. 1965. *Madness and Civilization: A History of Insanity in the Age of Reason*. Trans. Richard Howard. New York: Random House.

———— 1978. *The History of Sexuality: An Introduction*. Trans. Robert Hurley. New York: Pantheon.

———— 1979. *Discipline and Punish: The Birth of the Prison*. Trans. Alan Sheridan. New York: Random House.

Frappier, Jean. 1972. "Sur un procès fait à l'amour courtois." *Romania* 93: 145–193.

Gal, Susan. 1987. "Language and Political Economy." *Annual Reviews in Anthropology* 18: 345–367.

Gearing, F., T. Carroll, L. Richter, P. Grogan-Hurlick, A. Smith, W. Hughes, B. Tindall, W. Precourt, and S. Topfer. 1979. "Working Paper 6." In *Toward a Cultural Theory of Education and Schooling*, ed. F. Gearing and L. Sangree, 9–38. The Hague: Mouton.

Geertz, Clifford. 1973a. "Deep Play: Notes on the Balinese Cockfight." In Geertz, *The Interpretation of Cultures*, 412–453. New York: Basic Books.

———— 1973b. "Thick Description: Toward an Interpretive Theory of Culture." In Geertz, *The Interpretation of Cultures*, 3–32. New York: Basic Books.

Gergen, Kenneth. 1984. "An Introduction to Historical Social Psychology." In *Historical Social Psychology*, ed. K. J. Gergen and M. M. Gergen, 3–36. Hillsdale, N. J.: Erlbaum.

———— 1991. *The Saturated Self: Dilemmas of Identity in Contemporary Life*. New York: Basic Books.

———— 1994. *Realities and Relationships: Soundings in Social Construction*. Cambridge, Mass.: Harvard University Press.

Gibson, James J. 1979. *The Senses Compared as Perceptual Systems*. Boston: Houghton Mifflin.

Goffman, Erving. 1961. *Asylums: Essays on the Social Situation of Mental Patients and Other Inmates*. Garden City, N.Y.: Anchor.

Goodenough, Ward. 1994. "Toward a Working Theory of Culture." In *Assessing Cultural Anthropology*, ed. R. Borofsky, 262–273. New York: McGraw-Hill.

Goodman, James C. 1981. "Shiva's Scarlet Women." *ASIA* (Sept.–Oct.): 20–25.

Gove, Walter R. 1970. "Societal Reaction as an Explanation of Mental Illness: An Evaluation." *American Sociological Review* 35: 873–884.

———— 1980. "Labeling and Mental Illness: A Critique." In *Labeling Deviant Behavior*, ed. Walter R. Gove, 53–109. Beverly Hills: Sage.

Greenfield, Patricia M. 1984. "A Theory of the Teacher in the Learning Activities of Everyday Life." In *Everyday Cognition: Its Development in Social Context*, ed. B. Rogoff and J. Lave, 117–138. Cambridge, Mass.: Harvard University Press.

Gregor, Thomas. 1977. *The Mehinaku: The Drama of Everyday Life in a Brazilian Indian Village*. Chicago: University of Chicago Press.

Grob, Gerald N. 1973. *Mental Institutions in America: Social Policy to 1875.* New York: Free Press.

———— 1983. *Mental Illness and American Society.* Princeton: Princeton University Press.

———— 1991. *From Asylum to Community: Mental Health Policy in Modern America.* Princeton: Princeton University Press.

Gumperz, John, and Dell Hymes, eds. 1972. *Directions in Sociolinguistics: The Ethnography of Communication.* New York: Holt, Rinehart and Winston.

Habermas, Jürgen. 1975. *Legitimation Crisis.* Trans. Thomas McCarthy. Boston: Beacon.

———— 1984. *The Theory of Communicative Action,* vol. 1: *Reason and the Rationalization of Society.* Trans. Thomas McCarthy. Boston: Beacon.

———— 1987. *The Theory of Communicative Action,* vol. 2: *Lifeworld and System: A Critique of Functionalist Reason.* Trans. Thomas McCarthy. Boston: Beacon.

Hacking, Ian. 1995. *Rewriting the Soul: Multiple Personality and the Sciences of Memory.* Princeton: Princeton University Press.

Hall, Stuart. 1996. "Introduction: Who Needs Identity?" In *Questions of Cultural Identity,* ed. S. Hall and P. Du Gay, 1–17. London: Sage.

Hall, Stuart, C. Critcher, T. Jefferson, J. Clarke, and B. Roberts. 1978. *Policing the Crisis: Mugging, the State and Law and Order.* New York: Holmes and Meier.

Hallowell, A. I. 1955a. "The Ojibwa Self and Its Behavioral Environment." In Hallowell, *Culture and Experience,* 172–182. Philadelphia: University of Pennsylvania Press.

———— 1955b. "The Self and Its Behavioral Environment." In Hallowell, *Culture and Experience,* 75–110. Philadelphia: University of Pennsylvania Press.

Hannerz, Ulf. 1983. "Tools of Identity and Imagination." In *Identity: Personal and Socio-cultural,* ed. Anita Jacobson-Widding, 347–360. Atlantic Highlands, N.J.: Humanities Press.

Haraway, D. 1988. "Situated Knowledges: The Science Question in Feminism and the Privilege of the Partial Perspective." *Feminist Studies* 14: 575–600.

Harré, Rom. 1979. *Social Being: A Theory for Social Psychology.* Oxford: Blackwell.

———— 1984. *Personal Being: A Theory of Individual Psychology.* Cambridge, Mass.: Harvard University Press.

Harré, R., and L. Van Langenhove. 1991. "Varieties of Positioning." *Journal for the Theory of Social Behavior* 21: 391–407.

Harris, G. G. 1989. "Concepts of Individual, Self, and Person in Description and Analysis." *American Anthropologist* 91: 599–612.

Harvey, David. 1996. *Justice, Nature and the Geography of Difference.* Cambridge, Mass.: Blackwell.

Hatfield, Agnes B. 1987. "Coping and Adaptation: A Conceptual Framework for Understanding Families." In *Families of the Mentally Ill: Coping and Adaptation*, ed. A. B. Hatfield and H. P. Lefley, 60–84. New York: Guilford.

Haug, W. F. 1986. *Critique of Commodity Aesthetics: Appearance, Sexuality and Advertising in Capitalist Society*. Trans. Robert Bock. Minneapolis: University of Minnesota Press.

Heer, Friedrich. 1963. *The Medieval World: Europe, 1100–1350*. Trans. Janet Sondheimer. New York: Mentor.

Henriques, Julian, W. Hollway, C. Urwin, C. Venn, and V. Walkerdine. 1984. *Changing the Subject: Psychology, Social Regulation and Subjectivity*. London: Methuen.

Hill, Jane. 1995. "Junk Spanish, Covert Racism and the (Leaky) Boundary between Public and Private Spheres." *Pragmatics* 5(2): 197–212.

Hochschild, Arlie. 1983. *The Managed Heart: Commercialization of Human Feeling*. Berkeley: University of California Press.

Holland, Dorothy C. 1988. "In the Voice of, in the Image Of: Socially Situated Representations of Attractiveness." *IPrA Papers in Pragmatics* 2(1/2): 106–135.

——— 1997. "Selves as Cultured: As Told by an Anthropologist Who Lacks a Soul." In *Self and Identity: Fundamental Issues,* ed. R. Ashmore and L. Jussim, 193–221. New York: Oxford University Press.

Holland, D., and M. Cole. 1995. "Between Discourse and Schema: Reformulating a Cultural-historical Approach to Culture and Mind." *Anthropology and Education Quarterly* 26(4): 478–489.

Holland, D., and J. Crane. 1987. "Adapting to an Industrializing Nation: The Shango Cult in Trinidad." *Social and Economic Studies* 36(4): 41–66.

Holland, Dorothy, and Margaret Eisenhart. 1981. "Women's Peer Groups and Choice of Career." Final report. Washington: National Institute of Education.

——— 1990. *Educated in Romance: Women, Achievement and College Culture*. Chicago: University of Chicago Press.

Holland, Dorothy C., and Andrew Kipnis. 1994. "Metaphors for Embarrassment and Stories of Exposure: The Not-so-egocentric Self in American Culture." *Ethos* 22(3): 316–342.

Holland, Dorothy, and Jean Lave, eds. Forthcoming. *History in Person: Enduring Struggles and the Practice of Identity*. Santa Fe: SAR Press.

Holland, Dorothy C., and Naomi Quinn, eds. 1987. *Cultural Models in Language and Thought*. New York: Cambridge University Press.

Holland, Dorothy, and James R. Reeves. 1994. "Activity Theory and the View from Somewhere: Team Perspectives on the Intellectual Work of Programming." *Mind, Culture and Activity* 1: 8–24.

Holland, Dorothy, and Debra Skinner. 1987. "Prestige and Intimacy: The Cultural Models behind Americans' Talk about Gender Types." In Holland and Quinn, eds., 1987, 78–111.

—— 1995a. "Contested Ritual, Contested Femininities: (Re)forming Self and Society in a Nepali Women's Festival." *American Ethnologist* 22: 279–305.

—— 1995b. "Not Written by the Fate-writer: The Agency in Women's Critical Commentary in Nepal." *Folk: The Journal of the Danish Ethnographic Society* 37: 103–133.

—— 1996. "The Co-development of Identity, Agency, and Lived Worlds." In *Comparisons in Human Development: Understanding Time and Context*, ed. J. Tudge, M. Shanahan, and J. Valsiner, 193–221. Cambridge: Cambridge University Press.

Hollway, W. 1984. "Gender Difference and the Production of Subjectivity." In Henriques et al., 1984, 227–263.

Holquist, Michael. 1981. "Politics of Representation." In *Allegory in Representation*, ed. S. Greenblatt, 163–185. Baltimore: Johns Hopkins University Press.

—— 1990. *Dialogism: Bakhtin and His World*. New York: Routledge.

Howard, Donald R. 1966. *The Three Temptations: Medieval Man in Search of the World*. Princeton: Princeton University Press.

Huizinga, Johan. 1955. *Homo Ludens: A Study of the Play Element in Culture*. Boston: Beacon.

—— 1956. *The Waning of the Middle Ages: A Study of the Forms of Life, Thought and Art in France and the Netherlands in the XIVth and XVth Centuries*. Garden City, N.Y.: Doubleday.

Hutchins, Edwin. 1986. "Mediation and Automatization." *Quarterly Newsletter of the Laboratory of Comparative Human Cognition* 8(2): 47–58.

—— 1987. "Myth and Experience in the Trobriand Islands." In Holland and Quinn, eds., 1987, 269–289.

Inden, Ronald. 1990. *Imagining India*. Oxford: Blackwell.

Irvine, Judith T. 1980. "How Not to Ask a Favor in Wolof." *Papers in Linguistics* 13: 3–50.

—— 1985. "Status and Style in Language." *Annual Reviews in Anthropology* 14: 557–581.

—— 1989. "When Talk Isn't Cheap: Language and Political Economy." *American Ethnologist* 16(2): 248–267.

Ito, K. L. 1987. "Emotions, Proper Behavior *(hana pono)* and Hawaiian Concepts of Self, Person, and Individual." In *Contemporary Issues in Mental Health Research in the Pacific Islands,* ed. A. B. Robillard and A. J. Marsella, 45–71. Honolulu: University of Hawaii, Social Science Research Institute.

Jackson, W. T. H. 1960. *The Literature of the Middle Ages*. New York: Columbia University Press.

Jaeger, C. Stephen. 1985. *The Origins of Courtliness: Civilizing Trends and the Formation of Courtly Ideals, 939–1210*. Philadelphia: University of Pennsylvania Press.

Joas, Hans. 1985. *G. H. Mead: A Contemporary Re-examination of His Thought*. Trans. Raymond Meyer. Cambridge, Mass.: MIT Press.

Johnson, Richard. 1986–87. "What Is Cultural Studies Anyway?" *Social Text: Theory/Culture/Ideology* 16(Winter): 38–80.

Joravsky, David. 1989. *Russian Psychology: A Critical History*. Oxford: Blackwell.

Kay, Sarah. 1990. *Subjectivity in Troubadour Poetry*. Cambridge: Cambridge University Press.

Kelly, Amy. 1952. *Eleanor of Aquitaine and the Four Kings*. London: Cassell.

Kitayama, S., H. Markus, and C. Lieberman. 1994. "The Collective Construction of Self-esteem: Implications for Culture, Self, and Emotion." In *Everyday Conceptions of Emotion*, ed. J. A. Russell, et al., 523–570. Dordrecht: Kluwer Academic.

Kondo, D. K. 1990. *Crafting Selves: Power, Gender, and Discourses of Identity in a Japanese Workplace*. Chicago: University of Chicago Press.

Kozulin, Alex. 1986. "Vygotsky in Context." In Vygotsky, *Thought and Language*, trans. Alex Kozulin, xi–lvi. Cambridge, Mass.: MIT Press.

Kuhn, Manford, and Thomas S. McPartland. 1954. "An Empirical Investigation of Self-attitudes." *American Sociological Review* 19(1): 68–76.

Kuhn, Thomas. 1962. *The Structure of Scientific Revolutions*. Chicago: University of Chicago Press.

Kulick, Don. 1993. "Speaking as a Woman: Structure and Gender in Domestic Arguments in a New Guinea Village." *Cultural Anthropology* 8(4): 411–429.

Lachicotte, William S. 1992. "On the Borderline: Profession, Imagination and Authority in the Practice of Mental Health Care." Ph.D. diss., University of North Carolina at Chapel Hill. Ann Arbor: University Microfilms.

Lakoff, Robin. 1975. *Language and Woman's Place*. New York: Harper and Row.

Lancaster, Roger N. 1992. *Life Is Hard: Machismo, Danger, and the Intimacy of Power in Nicaragua*. Berkeley: University of California Press.

——— 1996. "Guto's Performance: Notes on the Transvestism of Everyday Life." Presented at the Department of Anthropology Colloquium, University of North Carolina at Chapel Hill, March 28.

Lave, Jean. 1988. *Cognition in Practice: Mind, Mathematics and Culture in Everyday Life*. Cambridge: Cambridge University Press.

Lave, Jean, and Etienne Wenger. 1991. *Situated Learning: Legitimate Peripheral Participation*. Cambridge: Cambridge University Press.

Leavitt, John. 1996. "Meaning and Feeling in the Anthropology of Emotions." *American Ethnologist* 23: 514–539.

Lederman, Rena. 1984. "Who Speaks Here? Formality and the Politics of Gender in Mendi, Highland Papua New Guinea." In *Dangerous Words: Language and*

Politics in the Pacific, ed. D. L. Brenneis and F. R. Myers, 85–107. New York: New York University Press.

Lee, Benjamin. 1985. "Intellectual Origins of Vygotsky's Semiotic Analysis." In Wertsch, ed., 1985, 66–93.

Lee, Benjamin, and Maya Hickman. 1983. "Language, Thought, and Self in Vygotsky's Developmental Theory." In *Developmental Approaches to the Self,* ed. B. Lee and G. Noam, 343–378. New York: Plenum.

Leontiev, A. N. 1978. *Activity, Consciousness, and Personality.* Englewood Cliffs, N.J.: Prentice-Hall.

LeVine, R. A. 1982. *Culture, Behavior, and Personality: An Introduction to the Comparative Study of Psychosocial Adaptation.* Chicago: Aldine.

Lévi-Strauss, Claude. 1966. *The Savage Mind.* Chicago: University of Chicago Press.

Lewis, C. S. 1936. *The Allegory of Love: A Study in Medieval Tradition.* Oxford: Clarendon Press.

Luhrmann, Tanya M. 1989. *Persuasions of the Witch's Craft: Ritual Magic in Contemporary England.* Cambridge, Mass.: Harvard University Press.

Luria, Alexander R. 1979. *The Making of Mind: A Personal Account of Soviet Psychology.* Ed. Michael and Sheila Cole. Cambridge, Mass.: Harvard University Press.

————— 1981. *Language and Cognition.* Ed. J. V. Wertsch. New York: Wiley.

Luttrell, Wendy. 1996. "'Becoming Somebody' (or Not): The Schooling of Gendered Selves." In *The Cultural Production of the Educated Person: Critical Ethnographies of Schooling and Local Practice,* ed. B. A. Levinson, D. E. Foley, and D. C. Holland, 93–117. Albany: SUNY Press.

Lutz, Catherine. 1987. "Goals, Events, and Understanding in Ifaluk Emotion Theory." In Holland and Quinn, eds., 1987, 290–312.

————— 1988. *Unnatural Emotions: Everyday Sentiments on a Micronesian Atoll and Their Challenge to Western Theory.* Chicago: University of Chicago Press.

————— 1990. "Engendered Emotion: Gender, Power, and the Rhetoric of Emotional Control in American Discourse." In Lutz and Abu-Lughod, eds., 1990, 69–92.

————— 1995. "The Gender of Theory." In *Women Writing Culture,* ed. Ruth Behar and Deborah A. Gordon, 249–266. Berkeley: University of California Press.

————— In press. "The Psychological Ethnic and the Spirit of Permanent War: The Military Production of Twentieth-Century American Subjects." In *The Invention of the Psychological: The Cultural History of Emotions in America,* ed. J. Pfister and N. Schnog,. New Haven: Yale University Press,.

Lutz, C., and Abu-Lughod, L. 1990. "Introduction: Emotion, Discourse, and the Politics of Everyday Life." In Lutz and Abu-Lughod, eds., 1990, 1–23.

——— eds. 1990. *Language and the Politics of Emotion.* Cambridge: Cambridge University Press.

Lutz, Catherine A., and Jane L. Collins. 1993. *Reading National Geographic.* Chicago: University of Chicago Press.

Lykes, M. B. 1985. "Gender and Individualistic vs. Collectivist Bases for Notions about the Self." *Journal of Personality* 53(2): 357–383.

Lynch, Michael. 1991. "Laboratory Space and the Technological Complex: An Investigation of Topical Contextures." *Science in Context* 4: 51–78.

MacAndrew, Craig, and Robert B. Edgerton. 1969. *Drunken Comportment: A Social Explanation.* Chicago: Aldine.

March, Kathryn. 1988. "Talking about Not Talking." Presented at the 87th American Anthropological Association Annual Meeting, Phoenix.

Markus, H. R., and S. Kitayama. 1991. "Culture and the Self: Implications for Cognition, Emotion, and Motivation." *Psychological Review* 98: 224–253.

Markus, Hazel, and Paula Nurius. 1987. "Possible Selves: The Interface between Motivation and the Self-concept." In *Self and Identity: Psychosocial Perspectives,* ed. Krysia Yardley and Terry Honess, 157–172. Chichester: Wiley.

Marriott, McK. 1976a. "Hindu Transactions: Diversity without Dualism." In *Transaction and Meaning: Directions in the Anthropology of Exchange and Symbolic Behavior,* ed. B. Kapferer, 109–142. Philadelphia: Institute for the Study of Human Issues.

——— 1976b. "Interpreting Indian Society: A Monistic Alternative to Dumont's Dualism." *Journal of Asian Studies* 36: 189–195.

Marsella, A., G. DeVos, and F. L. Hsu, eds. 1985. *Culture and Self: Asian and Western Perspectives.* New York: Tavistock.

Marsh, Diane T. 1992. *Families and Mental Illness: New Directions in Professional Practice.* New York: Praeger.

Marx, Karl. 1975/1845. "Theses on Feuerbach." In *Early Writings,* ed. Rodney Livingstone and Gregor Benton, 421–423. New York: Vintage.

McCall, George. 1987. "The Structure, Content and Dynamics of Self: Continuities in the Study of Role Identities." In *Self and Identity: Psychosocial Perspectives,* ed. K. Yardley and T. Honess, 133–145. Chichester: Wiley.

McCall, George J., and J. L. Simmons. 1978. *Identities and Interactions: An Examination of Human Associations in Everyday Life.* Rev. ed. New York: Free Press.

McConnell-Ginet, Sally. 1988. "Language and Gender." In *Linguistics: The Cambridge Survey,* ed. F. J. Newmeyer, 75–99. Cambridge: Cambridge University Press.

——— 1989. "The Sexual (Re)production of Meaning: A Discourse-based Theory." In *Language, Gender and Professional Writing,* ed. F. W. Frank and P. A. Treichler, 35–50. New York: Modern Language Association.

McDermott, R. P. 1974. "Achieving School Failure: An Anthropological Approach to Illiteracy and Social Stratification." In *Education and Cultural Process: Toward an Anthropology of Education,* ed. G. D. Spindler, 82–118. New York: Holt, Rinehart and Winston.

McHugh, E. 1989. "Concepts of the Person among the Gurungs of Nepal." *American Ethnologist* 16: 75–86.

McLeod, Enid. 1976. *The Order of the Rose: The Life and Ideals of Christine de Pizan.* London: Chatto and Windus.

Mead, G. H. 1934. *Mind, Self and Society.* Chicago: University of Chicago Press.

Miller, J. G. 1988. "Bridging the Content-Structure Dichotomy: Culture and the Self." In *The Cross-Cultural Challenge to Social Psychology,* ed. M. H. Bond, 267–328. Newbury Park: Sage.

Millon, Theodore. 1981. *Disorders of Personality. DSM III: Axis II.* New York: Wiley.

———— 1985. *Personality and Its Disorders: A Biosocial Learning Approach.* New York: Wiley.

———— 1990. *Toward a New Personology: An Evolutionary Model.* New York: Wiley.

Millon, Theodore, and Gerald L. Klerman, eds. 1986. *Contemporary Directions in Psychopathology: Towards the DSM-IV.* New York: Guilford.

Mines, M. 1988. "Conceptualizing the Person: Hierarchical Society and Individual Autonomy in India." *American Anthropologist* 90: 568–579.

Monat, Alan, and Richard S. Lazarus, eds. 1977. *Stress and Coping: An Anthology.* New York: Columbia University Press.

Morson, Gary Saul, and Caryl Emerson. 1990. *Mikhail Bakhtin: Creation of a Prosaics.* Palo Alto: Stanford University Press.

Murray, D. W. 1993. "What Is the Western Concept of the Self? On Forgetting David Hume." *Ethos* 21: 3–23.

Neilson, William A. 1967. *The Origins and Sources of the Court of Love.* Rpt. of 1899 ed. New York: Russell and Russell.

Neisser, Ulric. 1988. "Five Kinds of Self Knowledge." *Philosophical Psychology* 1(1): 35–59.

Newman, F. X., ed. 1968. *The Meaning of Courtly Love.* Albany: State University of New York Press.

Nuckolls, Charles W. 1992a. "Toward a Cultural History of the Personality Disorders." *Social Science and Medicine* 35(1): 37–47.

———— 1992b. "Notes on a Defrocked Priest: The Cynosure in South Indian Shamanic and American Psychiatric Diagnosis." In *Ethnopsychiatry,* ed. Atwood D. Gaines, 69–84. Albany: SUNY Press.

O'Barr, William, and Bowman Atkins. 1980. "'Women's Language' or 'Powerless Language'?" In *Women and Language in Literature and Society,* ed. Sally

McConnell-Ginet, Ruth Borker, and Nelly Furman, 93–110. New York: Praeger.

Obeyesekere, G. 1981. *Medusa's Hair: An Essay on Personal Symbols and Religious Experience.* Chicago: University of Chicago Press.

——— 1992. *The Apotheosis of Captain Cook.* Princeton: Princeton University Press.

Ortner, Sherry. 1984. "Theory in Anthropology since the Sixties." *Comparative Studies in Society and History* 26(1): 126–166.

Paden, W. D., ed. 1989. *The Voice of the Trobairitz: Perspectives on the Women Troubadours.* Philadelphia: University of Pennsylvania Press.

Page, Helán. 1994. "White Public Space and the Construction of White Privilege in U.S. Health Care: Fresh Concepts and a New Model of Analysis." *Medical Anthropology Quarterly* 8: 109–116.

Painter, Sidney. 1967. *French Chivalry: Chivalric Ideas and Practices in Medieval France.* Ithaca: Cornell University Press.

Paris, Gaston. 1883. "Lancelot du Lac, II: La conte de la charrette." *Romania* 12: 459–534.

Parish, S. 1991. "The Sacred Mind: Newar Cultural Representations of Mental Life and the Production of Moral Consciousness." *Ethos* 19: 313–351.

——— 1994. *Moral Knowing in a Hindu Sacred City.* New York: Columbia University Press.

Parker, I. 1992. *Discourse Dynamics: Critical Analysis for Social and Individual Psychology.* New York: Routledge.

Parsons, Talcott. 1951. *The Social System.* New York: Free Press.

——— 1961. "Social Structure and the Development of Personality." In *Studying Personality Cross-culturally,* ed. B. Kaplan, 165–200. Evanston: Row, Peterson.

——— 1972. "Definitions of Health and Illness in the Light of American Values and Social Structure." In *Patients, Physicians and Illness,* ed. E. G. Jaco, 2d ed., 107–127. New York: Free Press.

Paterson, Linda M. 1993. *The World of the Troubadours: Medieval Occitan Society, c. 1100–c. 1300.* Cambridge: Cambridge University Press.

Peterson, John H., Jr. 1988. "The International Origins of Alcoholics Anonymous." Presented at 12th International Congress of Anthropological and Ethnological Sciences, Zagreb.

Price, Laurie. 1987. "Ecuadorian Illness Stories: Cultural Knowledge in Natural Discourse." In Holland and Quinn, eds., 1987, 313–342.

Pryor, John B., C. M. LaVite, and L. M. Stoller. 1993. "A Social Psychological Analysis of Sexual Harassment: The Person/situation Interaction." *Journal of Vocational Behavior* 42: 68–83.

Quinn, Naomi. 1992. "The Motivational Force of Self-understanding: Evidence from Wives' Inner Conflicts." In *Human Motives and Cultural Models,* ed. R. G. D'Andrade and C. Strauss, 90–126. Cambridge: Cambridge University Press.

Quinn, Naomi, and Dorothy Holland. 1987. "Culture and Cognition." In Holland and Quinn, eds., 1987, 3–40.

Quinn, Naomi, and Claudia Strauss. 1994. "A Cognitive Cultural Anthropology." In *Assessing Cultural Anthropology,* ed. R. Borofsky, 284–297. New York: McGraw-Hill.

Raheja, Gloria G., and Ann G. Gold. 1994. *Listen to the Heron's Words: Reimagining Gender and Kinship in North India.* Berkeley: University of California Press.

Reidel, Brian. 1994. Personal communication.

Reiter, R. R., ed. 1975. *Toward an Anthropology of Women.* New York: Monthly Review Press.

Robbins, R. H. 1973. "Identity, Culture and Behavior." In *Handbook of Social and Cultural Anthropology,* ed. J. J. Honigmann, 1199–1222. Chicago: Rand McNally.

Robertson, D. W. 1962. "Some Medieval Doctrines of Love." In Robertson, *A Preface to Chaucer: Studies in Medieval Perspectives,* 391–503. Princeton, N. J.: Princeton University Press.

——— 1968. "The Concept of Courtly Love as an Impediment to the Understanding of Medieval Texts." In Newman, ed., 1968, 1–18.

Robins, Lee N. 1980. "Alcoholism and Labelling Theory." In *Readings in Medical Sociology,* ed. D. Mechanic, 180–198. New York: Free Press.

Robinson, David. 1979. *Talking out of Alcoholism: The Self-help Process of Alcoholics Anonymous.* Baltimore: University Park Press.

Rogoff, Barbara. 1990. *Apprenticeship in Thinking: Cognitive Development in Social Context.* New York: Oxford University Press.

Roiphe, Katie. 1993. *The Morning After: Sex, Fear, and Feminism on Campus.* Boston: Little, Brown.

Rosaldo, Michelle Z. 1980. *Knowledge and Passion: Ilongot Notions of Self and Social Life.* Cambridge: Cambridge University Press.

——— 1984. "Toward an Anthropology of Self and Feeling." In *Culture Theory: Essays on Mind, Self and Emotion,* ed. R. A. Shweder and R. A. LeVine, 137–157. New York: Cambridge University Press.

Rougemont, Denis de. 1956. *Love in the Western World.* Trans. M. Belgion. New York: Pantheon.

Rouse, Roger. 1995. "Questions of Identity: Personhood and Collectivity in Transnational Migration to the United States." *Critique of Anthropology* 15(4): 351–380.

Sahlins, Marshall D. 1995. *How "Natives" Think: About Captain Cook, for Example.* Chicago: University of Chicago Press.

Sanday, Peggy R. 1990. *Fraternity Gang Rape: Sex, Brotherhood and Privilege on Campus.* New York: New York University Press.

Sanders, W. B. 1980. *Rape and Woman's Identity.* Sage Library of Social Research no. 106. Beverly Hills: Sage.

Schade-Poulson, Marc. 1995. "The Power of Love: Raï Music and Youth in Algeria." In Amit-Talai and Wulff, eds., 1995, 81–113.

Scheff, Thomas J. 1966. *Being Mentally Ill: A Sociological Theory.* Chicago: Aldine.

Scheper-Hughes, Nancy. 1992. "Hungry Bodies, Medicine, and the State: Toward a Critical Psychological Anthropology." In *New Directions in Psychological Anthropology,* ed. T. Schwartz, G. M. White, and C. A. Lutz, 221–247. Cambridge: Cambridge University Press.

Schur, Edwin. 1980. *The Politics of Deviance: Stigma Contests and the Uses of Power.* Englewood Cliffs, N. J.: Prentice-Hall.

Schwartz, Gary, and Don Merten. 1968. "Social Identity and Expressive Symbols: The Meaning of an Initiation Ritual." *American Anthropologist* 70: 1117–31.

Scott, Robert A. 1969. *The Making of Blind Men: A Study of Adult Socialization.* New York: Russell Sage Foundation.

Selye, Hans. 1956. *The Stress of Life.* New York: McGraw-Hill.

Shepel, Elina. 1995. "Teacher Self-identification in Culture from Vygotsky's Developmental Perspective." *Anthropology and Education Quarterly* 26: 425–442.

Shotter, John. 1982. "Consciousness, Self-consciousness, Inner Games, and Alternative Realities." In *Aspects of Consciousness: Awareness and Self-awareness,* vol. 3, ed. G. Underwood, 27–61. London: Academic Press.

Shweder, R. A. 1991. *Thinking through Cultures: Expeditions in Cultural Psychology.* Cambridge, Mass.: Harvard University Press.

Shweder, R. A., and E. J. Bourne. 1984. "Does the Concept of Person Vary Cross-culturally?" In Shweder and R. A. LeVine, eds., *Culture Theory: Essays on Mind, Self, and Emotion,* 158–199. Cambridge: Cambridge University Press.

Siegler, Miriam, and Humphrey Osmond. 1974. *Models of Madness, Models of Medicine.* New York: Macmillan.

Skinner, Debra. 1989. "The Socialization of Gender Identity: Observations from Nepal." In *Child Development in Cultural Context,* ed. J. Valsiner, 181–192. Toronto: Hogrefe and Huber.

——— 1990. "Nepalese Children's Understanding of Themselves and Their Social World." Ph.D. diss., University of North Carolina at Chapel Hill.

Skinner, Debra, and Dorothy Holland. 1996. "Schools and the Cultural Production of the Educated Person in a Nepalese Hill Community." In *The Cultural Production of the Educated Person,* ed. B. A. Levinson, D. E. Foley, and D. C. Holland, 273–299. Albany: SUNY Press.

Skinner, Debra, Dorothy Holland, and G. B. Adhikari. 1994. "The Songs of Tij: A Genre of Critical Commentary for Women in Nepal." *Asian Folklore Studies* 53: 257–303.

Skinner, Debra, Alfred Pach III, and Dorothy Holland, eds. 1998. *Selves in Time and Place: Identities, Experience, and History in Nepal.* Lanham, Md.: Rowman and Littlefield.

Skinner, Debra, Jaan Valsiner, and Bidur Basnet. 1991. "Singing One's Life: An Orchestration of Personal Experiences and Cultural Forms." *Journal of South Asian Literature* 26: 15–43.

Smith, N. B., and J. T. Snow, eds. 1980. *The Expansion and Transformations of Courtly Literature.* Athens: University of Georgia Press.

Smith, Paul. 1988. *Discerning the Subject.* Minneapolis: University of Minnesota Press.

Spiro, Melford E. 1982. "Collective Representations and Mental Representations in Religious Symbol Systems." In *On Symbols in Anthropology,* vol. 3: *Other Realities,* ed. J. Maquet, 45–72. Malibu: Undena.

——— 1993. "Is the Western Conception of the Self 'Peculiar' within the Context of the World Cultures?" *Ethos* 21: 107–153.

Spradley, James. 1970. *You Owe Yourself a Drunk: An Ethnography of Urban Nomads.* Boston: Little, Brown.

Stevens, John. 1973. *Medieval Romance: Themes and Approaches.* London: Hutchinson.

Stone, Linda. 1978. "Cultural Repercussions of Childlessness and Low Fertility in Nepal." *Contributions to Nepalese Studies* 5(2): 7–36.

Stone, Michael H., ed. 1986. *Essential Papers on Borderline Disorders: One Hundred Years at the Border.* New York: New York University Press.

Strauss, Claudia. 1990. "Who Gets Ahead? Cognitive Responses to Heteroglossia in American Political Culture." *American Ethnologist* 17(2): 312–328.

——— 1992. "Models and Motives." In *Human Motives and Cultural Models,* ed. R. G. D'Andrade and C. Strauss, 1–20. Cambridge: Cambridge University Press.

Stryker, Sheldon. 1987. "Identity Theory: Developments and Extensions." In *Self and Identity: Psychosocial Perspectives,* ed. K. Yardley and T. Honess, 89–103. Chichester: Wiley.

Szasz, Thomas S. 1961. *The Myth of Mental Illness: Foundations of a Theory of Personal Conduct.* New York: Dell.

——— 1970. *The Manufacture of Madness: A Comparative Study of the Inquisition and the Mental Health Movement.* New York: Harper and Row.

Tannen, Deborah. 1990. *You Just Don't Understand: Women and Men in Conversation*. New York: Morrow.

Thompson, E. P. 1963. *The Making of the English Working Class*. New York: Pantheon.

Thomsen, Robert. 1975. *Bill W.* New York: Harper and Row.

Titunik, I. R. 1987. "Translator's Introduction." In V. N. Voloshinov, *Freudianism: A Critical Sketch*, ed. I. R. Titunik and N. H. Bruss, trans. I. R. Titunik, xv–xxv. Bloomington: Indiana University Press.

Todorov, Tzvetan. 1984. *Mikhail Bakhtin: The Dialogical Principle*. Trans. Wlad Godzich. Minneapolis: University of Minnesota Press.

Tolman, C. W., and W. Maiers, eds. 1991. *Critical Psychology: Contributions to an Historical Science of the Subject*. Cambridge: Cambridge University Press.

Townsend, J. M. 1976. "Self-concept and the Institutionalization of Mental Patients: An Overview and Critique." *Journal of Health and Social Behavior* 17(3): 263–271.

Traube, Elizabeth. 1992. *Dreaming Identities: Class, Gender, and Generation in 1980s Hollywood Movies*. Boulder: Westview.

Trosset, Carol S. 1986. "The Social Identity of Welsh Learners." *Language in Society* 15(2): 165–192.

Turner, Terrence. 1969. "Tchikrin: A Central Brazilian Tribe and Its Symbolic Language of Bodily Adornment." *Natural History* 78: 50–59.

Valsiner, Jaan. 1993. "Bi-directional Cultural Transmission and Constructive Sociogenesis." In *Sociogenesis Reexamined*, ed. W. de Graff and R. Mair, 47–70. New York: Springer.

van der Veer, René, and Jaan Valsiner. 1991. *Understanding Vygotsky: A Quest for Synthesis*. Oxford: Blackwell.

———— 1994. "Reading Vygotsky: From Fascination to Construction." In *The Vygotsky Reader*, ed. R. van der Veer and J. Valsiner, trans. T. Prout and R. van der Veer, 1–9. Oxford: Blackwell.

Van Gennep, Arnold. 1960/1909. *The Rites of Passage*. Trans. M. B. Vizedom and G. L. Caffee. Chicago: University of Chicago Press.

Voloshinov, V. N. 1986. *Marxism and the Philosophy of Language*. Cambridge, Mass.: Harvard University Press.

———— 1987. *Freudianism: A Critical Sketch*. Ed. I. R. Titunik and N. H. Bruss, trans. I. R. Titunik. Bloomington: Indiana University Press.

Vygotsky, L. S. 1930. "The Primitive Man and His Behavior." In *Etiudy po isotorii povedeniya*, ed. L. S. Vygotsky and A. R. Luria, 54–121. Moscow-Leningrad: Gosudarstvennoye Izdatel'stvo. (In Russian.)

———— 1960. "Development of Higher Psychical Functions (Razvitie vyshhih psihicheskih funktsii)." (In Russian.) Moscow: Izd. APN.

———— 1971. *The Psychology of Art*. Cambridge, Mass.: MIT Press.

———— 1978. *Mind in Society: The Development of Higher Psychological Processes.* Ed. M. Cole et al. Cambridge, Mass.: Harvard University Press.

———— 1984. "Child Psychology." In *The Collected Works of L. S. Vygotsky,* vol. 4. Moscow: Pedagogika. (In Russian.)

———— 1986. *Thought and Language.* Rev. ed. Cambridge, Mass.: MIT Press.

———— 1987a. "Imagination and Its Development in Childhood." In *The Collected Works of L. S. Vygotsky,* vol. 1: *Problems of General Psychology,* trans. Norris Minick, ed. Robert W. Rieber and Aaron Carton, 339–349. New York: Plenum.

———— 1987b. "The Problem of Will and Its Development in Childhood." In *Collected Works,* vol. 1, 351–358.

———— 1987c. "Thinking and Speech." In *Collected Works,* vol. 1, 39–285.

Weber, Max. 1978. *Economy and Society.* Ed. G. Roth and C. Wittich. Berkeley: University of California Press.

Weiner, Annette B. 1976. *Women of Value, Men of Renown: New Perspectives in Trobriand Exchange.* Austin: University of Texas Press.

Wertsch, James V. 1981. "The Concept of Activity in Soviet Psychology." In Wertsch, ed., 1981, 3–36.

———— 1985a. "The Semiotic Mediation of Mental Life: L. S. Vygotsky and M. M. Bakhtin." In *Semiotic Mediation: Sociocultural and Psychological Perspectives,* ed. Elizabeth Mertz and R. J. Parmentier, 49–71. Orlando: Academic Press.

———— 1985b. *Vygotsky and the Social Formation of Mind.* Cambridge, Mass.: Harvard University Press.

———— 1991. *Voices of the Mind: A Sociocultural Approach to Mediated Action.* Cambridge, Mass.: Harvard University Press.

Wertsch, James, ed. 1981. *The Concept of Activity in Soviet Psychology.* Armonk, N.Y.: M. E. Sharpe.

———— 1985. *Culture, Communication, and Cognition: Vygotskian Perspectives.* New York: Cambridge University Press.

Wertsch, James V., Norris Minick, and Flavio J. Arns. 1984. "The Creation of Context in Joint Problem-solving." In *Everyday Cognition: Its Development in Social Context,* ed. B. Rogoff and J. Lave, 151–171. Cambridge, Mass.: Harvard University Press.

Weston, Kath. 1990. "Production as Means, Production as Metaphor: Women's Struggle to Enter the Trades." In *Uncertain Terms: Negotiating Gender in American Culture,* ed. Faye Ginsburg and Anna Lowenhaupt, 137–151. Boston: Beacon.

Wexler, P. 1983. *Critical Social Psychology.* Washington: Falmer.

White, G. M. 1991. *Identity through History: Living Stories in a Solomon Islands Society.* Cambridge: Cambridge University Press.

———— 1992. "Ethnopsychology." In *New Directions in Psychological Anthropology*, ed. T. Schwartz, G. M. White, and C. Lutz, 21–46. Cambridge: Cambridge University Press.

———— 1993. "Emotions Inside Out: The Anthropology of Affect." In *Handbook of Emotion*, ed. M. Lewis and J. Haviland, 29–39. New York: Guilford.

Wilcox, John. 1930. "Defining Courtly Love." *Michigan Academy of Science, Arts and Letters* 12: 313–325.

Willard, Charity C. 1984. *Christine de Pizan: Her Life and Works*. New York: Persea Books.

Williams, Raymond. 1977. *Marxism and Literature*. Oxford: Oxford University Press.

Willis, Paul. 1981. *Learning to Labor: How Working Class Kids Get Working Class Jobs*. New York: Columbia University Press.

Willis, Susan. 1991. *A Primer of Everyday Life*. London: Routledge.

Wood, D. J., J. S. Brunner, and G. Ross. 1976. "The Role of Tutoring in Problem Solving." *Journal of Child Psychology and Psychiatry* 17: 89–100.

Wulff, Helena. 1995. "Interracial Friendships: Consuming Youth Styles, Ethnicity and Teenage Femininity in South London." In Amit-Talai and Wulff, eds., 1995, 63–80.

Young, Alan. 1996. *The Harmony of Illusions*. Berkeley: University of California Press.

Credits

Some of the material in Chapter 1 was originally published in Dorothy Holland, "The Woman Who Climbed up the House: Some Limitations of Schema Theory," in *New Directions in Psychological Anthropology,* ed. Theodore Schwartz, Geoffrey White, and Catherine Lutz (Cambridge: Cambridge University Press, 1992). It is used here with permission from Cambridge University Press.

Some of Chapter 2 is drawn from Dorothy Holland, "Selves as Cultured: As Told by an Anthropologist Who Lacks a Soul," in *Self and Identity: Fundamental Issues,* ed. R. Ashmore and L. Jussim (New York: Oxford University Press, 1997). It is used here with permission from Oxford University Press.

Chapter 4 is a modified version of Carole Cain, "Personal Stories: Identity Acquisition and Self-understanding in Alcoholics Anonymous," *Ethos* 19 (1991). It is used here with permission from *Ethos.*

Chapter 5 is a modified version of Dorothy Holland, "How Cultural Systems Become Desire: The Case of American Romance," in *Human Motives and Cultural Models,* ed. Roy D'Andrade and Claudia Strauss (Cambridge: Cambridge University Press, 1992). It is used here with permission from Cambridge University Press.

Portions of Chapter 10 are modified from Debra Skinner and Dorothy Holland, "Contested Selves, Contested Femininities: Selves and Society in Process," in *Selves in Time and Place: Identities, Experience, and History in Nepal,* ed. Debra Skinner, Alfred Pach III, and Dorothy Holland (Lanham, Md.: Rowman and Littlefield, 1998). They are used here with permission from Rowman and Littlefield Publishers.

Some segments of Chapter 12 were originally published in Dorothy Holland and Debra Skinner, "Contested Ritual, Contested Femininities: (Re)Forming Self and Society in a Nepali Women's Festival," *American Ethnologist* 22, no. 2 (1995). They are used here with permission from *American Ethnologist.*

339

Index

Fictitious names are in quotation marks.

341